A BRIDGE BETWEEN

SPANISH BENEDICTINE MISSIONARY
WOMEN IN AUSTRALIA

A BRIDGE BETWEEN

SPANISH BENEDICTINE MISSIONARY
WOMEN IN AUSTRALIA

KATHARINE MASSAM

Published by ANU Press
The Australian National University
Acton ACT 2601, Australia
Email: anupress@anu.edu.au

Available to download for free at press.anu.edu.au

ISBN (print): 9781760463519
ISBN (online): 9781760463526

WorldCat (print): 1200780874
WorldCat (online): 1200780878

DOI: 10.22459/BB.2020

This title is published under a Creative Commons Attribution-NonCommercial-NoDerivatives 4.0 International (CC BY-NC-ND 4.0).

The full licence terms are available at
creativecommons.org/licenses/by-nc-nd/4.0/legalcode

The ANU.Lives Series in Biography is an initiative of the National Centre of Biography at The Australian National University, ncb.anu.edu.au.

Cover design and layout by ANU Press. Cover photograph: Benedictine Oblate Sisters of New Norcia, early 1931, NNA W6-B3-4-108.

This edition © 2020 ANU Press

Contents

Foreword vii
Sr Veronica Therese Willaway OSB

Acknowledgements ix

Illustrations xiii

1. To Name and to Remember: The Reunion of 2001 1
2. The Company of St Teresa of Jesus at New Norcia, 1904–10 . . .35
3. Benedictine Oblates: Outsiders in Community 73
4. St Joseph's Native School and Orphanage:
   Workers at the Edge of the Town. 105
5. *Agencia Benedictina*: Burgos, Belgium and the Kimberley 131
6. Monastic and Missionary Sisters: 'Their Currency and Savings
   Were the Work' 165
7. Gathering New Energy: Abbot Catalan Recruiting in Spain,
   1947–48 211
8. Triggering the 'Second Part': Old School Patterns, a New
   Bindoon Community and Visiting the Villages Again. 239
9. Winding Together: 'The Grace of God Is Not Tied to Any
   Colour, Race or Nationality' 257
10. Spinning Apart. 309

Bibliography 357

Appendix 1: Numbers at a Glance 383

Appendix 2: Benedictine Missionary Sisters of New Norcia 387

Foreword

Sr Veronica Therese Willaway OSB

I am very honoured to be writing this foreword to welcome you to read this important book by Katharine Massam about the Spanish Benedictine Missionary Sisters of New Norcia.

This book is much more than words to me. It holds a significant part of my youth and history. I was one of the girls who lived with and was educated by the Benedictine Sisters, and at 14 years of age I entered the Congregation. Monastic and missionary life was not easy. It was a shock to my Aboriginal existence to overnight change my life and leave my peers behind to become a religious Sister. After some time, I came to realise how dedicated these Sisters were to their religious life and vocation to be missionaries working with Aboriginal people. Some people will find that hard to believe. I know New Norcia was also a place of suffering, and I know Katharine understands that too.

Walking together and listening has made this book possible. These values run deep for me. I am an Aboriginal person of the Yued and Whadjuk peoples of the Noongar Nation from the southwest of Western Australia. I am also a Benedictine Missionary Sister and have been a nun for over 60 years. The Yued traditional lands include the region where New Norcia is located. New Norcia is my family's cultural and spiritual home. My ancestors have had a close connection with New Norcia since not long after the Aboriginal mission was established there. This includes my great-grandmother Eliza Willaway (née Tainan). She was one of the Aboriginal women replaced in her role as matron of the mission when the first Spanish nuns arrived. She is included in this book too. My family is very proud of our long association with New Norcia and the Benedictine community there. Following the closure of the mission at New Norcia in 1974, my Congregation returned to live in Spain. I went with them and stayed there for three years before coming back to Australia. In the last 25 years I have been based in a Benedictine Missionary Sisters Congregation in Nebraska, USA.

Katharine is very well placed to write this book about the Spanish Sisters. She has written extensively about the history of women in the Catholic Church. She has had over 25 years' association with New Norcia, including being a member of the Archives, Research and Publications Committee for the Benedictine Community. I know the remaining Spanish Sisters have wholeheartedly supported Katharine writing this book and they have entrusted her with information, some of a sensitive nature, to faithfully tell their story.

This book about the Spanish Sisters and their experience as missionaries in the distant foreign land of Australia tells a story I am pleased to know. It is a careful step along the way to more storytelling and deeper listening. The curious title, *The Bridge Between*, is insightful. It reminds me that we can all build bridges when we share stories and listen well. It reminds me we are always 'between' hearing and understanding more.

This book has become part of my journey too. I remember first meeting Katharine in 1999 in Perth when she started to write the history of the Spanish Sisters. I have shared my story and insights of the Benedictine Sisters with her on many occasions in the intervening years. I accepted an invitation to attend a reunion with the 'mission girls' in 2001. The reunion was a very heartfelt occasion and showed the depth for feeling between the Sisters and past residents. Katharine was there too, and I saw how she listened. In 2015, I accepted another invitation and collaborated with Katharine in a workshop for theological students about monasticism at New Norcia. In 2016 we co-presented a session at the Conference on the History of Women Religious in Santa Clara, California. Through these activities, Katharine has become a dear friend. This book has been written slowly with patience, resilience and dedication. I warmly invite you to read it.

22 June 2020
Whadjuk Boodjar
Perth, Western Australia

Acknowledgements

Help and encouragement have come from many directions to sustain and enliven this project. My deepest debt is to the people who have shared their stories and photographs, inviting me into their memories of life as a Benedictine sister or a child in care at St Joseph's, usually over several conversations. Those interviews have been a privilege. Three stakeholder communities enabled the work and facilitated connections. I am grateful to the New Norcia Aboriginal Corporation, especially the members of the executive, Mary Nannup, Margaret Drayton and Paul Willaway, and to Mae Taylor whose careful initiative prompted the reunion of 2001. The Benedictine Missionary Sisters of Tutzing have been gracious hosts in Kalumburu, Madrid and Nebraska, where Sr Winfrieda Bugayong, Sr Maria Gratia Balagot, Sr Margargeta Wegscheid and Sr Pia Portmann made further introductions to the house of oblates in Barcelona, the Cistercian community in Valladolid, the Benedictine community of San José in Burgos, and to the families of the sisters. The generosity of the Benedictine Community of New Norcia also underpins this book. Abbot Placid Spearritt responded warmly to an initial enquiry with an invitation to 'come and see' what the archives might yield about the Spanish sisters. His vision for scholarship at New Norcia enabled the early stages of the project, and the hospitality of both the archives and the guesthouse of the Benedictine Community of New Norcia have remained a mainstay under the more recent leadership of Abbot John Herbert. Bernadette Taylor and her team at the guesthouse always smoothed the way, and the community's archivists Wendy McKinley, Leen Charles and Peter Hocking have contributed countless hours of professional expertise, regularly going the extra mile with patience and good humour. In particular, Peter Hocking's cheerful help and acumen, across a continent and three time zones, has been invaluable.

A BRIDGE BETWEEN

Research over decades is a rare freedom in contemporary academia. At the outset I was a member of the History Department at the University of Adelaide where a period of study leave made the first steps possible. The project was both fruitfully disrupted and ultimately enriched by my move to the United Faculty of Theology, and more recently Pilgrim Theological College, within what is now the University of Divinity in Melbourne. In a context where small group teaching is still valued and possible, students in the New Norcia intensives have engaged with the Benedictine story and the mission town, and expanded my understanding of how the site itself speaks. Along the way friends and colleagues have read and improved drafts, responded to papers and answered queries. I'm especially indebted to Edmund Campion, Graeme Davison and David Hilliard who read and discussed the full draft with typical generosity and insight, and to Kellie Abbot at the National Archives of Australia, Sally Douglas, Sarah Gador-Whyte, Stefano Girola, Anna Haebich, Andrew Hamilton, Kerrie Handasyde, Margot Harker, John Kinder, Margaret Malone, Lauren Mosso, Jill O'Brien, Carmel Posa, Randall Prior, Sharne Rolfe, Howard Wallace, David Whiteford at the State Records Office of Western Australia, and Naomi Wolfe, Indigenous Theologies Project Officer at the University of Divinity. Carlos Lopez, Kerry Mullan, Teresa De Castro and Fr David Barry translated material from historic handwriting. Stuart Fenner and Adrienne Maloney transcribed recordings. Joe Courtney made time to draft the maps and Alejandro Polanco Masa brought them expertly to life. Mary Nannup, Margaret Drayton, Paul Willaway and Sr Veronica Willaway advised on photographs and sought permissions. Merryn Gray, Carl Rainer, Lauren Murphy and Geoff Hunt brought technological magic and eagle eyes to the manuscript. The ANU.Lives editorial board and the editorial team at ANU Press were consistently perceptive and professional. Vivienne Halligan shared her family's stock of the sisters' embroidery. Patricia Weishaar with James Wahl and Chase Becker managed transport from Minnesota to Nebraska and back; and Helena Kadmos and Kevin Crombie made key trips to New Norcia to assist. Anne and Joe Courtney regularly made space for a visiting researcher in their home, and so did Sue Chapman, Helen Brash and Tim Featherstonhaugh, Phil and Imogen Garner, Tom Sutton, and the Fenner-Kadmos household. Kai Jensen, Jane Kelly, Kathleen Troup and Carole Carmody were always interested and insightful. The Dalton McCaughey Library is an ecumenical collection of visionary breadth and depth, resourcing conversations across the disciplinary boundaries. It has been a pleasure to share that conversation with good colleagues at Pilgrim and in the Catholic history seminar at the University of Divinity. I have also benefited from discussion with colleagues at the Australian Academy of the Social Sciences symposium on women and missions (Brisbane, June 2013), the University of Notre Dame symposium on the *Nun in the World* (London, May 2015), the US Conference on the History of Women Religious in St Paul (2013) and Santa Clara (2016), and the Third and Fourth International Monastic Symposia at Sant'Anselmo, Rome (2011, 2016), supported by funds from the Research Office at the University of Divinity and the Uniting Church in Australia, Synod of Victoria and Tasmania.

Some time before this project began I met my husband John H. Smith at a land rights demonstration. Later, we got to know each other at the monastery. He has been the sustaining constant through all the phases of this project. He has kept the kitchen humming and the household ticking beyond any rational accounting of tasks, while his commitment to good scholarship and to the Rule of Benedict informs and inspires my own. It is no platitude to say that without him this book would not have been completed. For this and for all, I am so grateful.

Katharine Massam

Illustrations

Figure 0.1: Map of Australia, showing locations in the text. xix

Figure 1.1: New Norcia cemetery, graves of the Spanish Benedictine Missionary Sisters, March 2017 3

Figure 1.2: Ms Mae Taylor, Sr Francisca Pardo, Sr Visitación Cidad, Fr Anscar McPhee and Sr Teresa González in the cemetery at New Norcia after the memorial service in October 2001 4

Figure 1.3: Teresa, Francisca, Pilar and Maria Gratia recording memories of the mission around the library table in Madrid, 2004 (left); Scholastica telling the stories of her photo album in Kalumburu, 1999 (right) 17

Figure 1.4: Sheila Humphries's painting *Life at St Joseph's*, within the liturgical display at the reunion, Mass of Thanksgiving, October 2001 20

Figure 1.5: Members of the reunion on the steps of the Abbey Church, October 2001. 32

Figure 2.1: Brother Friolán Miró and the residents of St Joseph's before 1904 42

Figure 2.2: The first Teresian community at New Norcia with residents of St Joseph's, 1904 43

Figure 2.3: Detail of Teresian arrival: Aboriginal matron with a cockatoo on her shoulder. 44

Figure 2.4: Detail of Teresian arrival: Teresa Roca and other sisters with St Joseph's girls behind 44

Figure 2.5: Fr Henry Altimira and Fr Planas with plans for the Drysdale River Mission 67

xiii

Figure 2.6: St Joseph's from the southern tower of St Gertrude's,
c. 1907. 67

Figure 2.7: St Joseph's girls assembled to show skills in weaving and
sewing, with the towers of St Gertrude's in the background 68

Figure 2.8: St Gertrude's College c. 1909, with the buildings
of St Joseph's to the left and cottages in the foreground 68

Figure 2.9: St Gertrude's and St Joseph's looking east c. 1908. 69

Figure 3.1: Interior of the Abbey Church 'before 1923' or as it
would have been on the morning of 1 July 1909 when Maria
Harispe made her profession as an oblate of New Norcia 76

Figure 3.2: Maria Harispe c. 1915 with St Joseph's residents. 77

Figure 3.3: A First Communion photo c. 1908 including the
Aboriginal matrons in the main doorway of St Gertrude's
College. 86

Figure 3.4: The St Joseph's girls with Aboriginal matrons
on the back verandah of St Gertrude's, c. 1908 86

Figure 3.5: The Sisters, dressed in Benedictine habits with
the St Joseph's girls, after December 1915 94

Figure 3.6: Mother Elias Devine, Easter 1933, aged 95,
'a woman of uncommon common sense' 95

Figure 3.7: Consuelo (centre) with Teresa (left), Maria (right)
and residents of St Joseph's, after September 1912 and before
December 1915. 100

Figure 3.8: Teresa Roca, one of the original Teresian community,
remembered in the *Notebooks* as setting out again in 1915
'without fear and with great confidence in God'. 102

Figure 3.9: Teresa Roca and Aboriginal girls working at embroidery
and crochet in the sewing room 103

Figure 4.1: Maria and children of St Joseph's near a swing,
with laundry in the background, c. 1912 106

Figure 4.2: Detail of Maria and the children. 107

Figure 4.3: Detail of laundry work at St Joseph's, after 1910. 107

ILLUSTRATIONS

Figure 4.4: The drawings that guided the renovation at St Joseph's in 1910 110

Figure 4.5: Cottages for Aboriginal workers and families in front of St Gertrude's College; St Joseph's rear left. 123

Figure 5.1: Home villages of the Benedictine sisters who arrived at New Norcia, 1921–33 (Cañizar de los Ajos, Cavia, Corella, Palacios de Benaver, Sasamón, Tapia de Villadiego and Villorejo)... 134

Figure 5.2: The village of Tapia de Villadiego, Burgos............ 134

Figure 5.3: Monastery of San Salvador, Palacios de Benaver, Burgos . . 143

Figure 5.4: Display of needlework by St Joseph's Girls, *St Ildephonsus College Magazine*, 1929, 7 147

Figure 5.5: Maria Harispe, c. 1925; the photograph that accompanied her obituary in the Perth *Record* 150

Figure 5.6: Emmaus House, Maredsous, Belgium, 2010. 157

Figure 5.7: Abbey church at the monastery of Maredsous, Belgium, 2010 157

Figure 5.8: Arriving at Pago Pago Mission in the Kimberley, 18 August 1931. Benedictine sisters at right in shoes and stockings, possibly Abbot Catalan in bare feet 158

Figure 5.9: Transferring to Drysdale River site, 1932 159

Figure 5.10: On the lugger *Koolinda*; Matilde, Escolastica and Hildegard with Fr Boniface and Aboriginal children 159

Figure 5.11: Gertrude, Escolastica and Hildegard with Aboriginal children on the steps of the first convent at Drysdale River, 1931 161

Figure 6.1: Benedictine Oblate Sisters of New Norcia early 1931 . . . 166

Figure 6.2: Benita and Felicitas en route to Belgium with Fr Paul Arza.. 177

Figure 6.3: Benita Gozalo to Abbot Catalan, June 1936.......... 179

Figure 6.4: Escolastica's sewing machine put to another good use, 1937... 186

Figure 6.5: Escolastica Martinez to Abbot Catalan, 1937 186

Figure 6.6: Interior of the church at Drysdale River c. 1947, Sister Magdalena Ruiz with a First Communicant 187

Figure 6.7: Interior of the church at Drysdale River c. 1947, sanctuary and two side altars, St Joseph and St Thérèse, patron of missions 188

Figure 6.8: Washing in the river, but wearing collars. 195

Figure 6.9: Washing as it was more usually done, without collars and with helpers. 195

Figure 6.10: Magdalena (seated), Ludivina and Maria (in apron) on a picnic at Drysdale River, c. 1939 196

Figure 6.11: Escolastica with her class at Drysdale River, 1932. 196

Figure 6.12: Fr Boniface Cubero with a camp oven on a picnic, 1930s 197

Figure 6.13: Posing for a photo on an excursion, 1930s: Hildegard (left), Escolastica (right), Matilde in front, local 'bush' men, woman in mission dress, and Benedictine monk with rifle 198

Figure 6.14: Josephine and Visitación with fishing nets at the beach, 1970s 199

Figure 7.1: The 12 who arrived at New Norcia in November 1948 on deck of the *Toscana* 232

Figure 7.2: Postulants on a picnic, 1949: Josefina Carrillo (standing left) and Amalia González (standing right) 235

Figure 7.3: Fatima Drayton brings a crêpe paper parasol from the school concerts forward at the reunion liturgy, 2001 238

Figure 8.1: First Community at Bindoon, c. 1949 243

Figure 8.2: A studio portrait to send to their families was a thank-you gift to the Benedictine sisters at Bindoon in the 1950s (Hildegard, Visitación, Florentina and Lucia). 244

Figure 8.3: Home villages of the Benedictine sisters to 1950, still focused on Burgos 250

Figure 8.4: Visitación Cidad under the fig tree, Murray Street, Perth, 1950 255

ILLUSTRATIONS

Figure 9.1: Back left to right: Cecilia Farrell, Ludivina Marcos and Mary Cidad. Front left to right: Angelina Cerezo, Dolores Vallejo, Magdelena Ruiz and Benita Gozalo, c. 1960 261

Figure 9.2: Veronica Therese Willaway, Pius Moynihan, c. 1962. . . . 261

Figure 9.3: Scholastica Carrillo, making cheese in the 1960s 264

Figure 9.4: Scholastica with cooking pots at Kalumburu, 1970s. . . . 264

Figure 9.5: Needlework was a sustaining tradition in the convent and at the school 267

Figure 9.6: New dining room at St Joseph's, 1956 273

Figure 9.7: St Joseph's marching team at rest, New Norcia sports day, 1960s 286

Figure 9.8: The novices and postulants playing hockey at the back of St Joseph's—Imelda and Josephine in white veils, Veronica centre and Pius right, c. 1959. Fowl yard in the background . . 303

Figure 9.9: Sr Veronica Therese with her family on the day of her final profession, 12 March 1966; left to right: Rose, Philomena, Veronica, Peter, Harold, Gabriel and Isobel 304

Figure 10.1: Young members from the Spanish house of formation in the late 1960s at Hildegard's tombstone in Zaragoza 313

Figure 10.2: Natividad Montero makes her profession as Sister Josephine, March 1964 at New Norcia. Students from St Gertrude's College and one of their teachers to her left, Felicitas, Veronica and Antonia to her right 313

Figure 10.3: Scholastica, Florentina and Visitación, and Kalumburu's cat, with chorizo made from the local wild boar that fed on the monastery's figs 322

Figure 10.4: Speeches during an annual dinner at the New Norcia hotel to celebrate the adult education classes, 1970s. Mr Peter Cuffley standing, Abbot Gregory Gomez and Br Anthony McAlinden to his right. 326

Figure 10.5: Chapel at the Girrawheen convent, showing tabernacle and wall cross by Robert Juniper. 333

Figure 10.6: *Ora et Labora* banner by Iris Rossen, now in the chapel of the Benedictine Missionary Sisters of Tutzing in Madrid . . . 333

Figure 10.7: The last of the community from New Norcia embarks for Barcelona, 20 March 1975; left to right: Margaret, Veronica, Dolores and Felicitas. 343

Figure 10.8: Benedictines and community assembled for the reunion liturgy, October 2001 351

Figure 10.9: The abbot greets the sisters at the monastery gate as the liturgy begins, Abbot Placid Spearritt and Sister Carmen Ruiz Besti. 351

Figure 10.10: Benedictine sisters (Veronica, Visitación and Carmen) with the congregation in the church for the reunion liturgy 353

Figure 10.11: Mae Taylor (left) and Anne Moynihan (Sr Pius) bring bread and wine for the Eucharist to Abbot Placid Spearritt and Dom Chris Power. The abbot is wearing the chasuble made by the novices in 1948 354

Figure 10.12: Praying the Lord's Prayer during the Eucharist 354

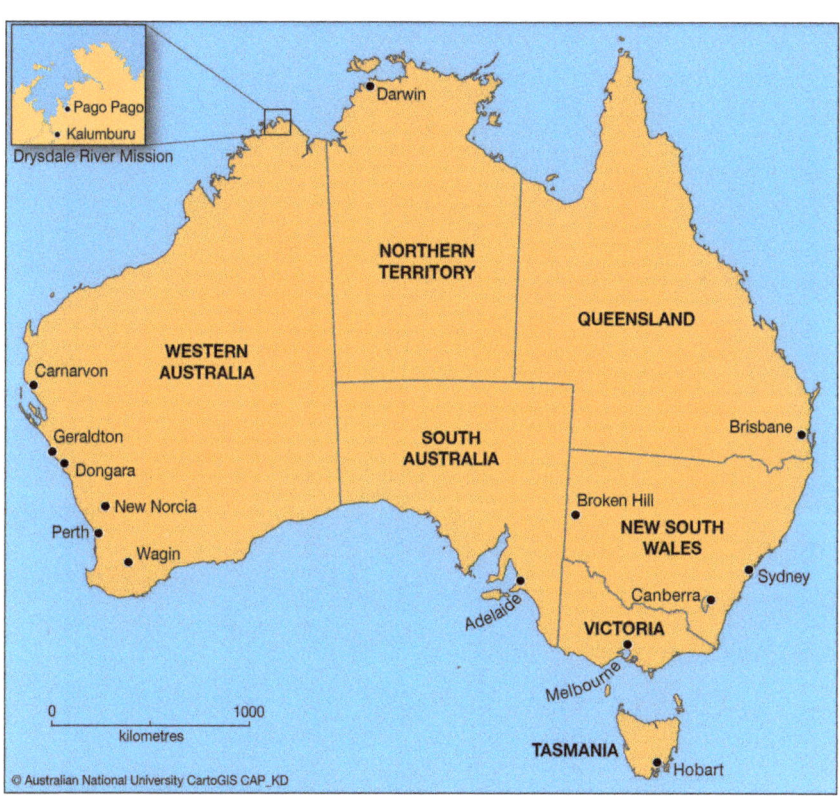

Figure 0.1: Map of Australia, showing locations in the text.

1

To Name and to Remember: The Reunion of 2001

'I am very thankful to be here. And there is something more in my heart, something I cannot say.' Sister Teresa González speaks firmly, with characteristic Spanish emphasis in the English she learnt in Australia 53 years ago. She speaks for us all, and we nod. We have sung an ancient liturgy of psalms to remember the eight Benedictine Missionary Sisters who are buried in the cemetery at New Norcia, in Western Australia, and 12 others who are in Spain, France and South Australia. It is the first time, so far as anyone knows, that the names of these women have been read together here, or anywhere.

The ceremony has been simple. In the open air, with the wind in the gum trees beyond the wall and the galahs striking out occasionally over the chant, we mark the graves of eight women who came from Spain to work with Aboriginal children in Australia's only monastic town. The evening light is clear, the sun is still warming the gravel and the wildflowers are fresh on the weathered graves. It is powerful to name and to remember.

Our vacant chairs still form a circle around the graves, and in the ring alongside the simple crosses of the Benedictine sisters there is another mound, unmarked. Sister Teresa and I stare at the baked ground: 'Is this Gracie?' I ask. I am guessing. I know a story from newspaper fragments. Like many of the women who grew up at St Joseph's Native School and Orphanage, Miss Grace Williams was born in the town and spent her life here. She did not know her father 'from America', and until she was four she had lived with her mother's people in a mission cottage.[1] Then, in 1899 or 1900 she was committed to the care of the monastery. She was one of the children living there when the first sisters arrived in 1904 to take over the running of St Joseph's from the monks. She was there as new buildings were built and as the Benedictine Missionary Sisters were made an official community of New Norcia. Grace never left. Whether poor health and bad eyesight determined things or whether *Pax*, the parish's newspaper, was right to report she had 'found her happiness in the secluded life of that Institution and in co-operating with the Benedictine sisters in their work for the native children' we do not know.[2] But when she died in 1956, aged 61, it was two years since she had taken the name 'Gertrude' and pledged herself to the Rule of Benedict as an oblate in private vows. Her funeral was a solemn occasion for the Benedictine monks and the sisters, as well as for family from New Norcia and Perth. She was buried in a Benedictine habit alongside the missionary women. But her grave was not marked. 'I think this is Grace Williams's grave', I tell Teresa. 'Grace? Ah yes! Gracie. She was very close to the sisters. The procession, the funeral, I think I was here.' Our liturgy did not name Grace or Gertrude Williams. Her grave might be part of the circle. But who am I to remember? How can I presume to know the story in her names?

Grace's grave disrupts the circle and makes space between sharp categories. I wonder what she thought of her insider–outsider status? So much of this story is like that, including my own part in it. I have known ever since I recorded long interviews with each of the sisters in 1999 that telling their story could not be an austere academic exercise. 'Don't praise anybody!' Teresa had warned. 'You will write what you like, of course, but don't praise anybody.' I quote her feisty injunction back to myself again and again, hearing the sisters' collective impatience with sentiment and the wariness that shadows conversations about their motivations and convictions. The deepest realities, 'these are what God knows', says Sister Visitación. Talking too much can trivialise decisions that lie beyond words. Discussion might belittle what it meant to live so far from home and family, to work so hard, and to believe or hope so fiercely that this was as God wished. They did not understand it. They learnt to distrust smooth, plausible words. There is pain now, with confusion and regret about what the institution meant in Aboriginal lives. 'We have much to pray for, and not much to be proud of', Visitación insists quietly. Naming needs time.

---

1   *Pax*, 22 July 1956, 3. See also Lois Tilbrook, *Nyungar Tradition: Glimpses of Aborigines of South-Western Australia 1829–1914* (Nedlands, WA: University of Western Australia Press, 1983), 230.
2   *Pax*, 22 July 1956, 3.

'Don't praise anybody!' It is a strange warning, but welcome. A promotional story will not do. These women have become my friends, and they are the link that binds my friendship with the Aboriginal women and men of New Norcia. They have also been missionaries, caught in the government policies that removed Aboriginal children from their families, committed to religious welfare before, and sometimes against, social justice and political rights. 'Don't *praise* anybody'. Teresa chooses her emphasis. Of course not, Sister. It is much easier to stereotype the mission enterprise as misguided, mistaken and cruel: to focus on abuse covered by institutional pride, to frame it all as more wilful oppression linked to destructive, arrogant religion. Much easier, but not good enough, not full enough, not fair. It would break hearts again but not heal them. And the Aboriginal women who have asked these sisters 'home' again and have gathered with them in the cemetery are hoping for healing, not heartbreak. Emotion runs deep. Even for us at the edge, tears are the most likely language. Women who have fought all their lives against the threat that their own children might end up in care are bringing their grandchildren to town, proud and keen that the next generation might meet 'the ladies who looked after Nanna'. It makes a difference how we name, how we remember.

Figure 1.1: New Norcia cemetery, graves of the Spanish Benedictine Missionary Sisters, March 2017.
Source: Author's collection.

Figure 1.2: Ms Mae Taylor, Sr Francisca Pardo, Sr Visitación Cidad, Fr Anscar McPhee and Sr Teresa González in the cemetery at New Norcia after the memorial service in October 2001.

Source: New Norcia Archives (NNA) W6-B4-4-213.

1. TO NAME AND TO REMEMBER

We are a small crowd in the cemetery. There will be hundreds in town tomorrow for bigger celebrations, at the Mass, the barbecue and the opening of a new museum display. This occasion, in the late afternoon on Friday 19 October 2001, is a New Norcia gathering: the community of Benedictine monks, some employees from the town, Aboriginal women and men who grew up in New Norcia, and just a few others who know the honoured guests. These guests, the visiting Benedictine sisters, have come back to New Norcia at the invitation of some of the women who grew up at St Joseph's. For two years and more, Mae Taylor has been building support for this extraordinary gathering. Back in New Norcia herself after her 1950s childhood spent at St Joseph's and working in the monastery kitchen, Mae shaped a daring plan. Moved by the visit of first one and then another individual sister to the mission town, she enlisted the support of the abbot's secretary and the blessing of the abbot to write to a string of church administrators seeking permission for five elderly Spanish women to travel to a reunion. It was a bold proposal but, with other local Aboriginal women, Mae persisted. Now Sisters Teresa González Francisca Pardo, Pilar Catalan, Visitación Cidad and Carmen Ruiz are here. They have flown halfway around the globe on airfares paid by their former students. In these extraordinary days, the former missionaries and the 'St Joseph's girls' retrace their experiences and celebrate, mourn, and pray. They remember, together. In the context of the people and the place that has itself shaped understanding, relationships are being tested, claimed, and renegotiated. Mae is in the crowd now, chuckling at one of the elderly sisters, 'one of my mothers', who takes a ritual bouquet apart to have flowers for another grave that she says needs attention. 'Always had her own idea', Mae says, grinning at the small rebellion, naming it, as a daughter might, and remembering.

There have been flowers for the sisters since they arrived in town more than a week ago. Mae, and her sister Sheila Humphries, had made sure of that. 'Welcome home', the card said. Were they home? Actually, Teresa, Francisca and Pilar live in Madrid; Visitación (Visi) has come from Kalumburu in the far north Kimberley; Carmen from Jamberoo in New South Wales. But New Norcia is as surely 'home' as any place could be for these Spanish sisters. Now in their seventies and eighties, they first lived here as young women. That experience has defined them as strongly as any in their lives. In Carabanchel, among many convents in that outer suburb of Madrid, they are the 'Australian Sisters'. Visi has brought greetings from Schollie, Sister Scholastica, who will not now leave the Kimberley.

Sister Anne, the Australian-Irish recruit who was once Sister Pius, has come from Perth, and Sister Veronica, once Marie, the oldest of the local Willaway girls, who joined the Benedictines as a teenager, has come from her convent in Nebraska in the United States to be with the Spaniards too. Like the Spanish, she has been part of the Benedictine Missionary Sisters of Tutzing since 1986, when the New Norcia community merged with that German-founded group, now strongest numerically in the Philippines and Korea. The New Norcia sisters are together again for the first time since their former congregation shifted its motherhouse from New Norcia to Spain in 1974.

Yesterday, sitting in the convent kitchen waiting for the kettle to boil there was a silence, broken as Sister Carmen mused: 'You know, we did not bring a pack of cards'. She met Sister Visi's sudden astonishment: 'My goodness, we have not seen each other for almost 40 years, and we are talking about cards! Can we find nothing to say?' The kettle boils, and the brisk Spanish exchange merges into afternoon tea, but the question lingers at the heart of the reunion. Re-create an old life where playing cards and checkers marked brief snatched holidays? Or talk of the realities since then, the changes, discoveries, losses, betrayals, pain, and enduring hopes? Or take the risk that there is nothing to say? 'Did we do nothing good?' Teresa has asked. Risk all the words that can never explain? If we name it, we must also remember.

Veronica Willaway and her sister, Rose Narkle, have sat together by the gravesites. They are Aboriginal Australians of the Yued people and their forebears were linked to the mission from its earliest decades after the two Spanish monks, Rosendo Salvado and Joseph Serra, made their way to the district in 1847. Their grandmother's grandmother, Eliza Tainan Willaway, spoke on behalf of the women and girls of the mission in the 1880s, in keeping with Salvado's nineteenth-century policy that Aboriginal women, not European nuns, would be his deputies as St Joseph's took shape.[3] Their parents, grandparents and forebears back to the time of the first missionaries in the 1840s are buried in this cemetery too. Veronica ran away from home, from one of the mission cottages, to join the sisters at the age of 14. 'Mum chased her with a broom one day', observes Rose unromantically, 'and she went to the sisters instead and stayed.' It was

---

3   For example, her speech of welcome to Cardinal Moran, *West Australian Catholic Record* (hereafter *Record*), 10 February 1887, 4; Katharine Massam and John H. Smith, 'New Norcia and Federation: A Story of Nation, Church and Race', *New Norcia Studies* 9 (2001): 13–14.

all of 500 metres across level ground from the cottage to the convent, 500 metres and a journey between worlds. Another local girl, Vera Farrell, was already there, professed as Sister Cecilia. Rose herself might have joined too, and there were four other former students of St Joseph's who did become postulants. Veronica stayed, from New Norcia to Barcelona, to a stint in the Kimberley, and now the United States. Later, much later, in an interview in Nebraska, Veronica disputes the implications of my draft and a summary of the Benedictine women. Her challenge means a lot. Getting this right matters to us both.[4] 'Well, let's put it this way', she proposes: 'They weren't feminine, nor were they motherly. They were not manly. They were just their own selves. They were there to be *religious*. And you know back then, that feminine would have been a bad thing.'[5] Interpretations diverge, demand precision and defy it, memories tangle, nuance matters. How do we name that?

That St Joseph's was a tough institution is beyond doubt. Efficiency and economy prevailed in a context that was sometimes barbaric. Generally anxious for government support and approbation, New Norcia did not challenge decisions unless they impacted on religious commitment. 'I am not prepared to sanction the fillings', noted the cost-conscious official on a request for a dentist to visit St Joseph's in March 1926, for example. There were prominent Catholic dentists in Perth, but no one at New Norcia sought their help or suggested the mission could contribute to the cost.[6] As a result, instead of the plan for 26 extractions and 44 fillings among the 25 girls at St Joseph's, including only one patient who would have more than two teeth pulled, there were only extractions: 66 in total. Grace Williams lost four teeth that day; one of her friends lost seven, and three others lost five.[7]

---

4   On dynamics in oral history interviewing, Laura Rademaker, '"We Want a Good Mission Not Rubbish Please": Aboriginal Petitions and Mission Nostalgia', *Aboriginal History* 40 (2016): 119–23, 138; Gillian Cowlishaw, 'On "Getting It Wrong": Collateral Damage in the History Wars', *Australian Historical Studies* 37 (2006): 181–202.
5   Veronica Willaway, Interview, Nebraska, 8 July 2012.
6   R. F. Stockwell, 'Henderson, Gilbert Dowling (1890–1977)', *Australian Dictionary of Biography*, National Centre of Biography, The Australian National University, adb.anu.edu.au/biography/henderson-gilbert-dowling-12975/text23449; published first in hardcopy 2005, accessed 5 November 2016.
7   E. E. Copping, Deputy Chief Protector of Aborigines, 'New Norcia Mission – Subsidy and General', State Records Office of Western Australia (SROWA) S2030 cons993 1926/0350, 12 February, 16 February and 15 March 1926.

There were also tyrannies and abuse initiated at St Joseph's itself. The stories have begun to surface and more will follow. At the time of the reunion, there are records of despair in archives and elsewhere. One trail from as late as May 1968 concerns a 15-year-old state ward whose hair was cut off, 'in a very short male style',[8] as punishment for running away to her home at Goomalling Reserve. The younger sisters were appalled at the archaic practice and the superintendent was somehow alerted, but the girl told him, 'Anyone can do anything to us and nobody cares'.[9] Her name is on the record, but this is not a public memory. Will she be at the reunion? Is her family coming? No one is sure.

For Rose Narkle and Veronica Willaway this reunion is a family gathering. When they arrived yesterday with nephews, nieces and grandnephews, I hoped I might see Paul, Rose's eldest son. But he will be in town tomorrow, Rose says, coming up for the day, with his uncle, the cousins, dozens of others. This is about family, remembered and not, named and unnamed.

At the beginning, Paul Willaway's friendship had connected me into this project. From the first days it was clear that the 'St Joseph girls' held keys to the Benedictine sisters' stories, and so I drove to Moora, the next town along the highway from New Norcia, to talk to Mary and Gloria and Fatima, three of the Drayton sisters. As we turned on the tape recorder, the first question was for me: 'So, how do you know Paul?' I explained we'd been students together at different Perth universities, he in Social Work at Curtin, me in Arts at the University of Western Australia. We'd both joined the Tertiary Young Christian Students, a group that shaped my ideas about social justice and Catholic commitment. At meetings when that group set about social analysis, Paul's single presence always brought the proportion of Aboriginal people among us way out ahead of the national statistical average. He was then my one Aboriginal friend. I dropped his name into the tape recorder at that first interview, claiming the history and grateful for the link. It was my first lesson in the relationships that sustain the memory of the Sisters and guard the telling of their story. There is power in the naming; we all know that.

*****

---

8   J. S. Beharell, Superintendent, to Commissioner of Native Welfare, 24 May 1968, Department of Child Welfare, 'Missions – Private – New Norcia – General Correspondence', SROWA S1099 cons2532 A0403 v1.

9   Beharell to Commissioner of Native Welfare, 24 May 1968. View from the younger sisters: Anne Moynihan, Interview, North Perth, 19 March 1999.

Named simply *Life at St Joseph's*, the painting by Yued artist Sheila Humphries was the focal point of the main liturgy of the reunion fortnight. It now hangs at the centre of the commemorative museum display. Sheila summed up her work, saying:

> The painting tells the story of our life in St Joseph's Orphanage. I was inspired to paint it with the love that I had, and the memories that I had, of the Sisters and the girls in the home.[10]

The first aim of this book is to reflect on what it means to hear those stories of love and memories. I hope to pay attention to the account of these missionary women that can be told only 'by heart'. The jumble of material in their scattered archives is not only emotional, personal and conflicting (as historical evidence often is) but also concerned above all with the things of the spirit, with the immaterial matters of the heart. Emotion has become a focus for historical reflection across many different periods, but religious belief is not strictly an emotion. The particular intersections of faith and passion that flow through this story make sense only theologically, not in rational or even psychological terms. What scholarly and human tools might we forge to help us explore 'soul' as a category of history? How might we set 'love' and 'faith', and also 'pain' and 'anger', alongside stories of race, class and gender that we already know shape the discussion of our past?

Public and also confidential accounts of neglect and great suffering in institutions like St Joseph's, and at New Norcia itself, have begun to fill the silences in the institutional records. Calls since the mid-1990s brought the harm done in and by institutions that failed to protect children from abuse into clearer view. Through the years of this project, the church's Towards Healing process, the state government's Redress scheme and, finally, the 2013–17 Royal Commission into Institutional Responses to Child Sexual Abuse sought to acknowledge and respond to crime and cover-up in the past, including five particular claims against two Benedictine sisters at St Joseph's.[11] More broadly, the allegations of inadequate

---

10   Sheila Humphries, Interview with Sr Anne Carter, New Norcia, 10 June 2002, *New Norcia Studies* 10 (2002): 36–37.
11   Royal Commission into Institutional Responses to Child Sexual Abuse, *Analysis of Claims of Child Sexual Abuse Made with Respect to Catholic Church Institutions in Australia*, Commonwealth of Australia, February 2017, 135, www.childabuseroyalcommission.gov.au/sites/default/files/REPT.0012.001.0001.pdf; accessed 26 March 2018. See also 'Towards Healing', Truth, Justice and Healing Council, www.tjhcouncil.org.au/support/towards-healing.aspx; accessed 26 March 2018; Redress WA (2008–2011), Find & Connect, 16 January 2012, last modified 12 February 2015, www.findandconnect.gov.au/guide/wa/WE00505#tab1; accessed 26 March 2018; Royal Commission into Institutional Responses to Child Sexual Abuse, *Final Report*, 15 December 2017, www.childabuseroyalcommission.gov.au/final-report; accessed 26 March 2018.

education, hunger, violence and fear of particular places associated with sexual predators cast a pall over all accounts of the institution. Members of the reunion shared their experience in the various enquiries, advocated for healing through roles at Yorgum, the Aboriginal Link-Up agency in Perth, with the New Norcia Aboriginal Corporation, in government departments and local reconciliation committees.[12] The pain and anger of those making the allegations must be heard, alongside their vehement hope that speaking out will raise awareness and ensure healing. Together with sufficient funding to assist survivors of abuse, healing also depends on wider recognition in the community that churches cooperated with government in an entrenched system that dispossessed Aboriginal people of their land and disrupted families over generations.

This is hard for the dedicated Benedictine women to hear. As they come to terms with the accusations there is shock and disbelief, disappointment and shame, stoic determination to listen well, and also gratitude that among the Aboriginal voices calling for justice some extend their hope for understanding and healing to include the Benedictines themselves. The institution was abusive, make no mistake; and yet the Aboriginal women insist on a more complex story. When descendants see a stolen childhood in photos on Facebook ('Those nuns look like Nazis') the women themselves comment warmly: 'Lovely Sister Carmen.' 'Sister Margaret: warrior woman!' 'Sister Teresa was our teacher. Everyone loved her. She taught us to dance.' 'We send our love.' While the narrative about injustice at St Joseph's is rightly aggressive, it is coupled with generous acknowledgment of the Benedictine sisters and of strong bonds with individuals among them.

This book draws on interviews with Aboriginal women who grew up with the Benedictine sisters, but it is not a history of St Joseph's Native School and Orphanage. That work with a focus on the experience of the children in care remains to be done, and I hope by an Aboriginal historian. This book is a history of the group of Benedictine Missionary Sisters whose story taps a rich vein of memory below the surface of the Spanish Benedictine mission of New Norcia. It gathers a fragmented story from the margins of the archive and offers a point of entry into material to support further work. I will not be able tell a complete and comprehensive

---

12 'New Norcia Healing Camp: The Road to Healing', *Yorgum Newsletter*, March 2014, n.p.

story, but it may be that by reflecting on why a smooth account is not possible we can come to understand more of what it means for historians, and all Australians, to hear stories such as those told by and about the Benedictine Missionary Sisters.

Remembering in context

From 1904 until 1974 the hidden lives of the Benedictine Missionary Sisters of New Norcia stood at the heart of the complex dynamics of the famous mission town. Through the nineteenth century New Norcia's founder, Rosendo Salvado, had steadfastly refused offers from European women, and especially Spanish Benedictine women, to join his monastic foundation among the Yued people of the Victoria Plains.[13] On Salvado's death in 1901, the decision of his successor to invite a group of nuns to replace Aboriginal matrons at St Joseph's Native School and Orphanage triggered the events that established the missionary sisters as a diocesan congregation within the mission and saw the expansion of their work in succeeding decades to the Kimberley (1931), Bindoon (1948), Spain itself in 1958, and Perth's suburbs in 1973. Their collective biography touches the most pressing questions in Australian historical writing, bringing issues of race, gender and class together in a crucible of religious commitment. Their story offers a close study of the development of a community that was transnational in scope and holds wide significance.

The pages that follow focus on the Benedictine sisters in order to demonstrate the fundamental significance of the emotional and physical work of the institution they ran and the network of relationships that shaped their lives. From the South American and Mexican foundresses, through the chain migration of young women who travelled from villages near Burgos in the north of Spain to join them in the 1920s, 30s, 40s and 50s, to the Anglo-Celtic and Aboriginal Australians who joined in the 1950s the Benedictine Missionary Sisters navigated between boundaries. They were Spanish-speaking Catholic women in Protestant, White Australia, they were 'sisters' not monks in a monastic town, they were missionaries in an institution that began as a whitewashed hut among the other whitewashed huts that housed Aboriginal families,

---

13   For example, Rosendo Salvado to Venancio Garrido, 20 March 1866, Salvado Correspondence by Teresa De Castro and David Barry OSB, New Norcia Archives (NNA) 2-2234A/21.069.

they exercised authority over the children of those families on behalf of a coercive government as they sought to modernise and professionalise first the school at New Norcia and then the childcare centre in Perth's northern suburbs to provide alternatives for the people. The reunion of key members with the Aboriginal women who had grown up at St Joseph's in 2001 points to the significance of their memory and of this story for the future of reconciliation in Australia.

The history of Australia's Spanish Benedictine women connects with vibrant scholarly conversations about the history of Catholic women religious ('nuns' and 'sisters') internationally. This field has shifted well away from devotional or hagiographical accounts to embrace the insights of feminist and post-colonial history and theology, alongside new digital technologies.[14] Sustained by two thriving networks with regular conferences, recent scholarship on women religious is taking account of the transnational significance of their communities, the complexity of religious identities, and the subtleties of convent engagement in political and social concerns.[15] The contribution of Catholic women religious to education, nursing and pastoral work has been recognised gradually since the rise of women's history in the 1960s and also subjected to more sophisticated questions.[16] This book about New Norcia's sisters stands alongside the growing literature on 'oblate' congregations and Black American women religious, and adds the unique Spanish-speaking missionary community to the work on predominantly Irish communities

---

14 Deirdre Raftery, 'The "Third Wave" Is Digital: Researching Histories of Women Religious in the Twenty-First Century', *American Catholic Studies* 128 (2017): 29–50.

15 See especially the international bibliographies maintained by History of Women Religious of Britain and Ireland, historyofwomenreligious.org/women-religious-bibliography/, and research resources curated by Conference on the History of Women Religious: www.chwr.org/research-resources; accessed January 2019.

16 For example, the special issue on women religious *Paedagogica Historica: International Journal of the History of Education* 49 (2013); Janice Garaty, Lesley Hughes and Megan Brock, 'Seeking the Voices of Catholic Teaching Sisters: Challenges in the Research Process', *History of Education Review* 44 (2015): 71–84; Carmen Mangion, 'Developing Alliances: Faith, Philanthropy and Fundraising in Nineteenth-Century England', in *The Economics of Providence: Management, Finances and Patrimony of Religious Orders and Congregations in Europe 1773–1931*, ed. Maarten van Dijck, Jan de Maeyer, Jimmy Koppen and Jeffrey Tyssens (Leuven: Leuven University Press, 2013); Susan O'Brien, *Leaving God for God: The Daughters of Charity of St Vincent de Paul in Britain, 1847–2017* (London: Darton, Longman & Todd, 2017).

in Australia.[17] It also contributes a close study of a Catholic community to historical work on women missionaries in Australia where the emphasis so far has been on Protestant experience, and brings Western Australia into focus within a larger narrative of Catholic history and women's history, often more informed by archives from the eastern seaboard, especially in Sydney and Melbourne.[18]

New Norcia is central to the history of religion in Australia, and both the monastic town and its charismatic founder already have a profile in histories of nineteenth-century missionary enterprise, as well as of empire and culture.[19] The mission founded in the Kimberley in 1908 by monks from New Norcia has also received attention, especially in studies of Aboriginal experience by Ian Crawford and Christine Choo.[20] As the source materials about Salvado and his work grow richer for English-language readers there is a need to examine the mission in the south that

---

17   Rosa Bruno-Jofré, *The Missionary Oblate Sisters: Vision and Mission* (Montreal: McGill-Queen's University Press, 2005); Diane Batts Morrow, *Persons of Color and Religious at the Same Time: The Oblate Sisters of Providence, 1862–1860* (Chapel Hill: University of North Carolina Press, 2002); M. Shawn Copeland, 'Building up a Household of Faith: Dom Cyprian Davis OSB and the Work of History', *US Catholic Historian* 28, no. 1 (2010): 53–63. On Australian communities, M. Rosa MacGinley, *A Dynamic of Hope: Institutes of Women Religious in Australia* (Darlinghurst, NSW: Crossing Press, 2002); Stephanie Burley, 'An Overview of the Historiography of Women Religious in Australia', *Journal of the Australian Catholic Historical Society* 26 (2005): 43–60; and for recent examples of Australian community histories, Mary Ryllis Clark, *Loreto in Australia* (Sydney: University of New South Wales Press, 2009); Margaret Walsh, *The Good Sams: Sisters of the Good Samaritan 1857–1969* (Mulgrave, Vic.: John Garrett Publications, 2001).
18   Patricia Grimshaw, 'Rethinking Approaches to Women in Missions: The Case of Colonial Australia', *History Australia* 8 (2011): 7–24; Regina Ganter and Patricia Grimshaw, 'Introduction: Reading the Lives of White Mission Women', *Journal of Australian Studies* 39 (2015): 1–6. On women across the churches, Anne O'Brien, *God's Willing Workers: Women and Religion in Australia* (Sydney: University of New South Wales Press, 2005).
19   Tom Stannage, 'New Norcia in History', *Studies in Western Australian History* 29 (2015): 125–30; George Russo, *Lord Abbot of the Wilderness: The Life and Times of Bishop Salvado* (Melbourne: Polding Press, 1980); Rosendo Salvado, *The Salvado Memoirs: Historical Memoirs of Australia and Particularly of the Benedictine Mission of New Norcia and of the Habits and Customs of the Australian Natives*, trans. E. J. Storman (1977; Nedlands, WA: University of Western Australia Press, 1998); David Hutchinson ed., *A Town Like No Other: The Living Tradition of New Norcia* (1995; Fremantle, WA: Fremantle Arts Centre Press, 2007). For current research trends, see the journal *New Norcia Studies*; and John H. Smith, ed., *Rosendo Salvado: Commemorating Two Hundred Years* (New Norcia: Benedictine Community of New Norcia, 2014).
20   Ian Crawford, *We Won the Victory: Aborigines and Outsiders on the North-West Coast of the Kimberley* (Fremantle, WA: Fremantle Arts Centre Press, 2001); Christine Choo, *Mission Girls: Aboriginal Women on Catholic Missions in the Kimberley, Western Australia 1900–1950* (Crawley, WA: University of Western Australia Press, 2001).

continued on the strength of his legacy.[21] New Norcia's institutions in the twentieth century have received comparatively less attention although they remained central to the lives of Aboriginal Australians. That there were Spanish women involved in the work, and that the community came to include Anglo-Australian and Aboriginal Australian sisters, remains largely unknown. *A Bridge Between* addresses that silence.

Without pretending a complete history is possible, this book traces the story of the Benedictine sisters who worked in the mission town. By honouring a stream of memory that bubbles just below the surface of the written history of New Norcia, I hope to prompt more conversation and encourage the gathering of further material for reflection. Again and again, this story is about the commitment—to a community and the people involved, to a way of life, to God—that formed a thread of meaning to link realities that threatened to spin apart.

The existing material is scattered and elusive. The archives at New Norcia are rich in glimpses of sisters, 'crunching across starlit gravel … wrapped in meditation',[22] but scant on detailed depictions. It is simple to find affirmations 'that no band of Benedictine missionaries ever showed a nobler spirit of sacrifice',[23] and even straightforward to find their photographs, but it is much harder to name the members of this group or describe what they did. Public memory swings between quaint women gliding to chapel in the dawn light and fierce disciplinarians pulling children into line by the earlobe. The record has been strong on 'finding happiness in the secluded life'[24] but silent on the intense interactions and flashes of creativity that marked the reality of days in the school, the sheer hard work of the laundry, the challenges and accomplishments of the kitchen. Much was never recorded, and a bonfire instigated by the Benedictine women when they left Australia destroyed children's schoolbooks and class work and all the odds and ends that would never be used again.

---

21 The Abbey Press is publishing primary material with the intention of resourcing fresh scholarly work; for example, Théophile Bérengier, *New Norcia: The History of a Benedictine Colony in Western Australia 1846–1878*, trans. Peter Gilet (Northcote Vic.: Abbey Press, 2014); Rosendo Salvado, *Report of Rosendo Salvado to Propaganda Fide in 1883*, trans. Stefano Girola (Northcote, Vic.: Abbey Press, 2015). Salvado's diaries transcribed and translated into English by Teresa De Castro and David Barry are forthcoming. On Salvado's correspondence, see Teresa De Castro, 'Westaustralianae: New Norcia's Archive', www.geocities.ws/CollegePark/Field/4664/Historyserver/westraliana/index.htm; accessed January 2019.
22 'New Norcia Today', *St Ildephonsus College Magazine*, 1929, 5–9.
23 'First Sisters at Drysdale River Mission', *St Ildephonsus College Magazine*, 1931, 34–40.
24 *Pax*, 19 September 1954, 4.

At first, it seemed all that remained were the buildings themselves. When I taught history at the University of Western Australia in the 1990s I brought groups to stay at the 'Old Convent', and it was never quite clear who the mysterious Spanish sisters had been, how they had connected to the Benedictine traditions the students had come to see, or why the museum and art gallery occupied their building without telling their story. Preparation for the 2001 reunion itself prompted work to restore some awareness of the women in the mission, with artefacts and accounts of life at St Joseph's gathered into an exhibition in the former convent chapel. It is a first step, a collaboration that might see New Norcia commemorated as a 'site of conscience', one day, in the future.[25] In the museum storerooms (areas the Benedictine sisters see as former classrooms and dormitories) there are artefacts that survived because they were still needed: statues from the chapel and classrooms, washing machines, sewing machines, cooking pots and kitchen utensils, sporting trophies, stray toys and oddments of clothing. They build a picture.

The photographs are even more evocative. They are held in the archive at New Norcia and with the communities in Spain and the Kimberley, both promotional and documentary shots taken for publication over the years, and family snaps. Some appear in these pages but several of the most dynamic remain unpublished as families reserve the right to their own privacy or respect the rights of others. As the footnotes indicate, some of those have been entrusted to the Storylines project at the State Library of Western Australia who will manage protocols about access. A treasure in one context is a trigger in another. Not many of the images are catalogued, but they illustrate and deepen the conversations. As stories flow in some 30 interviews in Spanish and English, identities emerge from the uniform rows, and individual faces match with names and dates. In Kalumburu, while the air-conditioner hums, Schollie and Visi take me through their albums, with images of mentors and earlier generations mixed in with their own 40-plus years in the north. There will be several visits to Spain, to the community in Madrid, their ongoing outreach in Barcelona, and Valladolid where the library holds the relevant newspapers. I stay with the Sisters, in the residence they founded for students, in various convent guesthouses as the search for material fans out, sharing their life

---

25 For example, Bonny Djuric, Lily Hibberd and Linda Steele, 'Transforming the Parramatta Female Factory Institutional Precinct into a Site of Conscience', *The Conversation*, 4 January 2018, theconversation.com/transforming-the-parramatta-female-factory-institutional-precinct-into-a-site-of-conscience-88875; accessed 2 April 2018.

and included in their network of hospitality. Each visit includes Burgos, Napoleon's capital and then Franco's, surrounded by the farming villages that were home to most of New Norcia's missionaries and the network of Benedictine connections that brought them to Australia. On the first visit, I photocopy images; later, when technology catches up with the needs of this project, we take precious selections to be scanned. There is only one copy of a photo of Sister Teresa at the piano with her first student, and her reminder is earnest: 'Do not hurt my photo!' The material matters: it names relationships.

The written sources are scattered in Spain and in Belgium as well as in various archives in Australia. Some material in government files and at New Norcia is rightly restricted to family members of the children whose names it also records, some material in Spain was lost as religious houses were burnt in the Spanish Civil War, other fires claimed material written by the sisters because 'anyone might read them'.[26] The *Notebooks* of Sister Felicitas from the 1920s were the closest thing the community had to a diary but Teresa burnt them in the 1980s. Their fate comes to light in a typical group interview upstairs in the airy Madrid convent: Teresa, Francisca and Pilar respond to my questions in Spanish; Sister Maria Gratia from the Philippines takes notes to help keep track of the recording later. She is their community leader and has known these Spanish sisters since they merged with her Tutzing community in the 1980s but she has not heard the mission stories before. 'But why?' asks Gratia, 'Why did you burn them? That was our history.' Teresa had made a summary in Spanish, then edited it again to translate it into English. 'Maybe I was wrong', she concedes. As the new superior she had sat lightly enough to convent conventions—her Christmas gift to each sister that first year was a small Swiss Army pocket knife—but the *Notebooks* had been too full of the hard work and loneliness that traumatised her predecessor: 'Sister Felicitas was always crying, every day picking stones, every night crying'. Judged unedifying, the shadow of the *Notebooks* survives to show above all what the later generation thought should be preserved.

---

26   Teresa González in Teresa González, Pilar Catalan, Francisca Pardo and Maria Gratia Balagot, Interview, Madrid, 9 July 2004.

Figure 1.3: Teresa, Francisca, Pilar and Maria Gratia recording memories of the mission around the library table in Madrid, 2004 (left); Scholastica telling the stories of her photo album in Kalumburu, 1999 (right).
Source: Author's collection.

In the same way, some rare letters from the Benedictine women themselves testify to expectations and the quality of relationships as much as they provide details of the life. There is a trail in Spanish and English of official documentation and letters, and it is especially letters written by the third abbot of New Norcia, Anselm Catalan, that provide a narrative spine to the account of the Spanish sisters. Writing to contacts in Spain to promote the mission, explaining the work to prospective recruits, negotiating migration requirements, discussing the sisters with other monks, and corresponding directly with the women themselves, the abbot indexed his carbon copies annually—placing the sisters in their own category, not monks, not officials, not members of the public. In asides and against the grain of the discussion, these letters carry an elusive but invaluable imprint of the Benedictine women's lives. Beneath these scattered documents, there is the rich vein of memory that energises the stories of 70 years and more of the sisters' interaction with the town and its people. These are the memories, of love and also of pain, that the women sought to name in their reunion.

To honour that reunion and those memories, this is an account of the Benedictine Missionary Sisters of New Norcia. They were a group of 58 women in all, who travelled to Australia between 1904 and 1958 and ranged in age from 13 to 94. Most of the sisters were Spanish, like the monks of New Norcia, from villages in the north near Burgos, and, like the monks, they arrived in Australia as teenagers, with little English and even less understanding of their new country. They came for different reasons: protesting 'do not ask me why! I came because I came', or 'to work for the mission', or because 'I had an intuition I would be a nun, but I did not know the when or the how, and the abbot made it easy'.[27] For some, their families supported their going, and the church was a recognised opportunity for adventure, travel, livelihood or holiness. For others, leaving Spain was a wrench that never healed completely, a break from potential and actual careers, motherhood and community, family and other support structures; all left behind because God (or the abbot) asked. Pledged to the Benedictine vows of obedience, stability and 'conversion of life', some stayed 'forever' knowing they belonged; others left within weeks, or felt they should have. All of them seemed to wonder at their commitment and the struggle it brought them, and they variously learnt to laugh at the new life, to love it, or to find ways to survive. Over the years, they were joined in Australia by some of the Aboriginal young women from St Joseph's, two in particular in the 1950s who found an expression of their own identity in the religious community. Five others, European Australians from Perth and one New Zealander, were also drawn to the community through circumstances as diverse as the Spanish women before them.

St Joseph's was a hub for work that the town took for granted. Here the sisters provided basic primary education and hands-on training in domestic work. In rosters with the older girls (at times including everyone aged nine or over), they cooked, washed, sewed, and had responsibility for a full range of domestic and farm tasks, from cleaning the abbey church and decorating the altar with flowers and fine linen, to unblocking the town's sewers using coat hangers. They had branch houses in the Kimberley from 1931, in Bindoon from 1948, in Madrid, Samos, Zaragoza, Barcelona, and Madrid again in the 1960s and, from 1973, in Girrawheen, on the northern fringe of Perth, where they ran the first government-funded community childcare centre.

---

27 Illuminada Perez [Sr Florentina], Interview, Burgos, September 2010; Teresa González, Interview, Madrid, 17 May 1999; Visitación Cidad, Interview, Madrid, 29 July 2010.

The chapters that follow trace the sisters' years at New Norcia through four distinct phases, reflecting changes in personalities, circumstances and policies of both church and government. The chronology moves broadly from the community's foundation over a decade from 1904 to 1915, through a time when their status within the church was regularised and codified in the 1930s, to a period of regeneration in the later 1940s, and then departure from New Norcia in the mid-1970s. Throughout the changes in each of those phases, the Benedictine women were forever 'between'. They defied simple labels and were often identified simultaneously in contradictory roles. They were women of prayer, drawn together across racial and ethnic boundaries, working within the various hierarchies of church and state. Competing ideals and demands held them in constant, but often muffled, conversation. As missionary women also vowed to a contemplative life of prayer and work, they were negotiating with Catholic tradition along the boundaries of women's holiness and feminine spirituality. As Spanish women, identified racially as 'Mediterranean' and classified officially as 'aliens', they worked with Aboriginal children in English-speaking, White Australia and spoke the language of citizenship in unfamiliar cadences. As working women charged with professional duties in the school and childcare centres, they juggled the need for access to training with community life, limited recognition of their roles and pragmatic insistence that the show must go on. As domestic workers in a rural farming community, they traded their capacity to labour without complaint with the personal cost of broken health and neglected development. Among themselves, the sisters fought changes that would make any of the demands unimportant, even as experience showed that no individual (and perhaps no community) could meet them all.

Definitions of holiness and femininity, citizenship and motherhood, meaningful work and authority overlapped and tangled with each other as speakers in the conversations multiplied. From the government official promoting assimilation, to the woman psychologist tired of being treated 'as if I were a man'; from church instructions on fasting and forms of prayer, to monks who found their laundry shrunken; from the toddler always hiding in the skirts of Reverend Mother, to the homesick runaway returned by police; from the Sister no one visited in hospital, to the one spared dirty work in the kitchen; from the university summer schools on Aboriginal education, to the school concerts featuring Spanish folkdances: these women found their lives framed by complex and competing claims. And those wider dialogues in turn shaped a deeper negotiation: in the routines of a tough institution, the sisters and the children in their care held a muted but intense conversation that spoke simultaneously of motherhood and vowed virginity, obedience and decision-making power, forced removal from families, separation, abandonment, childhood and love.

The reunion unfolds

It is all there in Sheila Humphries's painting *Life at St Joseph's*. The painting is shown here not as it hangs in the museum but as it was during the central liturgy of the reunion in the parish church, surrounded by other symbols of the life and work of the women of St Joseph's.

Sheila's description of her work begins at the centre of her image and names the core relationships:

> If you look at the picture, in the centre you will see the girls [with the] Aboriginal sitting symbol portraying the girls in the different colour uniforms we had throughout the years that we were in here. Around us you will see in black and white the Aboriginal figure again, showing the nuns ... how we were always protected by them, their love surrounded us, everyday life was around us.[28]

Figure 1.4: Sheila Humphries's painting *Life at St Joseph's*, within the liturgical display at the reunion, Mass of Thanksgiving, October 2001.
Source: NNA W6-B4-4-208.

---

28 Humphries, Interview with Sr Anne Carter, 10 June 2002.

There are two separate circles, one of the children, one of the nuns, and they are coded in separate roles in the colours of institutional dress. But a common symbol represents them both, and one circle encloses the other. Imprisoning? Restricting? No, Sheila says: Protecting. Surrounding. The sisters' love and the details of the everyday surround the girls. Her commentary connects the girls' day-to-day experience directly with the sisters' own situation and the disruption of their ordinary circumstances:

> Everyday life was around us, they left their homes, their parents, their families, came out to Australia. Most of them were only teenagers like ourselves, they came out to look after us, knowing very little English.[29]

A strong critic of the monastery in other contexts, Sheila goes on to remark on everyday life in the orphanage:

> I'm not denying there were times it was bad, there were times when I wished that Mum and Dad were near, but the Sisters were always there for us. It wasn't just an institution, it was a home where people loved us and looked after us.[30]

The love that the painting records was expressed in simple gestures of companionship. There is another frame in the image beyond the central circles. 'Everyday life was around us', Sheila says. Everyday life involved shared traditions and a shared place:

> In the picture you will see different colour dots in the background, representing the earth, grass, and different colours of flowers. The circles on the picture represent the different areas that we went to for walks with the nuns, as you can see the walk sign and the travel sign is all over the picture. … We travelled all over New Norcia as children with the nuns … with picnic spots, and areas that we went to swimming, picking wildflowers, chasing rabbits and ducks, and in the rivers catching gilgie for the nuns and the priests. … When we'd go on picnics we used to chuck 'em on the fires and the Sisters used to have a feed with us, so we had our bush tucker.[31]

---

29   Humphries, Interview, 10 June 2002.
30   Humphries, Interview, 10 June 2002.
31   Humphries, Interview, 10 June 2002.

The sisters and the girls shared life in a Catholic mission, and life in the Australian country town, essentially on a large farm. They found symbols of a shared Catholic identity in the bush. The painting itself, and Sheila's commentary on it, elides the memory of the bush and the traditions of Catholic belief. The prayer of the rosary, a meditation on the life of Mary the mother of Jesus, who is traditionally dressed in blue, winds through the painting in blue beads that merge with the blue of the local river:

> The large blue dots in the painting represent the rosary which was part of our daily life. We said the rosary everyday, and that was very, very dear to us. The river, the dark blue dots that run through the centre of the picture, is the river that runs through New Norcia, the Moore. We spent many, many happy hours in that river, with the nuns, we grew up with the nuns.[32]

Local flowers, identified in the painting with picnic sites and regular walks, also defined sacred spaces for annual processions and adorned the chapel:

> The flowers, we used to pick a lot of everlastings when they were in bloom. … The wattle meant a lot to us because, each year, at Corpus Christi, we used to sprinkle the path where we walked in procession from the church through the two colleges, and then back to the church. The road used to be sprinkled with wattle blossom right through, and we walked over that. Kangaroo paws we used to pick and bring back. A lot of flowers we picked, the Sisters would put them in the church, in our little chapel.[33]

The girls, the sisters, everyday life of traditional devotion and connection with place, and the relationships between them—all accumulated to endorse the institution as a home. Sheila's account stresses above all that it was a home. It was a home in the institutional sense: 'we were *in here*'. But it was not just an institution, 'it was a home where people loved us and looked after us'. Sheila points to relationships with the other girls, with an absent mum and dad, with the sisters who were near as the first step in explaining St Joseph's.

The relationships, the bonds of shared experience, hold the many stories of St Joseph's and the sisters on a common horizon. They are my point of connection to the story as a researcher and also the barrier that separates me from it. The written records cannot carry the emotional weight of this story. I have relied on the girls, now women, who grew up at St Joseph's,

---

32   Humphries, Interview, 10 June 2002.
33   Humphries, Interview, 10 June 2002.

and the young women, now elderly nuns, who travelled up the gravel road to work at the mission. Standing outside both those experiences, my task was daunting. But it was the reunion of 2001 that offered a way forward. As I shared the preparation and the events of the reunion fortnight living alongside the sisters as a general historical rouseabout for the gathering and museum display, I could recite the 'historical facts' as steadily as anyone. I knew from the documents that the institution of St Joseph's itself goes back to 1867, the time of New Norcia's founder. But in 1933 Andrea Pardo, then aged 16, and Pilar Catalan, then aged 15, travelled to New Norcia and became Sister Francisca and Sister Placida. In 1948 Amalia González a 22-year-old teacher, also arrived in Australia from Spain with 11 other young women and became Sister Marie Therese, later Teresa. In 1950 another six sisters joined them, including Visitación Cidad, then 18, and Carmen Ruiz, then 26. It was the women who were children in the 1940s and 1950s when these sisters arrived who lobbied for and financed the reunion, who stood laughing and crying on the steps of the church 50 years later for one more photo, and one more with the grandkids. It was in these years that policies of racial assimilation and disruption of Aboriginal families were at their height in Western Australia. It was in these years that confidence that St Joseph's was doing good and important work was strongest. Yet the 'facts' were full of ambiguities. As the reunion took shape, the ability to question old assumptions, and to challenge and repudiate them, but to remain committed to the relationships that had been forged was a hallmark of the many and varied interactions. I saw ambiguity ignored. It was transcended by the business of the reunion and the work of remembering itself.

At the reunion, St Joseph's was the centre of life again, and the stories took their meaning from that common centre—even the stories that could not yet be uttered or resolved, as much as those that could not be contained. In silent gestures and in the overflow of words, the stories that sustained the relationships reverberated. They were retold one-to-one, or sitting together in the kitchen, in the monastery parlour, and in the car; polished for journalists, committed to private diaries, incorporated into art and poetry, ritualised and relived in liturgies, laughed over, cried for, expressed in a hug or a hand on the shoulder or paused in a careful turning away. Reducing the experience of being 'a St Joseph's girl' or 'a Spanish missionary Sister' to a single narrative was not possible and was not the point. It was the many stories, even the competing and conflicting stories told by the same person, that forged the deepest and most lasting foundation for understanding.

In fact, it had been in the reaction against a single, simplifying narrative that talk of a reunion with the Benedictine women had gathered momentum. The documentary *The Habits of New Norcia* went to air with accompanying press late in 2000 and presented the town's Aboriginal institutions as an unmitigated failure.[34] Reeling from the experience of seeing their childhoods televised as a stereotype of deprivation, the Aboriginal community had split over who had been interviewed, whose story had been used, how the tapes had been edited, and why anyone thought this would bring an apology from the government anyway. No one argued for a sunny vision of simple rural upbringing or triumphal missionary success, but harsher selections that were also too simple did not help either. In planning for the reunion, New Norcia's women made a choice to include other memories of love and home alongside those of hardship and suffering.

The Christian theologian Miroslav Volf has drawn on his own memories of abusive interrogation to explore what it means to remember 'rightly'; the reunion was an affirmation that, in Volf's words, 'we are not just shaped by memories; we ourselves shape the memories that shape us'.[35] Throughout the days of the reunion, identity as a community was being 'stitched together' to form a 'veritable patchwork quilt … from the growing mountain of discrete multi-coloured memories'.[36] As part of the process, individuals discarded some stories, featured others, and worked yet other strands into the background. Volf argues that making decisions about the pattern of stories that help constitute our identity is part of being human, a process of individual design that 'will depend greatly on how we sew our memories together, and how others—from those closest to us all the way to our culture as a whole—sew them together for us'.[37] Acknowledging as full a reality as possible provides the strongest foundation. Every human quilt of identity must include dark, tattered, coarse and ugly memories, if we are truthful and remember honestly. Those memories, Volf argues, can support hope for reconciliation.

---

34 *The Habits of New Norcia*, dir. Frank Rijavec, with Harry Taylor and Carmelo Musca (Eight Mile Plains, Qld: CM Film Productions, 2000).
35 Miroslav Volf, *The End of Memory: Remembering Rightly in a Violent World* (Grand Rapids, MI: William B. Eerdmans, 2006), 25.
36 Volf, *End of Memory*, 25.
37 Volf, *End of Memory*, 25.

1. TO NAME AND TO REMEMBER

The reunion was a conscious statement about reconciliation. It was also political, as every meeting of Aboriginal Australians and mission authorities is and was political. But it was driven by concerns that placed it outside the lines of argument about the racism of the past. When talk of inviting the sisters 'home' began, it was fuelled by a longing for relationships and by a recognition of the significance of being together in the right place to talk and reconnect. Plans were mulled over in private, and it was only slowly that the possibility of some public acknowledgment of the sisters' visit grew as an idea.

The reunion was about bonds between people, not structures. It brought together people who had publicly and vehemently criticised the sisters and the institutions at New Norcia with others who had literally spent their savings to finance their return. Most often the women and men who gathered could talk in more than one voice, from more than one standpoint, about their childhoods. Again and again, the reunion was about relationships that had persisted through dreadful, and sometimes wonderful, experiences and that had held firm over many years. In a context where so much had been stolen, there were still relationships to be acknowledged and honoured, in order that, as Sheila Humphries said, summarising for the others, 'people will know there was love in this home'.[38] St Joseph's should not have been their home, but that is not the end of the story. The Aboriginal women themselves claim a more complex account of the Benedictine sisters.

The process of acknowledging complexity to see more clearly and get closer to realities is analogous to the naming of St Joseph's itself. In the first place, the buildings on the southern edge of the town are sometimes not named; the standard public accounts can erase the communities of women from Australia's only monastic town. But then, below the horizon of spires and towers that mark out the public history, other accounts multiply. For example, the complex that was called 'St Joseph's Native School and Orphanage' by the government was 'the convent' or sometimes 'the laundry' for the monks, as it was just 'our place' to the sisters who lived there, and 'The Girls' House' for the Aboriginal children who also lived there, in contrast to 'The Boys' House' on the other side of town. Furthermore, when in 1974 the sisters made their sudden decision to leave and return to Spain, the same complex became the 'New Norcia

---

38 Humphries, Interview, 10 June 2002.

Museum and Art Gallery', housing exhibitions about the farm and the founder and the art collection, with no mention of the convent until 2001 when the exhibition in which Sheila's painting hangs was opened in the space that had once been the chapel. All of the names for the complex were accurate; but each name became more accurate alongside the other names. So also the single stories, powerful in themselves, gained another layer of meaning when brought into dialogue and relationship with other strands of stories. And when the competing claims came into conflict in the conversation, then it was the relationships, especially the bonds of shared experience, that demanded attention, made ongoing conversation possible, and encouraged continuing stories.

Storytelling, the incremental and slow process of forging common memories from different histories, is at the heart of reconciliation for an increasing number of commentators. Elizabeth Pike, a Noongar woman from the south of Western Australia, now a writer in residence at the Aboriginal Catholic Ministry in Melbourne, says good relationships across cultures in Australia could hinge on storytelling:

> [O]ne of the most simple and yet one of the strongest means [for bringing Aboriginal and non-Aboriginal Australians together] is the tremendous power of 'story'. Before we can learn to get along, we have to get to know each other, in order to build firm relationships. Because we are such a minority group in the community, it is often very difficult for non-Indigenous people to meet us. It has often been my experience that when contact is made with genuine people, barriers are often broken down quickly. However, when this is not possible, the power of story can awaken the awareness and begin to stir the compassion needed in the depths of one's being. It requires very little intelligence to know that 'love' cannot be bought, sold or legislated in a document and love is what relationships are founded on.[39]

Here Pike is in tune with the international literature that argues for reconciliation as a dimension of spirituality. Approached theologically or understood as a spiritual task, reconciliation emerges most surely from ongoing relationships, from listening to the stories at the deepest level rather than simply from well-managed strategies or well-intentioned therapies. In particular, sharing stories to search for points of connection

---

39 Elizabeth Pike, 'Reconciliation, or Conciliation through Restoration?', in *Developing an Australian Theology*, ed. Peter Malone (Strathfield, NSW: St Paul's Publications, 1999), 38–39.

breaks down barriers. At New Norcia those connections and resonances that keep their shape in more than one narrative might well include the rosary, the Corpus Christi processions, the shared picnics, and the river. Furthermore, it is the stories told 'against the grain' of well-worn narrative tracks that probably contribute most to the healing of reconciliation.[40] In particular, as Robert Schreiter, a contextual theologian from North America, argues, it is in moments when the initiative lies with the people who have been without power and whose voices have not been heard that the potential for reaching common understanding is greatest. The invitation to us from the past pupils of St Joseph's to hear the sisters' stories and their own stories of the sisters at the reunion is all the more important in this light.

It is not just the telling of stories alone that advances understanding. Simply layering in another account, watching the contradictions, is just confusing without some signposts for the discussion. The international experience is full of examples of groups 'speaking past each other' with the best will in the world.[41] But it was Herodotus long ago who pointed out that history has always involved interpretation, that the very word 'historeo' means both 'I gather the evidence' and 'I tell my story'. It was the distinguished Australian historian Keith Hancock who reflected on Herodotus as he offered a rubric for understanding the past. Hancock argued that good historical interpretation demanded three things: attachment, justice and span.[42] This three-part hermeneutic for historical storytellers is still useful. It echoes in the rubric proposed by Rowan Williams where the past is both 'familiar' and 'strange', and in Catherine Chin's quest for the 'radiance' of history, encountered through empathetic and stubborn engagement with 'otherness that can never be entirely domesticated'.[43] Both the process of research and the stories we tell out of that work depend for their integrity on engaging deeply with the fragments and memories of the past and recasting them onto new canvases that have both breadth and depth. Historians know well that simply hearing alternative voices

---

40   Robert J. Schreiter, *Reconciliation: Mission and Ministry in a Changing Social Order* (Maryknoll, NY: Orbis Books, 1992), 45.
41   Charles Villa-Vicencio, 'Telling One Another Stories: Towards a Theology of Reconciliation', in *The Reconciliation of Peoples: Challenge to the Churches*, ed. Gregory Baum and Harold Wells (Maryknoll, NY: Orbis Books, 1997), 30–42.
42   W. K. Hancock, *Professing History* (Sydney: Sydney University Press, 1976), 2, 4–7.
43   Rowan Williams, *Why Study the Past? The Quest for the Historical Church* (London: Darton, Longman and Todd, 2005), 10–11, 88–95; Catherine Chin, 'Marvellous Things Heard: On Finding Historical Radiance', *The Massachusetts Review* 58 (2017): 478–91.

is more likely to open questions than to settle them, and sitting with competing interpretations is not the same thing as resolving a narrative line. Increasingly, readers appreciate that meaningful conversation with the past requires a common acknowledgment of divergent experiences and a commitment to search for 'symbols that unite and stories that bind'.[44] As Inga Clendinnen asks in her work on encounters between Aboriginal Australians and early Europeans: 'Why concoct a single, simple and therefore necessarily false tale and call it Australia's history? Why not a cornucopia of true stories which would tell us what happened?'[45] She urges a 'dance' of history that is disciplined by past realities and distinct from fiction and also alert to the power of myth and legend. Against tight certainties of the history warriors she recommends a 'crabwise approach, eyes swivelling sideways, backwards, forwards, with equal intensity, because while the past is the past, it is not dead'.[46] As historians of Australia have been saying increasingly since the 1990s, deep understanding does not necessarily involve dichotomous choices but might require more inclusive reading of the multivalent evidence of, for example, 'resistance to' and 'co-operation with' and 'flight from' and 'abuse by' and 'interpretation of' colonising powers.[47] Reconciliation is forged slowly in relationship and conversation.

For Hans-Georg Gadamer, a philosopher concerned with the practical implications of how we understand language, the reconciling conversations depend on a 'fusion of horizons' if they are to arrive at common and enabling memories.[48] The metaphor is a striking one, especially for New Norcia. For travellers, the town rises distinctively against the horizon of the Victoria Plains, a sudden Spanish apparition, or puzzle, or even disruption, on the Great Northern Highway. Against the horizon it provokes particular questions and requires specific stories. In the town itself, and especially overnight, the sky is vast. The limitless horizon prompts the need for bearings within a cosmic hinterland and recasts the

---
44   Villa-Vicencio, 'Telling One Another Stories', 32.
45   Inga Clendinnen, *True Stories* (Sydney: ABC Books, 1999), 101.
46   Clendinnen, *True Stories*, 103; Stuart Macintyre and Anna Clark, eds, *The History Wars* (Melbourne: Melbourne University Press, 2004).
47   Lorenzo Veracini, 'Of "Contested Ground" and an "Indelible Stain": A Difficult Reconciliation between Australian and Its Aboriginal History during the 1990s and 2000s', *Aboriginal History* 27 (2003): 225–39.
48   Hans-Georg Gadamer, *Truth and Method*, 2nd rev. ed., trans. J. Weinsheimer and D. G. Marshall (New York: Crossroad, 1989); Hans-Georg Gadamer, *Hans-Georg Gadamer on Education, Poetry, and History: Applied Hermeneutics*, ed. Dieter Misgeld, Graeme Nicholson, Lawrence Schmidt and Monica Reuss (Albany: State University of New York Press, 1992).

parameters of the town.⁴⁹ Gadamer suggests that the telling and hearing of stories so as to find where the horizons meet is crucial to reconciliation. This involves more than analysis of different perspectives, although the differences are not to be ignored, and more than empathy, although mutual empathy is taken for granted before real storytelling occurs. Reconciliation requires a shift of perception and a mutual recognition of the deepest dimensions of reality that stories can express. When meaning 'happens', to use the verb that theologian Sandra Schneiders applies to interpretation of text, it is because the horizons of the world of the listener and the world of the storyteller have fused, each expanding to forge a new understanding.⁵⁰ A fusion of horizons enables people with different stories to recognise the experience behind each other's words and metaphors, to 'crack the code' so as to embrace a more complex (not neater) reality:

> [The fusion of horizons] always involves the attainment of a higher universality that overcomes, not only our own particularity, but also that of the other. The concept of the 'horizon' suggests itself because it expresses the wide, superior vision that the person who is seeking to understand must have. To acquire a horizon means that one learns to look beyond what is close at hand—not in order to look away from it, but to see it better within a larger whole and in truer proportion.⁵¹

This necessarily acknowledges what the American public historian Michael Frisch calls a 'shared authority' between many strands of evidence, and the development of strategies for 'shared authorship' between the public record and other storytellers. In this vision, scholarly work is another tool for community understanding.⁵² It implies, as Robert Orsi, historian of American Catholicism, argues, that fieldwork is 'not a matter of taking notes, but of comparing them',⁵³ and that research is an encounter that changes people. Most fundamentally, it recognises that the process by which we discover meaning is one of dialogue. This is remembering and storytelling from what might be called a meditative stance, not just a political, intellectual, or administrative one.

---

49 See similarly Abbot Placid Spearritt, *Friends of New Norcia Newsletter*, 23 December 2001.
50 Sandra M. Schneiders, *The Revelatory Text: Interpreting the New Testament as Sacred Scripture* (San Francisco: HarperSanFrancisco, 1991).
51 Gadamer, *Truth and Method*, 272.
52 Michael Frisch, *A Shared Authority: Essays on the Craft and Meaning of Oral and Public History* (Albany: State University of New York Press, 1990), xix–xx.
53 Robert Orsi, *Between Heaven and Earth: The Religious Worlds People Make and the Scholars That Study Them* (Princeton, NJ: Princeton University Press, 2005), 174.

In his book on what it means to remember 'rightly', the work that seems to point towards so many themes of the reunion, Miroslav Volf argues that the infinite horizon of Love and Grace is definitive for people of faith. This is the horizon that enables a meditative, and essentially 'gracious', stance. Volf explores how a God who is Love both challenges and enables people of faith to make memory 'a bridge between adversaries instead of a deep and dark ravine that separates them'.[54] Far from recommending that conflict should just be ignored or forgotten, Volf holds that memories, including those of injustice and suffering, can become salutary, not destructive; they can be 'redeemed and transformed' without denial or repression.[55] This is hard spiritual work, but in a secure context, where experiences have been recounted truthfully and moral judgement has been made and accepted, ultimately (and Volf means that literally, at the end time, in God's new creation), memories of suffering will have no power. In the redeemed world of Love and Grace, the memories of wrong will 'not-come-to-mind', as a consequence of God's gift of healed relationships in a redeemed world. In the meantime, in the imperfect world in which the reunion took place, the promise of the infinite horizon means 'every act of reconciliation, incomplete as it mostly is … stretches itself toward completion in that world of love'.[56]

The work of reconciliation at New Norcia is far from complete, but the gathering in 2001 was lived out in the hope of 'a world set aright'. It even offered glimpses of that reality. The reunion at New Norcia did not bring people together as adversaries. It could have done so, easily. Missionary denial and pride could have met Aboriginal accusation and blame, or hierarchical condescension could have met feminine disdain, and the occasion could have become a series of textbook cases of what Volf calls 'contractual' interactions based on the logic of what is supposedly or actually deserved. Instead, the reunion was lived out of a 'logic of grace', marked by 'covenantal' relationships where people assumed they belonged together.[57] The 'members of the reunion' gave priority to the relationships between them and were generous to each other, as they knew God to be generous on the infinite horizon. They shared relationships forged in the context of the mission town where the girls saw that the sisters were 'teenagers like us', 'always there for us', and where the sisters held

---

54   Volf, *End of Memory*, 35.
55   Volf, *End of Memory*, 144–45.
56   Volf, *End of Memory*, 150.
57   Volf, *End of Memory*, 144n36.

that they had come 'to help the people, to serve', being adamant that 'God does not exploit' (even when, as Abbot Placid observed, 'monks and institutions do'). Those relationships gave an expectation of ongoing connection and the hope of further, ongoing, reconciliation. Memory became not only a 'space of experience' in which the past entered the present but also a 'horizon of expectation' stretching the present forward towards a new way of relating in future.[58]

The gradual breaking open of new meaning in this kind of storytelling seems to me to be akin to the monastic practice of sacred reading, *lectio divina*, the slow mulling over sacred text taught by the desert monastics in the third and fourth centuries. The steady listening that stretches and transforms reality is an ancient and particularly Benedictine approach to prayer, human healing and growth. It recognises that meaning is an event, an active process for the listener who takes the story to heart. This style of engagement is not about gathering information or seeking 'raw facts' but much more about the potential for change at the level of being. It echoes the teaching of Miriam-Rose Ungunmerr-Baumann that 'deep listening', or *dadirri* in the language of her Ngangikiurungkurr people from Daly River, is central to healing. The reciprocal process of paying attention, practising 'quiet, still awareness—something like what you call contemplation'—opens new layers of meaning.[59] The invitation to access 'the larger whole' through stories told and heard is an invitation to encounter the evidence of the past in a dialogue that is potentially transformative.[60] This style of deep listening as part of research involves being open to living out new relationships.

* * * * *

---

58 Reinhart Koselleck, *Futures Past: On the Semantics of Historical Time*, trans. Keith Tribe (Cambridge, MA: MIT Press, 2004), 287–88; Volf, *End of Memory*, 98–100.
59 Miriam Rose Ungunmerr-Baumann, '*Dadirri*: Listening to One Another', in *A Spirituality of Catholic Aborigines and the Struggle for Justice*, ed. Joan Hendricks and Gerry Heffernan (Brisbane: Aborigines and Torres Strait Islander Apostolate, Catholic Archdiocese of Brisbane, 1993), 34–37. For work that approaches Indigenous trauma using *dadirri* as the research method, see Judy Atkinson, *Trauma Trails, Recreating Song Lines: The Transgenerational Effects of Trauma in Indigenous Australia* (North Geelong, Vic.: Spinifex Press, 2002).
60 Gadamer, *Truth and Method*, 379.

Figure 1.5: Members of the reunion on the steps of the Abbey Church, October 2001.
Source: *Newsletter of the Aboriginal Corporation of New Norcia*, 2008.

The final public statements of the reunion encapsulated the whole. At the opening of the new museum exhibition on 'Life at St Joseph's', Abbot Placid spoke for the community, thanking contributors and the people gathered at the opening. Sheila Humphries spoke for the former students and introduced the primary school girls, who, dressed in white frocks in the best New Norcia tradition, gave bunches of red roses to each of the sisters. Then together, Sister Francisca and Mae Taylor unveiled the exhibition plaque. At the very end, Sister Teresa spoke again on behalf of the Benedictine women, taking her turn on the stage at the front of the school hall at St Joseph's. The hall had not been there in her time at the school, but it was not unlike the classroom she fronted as a young teacher in the early 1950s, and she addressed a crowd of former students, now with their grandchildren on their knees.

Without notes, without rehearsal, and almost without warning, her words commanded attention at the end of the long day. Remember New Norcia, she said; remember why the sisters came, remember the good that they hoped New Norcia would stand for, remember above all the relationship that stands firm over decades. It was that relationship that made her exhortation both possible and compelling and brought a common horizon into view. No one in that room could doubt the validity and depth of the bonds between the sisters and the people. They knew enough of each other's stories to begin to grasp the larger whole. On behalf of the sisters, Teresa's final words were simply of thanks. Flipping the dynamic of acknowledgment, she spoke frankly of the love that fused their realities: 'We came to teach you and you have taught us. You are in our hearts. It is good to know that we are in your hearts'. There were no further words, just applause as proceedings ended and movement as people converged at the edge of the room for photographs. The former students presented a banner to the sisters, with signatures and handprints: to name and to remember.

2

The Company of St Teresa of Jesus at New Norcia, 1904–10

On 6 June 1908 Sister Maria Harispe, a member of the Company of St Teresa of Jesus, wrote to Father Henry Altimira, secretary to New Norcia's second abbot Fulgentius Torres. After nine months at New Norcia and approaching her third year in temporary vows as a lay sister with the Teresian community of missionary teachers, the 26-year-old wrote to Henry Altimira as someone she trusted and who knew the background of her situation. She wrote in her own hand, and in Spanish, the language of Paraguay, her home country. Faced with a disintegrating community and an imminent departure from New Norcia, Maria asked to remain at the West Australian mission. Her letter was not intended to be more than a personal statement, but it held the seed of the new style of monastic missionary presence that would emerge from the ashes of the Teresian community to become the Benedictine Missionary Sisters of New Norcia. Maria's urgent hopes for a future at New Norcia named priorities and pitfalls that had haunted the Teresian enterprise and would remain powerful themes in the lives of all the Spanish women who were involved at the mission through the next seven decades. This chapter sets the experience of these first Spanish missionary sisters in the context of their congregation's foundation in Barcelona and then focuses on the Teresian years at New Norcia, between 1904 and 1910, to tease out the themes of religious commitment, of ethnic and racial identity, of gender and institutional hierarchies, of class and educational opportunity that were formative of later patterns at St Joseph's.

We begin with Maria's letter because it encapsulates the crisis that marks the end of the Teresian story at New Norcia and because it points towards new and different structures. She probably wrote her letter upstairs in the south-west tower of St Gertrude's College. The fine new building bore the Teresian crest, but only the southern tower, accessible by a back stairway, was serving as a convent for the Teresian sisters, as the newly arrived Sisters of St Joseph of the Sacred Heart, Irish-Australian members of Mary MacKillop's group, had the front door keys and were launching the first year of St Gertrude's school downstairs.[1] Maria's letter, in response to this and much else, asked Father Altimira to help her persuade the abbot to keep her on as a worker and to send her to the new mission he was planning in the Kimberley. Her request came after careful and unromantic discernment of her decision through the wintery rains of June and flowed from faith that God had inspired her overriding commitment to missionary work with the Aboriginal people:

> After having commended to the Lord the matter which you already know, and especially during this month, and after having asked Him with all the sincerity of my heart for the grace to know His most holy will about putting my desires into operation, I find myself determined to follow this way of abnegation and sacrifice for His love. Since as far as I can understand, although no angel from heaven came down to reveal it to me, I think it will be God's will when He gives me these desires. Therefore I ask you sincerely to intercede for me with Reverend Father Abbot that he may deign to admit me for the mission of the north, which one who although [a] miserable and cowardly soldier is offering herself as a volunteer.[2]

---

1   On the early days of St Gertrude's, see Marie Therese Foale, *The Josephites Go West: The Sisters of St Joseph in Western Australia 1887–1920* (Fremantle, WA: University of Notre Dame Press, 1995), 68–75; Anne Carter and Elizabeth Murphy, *A Rich Harvest—St Gertrude's College* (South Perth: Sisters of St Joseph of the Sacred Heart, 2006), 6–9, 20–26. On the move to the south-west tower of the 'New College', 'Chronicle of the Benedictine Community of New Norcia' (hereafter *Chronicle*), 17 August 1907, 14 March 1908, New Norcia Archives (NNA). See also Katharine Massam, '"To Know How to Be All for All": The Company of St Teresa of Jesus at New Norcia 1904–1910', *New Norcia Studies* 15 (2007): 44–52.
2   Maria Harispe to Henry Altimira, 6 June 1908, in the 'Canonical Visitation to the Community of Teresians of St Gertrude's New Norcia, October 1907', trans. David Barry, OSB, NNA 01717 (hereafter *Visitation*), 82.

She signed herself with her full name in religion, Sister Maria Teresa de Jesus Harispe, and went on to detail her motivation for volunteering for the new mission. She documented her sense of call to the work and her particular promise to 'sacrifice' her own family connections in favour of a missionary life. She stressed her commitment to the Aboriginal people, who, in the Spanish of her day, were matter-of-factly 'blacks' and 'savages', 'despised by the majority of people' but loved by Maria:

> First, because since I heard that a house was going to be founded in Australia for the natives I always had the desire that they might send me. Secondly, so to live separated from the world and above all from my relatives which sacrifice I offered the Lord in a special way on the day of my religious profession. Thirdly, out of the compassionate love which I have towards the blacks for being so despised by the majority of people. Fourth, because I would desire to sacrifice my life for the savages and I would consider myself very happy if I could finish my life amongst them.[3]

She hesitated to tell the abbot's secretary of three requirements she saw as essential to her offer, but with a frank admission of her fear she would be laughed at she explained her hopes that she could continue to be identified as a religious sister, even as she sought to align herself with the Aboriginal people for the rest of her life:

> Concerning the conditions I will speak to you when I see you since I think that they are as it were some three conditions and indispensable which if I put them to you I have no doubt that you will laugh. Shall I put them to you? Yes. Firstly, that I may always be able to use the religious habit even though it be of sackcloth. Secondly, that they may regard me as a native as far as my clothing and other necessities. Thirdly, a plot of land when I die and a requiescat in pace.[4]

Maria's letter pivots between stages in her life: she will not renew her vows with the Teresians, and she will transfer to New Norcia's structures. It also serves to introduce the four powerful themes that marked the identity of the Teresian sisters and also threaded through the experience of later missionary women at New Norcia. They were Spanish, or if not born in Spain they were Spanish speakers from Spanish colonies, who had left their own empire to work in an outpost of Great Britain. From Mediterranean

---

3   *Visitation*, 83.
4   *Visitation*, 83.

and South American countries, they were also olive-skinned, ready to identify with the Aboriginal people and in a dubious position in the racial hierarchies that preoccupied White Australia.[5] They were missionaries for Catholicism who spoke a language of faith and salvation that they hoped to offer to the people they encountered. The prevailing Protestant assumptions in Australia alarmed and dismayed them. They were sisters, members of a community of religious women, and in this they belonged to a category that might be named even more powerfully as 'not monks'. On each of these counts, and framing them, they were outsiders, falling between categories and frequently separated from direct decision making. An account of the congregation's foundation in nineteenth-century Barcelona frames the hope expressed by their Teresian superiors in Spain: that at New Norcia, the community would 'know how to be all for all'.[6]

The Company of St Teresa of Jesus

A 36-year-old priest of the Diocese of Barcelona, Enrique Ossó y Cervelló, established the Company of St Teresa of Jesus in 1876. A teacher of mathematics at the diocesan seminary, Osso had a devotion to the sixteenth-century Carmelite foundress, Teresa of Avila, and a conviction that Christian education was the only thing that could transform society and draw it into Christ. The organisation of missionary teachers that he drew together, initially eight young women, was pledged to missionary outreach, drawing inspiration from Teresa of Avila. The present-day Teresians, now with communities in 23 countries, remember that Osso told the founders they were committed to:

> A work of zeal to make you other Teresas in so far as possible, so that you might be foremost in promoting the honour of Jesus. Praying, teaching, and sacrifice is the honour of the Society.[7]

As Osso wrote textbooks for the Teresian schools, the new group expanded rapidly from Barcelona to South America, in particular to Uruguay, Paraguay and Mexico. Young women from those countries

---

5   On the 'non-white' status of Spain, see Marilyn Lake and Henry Reynolds, *Drawing the Global Colour Line: White Men's Countries and the Question of Racial Equality* (Melbourne: Melbourne University Press, 2008), 24, 101, 105; J. Lyng, *Non-Britishers in Australia: Influence on Population and Progress* (Melbourne: Macmillan and Melbourne University Press, 1927), vi–vii, 4–5.
6   Saturnina Jassa to Fulgentius Torres, 30 April 1908, *Visitation*, 41.
7   Company of St Teresa of Jesus, www.teresians.org; accessed 25 April 2007.

joined them, including Maria Harispe, a French citizen from Paraguay, and Consuelo Batiz from Mexico. These two recruits, along with Teresa Roca from Barcelona, would become particularly important for the New Norcia story.

Osso also set up a teacher-training institute in the motherhouse in Barcelona. This Colegio Teresiano, now a prestigious secondary school, was one of the first buildings designed and built by Antoni Gaudí in 1889 and was full of the intriguing detail that would mark his style. Osso was uneasy about its high style and quirkiness; in response Gaudí was reported to have told his friend the founder: 'To each his own Fr Henry. You say Mass so that I may build houses'.[8] That division of labour settled, he ensured a building that reflected the Teresians' unusual commitment to education, both in their investment in professional training for the women who would teach and in what they would offer to children, especially girls, in mission countries. The founder was fond of remarking that '[t]he world has always been what women made it',[9] and education was a key to shaping their influence.

So, it was not so surprising that Fulgentius Torres, new abbot of the Benedictine mission at New Norcia, would think of the Teresians when he was seeking a community of women religious who could work with the Aboriginal women and girls at New Norcia. In fact, after ensuring the return to New Norcia of the body of Rosendo Salvado, New Norcia's founding abbot, from St Paul's Outside the Walls in Rome where he had died in December 1900, Torres announced that his highest priority would be to find women to take charge of what the Western Australian Government called 'St Joseph's Native School and Orphanage'. Archbishop Casanas of Barcelona recommended the Teresians. They honoured the Black Madonna, patroness of Barcelona, and they regarded her shrine, downhill from the monastery of Montserrat, as a place of particular inspiration.[10] Torres himself, as a monk of Montserrat, had met both the founder and the first sisters in 1885 and had kept track of the community over some

---

8   'Colegio de las Teresianas', Gaudi Barcelona Club, www.gaudiclub.com/esp/e_vida/teresian2.html; accessed 25 April 2007.
9   Enrique de Ossó y Cervelló, *Escritos* (Barcelona: Ediciones STJ, 1976), 207, cited by Pope John Paul II in his homily at the canonisation, 16 June 1993, w2.vatican.va/content/john-paul-ii/es/homilies/1993/documents/hf_jp-ii_hom_19930616_canonizzazione-madrid.html; accessed 15 April 2018. See also Alejandro Fernandez Pombo, *Saturnina Jassá de la Compañia de Santa Teresa de Jesús* (Barcelona: Ediciones STJ, 1991), 135.
10 'Quienes Somos', Compañia de Santa Teresa de Jesús, www.stjteresianas.org/quienes-somos/lugares-significativos/; accessed 12 October 2018.

25 years since.[11] In Spain again on behalf of the mission, Abbot Torres made contact with the superior general Mother Teresa Blanche, and the monastery's community diary or *Chronicle* records that a contract was approved on 8 June 1903.[12]

At three o'clock in the afternoon of 25 August 1904, a party of nine Teresian sisters arrived in buggies at New Norcia. Two of the monks had met them from the steamer *Stuttgart* at Fremantle, the abbot and the prior went to greet them on the road while the bells rang out, and 'the whole community' went to the mission church to chant the *Te Deum* in thanksgiving.[13] The sisters, travelling in black, cape-like habits and plain black veils, would remember they 'were given a warm welcome by the girls who had adorned themselves with bush flowers in their hats'.[14] Sure enough, in the photograph to commemorate the new community at St Joseph's the same wide-brimmed almost ostentatious hats marked the young women from the children in straw boaters and the new arrivals in their tight veils. Two members of the Teresians' provincial council, Mother Teresa Pla and Mother Josefa Beltran, had come to learn about their new foundation firsthand; the seven other travellers, Montserrat Fito, Consuelo Batiz, Felipa Sanjuan, Maria Teresa Vilar, Leonor Bargallo, Teresa Roca and Carmen Mayordom, would stay 'to care for the education of the girls'.[15]

On 11 December 1904, responsibility for St Joseph's passed into the hands of the Teresians. Only two of the community moved to the orphanage, a whitewashed wooden cottage dating from 1861, but all 'helped during the day'. They expected to move out of the two-storeyed guest house in front of the church and into their own new convent and school when construction was complete. Building had begun as they had left Europe, and the monks, perhaps unaware of the high standards set by Gaudí's

---

11   Torres to unnamed cardinal, 19 December 1907, *Visitation*, 60; [Torres, Fulgentius], *The Torres Diaries, 1901–1914: Diaries of Dom Fulgentius (Anthony) Torres y Mayans, O.S.B., Abbot Nullius of New Norcia, Bishop Titular of Dorylaeum, Administrator Apostolic of the Kimberley Vicariate in North Western Australia*, trans. Eugene Perez, ed. Rosemary Pratt and John Millington (Perth: Artlook Books, 1987), 12.
12   *Chronicle*, 8 June 1903.
13   *Chronicle*, 25 August 1904.
14   'Origen de la Congregacion de las Hermanas Benedictinas Misioneras de New Norcia, Western Australia' unpublished typescript from the notebooks of Sister Felicitas Pampliega c. 1921–c. 1967, transcribed and edited by Sister Teresa González, Madrid c. 1980, Archives of the Benedictine Missionary Sisters of Tutzing (ABTM) (hereafter *Notebooks*, Madrid), 1.
15   *Chronicle*, 22 August 1904.

motherhouse, expected the facilities 'to be magnificent'.[16] Recording the transfer, the *Chronicle* interlaced the three strands of Spanish identity, missionary vocation, and the call for women, as 'sisters-not-monks', suited to work with women:

> Brother Friolán Miró today began to follow all the acts of the community; till today for the last 30 years he has had charge of the education of the Aboriginal girls. He educated, cared for and watched over them day and night, doing as much as a mother could have done for them. The *great inconvenience* is obvious to anyone who thinks about it, which is the reason why the Abbot has not rested until he could bring out the Teresian Sisters of recent formation of D. Enrique de Osso priest; they have taken charge of the aforementioned girls, caring for them better than the virtuous and patient Br Miró and without the danger that resulted. He only goes to the college to sleep, the aim being to act as interpreter for the Sisters should anything happen since they do not yet understand the girls' language.[17]

The account is expansive by the standard of the *Chronicle*'s brief entries, marking an important occasion. The Teresians brought a religious identity as sisters to the work that local women, including Judith Butler as schoolmistress and Eliza Willaway as one of the Aboriginal matrons, had been doing alongside Brother Miró.[18] The Teresians took up the missionary tasks of care and education, and they faced these as Spanish women unable to speak 'the girls' language'. (This intriguing phrase might suggest something other than English, but probably reflects the *Chronicle*'s own distance from English rather than another lingua franca. Certainly by 1908, it was English that the Teresians were struggling to understand as they interacted with the St Joseph's girls.)

---

16 *Chronicle*, 27 July 1904, 24 September 1904.
17 'Notes on the Teresian Sisters in New Norcia', trans. Fr David Barry, NNA 01717, original emphasis; *Chronicle*, 11 December 1904.
18 Katharine Massam, 'Cloistering the Mission: Abbot Torres and Changes at New Norcia 1901–1910', *Australasian Catholic Record* 89 (2012): 13–25.

Figure 2.1: Brother Friolán Miró and the residents of St Joseph's before 1904.
Source: NNA 73609P.

The abbot had high hopes for the missionary women, but these were unrefined times at New Norcia. A monk wanting a bath still used the 'ram's trough' in a paddock, and the lay brothers did the laundry in the river.[19] Practical demands came first. Perhaps it is the matter-of-fact announcement in the *Chronicle* two days after the sisters took over at St Joseph's that reveals most about the expectations of their work. The diarist noted: 'The Teresian Sisters have made a habit for Fr Alcalde. They are also mending the old habits of the community'.[20] Three months later the diarist celebrated the expansion of the domestic work at St Joseph's, announcing that 'for the first time the girls of the College have washed the clothes of the community'.[21] Whether this was the kind of work the Teresians expected their school to be doing, the *Chronicle* does not say, but later events suggest it was not. Teacher education, missionary vocation and refined taste all paled beside the expectation that the women would do the washing and mend the clothes.

---

19 *Chronicle*, 31 January 1905, 13 March 1905.
20 *Chronicle*, 13 December 1904.
21 *Chronicle*, 13 March 1905.

Figure 2.2: The first Teresian community at New Norcia with residents of St Joseph's, 1904.
Source: NNA 73743P.

There are no photographs of the community at work, but we do have an image of the group at St Joseph's taken soon after the sisters arrived, posed in careful rows. As discussion of the photographic collection at New Norcia as a whole has shown,[22] the image marking the occasion of the Teresians' arrival reveals but also conceals. The image is one of half a dozen or so photographs of the sisters in their time at New Norcia. They are always pictured with the St Joseph's girls. Unlike later communities of sisters at New Norcia, there are no group photos of the Teresian sisters by themselves or in informal settings. In a context where the Western Australian Parliament was moving towards the 1905 legislation on Aboriginal people, the so-called Protection legislation that actually introduced greater segregation and separation from families, the anxiety about St Joseph's that comes through in the monastery *Chronicle* was not unique.

The arrival photograph was one answer to that anxiety, perhaps. As with any historical evidence, however, we cannot be absolutely sure of what we are seeing. Some of the women in this picture meet our gaze, and some

---

22   For papers from the 2014 symposium 'Ways of Telling: Images of Salvado and the New Norcia Mission'; see *New Norcia Studies* 22 (2015).

avoid it. The children scowl, squint or face the camera calmly. Teresa Roca, the lay sister seated on the right, seems lost in thought as one girl rests a hand on her shoulder and another chooses not to. No one smiles, but the Aboriginal matron on the far left has a white cockatoo on her shoulder, tucked in close under the brim of her hat. A subversive gesture or a signal of the daily reality? We can speculate but we cannot know what the women are thinking or how they are feeling.

Figure 2.3: Detail of Teresian arrival: Aboriginal matron with a cockatoo on her shoulder.
Source: NNA 73743P.

Figure 2.4: Detail of Teresian arrival: Teresa Roca and other sisters with St Joseph's girls behind.
Source: NNA 73743P.

Our focus for the moment is on the Teresian sisters. Like missionary women in many other contexts, their history is written in the 'white ink' of discounted experience.[23] The milky white ink is often lost between the lines, or visible only through accounts of other people, such as photographs for the Catholic press and administrative records that trace their interaction with the church and the state. Occasionally, we get a sense of personality and the echo of a personal voice in those records, and even more so in the letters they wrote to the abbot and other officials, usually written in times of crisis—as Maria Harispe's letter was written to Henry Altimira, for example. More often, we only have glimpses to piece together and passing remarks in other accounts to rely on.

Take, for example, the account of Maria Harispe's own arrival at New Norcia. She came not with the foundation party but three years later, in 1907. Our main source for this information is a shipboard diary kept by a young monk travelling in the abbot's party of nine, probably one Miguel Angel Estremera. As the German liner *Seydlitz* set out from Genoa in July 1907 he kept note of the distance travelled and the miles that remained until Fremantle; he recorded heat, thirst, seasickness, sightings of whales and of rainbows. Like many diary writers, he kept an eye lightly on his reader, apologising for smudges and 'the badly chosen selection of events of our journey'.[24] He took his readers into his confidence a little. We know he respected the abbot, who threw a medal of St Benedict overboard, 'so that the sea may calm itself'[25] and they could celebrate Sunday Mass. He noted the success of a concert and the abbot's work as accompanist ('Well done Father', applauded Miguel, 'A Protestant public! All for the greater glory of God!'[26]), as he noted the concert seating—children apart, gentlemen at one table, religious persons (including himself) at another, and then, with the ladies, there were also 'the Sisters'. These sisters, and all of the party except the abbot, were seasick as they crossed the equator and for days afterwards. But the weather calmed and they recovered, and after five weeks at sea they stood on deck together to watch the Australian coast appear. At the last, he names Abbot Torres and the five other Benedictine men, 'plus' he says, 'four Sisters of the Congregation of St Teresa of Jesus and a Spanish married couple'.[27]

---

23   Gerda Lerner, *The Majority Finds Its Past* (Oxford: Oxford University Press, 1981), 145–59.
24   'Viaje de Génova a Nueva-Norsia (Australia)', trans. Carlos Lopez, NNA 00033 (hereafter *Viaje*), Sunday 18 August 1907.
25   *Viaje*, 3 August 1907.
26   *Viaje*, 5 August 1907.
27   *Viaje*, 18 August 1907.

These he does not name, and we have no shipboard diary for them. We know that they were travelling with the abbot and his party, and at New Norcia they knew to expect the woodworker and sculptor Juan Casellas and his wife Catalina, as well as the four sisters whose names they did not know.[28] As the diary draws to a conclusion Miguel explains the party's shared purpose in terms that had been popular in Spanish missionary literature since the sixteenth century. They had shared this journey, he says, 'for the Greater Glory of God, to profit our own souls and the Mission, whose purpose is to procure salvation for the Blacks who dwell there'.[29] The journey was nearly over, and the party would be testing their assumptions against the reality of the new place. Let us follow the account for just a little longer.

It was Sunday, so there was only one train that day from the port at Fremantle to the city, Perth. Waiting to catch it, the party attracted attention. Whether because of their dark skin, their monastic clothes, or their Spanish talk, Miguel did not know or say, but he recorded the jolt, in national terms:

> I was surprised that these English, famed for their indifference and education, were perplexed to see us; such was their astonishment that they stopped and laughed as though we were strange beasts.[30]

Even at its port, Western Australia was homogenous enough to know whom to label strange. The diary rushes on, but all of a sudden everything is compared to what he had known at home: the train was inferior to Spanish railcars; the views from the window were not pretty, all billboards; the hotel lunch had no wine, although they asked, only sherry with dessert. And then Perth itself. It was larger in size than Barcelona, but not as beautiful: it was all trams, asphalt, more timber than stone; in fact, he says, 'I would not give ten cents for it'.[31] He was a little more relaxed about the large park with walkways, the river—wider than the Ebro at Tortosa—and the Catholic cathedral, 'raised by the Brothers from the Mission',[32] where in the evening a good congregation gathered for devotions with a sermon in English and sung litanies. But we can hear the writer's shock and a reassertion of Spanish assumptions.

---

28   *Chronicle*, 19 August 1907.
29   *Viaje*, 18 August 1907.
30   *Viaje*, 18 August 1907.
31   *Viaje*, 18 August 1907.
32   *Viaje*, 18 August 1907. As Frances Stibi shows, this was a widespread misunderstanding about the role of the Benedictines in Perth. See 'Cathedral Construction: Building the Cathedral of the Immaculate Conception', *New Norcia Studies* 14 (2006), 1–13.

The next day, the party set off at eight in the morning for Mogumber by train, a journey of four-and-a-half hours, and the prose expands again. The writer appreciated what he saw: eucalyptus forests and green fields, stations that 'find themselves all alone';[33] and then a further journey from Mogumber in 'carts';[34] until suddenly, 'a great surprise to the traveller to see such a beautiful town spring out of the forest'.[35] They were welcomed with New Norcia's ritual of everybody turning out on the road. Miguel's travel diary was approaching its conclusion and he records it this way:

> At half past three we alighted and were made welcome by the gathered community, the boys school and the girls school and other inhabitants, their children blacker than coal. Under an arch with the English and Spanish flags and many banners, we crossed towards the church to sing a *Te Deum* in thanks. Afterwards we went to eat and to install ourselves.[36]

But you have not arrived until you know where you are, so the next day there was a full tour, and Miguel celebrated what he saw, again in national terms. It surpassed Europe; it surpassed 'the [local] English':[37]

> [W]e visited the various parts of the Monastery, the girls' school close to being finished; would that Europe had such a thing, it is no wonder that the English seem astonished [as] … there is nothing like it in all Australia.[38]

The diary keeper is becoming less of a stranger at every step. As they walk around the town he catalogues the signs of progress—the mill, the saw, the noodle-making machine, the engine configured as at home, the workshops, harvesters and brick kiln. 'In other words', he sums up, 'thanks be to God and to the Abbots that have governed here, we lack for nothing.'[39] In a burst of generous acknowledgment he adds: 'Thanks also to the freedom given by the English government'.[40] Then he signs off, with the initials for the Latin declaration, 'May God be glorified in all things': UIOGD.

---

33 *Viaje*, 18 August 1907.
34 *Chronicle*, 19 August 1907, records the urgent borrowing of two coaches from the neighbouring Clune and Lanigan families to add to the monastery's trap, so they could meet the party in style.
35 *Chronicle*, 19 August 1907.
36 *Chronicle*, 19 August 1907.
37 *Chronicle*, 19 August 1907.
38 *Chronicle*, 19 August 1907.
39 *Chronicle*, 19 August 1907.
40 *Chronicle*, 19 August 1907.

Meanwhile, at the southern end of town, the newly arrived superior of the Teresian community, Sister Crisanta Lopez, was sitting down at the table with her community—three other new arrivals and five who had been at the mission for three years. As she sat down, Crisanta, also thanking God, made an impact on her sisters with a very different view of the journey Miguel has described. Apparently she exclaimed: 'Thanks be to God we can eat free of the presence of the monks! We are full of monks, up to the top of the head'.[41] Sister Carmen, one of the established group, was credited by the others as advising Crisanta that 'the Abbot was a kind man'. At the table the old community of five (Carmen Mayordom, Maria Teresa Vilar, Felipa Sanjuan, Leonor Bargallo and Teresa Roca) went on to tell the newcomers (Crisanta Lopez, Luz Castañada, Dolores Sol de Vila and Maria Harispe) 'all that could be known' about Abbot Torres, including prudent advice that 'she should be somewhat careful with him'.[42]

Perhaps they included some stories of the former superior, Montserrat Fito, and her deputy in charge of the school, Consuelo de la Cruz Batiz, who had been recalled to Spain just five weeks earlier on 11 July 1907. Perhaps, but the subject was raw. The sudden order from Barcelona recalling both sisters had fallen 'like a bomb' on the whole town.[43] The Teresians were 'not able to get out of the amazement that the decision of the superiors … has caused them'. The 15 Aboriginal residents at St Joseph's withdrew their participation from public prayer and 'spent two days in which, in the Church, they could not respond to the Priest leading the Rosary', perhaps through sorrow, or in protest, or maybe both.[44] Two girls left St Joseph's and hid under the arches of the 'New College' with a wild plan to meet up with one of the workers. When they were discovered, the sisters initially accepted 'their sadness at the departure of Sr Consuelo' as a plausible excuse.[45] The monks recorded that Montserrat's departure was 'what the Aborigines and Europeans of these environs want'.[46] She had opposed Consuelo. The loss of Consuelo herself was a great blow. The *Chronicle* is clear that the mission owed her 'so much gratitude, more than to all the other Sisters combined'.[47] She was one 'who has earned the respect of the Aborigines in the village and in particular the girls in the College (of which she had been in charge since the Sisters started to

---

41   Teresa Roca, 30 October 1907, *Visitation*, 10.
42   Teresa Roca, 30 October 1907, *Visitation*, 10.
43   *Chronicle*, 6 July 1907.
44   *Chronicle*, 11 July 1907, 18 July 1907. On the numbers at St Joseph's over time, see Appendix 1.
45   *Chronicle*, 22 July 1907.
46   *Chronicle*, 5 July 1907.
47   *Chronicle*, 16 July 1907.

run it), and not excluding the Aboriginal people who admired her and venerated her very much'.[48] There had been a rift between the two local leaders, and Barcelona attempted to resolve it by recalling them both and sending a new superior.

The local community was reeling. The monastery's *Chronicle* observed that '[t]he jealousy of the superior has taken from the Mission the Sister who has worked the hardest for the Mission itself'.[49] As Abbot Torres eventually explained to the Teresian superior general, Sister Consuelo had been at the core of his hopes for the new school, simply 'the Sister who in the judgement of those close to her and of strangers could have been put in charge of the college both of white girls and of native girls without delay'.[50] But now, arriving home to the new situation and after a voyage where 'neither the new superior nor any of the Sisters ... asked one question about the Sisters here or about the people and things in the mission', Abbot Torres could not bring himself to make the customary courtesy call to the sisters who had been waiting for his return.[51] As the new superior, and the one sent to replace Consuelo in the school, Crisanta Lopez walked into a context where all of New Norcia's communities were alarmed and confused. She would have been well-advised to go gently.

Whatever the sisters said around the table at that first meal, we know it was not a good beginning for Crisanta. The fragments of their lunchtime conversation survive because within three months Abbot Torres and his secretary Henry Altimira were conducting a canonical visitation into the governance of the Teresian community, recording accusations and counter-accusations among the sisters. Within six months Mary MacKillop's Sisters of St Joseph (Josephites) arrived to teach in English at the girls' school. And in another six months the abbot and the Teresian superior in Barcelona were exchanging telegrams and letters, each threatening the other with withdrawing or banishing the sisters and leaving the other party to explain to the Congregation for the Propagation of the Faith in Rome. In late November 1907 Crisanta and Luz returned to Spain, and Sister Felipa Sanjuan, who had made her final profession at New Norcia in August only the year before, became the new stop-gap superior.[52]

---

48 *Chronicle*, 5 July 1907.
49 *Chronicle*, 11 July 1907.
50 Fulgentius Torres to Saturnina Jassa, Superior General of the Company of St Teresa of Jesus, 3 May 1908, *Visitation*, 43.
51 *Chronicle*, 21 and 24 August 1907.
52 *Record*, 11 August 1906, 17; *Chronicle*, 23 November 1907.

In April 1908 the newly elected superior in Barcelona, Saturnina Jassa, and her councillor, Teresa Pla, wanted to renew the commitment to New Norcia. But the abbot's secretary advised them to stop trying to solve the situation: 'I understand the sign INRI has been well and truly fixed on this cross', Altimira wrote, 'it only remains to bear the burden of disappointment'.[53] On 10 October 1908 a further four Teresians were recalled. All three who remained—Maria Harispe, Leonor Bargallo and Teresa Roca—petitioned the abbot to be permitted to stay and work at New Norcia or in the new mission in the north. Maria's hope could be accommodated with the support of the monks because her temporary vows as a Teresian expired in July 1909 but Leonor and Teresa were bound to obedience in permanent vows. They were finally recalled to Spain, and in February 1910 Maria Harispe was alone in charge of St Joseph's. How did it come to this?

At the centre of what we know is the report of the canonical visitation and the letters and telegrams collected with it. These valuable documents were preserved at New Norcia when other Teresian material that might have given more background was burnt during the Spanish Civil War. Through the visitation records, the three categories of identity that Maria's letter itself introduced—ethnicity, spirituality and gender—emerge as important touchstones. When we put the quasi-judicial record of 1907 alongside the day-to-day *Chronicle* kept by the Benedictine monks to record their own life in the town, we have glimpses of the impact of a fourth category: race. What did it mean for the Teresians to be Spanish, missionaries, and members of a vowed community? How did these categories of identity intersect with the markers of 'Whiteness' that implicitly shaped the dynamics of the mission town?

Spanish identity

The importance of Spanish identity had preoccupied New Norcia's monks as they framed the first invitation to women to share the work of the mission. At a 'Community Council' held on 6 October 1902, a mere four days after the abbatial election that confirmed Fulgentius Torres as Salvado's successor, and only four days before Torres left for Europe, the monks had five items of business to determine. They agreed unanimously on buildings first and last: to complete the addition of the third floor to

---

53   Henry Altimira to Teresa Pla, 8 June 1908, *Visitation*, 48.

the existing monastery and to plan for a new structure on the hill near the post office. The proposal 'afterwards to construct a house for the girls; to bring nuns to educate them'[54] drew so much discussion 'about what nuns would be suitable and of what nationality'[55] that there was, however, no formal vote. The *Chronicle* considered the options in terms of location, with support divided between the Sisters of the Good Samaritan, founded in 1857 by John Bede Polding, the Benedictine archbishop of Sydney 'in that capital', others who favoured 'those in Perth or Fremantle', and still others 'who wanted them from Spain'.[56] Vote or no vote, the *Chronicle* concluded that 'this last position [Spain] was agreed on, and Benedictines are preferred'. The remaining item, that Salvado's body should be brought back to a tomb in the church, was simply referred to the new superior to sort out. In Europe, negotiating that return at the same time as he sought women for the mission, Abbot Torres's decision to invite the Teresians gave priority to the women's Spanish identity and formation as missionaries over any familiarity with the Benedictine structures or way of life.

The Teresians fell between categories. Ethnicity united them with the monks but divided them from the norms of both the English and Irish colonists and of Aboriginal Australians. In his visitation to the convent in 1907 Torres noted the sisters were using more than a whole jar of coffee every day at breakfast; he thought it important enough to record, although he did not comment further on the custom or its economy.[57] He did indicate more clearly that daily classes in arithmetic and Castilian or Spanish grammar were a problem, because 'they don't study English, nor does the superior recommend it'.[58]

Language was an early and enduring barrier. That the Teresian sisters did not share the language of the girls and had no capacity to teach in it emerged as a major issue, alongside the sheer distance between Spain and Australia that made the communication of the abbot's expectations, and the response and oversight of the Barcelona superiors, so difficult. Torres had clearly expected that English-speaking members would be sent from the beginning. When only Consuelo of the original seven had any grounding in English, the mission had invested in increasing her capacity,

---

54   *Chronicle*, 6 October 1902. On the foundation of the Sisters of the Good Samaritan, see Margaret Walsh, *The Good Sams: Sisters of the Good Samaritan 1857–1969* (Mulgrave, Vic.: John Garrett, 2001).
55   *Chronicle*, 6 October 1902.
56   *Chronicle*, 6 October 1902.
57   *Visitation*, 3.
58   *Visitation*, 5, 8.

perhaps through lessons with the former schoolmistress or another local, 'so as to have her made ready' to head the integrated school.[59] But then, as we have seen, the abbot was confronted with Consuelo's withdrawal in 1907 and her subsequent transfer to a Teresian school in Valencia.

Without Consuelo to bridge the language barrier between the Teresians and their charges, the school was in dire straits. The abbot had written ahead from Spain to reassure the community that among the four new Teresians 'there is one who can speak English'.[60] 'Thank goodness for that at least', the *Chronicle* had remarked.[61] But this was Sister Crisanta who in December 1907, after less than four months in Western Australia, had so mismanaged her office as local superior that she was on her way to Spain again. With a second superior returning in crisis, the Teresian leadership in Barcelona asked the abbot to do them the favour of applying to Rome to close the Teresian house at New Norcia and to 'take all the necessary steps to provide substitutes there for our community'.[62] Teresa Blanche's letter was full of regret and defeat. She acknowledged 'only God can measure our pain on seeing so many efforts brought to nothing'[63] and hoped 'the divine wisdom may draw from so much grief some small atom of glory'.[64] Nevertheless, she alerted Torres that some of the sisters found 'the present conditions [at New Norcia] foreign to their vocations',[65] and furthermore implied they would take a lawsuit against the abbot to Rome if he did not petition Rome to close the house.[66]

Abbot Torres remained focused on the school and his hope that the Spanish sisters might teach in English. In December 1907 he was not ready to give up on the Teresian community at New Norcia or the possibilities for St Gertrude's.[67] Implacably, Torres replied to the superior in Barcelona that she could seek permission from Rome herself for the closure. He expected they would approach the authorities (and later claimed to have been 'waiting for the fulfilment of the threat'[68]) but felt himself that patience might lead to improvement. He would not release the sisters from their commitment to New Norcia. 'No', the abbot wrote back in January 1908,

---

59   Torres to Pla, 3 May 1908, *Visitation*, 45.
60   *Chronicle*, 19 July 1907. On Crisanta as the English speaker, Torres to Saturnina Jassa, 3 May 1908.
61   *Chronicle*, 19 July 1907.
62   Teresa Blanche to Fulgentius Torres, 18 December 1907, *Visitation*, 38.
63   *Visitation*, 38.
64   *Visitation*, 38.
65   *Visitation*, 38.
66   Henry Altimira to Teresa Pla, 8 June 1908, points out this implication, *Visitation*, 48.
67   *Visitation*, 48.
68   Torres to Jassa, undated letter but by internal evidence 3 May 1908, *Visitation*, 43.

'Wait and see if some sister or sisters reach the stage of being able to teach the white girls.'[69] In the meantime, he persuaded the Sisters of St Joseph who were already running primary schools in his far-flung diocese to send teachers to New Norcia for the new school year. On 8 January 1908 Sister La Merci, assistant to Mother Mary MacKillop, gave him the support he was looking for when she telegraphed from Sydney that the congregation would send teachers 'at least for the next term'.[70] Clearly aware of the tensions growing in the town, she also indicated that they were open to taking over the 'native girls' if, as everyone judged likely, the Teresian sisters did not continue.[71]

In Barcelona, however, the changes in the Teresian leadership that saw the election of the experienced missionary Saturnina Jassa meant there was new energy for the Australian house. Early in 1908 Mother Teresa Pla, drawing on her firsthand knowledge of New Norcia gathered in the four months she spent there with the foundation community, wrote that they would send someone who not only spoke English but who also had qualities valued highly as part of the Spanish national character. She proposed someone 'competent, faithful, zealous for good works' who had taught English for some years. Teresa Pla also offered to come herself to 'settle things down'.[72]

The offer was no longer welcome. Only weeks before, Torres had been hoping for this, 'to gain time and see if the Superior General of the Teresians was taking better counsel'.[73] But now, in March 1908, with Torres heading to the Kimberley on behalf of the new mission, Henry Altimira replied to Barcelona that 'the English religious', the Josephites, were in place, and the monastery was no longer resisting the withdrawal of the Teresians. Recent 'events' had cast doubt over any Teresian future at New Norcia:

> In view of what has happened because of the three English religious having been put in charge of the college of the white girls duly authorised for it ... I beg to notify you that if you are still determined to withdraw ... the abbot will not place the least difficulty in your way.[74]

---

69 Torres to Blanche, 29 January 1908, *Visitation*, 39.
70 *Chronicle*, 8 January 1908.
71 *Chronicle*, 8 January 1908.
72 Pla to Torres, 28 April 1908, *Visitation*, 43.
73 Torres to Jassa, 3 May 1908, *Visitation*, 43.
74 Altimira to Blanche, 12 March 1908, *Visitation*, 39.

He does not say explicitly what 'has happened' at New Norcia, but by then the message was clear: 'Don't bother to come. The Spanish sisters need to leave.' The English speakers who could run the school had priority over the Spanish sisters whose conflict with them was about more than language, as we shall see. What was at stake both in Barcelona and in the minds of the Teresians at New Norcia who were petitioning to stay was their missionary vocation.

Missionary identity

The arrival accounts and Maria Harispe's letter both gave a high priority to the work to evangelise and to be with the Aboriginal people. The same concern runs through the pages of the report on the canonical visitation. Some of the key difficulties in the community related to Sister Crisanta's lack of understanding as the new superior about how the missionary work was conducted and also perhaps about how much hard work, both domestic and on the farm, the Teresian sisters were doing alongside the St Joseph's girls. Photographs of a child practising the weaving that produced cinctures and other cords for the liturgy and a toddler sweeping with the twig broom that were taken to record the life at St Joseph's at the time give a much more tranquil picture than the account the established sisters gave the abbot. He recorded that, according to Sister Felipa Sanjuan, Crisanta struggled to assert her authority over the demands of mission work:

> The superior has said that she can't work with due freedom, that she came to be superior and not a slave. ... The Sisters with due circumspection, drew her attention to the inconveniences which were caused by leaving the native girls alone in bed and letting them rise at their pleasure and without any supervision. The superior answered them: 'You are opposing what I am laying down.' Everyday with the exception of Monday when they are with the clothing, the girls who can't assist at class are without any supervision, with the weekly change of sisters in charge of the native girls, what one sister does the other undoes. The superior declared she would prefer to be in gaol rather than continue here in New Norcia.[75]

---

75   Felipa Sanjuan, 28 October 1907, *Visitation*, 5.

Other sisters echoed the concerns with the need to focus on the work in the school, to supervise the girls on walks and at work, and, a little surprisingly, on the freedom that the mission context gave the sisters in relation to the local superior because they could enlist the support of the abbot against her. A lay sister, Dolores Sol de Vila, put it to Torres that they were clashing with the superior over their access to the alternative authority of the monastery. Abbot Torres (or Father Altimira) recorded Dolores's summation of Crisanta's accusation in direct quotation marks: 'The ease we sisters have here in New Norcia of having recourse to the prelate, making clear what we judge necessary, and in this way they cannot suffocate us as happens in other parts'.[76]

The full cooperation with the monastery that the Teresians were apparently claiming at New Norcia is especially interesting in the context of the wider literature on women's missionary work. Frequently, 'missionary' was an implicitly male term.[77] The monks or the priests or the male ministers were the 'missionaries' and the women—whether accompanying nuns, or ministers' wives, or single women teachers, nurses and occasionally doctors—were framed as assistants, associates and helpmates. Salvado had distinguished the Sisters of Mercy from the 'missionaries' in his original party,[78] and in the twentieth century New Norcia's *Chronicle* revealed a similar assumption, even as it paid tribute to Consuelo as an extraordinary missionary. Documenting the emotional impact of her sudden recall to Spain in a week when she was 'feeling it' and 'quite upset … through her sorrow'[79] the diary keeper praised her for transcending her gender:

> [Sr Consuelo] was perhaps never more distinguished than in what has been seen in these days, seeing that she had to overcome [the limitations of] her sex and condition, with her untiring perseverance in working without reserve for the good of the Aborigines, using her great talent in this. She has gained such great respect and love that the sorrow and tears at her departure were common to both the Aborigines and the European women.[80]

---

76   Dolores Sol de Vila, 28 October 1907, *Visitation*, 12.
77   Philip M. Kulp, ed., *Women Missionaries and Cultural Change*, Studies in Third World Societies 40 (Williamsburg, VA: Department of Anthropology, College of William and Mary, June 1987); Leslie A. Flemming, ed., *Women's Work for Women: Missionaries and Social Change in Asia* (Boulder, CO: Westview Press, 1989); Fiona Bowie, Deborah Kirkwood and Shirley Ardener, eds, *Women and Missions: Past and Present; Anthropological and Historical Perceptions* (Providence, RI: Berg, 1993).
78   Katharine Massam, 'Missionary Women and Holy Work: Benedictine Women in Western Australia', *Journal of Australian Studies* 39 (2015): 44.
79   *Chronicle*, 6 July 1907 and 16 July 1907.
80   *Chronicle*, 11 July 1907.

Clearly appreciated by the monks as well as the Aborigines, and with a particular bond with the European women in town, Consuelo subsequently made choices that show how deeply she valued her missionary work.[81] That she and other Teresians claimed their own vocation as missionaries and not simply 'helpmeets' challenged the assumptions of the day and disrupted their own community.

In writing to the cardinal in Rome with oversight of Catholic missionary work around the world in June 1908, Abbot Torres assumed that the women were 'helpers', not missionaries in their own right. In his letter supporting the requests of Leonor Bargallo and Teresa Roca to be released from their commitment to the Teresians, Torres foreshadowed the informal group of Benedictine oblates that would take their place:

> For the rest, Your Eminence, the Institute of Religious Oblates of our Holy Father St Benedict in these regions whose primary duty would be to help our Benedictine missions amongst the Aboriginals would I think contribute to the greatest good and be an ornament of the holy Roman church. It would moreover, turn into the best help of our missionaries who only at great risk of their spiritual life can take care of young women and native girls in teaching them sacred doctrine.[82]

His concern with the moral threat that would be overcome by having women to evangelise women echoed the original call to the Teresians in 1904. It related directly to the third dimension of identity that is entwined in the details of the visitation, that of gender or of the Teresians as sisters, not monks.

Identity as sisters-not-monks

The record of the visitation is overwhelmingly concerned with tensions that arise from understandings of gender and the appropriate role of women in the church. The impetus for the visit came in the first place (it seems) from complaints by the Teresians to Torres that the local superior (both Crisanta Lopez and her predecessor Montserrat Fito) was interfering with their consciences, asking individuals why they had not received communion, and refusing to call the extraordinary confessor

---

81 See Chapter 3.
82 Torres to unnamed cardinal, 5 June 1908, *Visitation*, 80.

when they requested him. They did request him often—so much so that the depositions all agree almost in the precise wording that Crisanta Lopez used to tell her community to stop requesting the extraordinary confessor. She claimed that the extraordinary confessor was becoming the ordinary one and the superiors (probably in Barcelona, but perhaps of the monastery) had told the local superior not to go along with this. Such a refusal is in breach of canon law. As a result, Torres removed Crisanta Lopez from office.

Exactly what was going on in the repeated requests for the extraordinary confessor is open to interpretation. Perhaps the Teresians were scrupulous, or the ordinary confessor was hopeless, or the community simply preferred Planas and Altimira (the senior monks who were the extraordinary confessors) to Fr Mateu (the resident diocesan priest appointed as ordinary confessor), or perhaps they were playing the local superiors against the monastery. Or perhaps, and this is what Abbot Torres saw, the superior was usurping priestly authority and restricting the women's access to the sacramental life of the church.

There was more than just the restriction on access to confession to support Torres in this view. Crisanta Lopez had also prevented visits to the Blessed Sacrament in the church, telling the sisters instead to make the daily devotional act required by their directory in the convent chapel, where the Sacrament was not reserved. There were also practices that looked like the ritual exercise of authority, and these, Torres discovered in some alarm, were common to most Teresian houses. As the sisters remembered, tension between Montserrat Fito and Consuelo Batiz had included Consuelo's objection to the practice. Each day the sisters were required to kneel or prostrate themselves at the feet of the superior to seek absolution of their faults. Sometimes this followed a gathering of the house in chapter session where they accused each other of faults against the common life, but not always. When they left the convent building, they were also expected to kneel and ask the superior's permission. Torres was amazed, even though 'we ourselves have been eyewitnesses of this'.[83] He summed up the difficulties to the cardinal as a usurpation of authority and as a mimicking of priesthood in particular:

> The religious of the Society of St Teresa of Jesus labour under the greatest ignorance concerning the true subjection and obedience due to prelates.

---

83   Torres to unnamed cardinal, 19 December 1907, *Visitation*, 64.

> The Sisters come together regularly at night time before they sleep before the feet of the superior, so that kneeling they ask a blessing as from a priest. The superior … imploring the help of God and St Teresa makes the sign of the cross over the one asking and presents her hand to be kissed … having accused themselves of faults … the superior at the pre-arranged time sits apart in a seat placed like a sacred minister there awaiting each member of the community.[84]

Shifting ground a little in his conclusion, the abbot lamented the harsh dictatorial demands that had replaced 'the love which is necessary to render light and sweet the yoke of Christ our Lord'.[85] It is clear from the testimonies that the local superior was behaving erratically and was probably unsuited to the role, but the crisis came to a head because she appeared to lack the Christ-like and womanly quality of gentleness, on the one hand, while clutching after priestly power of decision making and care of souls, on the other.

Governance and the sisters' independence from the local bishop were also at issue. Like Mary MacKillop's Sisters of St Joseph in the 1870s, the Teresians had drafted constitutions that enshrined obedience to Rome through their own superiors, rather than a structure of distinct houses answerable to a local bishop. The central structure was part of 'the spirit of the Company'.[86] It was identified with the founders, including Saturnina Jassa and Teresa Pla, who were both involved in decisions about the mission to Australia.[87] But in July 1903 Rome rejected these first constitutions and approved a revised version that emphasised the authority of the local bishops. The Teresians welcomed the changes as a 'new grace' that affirmed the work of the congregation overall, but exactly how the revisions would affect local decision making was left to evolve. In 1905 the leadership issued a 'Directory' that included customs previously revoked by the approved constitutions, including the in-house practices of accusation and confession. Not surprisingly, different sisters came to different conclusions about the relative authority of the two documents. Torres found he was the first bishop to conduct a visitation of any house so far as the sisters at New Norcia knew. One sister believed that 'in certain customs of the house not even the Pope could interfere',[88] while another

---

84 *Visitation*, 64.
85 *Visitation*, 64.
86 Fernandez Pombo, *Saturnina Jassá*, 117, 126, citing *La Compañia de Santa Teresa de Jesús 1876–1932* (Barcelona: Ediciones STJ, 1969), 351.
87 Fernandez Pombo, *Saturnina Jassá*, 126.
88 Reported of Sr Montserrat, 30 October 1907, *Visitation*, 70.

held that 'if the superior general did not order it she would not do it, even if twenty abbots or bishops ordered it'.[89] Abbot Torres was also bishop of the extensive network of parishes within the abbey nullius of New Norcia. A small scrap of paper in the monastery's copy of the approved Teresian constitutions, placed between the pages sometime before 1910 gave quick access to precisely those sections on local governance.[90] It is not there by accident. The findings of the visitation and the letters Torres wrote to superior general Saturnina Jassà and to the cardinal heading the Congregation of the Affairs of Religious in 1907 and 1908 crackle with indignation and astonishment that the Teresian superiors would assume so much autonomy.[91]

While the bishop's difficulties with the structures and with the particular superior in charge were significant, they did not in themselves trigger the loss of confidence in the community that overtook Torres in February 1908. One particular incident at the start of the school year effectively sealed the fate of the community. Recorded only obliquely, the fragments nevertheless show that tensions about race fanned other smouldering issues into an open blaze.

Race, and identity as not-White

While the correspondence between the Spanish superiors traced concerns about language and women's spiritual authority, the *Chronicle* recorded that the Aboriginal girls were also apprehensive. With Torres and the Teresians, they had seen the tension erupt one night just after Christmas 1906, when a group of 32 Aboriginal men had raided St Joseph's and St Mary's, breaking windows, fences and flowerpots. Historians have read the incident as an effort by fathers to free their children after changes in New Norcia's administration made the institutions a target. The press in Perth had already noted the shift from the outward-looking mission of Salvado's era towards a more aloof institution under the new abbot.[92] Aboriginal voices implicate Torres in changes that were insensitive and

---

89   Reported of Sr Luz, 29 October 1907, *Visitation*, 69.
90   *Constituciones de la Compañia de Santa Teresa de Jesús* (Barcelona: Tipografia Tersiana, Calle de los Angeles 22 y 24, 1903).
91   *Visitation*, 26–32, 33, 39, 60.
92   Lady Visitor, 'New Norcia Mission', *Western Mail*, 18 January 1902, 11; Massam, 'Cloistering the Mission', 16–18; Anna Haebich, *Dancing in Shadows: Histories of Nyungar Performance* (Crawley, WA: UWA Publishing, 2018), 163–67.

cruel. From Eliza Willaway's remark to one visitor that 'he [Abbot Torres] noo [sic] understand yet' to letters of complaint to the government from Felix Jackimarra and George Shaw, two of the leaders of the Christmas raid, protesting that New Norcia was no longer a home for Aboriginal people, tension was rising.[93] Following the damage to St Joseph's, Shaw, Lucas Moody and Emmanuel Jackimarra were arrested and jailed for three months. The monastery distanced itself from the men and referred their families to the Chief Protector of Aborigines for support. The *Chronicle* noted they were not mission families but 'from Catabody', somehow suddenly ignorant of ties that went back to Salvado in the 1860s.[94] Approaching the first anniversary of that raid, the Aboriginal residents of St Joseph's saw the changes to their institution in racial terms. As firmly as any official of the White Australia policy, they drew a distinction between the Teresians from southern Europe and the Irish-Australian Josephites.

By December 1907 Abbot Torres was resisting the withdrawal of the Teresians, on the one hand, while also arranging for English-speaking teachers to open the school to 'white girls' in the new year. Three Sisters of St Joseph arrived a month later and commenced classes on Thursday 13 February 1908. The beautiful if sparsely furnished building of St Gertrude's had more than enough space for the two pupils, one aged about 11 and the other aged 18, who started school that week.

On the following Monday, 17 February 1908, a washing day, Abbot Torres was called away from a meeting to deal with a dispute. Only a serious argument would have warranted such urgent and personal attention. Sister Leonor Bargallo and Sister Maria Vilar had come to the monastery parlour to complain to the abbot. The issue was 'the washing of the white girls, students of the College'.[95] Maria Vilar spoke strongly and asserted three times that she had the support of the whole community: 'so say all of us', noted the *Chronicle* archly.[96] That the matter was grave and gave the abbot 'great displeasure' was underlined in the *Chronicle*'s hope for

---

93 Haebich, *Dancing in Shadows*, 168–69. Eliza Willaway reported by the 'Lady Visitor', *Western Mail*, 18 January 1902, 11; 'Treatment of Natives. New Norcia. Complaints re George Shaw and Felix Jackimarra', State Records Office of Western Australia (SROWA) S1644 cons652 1911/0473.
94 'New Norcia: Case against George Shaw and Others', SROWA S3054 cons968 1907/0505; 'Police, New Norcia Re: Arrests', SROWA S3005 cons255 1907/0108; *Chronicle*, 1, 11, 12 January 1907. See also Anna Haebich, *For Their Own Good: Aborigines and Government in the South West of Western Australia 1900–1940* (Nedlands, WA: University of Western Australia Press for the Charles and Joy Staples South West Region Publications Fund, 1992), 17–18.
95 *Chronicle*, 17 February 1908.
96 *Chronicle*, 18 March 1908.

'God [to] have mercy on them!'[97] The abbot saw it as trouble 'from those from whom he least expects it'[98]—those Teresian sisters who had been at New Norcia since 1904. It was at this point that Torres dropped any idea that the Teresian community might remain at the mission.[99]

We do not know exactly what happened, or did not happen, in the laundry. Through the following week, the older Aboriginal girls (who would have been working in the laundry) were also making their own judgements. By the next Sunday at least six, possibly more, had left St Joseph's. Recording the departures, the *Chronicle* was succinct and pithily named the common cause that united the Teresians and the Aborigines as 'race':

> Today another girl who is already of age left the Teresian Sisters, and four others went with her. How much these natives can not endure the presence of the whites, and our Teresians do not suffer less for the same reason![100]

Clearly, both the *Chronicle* and the Aboriginal girls as reported by the diarist assumed that the Teresians were not white, or at least not in the same way as the Australian Josephites and their pupils were white. Even as the *Chronicle* seemed concerned to show the calm of that same Sunday following the dispute and recorded that everyone at St Gertrude's was at Mass and then Vespers together, there was also the subtle divide in the congregation of 'white girls and the Josephite Sisters … equally the native girls with the Teresian Sisters'.[101] That division played into the dynamics about who would take on the domestic work of the college and triggered the Teresians' explosion about the washing. They had been prepared to wash for the monks and work with the Aboriginal girls to do this, but they refused the new expectation that they would wash for other women and 'white girls'.

It looked to the monastery as though the Teresians were 'immoral'.[102] This was a strong judgement and the *Chronicle*'s conviction that the offence was 'against the abbot'[103] probably means they were seen as having broken

---

97 *Chronicle*, 17 February 1908.
98 *Chronicle*, 17 February 1908.
99 *Chronicle*, 12 March 1908.
100 *Chronicle*, 23 February 1908.
101 *Chronicle*, 23 February 1908.
102 *Chronicle*, 23 February 1908.
103 *Chronicle*, 29 February 1908.

their vows of obedience. In a letter to Saturnina Jassa begun on 3 May 1908, Abbot Torres was more explicit about the fact of the problem but gave no details:

> Meantime the Sisters here began to suffer from various ideas and especially with the presence of other religious and so it was that in a paroxysm of pique they did what afterwards they have regretted and to no purpose.[104]

Torres underplayed the cause as a skirmish between the women, yet for the monks there was no coming back from it. The sisters sought a compromise. Sister Felipa consulted Father Henry about a way to 'undo what they had done',[105] but he could only advise her to ask for tickets to Spain.[106] It became clear that Sister Maria Vilar had acted on her own initiative on 17 February and that, far from unanimously supporting her, four of the community knew nothing about it. Leonor wrote to the abbot to apologise for her part in the conflict. Maria Vilar along with the others deeply regretted 'the displeasure' and the stand-off that resulted. As they began to understand that their whole future at New Norcia was in jeopardy, the keeper of the monks' diary noted 'there are those who are weeping' about 'the blind alley' they had gone down.[107]

Sorrow was not a lever for change. The *Chronicle* argued it was only God who would console the sisters, not the monks, 'because for us after what happened that is morally impossible'.[108] Perhaps resolution was impossible because, while the Teresians were sorrowful about the outcome, they were not in fact repenting of their refusal to do the washing. On 4 April 1908 Felipa and two others sought an interview with Torres and offered a crucial clarification. The *Chronicle* records 'they said to him, "that they did not want to do the washing of the white girls, as they were not their servants and had nothing to do with them"'.[109]

The two groups were living out a policy of separation in any case. At the same time as the abbot's secretary was encouraging the Teresians to withdraw from New Norcia, the word came from the monastery for the Aboriginal girls to move into the new college of St Gertrude's,

---

104 Torres to Jassa, undated letter c. October 1908, *Visitation*, 43.
105 *Chronicle*, 29 February 1908.
106 *Chronicle*, 29 February 1908.
107 *Chronicle*, 18 March 1908.
108 *Chronicle*, 18 March 1908.
109 *Chronicle*, 4 April 1908.

'sleeping on the top floor'.[110] The move was not about integration, as they continued to 'work, eat and study in the old [St Joseph's]'.[111] When one of the Teresian sisters sought 'permission to take the native girls to the room [downstairs] on the left of the College Chapel for recreation' she was refused. The abbot 'did not judge it fitting'.[112] The *Notebooks* of the Benedictine Missionary Sisters comment that Sr Maria Harispe and the smallest children spent two years in this 'dance of comings and goings', going to bed early and rising early to avoid giving trouble and 'all this because of the discrimination between blacks and whites'.[113] The southern tower still bore the Teresian crest in marble, and the recently installed foundation stone at the front door still announced the intention to bring Christian teaching to *puellis indigenis* but neither the Aboriginal girls nor their Teresian teachers could walk past it. Abbot Torres began planning to refurbish the old St Joseph's cottage as a second convent and school.

When St Joseph's was renovated and updated over the two years leading up to August 1910, a preliminary makeover concerned race. In August 1908 the *Chronicle* noted one of the community's artists, Brother Salvador, was restoring the image of the Blessed Virgin Mary that had been at St Joseph's 'for years'.[114] This was a devotional image that hung in the dormitory in which Mary 'appeared to be a person of mixed blood'.[115] Perhaps the painting was New Norcia's copy of Mary as 'Our Lady of Guadalupe', a title made famous through Spanish missions to the Americas. We know Abbot Salvado was given such an image, among others, and that it has been restored.[116] Whether or not Brother Salvador was working on the Guadalupe Madonna, the instructions he was given betray much about New Norcia's ideals of holiness, feminine beauty and race. Brother Salvador's task was to correct the impression of Mary's mixed descent. He did this successfully in the opinion of the *Chronicle*, leaving it 'as new, as it has not been known before'.[117] Intriguingly, at the same time, the dark, carved features in Juan Casellas's image of Our Lady of Montserrat, icon of Spanish and Catalan identity, were an undisputed treasure of the monks' chapel. It was not skin colour as such but the Madonna's mixed

---

110 *Chronicle*, 12 March 1908, on the letter to Barcelona, 14 March 1908.
111 *Chronicle*, 12 March 1908, noting a move to the new college 'last Saturday', 7 March.
112 *Chronicle*, 23 March 1908.
113 *Notebooks*, Madrid, 5.
114 *Chronicle*, 6 August 1908.
115 *Chronicle*, 6 August 1908.
116 *Chronicle*, 6 August 1908; Dom Christopher Power, OSB, email correspondence, 28 April 2014.
117 *Chronicle*, 6 August 1908.

heritage that triggered the intervention at St Joseph's. The *Chronicle* approved of the restoration, and the image was blessed in a ceremony on the feast of the Assumption a few weeks later.[118] We can only imagine the impact on the Aboriginal girls and the sisters; 'half-caste' could no longer stand as 'holy'.

At the practical level of building work, the *Chronicle* recorded steady progress. The renovations included a verandah, newly concreted and painted; new bathrooms; a better stove, moved from the monks' novitiate; and dormitory buildings freshly plastered, painted and with galvanised iron roofing instead of thatch. Large water tanks and a new laundry were also noted as 'giving very good results'.[119] When it was complete the monks recorded the praise it attracted from the Josephites at St Gertrude's. They thought it looked like a 'true College for Girls, such as you might find in various important towns, not excluding some colleges in Perth'.[120] To emphasise the good comparison the diary-keeper inserted 'white' above the reference to girls' colleges elsewhere, clarifying both the high praise and the prevailing assumptions about real education.[121] Certainly the dedicated facilities at St Joseph's were superior to the makeshift and cramped schools in many Catholic parishes in Perth. The new buildings also blended with the cottages that housed the Aboriginal families and the low rise of the monastery itself some distance away. But everyone could see they did not match the neighbouring towers of St Gertrude's and the generous classrooms available there; in fact, there was no mention of classrooms in the St Joseph's renovation at all. For the Aboriginal people there was also another issue. The most striking new feature was a high dividing wall.

Enclosure was a powerful theme in monastic life, especially for women, but this wall organised space along racial rather than religious lines. There had been no move towards a formal cloister for the Spanish sisters before 1910, and this move sequestered them with, not apart from, the Aboriginal girls. The monastery's *Chronicle* gives the only accounts we have of reaction to this change, and the focus is on the horrified response of the Aborigines. As well as dividing the white and native colleges, the *Chronicle* read reactions against the wall as a sign of lack of civilisation.

---

118 *Chronicle*, 15 August 1908.
119 *Chronicle*, 16 October 1908. Also 26 September 1908, 17 October 1908, 25 January 1910, 22 April 1910, 10 May 1910, 28 May 1910, 8 June 1910, 23 June 1910, 8 August 1910.
120 *Chronicle*, 17 July 1910.
121 *Chronicle*, 17 July 1910.

The Aborigines' nickname for the new enclosure, 'Golden Gaol', suggested a wry appreciation of the quality of the work but was also a clear rejection of the project. Perhaps they intended to echo the name given to the Salvation Army's house in Perth, the 'Golden Gate', where young women also worked in a laundry.[122] On the day it was completed in February 1910, the *Chronicle* recorded in some bewilderment:

> Finished the brick enclosure near the college of the native girls, and God knows who it will be useful for because the coloured people both within and without abhor nothing so much as the 'Golden Gaol' as one of the girls who escaped from it called it recently. The place is spacious and beautiful and can only be hated by bush people.[123]

The escape the *Chronicle* referred to may have been as simple as the dignified exit described a few weeks earlier when Katie Yapo, one of the older girls, nearly 15, simply left quietly after supper 'having served the rest of her companions'.[124] It was a week when the sisters themselves were in turmoil about their own departure for Spain, but, touching on the realities of institutional life, the *Chronicle* discounted other likely reasons for Katie's decision: 'nothing about repression on the part of the sisters nor about a quarrel with her companions'; she had told her friends she was leaving 'because she didn't want to be in the college any longer'.[125] Whether trauma or simple choice lay behind her move, that she had wanted to be there but now had changed her mind, is significant, as it is significant that the 'Golden Gaol' had only recently been nicknamed a prison. What had changed, the *Chronicle* said clearly, was the wall:

> The true reason [for her leaving] seems to be on seeing how advanced they were with the walled enclosure of the college which stinks for them as it does for all the natives in the village. They all regard it as a prison.[126]

---

122 Penelope Hetherington, *Paupers, Poor Relief and Poor Houses in Western Australia 1829–1910* (Crawley, WA: University of Western Australia Publishing, 2009), 132.
123 *Chronicle*, 18 February 1910.
124 *Chronicle*, 30 January 1910. See Catalina Yapo in *Aborigines of New Norcia 1845–1914*, ed. Neville Green and Lois Tilbrook (Crawley, WA: University of Western Australia Press, 1989), 170.
125 *Chronicle*, 30 January 1910.
126 *Chronicle*, 30 January 1910.

Declaring itself against their protest by condemning the illicit trysts that freedom would make possible, the *Chronicle* inadvertently confirmed the high value that the young Aboriginal women placed on 'liberty', against the new situation the sisters found themselves supporting. 'Praised be God', the writer observed ironically, 'In this way [by leaving] they will have an opportunity to give themselves to X. … They are not worried about the hunger they will have to endure for the sake of this liberty [sic]'.[127] The walled enclosure defined a racial and gendered zone. The assumption that protection and even privilege lay inside it reflected a shift in the missionary approach at New Norcia. Significantly, the Aboriginal girls shared the enclosure with the Spanish sisters.

The evolution of two distinct schools began as a pragmatic response to the situation where the Spanish speakers could not teach in English but became firm mission policy in response to conflict or the fear of conflict between the two groups. The Sisters of St Joseph were open to having Aboriginal children in their school, but the girls themselves were voting with their feet against integration. Some were willing to cross the divide but risked unleashing controversy. For example, in 1908 one of the diocesan priests resident at New Norcia had made a unilateral decision to 'put the young native girl in the College with the white girls'.[128] We do not know the name of either the student or the priest or what motivated the move, but the *Chronicle* recorded that Henry Altimira, missionary trained by Salvado, trusted confidant of the Teresians, efficient secretary to the abbot and, by this time, also the monastery's procurator, 'disapproved of his action and condemned it strongly'.[129] Fr Altimira would have been well aware of the unrest and anxiety among the Aboriginal girls due to the new school. Probably he also had the power to have reversed the priest's decision.

---

127 *Chronicle*, 30 January 1910.
128 *Chronicle*, 12 June 1908.
129 *Chronicle*, 12 June 1908.

Figure 2.5: Fr Henry Altimira and Fr Planas with plans for the Drysdale River Mission.
Source: NNA 24821P.

Figure 2.6: St Joseph's from the southern tower of St Gertrude's, c. 1907.
Source: NNA 74603P.

Figure 2.7: St Joseph's girls assembled to show skills in weaving and sewing, with the towers of St Gertrude's in the background.
Source: NNA 74904P.

Figure 2.8: St Gertrude's College c. 1909, with the buildings of St Joseph's to the left and cottages in the foreground.
Source: NNA 74616P.

Figure 2.9: St Gertrude's and St Joseph's looking east c. 1908.
Source: NNA 74408P.

The *Chronicle* records an irate scene.[130] The priest found the procurator talking with some young monks and an Aboriginal man. He confronted Altimira, 'attacked him', the *Chronicle* says, and told him he was going to kill him. The diary-keeper, 'one who heard', took the threat seriously. Not missing a beat, Altimira told him, effectively, to put it in writing. Diffusing the situation with good sense and wit, Altimira got the priest's 'indignant' promise to commit the complaint to paper. Two-and-a-half hours later, the long letter that was slipped under the procurator's door did not repeat the death threat. Instead, it explained 'in very different terms' why the priest had tried to make a place for the girl at St Gertrude's. We do not have the letter, or any further detail at all, but there is something poignant about the furious exchange falling back into ordered account and then silence. The changes at the girls' schools stirred deep emotion but had an unassailable momentum.

---

130 *Chronicle*, 12 June 1908.

The hope that St Gertrude's would be a school for Aboriginal girls to rival anything in Europe sat awkwardly in New Norcia's continuing history. The foundation stone's commitment to *puellis indigenes* came to be translated as education for 'Australian girls',[131] and while some Aboriginal people remembered the new buildings had started out 'for the natives', they gave credit to Salvado, not Torres.[132] Where Torres's original intention was acknowledged, the reasons given for the change were fuzzy. They included an initial lack of realism on Torres's part, as he had 'underestimated' the degradation of the Aboriginal people in the south, and implied the resistance of farming families to send their daughters to a mixed boarding school. Both of these ignored the decisions the Aboriginal girls themselves were making and discounted the situation the Teresian sisters faced as their involvement in the project dissolved. St Joseph's continued as a separate institution with a small, much less ambitious school. Overall, the focus on the institutions for children suggested a narrower vision, less sympathetic to engagement with Aboriginal people, and one that prompted rather than responded to the departure of many Aboriginal workers and their families from the town. Bernard Rooney and Anna Haebich argue that the second abbot's policies actively caused the 'Yued diaspora', driving Aboriginal families from New Norcia to fringe camps and other institutions, as the mission sold farmland to fund new buildings and expansion in the Kimberley.[133] The opening of the new boarding colleges came to mark a 'new era' as the town focused on education, rather than on missionary work.

*****

The Teresian sisters had come as missionaries to the Aboriginal people and, as Maria Harispe's letter shows, were looking for ways to live out that commitment 'for the mission' but not through domestic work in another congregation's school. Neither did the abbot's proposal that they should continue at New Norcia and be answerable to him make any sense to this group. If Maria Harispe, Leonor Bargallo and Teresa Roca saw their future continuing 'to assist the native girls',[134] it would have to be, as Torres

---

131 For example, *The Golden Career of St Gertrude's College, New Norcia 1958* (New Norcia: The Abbey Press, [1958]) (NNA).
132 Harold Willaway, cited in Haebich, *For Their Own Good*, 17n34.
133 Bernard Rooney, *The Way of the Boorna-Waangki: A Tale of Cultural Endurance* (Melbourne: Abbey Press, 2014), 111; Haebich, *Dancing in Shadows*, 163–64; Bob Reece, '"Killing with Kindness": Daisy Bates and New Norcia', *Aboriginal History* 32 (2008): 137–38.
134 *Chronicle*, 25 February 1910.

knew, a new commitment to the work of New Norcia in particular. Facing this reality, even the finances for their travel caused conflict. The Teresian community could not decide to stay without the support of the abbot, but neither could the abbot send them home without the approval of their councillors. When Barcelona refused the mission's request to pay for tickets, New Norcia responded with the news that the sisters would not travel until their pensions had built up to the amount needed for a third-class berth.

In the negotiations with the Barcelona leadership over payment for the sisters' fares, Torres and Altimira also found themselves dealing with women who, on the one hand, were willing to argue the toss about who funded the travel (Barcelona paid in the end) and, on the other, to call on the authority of their own spiritual heritage to assert their right to keep the house open. Mother Saturnina Jassa did not expect Abbot Torres to make a decision about the foundation for her; she was expecting to discern for herself what God intended in the debacle:

> Who knows whether we needed to pass through this mighty tempest so that the daughters of the great Teresa who loved souls so much might be extended in those distant countries and contribute not a little to the Christianisation of peoples.[135]

In the end, however, she had to acknowledge that the sisters and the monks were not going to be able to agree. In convoluted Spanish that probably reflected the stress of the situation, she complained of the 'succession of misunderstandings', especially to do with the qualities suited to the work there:

> I understand that a large part of the personnel ... was not suitable for the nature of a mission in which the principal role is played by the glory of God which has to be carried out to the end in those points mentioned through various manifestations of Christian charity.[136]

Then she gathered herself together and summed up what she thought New Norcia required: 'That is to say, knowing how to be all for all'.[137] She went on to suggest ways in which she could even now make sisters available, who had enough English, and the right 'zeal for souls'.

---

135 Jassa to Torres, 30 April 1908, *Visitation*, 42.
136 *Visitation*, 41.
137 *Visitation*, 41.

Abbot Torres did not accept Saturnina Jassa's offer. Neither was he able to accept the offer from Leonor Bargallo and Teresa Roca that they stay on. No dispensation from their vows arrived. They left New Norcia to sail for Spain in February 1910.[138] Maria Harispe had taken new vows as a Benedictine oblate in July 1909, when her temporary profession with the Teresians expired. She continued to superintend the complex in the shadow of St Gertrude's for two years, with help from one of the Josephites as a teacher, until in 1912 a small community began to gather around the work at St Joseph's.

The tensions of the Teresian years did not disappear. The women continued to wrestle with ethnicity and racial difference, spirituality and expectations of women's work in the crucible of monastic and missionary commitment. In a sense, 'Benedictine Oblate Sisters', as they came to be known, took on Saturnina's challenge; they were willing to embrace 'being all for all'.

---

138 *Chronicle*, 5 February 1910. See also Chapter 3.

3

Benedictine Oblates: Outsiders in Community

For a decade following the departure of the Teresians, Maria Harispe was at the centre of a small household among the mission cottages that assembled almost by accident. By 1915 there were four missionary sisters. They were thought of as 'Spanish', although only Teresa Roca actually came from Spain. Maria Harispe and Consuelo Batiz were from the former Spanish colonies of Paraguay and Mexico. Elias Devine had come from Ireland via France and India. Their community was fragile, and their status as 'missionary oblate sisters' was informal and even contradictory, but this group of outsiders persisted and grew.

This chapter traces their transition from individuals gathered together on their own initiative into a group with a shared identity sustained by their commitment to St Joseph's and the Benedictine mission more broadly. From the strands of their outsider status they began to weave a distinctive community at the edge of the Benedictine town. In the warp and weft of daily contact with the Aboriginal women and girls, the missionary women meshed together a complex institution that linked several categories: it was part convent, part mission and training school, part government institution, and also, poignantly, part 'home'.

From Teresians to the first Benedictine oblate

When the Teresian community split in October 1908, leaving Maria Harispe, Teresa Roca and Leonor Bargallo at New Norcia, the leadership in Barcelona told Abbot Torres that none of the sisters remaining could lead an independent house, let alone found a religious family.[1] Structurally there were reasons against it. Maria and Teresa were both *ayudante* or lay sisters, 'helpers' to the better-educated choir sisters, and Leonor, while a choir sister, had made her final profession only in March 1905 at New Norcia, now a suspect and unstable environment from a Teresian point of view.[2] Abbot Torres was not opposed to a separate community with external governance, as his dealings with the Presentation Sisters and the Sisters of St Joseph in other parts of the diocese show, but by 1908 he had little reason to trust Teresian judgement on leadership. To keep Spanish missionary women at St Joseph's, he was already thinking about another model that would reconfigure them as Benedictines. An 'Institute of Religious Oblates' would preserve the best of what the Teresian community had been doing while ensuring that the monastery was the sole authority directing the work.[3]

The significance of 'oblates' within the Benedictine tradition was growing in the early twentieth century. The practice, recorded in the sixth-century Rule of St Benedict, of parents making a gift or 'oblation' of a child to a monastic community meant that for centuries of Benedictine history 'oblates' were children who lived within the monastery and often (though not always) went on to become monks or nuns. The word 'oblate' also came to include others, however, of whatever age, who sought to live the Rule and to see the world through a Benedictine lens.[4] Oblates were recognised by William, Abbot of Hirschau, in the mid-eleventh century and by the Lateran Council in 1215 as laypeople affiliated to a monastery.

---

1 Teresa Blanche to Fulgentius Torres, 18 December 1907, 'Canonical Visitation to the Community of Teresians of St Gertrude's New Norcia, October 1907', translated by David Barry, NNA 01717 (*Visitation*).
2 'Chronicle of the Benedictine Community of New Norcia' (hereafter *Chronicle*), 20 March 1905, NNA.
3 Torres to the cardinal in charge of the Sacred Congregation of Bishops and Regulars, 5 June 1908, *Visitation*.
4 [Benedict of Nursia], *RB 1980: The Rule of St Benedict in Latin and English with Notes*, ed. Timothy Fry (Collegeville, MN: Liturgical Press, 1980), chapter 59; Linda Kulzer and Roberta C. Bondi, *Benedict in the World: Portraits of Monastic Oblates* (Collegeville, MN: Liturgical Press, 2002).

There was a distinguished tradition of Benedictine oblate women. Elena Conaro Piscopia, the first woman awarded a doctorate in a Western university, became a Benedictine oblate in Padua in 1665, bound into monastic life through her interests in philosophy and theology.[5] More famously, the members of the community that gathered around Frances Ponzani in fifteenth-century Rome were affiliated with the local Olivetan Benedictine monastery in the 1430s.[6] These women were dedicated to prayer and work with the poor and came to be known as an 'Institute of Oblates'. Torres picked the same term for New Norcia.[7]

By the nineteenth century, Benedictine groups that had been exiled or dissolved during the upheavals of the Reformation and the French Revolution were being refounded, and, as European monasticism was revived and organised,[8] provisions for oblates were codified. The American-Cassinese Congregation wrote regulations for their oblates in 1884 that were widened to include other Benedictine communities in 1889 when Leo XIII acknowledged as secular oblates (*oblati seculares*) those who 'for their friendliness and good offices have been admitted as *confratres* of any Benedictine monastery or congregation'.[9] Leo formally approved 'Statutes and Rules of Secular Oblates of St Benedict' on 17 June 1898. These guidelines did not bind members as strongly as the statutes of a religious order or congregations, but, as revised on 23 July 1904, they gave Abbot Torres a structure for new arrangements at New Norcia.

Initially, the abbot proposed that all three remaining Spanish speakers would become oblates of New Norcia. The situation was clearest for Maria Harispe, whose vows as a Teresian expired at midnight on 1 July 1909. Hours later, on the morning of 2 July 1909, Maria renewed her commitment to poverty, chastity and obedience, not in the context of

---

5   Francesco Ludovico Maschietto, *Elena Lucrezia Cornaro Piscopia (1646–1684): The First Woman in the World to Earn a University Degree* (Philadelphia: St Joseph's University Press, 2007).
6   Judith Sutera, 'The Origins and History of the Oblate Movement', in *The Oblate Life*, ed. Gervase Holdaway (Collegeville, MN: Liturgical Press, 2008), 33–34.
7   *Oblate Formation Booklet for Oblates Associated with St Vincent Archabbey* (Latrobe, PA: The Abbey, 2002), 52.
8   A. G. Dickens, *Late Monasticism and the Reformation* (London: Hambledon Press, 1994); Maria Crăciun and Elaine Fulton, *Communities of Devotion: Religious Orders and Society in East Central Europe, 1450–1800* (Farnham, Surrey: Ashgate, 2011); Bruce L. Venarde, 'Recent Western Christian Historiography', in *Encyclopedia of Monasticism*, ed. William Johnston, vol. 1, *A–L* (Chicago and London: Fitzroy Dearborn, 2000), 596–99.
9   *Oblate Formation Booklet*. See also Philip Almond, 'Oblati', *The Catholic Encyclopedia: An International Work of Reference*, ed. Charles Herbermann (New York: Appleton, 1911), www.newadvent.org/cathen/11188a.htm; accessed 2 April 2018.

a religious community, but as a private undertaking witnessed by the abbot in New Norcia's parish church. Then immediately, so that the separate ceremony was remembered as part of the first, Maria Harispe made a further commitment as an oblate of St Benedict. Here she made the traditional Benedictine pledges of stability, obedience to the abbot, and life according to the Rule of Benedict. This was also probably the occasion when she changed her name: no longer Maria Teresa but now Maria Escolastica, in honour of St Benedict's sister.[10] It was the feast of the Visitation, marking the journey made by Mary the mother of Jesus to Elizabeth the mother of John the Baptist. The *Chronicle* noted the feast in the context of Maria's new status. For those who cared to hear, the liturgies of the day carried echoes of courageous women who travelled into unknown territory.[11]

Figure 3.1: Interior of the Abbey Church 'before 1923' or as it would have been on the morning of 1 July 1909 when Maria Harispe made her profession as an oblate of New Norcia.
Source: NNA 74667P.

---

10 Most often she is simply Maria or Mary, but the *Chronicle* is clear about her new second name.
11 Luke 1:39–56.

Figure 3.2: Maria Harispe c. 1915 with St Joseph's residents.
Source: Detail of NNA W7-A3-4-494.

Maria Harispe was, the *Chronicle* believed, the first person in Australia to pledge allegiance to the Rule of Benedict as a secular oblate. New Norcia had other oblates already, including several diocesan priests and the painter-decorator Br Salvador Alberich, who lived within the monastic cloister, but Maria's status was distinctive. She was a woman committed to the work of the Benedictine community but living separately, with the Aboriginal people. The monastery recorded the new step carefully, hoping it augured well for Benedictines in general:

> Sr Maria Harispe yesterday completed her year of religious profession, and as her vows were temporary, she is free from her Superiors in the Company of St Teresa of Jesus. Today, the day of the Visitation of Our Lady, she made vows of poverty, chastity and obedience before the Rt Rev Abbot. At once she received the scapular of a Benedictine Oblate, the Oblation following immediately. Thus it seems she is the first Benedictine Oblate in Australia, and may such an act have favourable results for Our Holy Order. The consecration to God and the offering to St Benedict took place in the church. May all be to the honour and glory of God our Lord and of our glorious Father St Benedict.[12]

Maria's own response is not recorded, but the move was certainly in keeping with the request she had put to Fr Altimira a year earlier, to continue to work with the Aboriginal people as a religious sister and to wear religious dress. Apart from the new Benedictine scapular, at this stage Maria continued to wear her Teresian habit.[13] Teresa Roca and Leonor Bargallo had also petitioned Rome through the abbot to take a similar step. They put their request on two grounds, both concerned with preserving what they valued in their present circumstances.

Both of the grounds for transfer were relational. First, Leonor and Teresa said they feared for their religious vocations if they had to rejoin the group they had denounced in the visitation of 1907. Relationships were so damaged, they told the Roman officials, that they expected to be expelled or ostracised by 'the continual vexation which is all they can promise themselves on the part of their major superiors and even on the part of the rest of the members of their Institute'. Second, they wanted to continue to work at New Norcia, 'co-operating' with the Benedictines 'in their

---

12   *Chronicle*, 2 July 1909. For Salvador Alberich's oblate profession, see *Chronicle*, 1 November 1906.
13   *Chronicle*, 8 December 1915.

work of evangelisation for the Australian Aborigines, taking care in particular of the education of the girls'.[14] Like Maria, their commitment was to St Joseph's.

Abbot Torres supported and perhaps encouraged Teresa and Leonor in their request for a dispensation, carefully preserving copies of their letters to Rome within the report of the canonical visitation. Their situation was, however, more complex than Maria's, and negotiations inched along in Rome without much promise. Meanwhile, the Teresian leadership in Spain assumed that by allowing (or perhaps compelling) the three sisters to remain, Abbot Torres was in breach of a directive from the Congregation of the Affairs of Religious in 1909 that all the Teresians should withdraw. They 'made so much noise to obtain their return'[15] that Torres was accused of impeding the congregation and began to fear he had put his own position as abbot in jeopardy.[16]

By January 1910, when Torres was in Rome in person, he was balancing concern about his own standing with the situation of the Teresians and negotiations on other matters, including the boundaries of the new mission in the Kimberley. He avoided the general procurator for the Benedictines in Rome and also took care not to cross paths with Cardinal Vives, the official in charge of the Congregation of Religious, until he knew how matters stood.[17] When he did meet with Cardinal Vives to discuss New Norcia and the Teresians, Torres made a careful record, so there are two accounts of his interview: one in his diary and the other a more reflective letter that he sent to New Norcia's procurator, Henry Altimira, on 29 January after the decisions were made. By both accounts, when Torres met Vives he made no attempt to persuade the cardinal that women vowed to another congregation should be released to work at New Norcia. Quite the contrary: he chose his moment to detail the five

---

14   Petition of Leonor Bargallo and Teresa Roca to the Sacred Congregation of Bishops and Regulars, 25 May 1908, *Visitation*.
15   Torres to Altimira, reporting the view of Cardinal Vives, 29 January 1910, trans. Fr David Barry, OSB, NNA 01717, 23.
16   *Chronicle*, 25 February 1910, referring to the January letter from Torres explaining this received that day. See also *The Torres Diaries 1901–1914, Diaries of Dom Fulgentius (Anthony) Torres y Mayans, O.S.B., Abbot Nullius of New Norcia, Bishop Titular of Dorylaeum, Administrator Apostolic of the Kimberley Vicariate in North Western Australia*, trans. Eugene Perez, ed. Rosemary Pratt and John Millington (Perth: Artlook Books, 1987), 208–9, 210, 211.
17   Torres to Altimira, 29 January 1910; *Torres Diaries*, 210–16.

years of grief the Teresians had caused him and assured the cardinal that everything was arranged 'so when they left the Sisters of St Joseph of the S[acred] H[eart] would immediately take charge of the native girls'.[18]

Should we wonder if there was a subtext here? To make a case against the Teresians would diffuse any suspicion that New Norcia had defied directives for their return. The presence of the Josephites as willing alternative workers was crucial, and the cardinal took the implication that the Spanish women were no longer needed.[19] He concluded that the abbot should cable New Norcia with the message 'Sisters to leave for Spain – Torres'.[20] This was sent on 29 January 1909.

It was important to Torres that the telegram was sent in his own name. He knew his competence to act was under suspicion, and he was at pains to note the cardinal's direction: 'You should be the one to send them to Spain without the name of my Congregation being mentioned'.[21] That the public directive was allowed in his own name presumably signalled the 'fuss' about his leadership created by the Teresian lobby in Spain had come to nothing. Relief suffused Torres's diary entries that the work of the mission and his own place in it were both still well-regarded in Rome.

The telegram was, however, deliberately ambiguous. Addressed to 'Sisters', it left Maria with the choice to stay or to leave. The hope for an institute of oblates likely remained alive at the back of the abbot's mind. Torres's diary shows he remembered Maria's commitment and knew she would not want to return to South America. His letter to Fr Altimira begun on the day he issued the directive to leave acknowledged the confusion the telegram would have caused his deputies at New Norcia when they saw he had signed something requiring 'that the poor women are to travel to Spain'.[22] Reworking his notes into a fuller account, Torres walked his procurator through events that led up to the recall in a letter of 28 small pages. He began to discuss the 'principal point' of the sisters on page 5 but nevertheless spent the next 15 pages tracing events that left him reassured the Roman authorities supported him to 'continue in Australia until [he] left [his] bones there'.[23] Only after establishing that context

---

18 Torres to Altimira, 29 January 1910; *Torres Diaries*, 210.
19 *Torres Diaries*, 210.
20 Torres to Altimira, 29 January 1910, 25; *Chronicle*, 25 January 1910. *Torres Diaries*, 211, records the cable was sent at 10.30 in the morning on Saturday, 23 January 1910.
21 Torres to Altimira, 29 January 1910, *Visitation*, 22; *Torres Diaries*, 211.
22 Torres to Altimira, 29 January 1910, *Visitation*, 5.
23 Torres to Altimira, 29 January 1910, *Visitation*, 20.

carefully did he recount the discussion of the Teresian community itself. There was a clear implication that all three Spanish women would be willing to remain at New Norcia but that Cardinal Vives advised against it, as 'they themselves could afterwards change their minds … and give [Torres] cause for regret'.[24] After the cardinal indicated the abbot would be the one to recall the sisters, Torres was concerned 'to avoid future sorrows'; presumably, he did not want conflict with the Teresians if Maria stayed behind. While confident that two Teresians would leave, he warned he could not 'give an assurance' about 'the third who had completed temporary vows'.[25] Torres reported that this 'preoccupied' the cardinal who 'thought that by being the only one to stay she would be abandoned',[26] but their combined judgement in the end was to leave the decision to Maria, phrasing the telegram to apply to 'Sisters'. The cardinal apparently mused: 'If the three come, fine, if the other remains, also [fine] since she does not belong to the Congregation'.[27] The published diary is brusque at this point, implying Torres himself saw no difference in Maria staying or going, but the letter is more considered and clarifies that he was noting the cardinal's remarks. For himself, Torres observed that thus the 'business of *the Teresians* has ended'.[28] He emphasised Teresians and left open the implication that another, different, group might replace them.[29] The letter went on in some sympathy for the departing women, 'whether two or three', to imagine them waiting to embark and praying God would give them a good journey.[30]

Sure enough, by the time the letter arrived at New Norcia, Teresa Roca and Leonor Bargallo had obeyed the telegram and left. They departed, the *Chronicle* judged, 'with the greatest feeling and repugnance that there could be'.[31] At five o'clock in the morning on Saturday 5 February 1910, a neighbour drove the monastery coach through the dawn light to the nearest railway station at Mogumber. The women did not understand why Fr Altimira was determined to go in the other direction, to the mission house at Wyening, instead of seeing them onto the train. The *Chronicle* did not explain either, except to call this a 'moral impossibility' and

---

24 Torres to Altimira, 29 January 1910, 21.
25 Torres to Altimira, 29 January 1910, 24.
26 Torres to Altimira, 29 January 1910, *Visitation*, 24; *Torres Diaries*, 211.
27 Torres to Altimira, 29 January 1910, 25. The *Torres Diaries* also imply this was Torres's own view.
28 Torres to Altimira, 29 January 1910, 25, original emphasis.
29 Torres to Altimira, 29 January 1910, *Visitation*, 25; *Torres Diaries*, 211, refers to 'Sisters' in general.
30 Torres to Altimira, 29 January 1910, 26–27.
31 *Chronicle*, 5 February 1910.

acknowledge that 'no-one went with them and this increased their feeling'.³² Such a cool farewell would signal they were being sent from Australia, not released reluctantly on Teresian initiative.

As the abbot hoped, they did have a smooth journey. At Marseilles they received a 'consolatory' letter from Saturnina Jassá, the new Teresian superior, promising to treat them kindly. They forwarded this to New Norcia, perhaps to reassure Maria and the monks. Saturnina wrote to New Norcia directly to let the monks know when Teresa and Leonor arrived safely in Barcelona, to express surprise that only two of the missionaries had travelled, and to encourage Maria to follow. That letter has not survived, but reportedly it advised Maria to appeal to the Holy See for support to leave. The *Chronicle*, noting that advice, observed that the Teresians already knew Maria had decided to remain, as the letter sent to Marseilles had been addressed to Leonor and Teresa only.³³

Throughout the changes, Maria kept the focus on the new commitment she had made. When the telegram recalling 'Sisters' arrived, she reminded the New Norcia monks that the order to leave did not apply to her as she was no longer a Teresian. She also reinforced the particular vow she had made to separate from her natural family in South America and simply reiterated that 'if allowed' she would remain.³⁴

Maria intended to live with the Aboriginal people according to her original request.³⁵ Torres assured the cardinal 'she could continue with the *nativas*', literally the 'female natives' not differentiated by age, and that the Josephites would assist her.³⁶ The original of Torres's diary and his letter are virtually identical at this point, casting Maria as a missionary and companion to the Aboriginal women and girls and the Josephites as her helpers, presumably as teachers but perhaps in other roles also.³⁷

---

32   *Chronicle*, 5 February 1910.
33   *Chronicle*, 8 April 1910.
34   *Chronicle*, 25 January 1910.
35   Maria Harispe to Henry Altimira, 6 June 1908, *Visitation*, 82; *Torres Diaries*, 211.
36   Maria Harispe to Henry Altimira, 6 June 1908; *Torres Diaries*, 211.
37   Torres to Altimira, 29 January 1910, 24; also unpublished 'Diary of Abbot Torres', NNA 2234A-41-023/024. Both accounts report Torres thought Maria '*continuaría con las Nativas ayudandola las Religiosas de S. José*'.

In terms of the public history of the Benedictine Missionary Sisters it is significant that the version of the abbot's diary published in the late 1980s reversed the initiative, claiming Maria would 'assist' the Josephites. This translation also assumed the work would be with 'native girls'.[38] The misreading that downplayed Maria's responsibilities is consistent with the popular accounts of New Norcia's history that obscure the women and stress the arrival of boarding-school education. The deeper memory would be of Maria as a 'founding Mother'[39] whose perseverance shaped a community at St Joseph's. Linked to the monastery, integral to the mission town, and therefore also bound into the government's policies on Aboriginal affairs, St Joseph's also emerged paradoxically as separate from and distinctively 'outside' the world of the decision makers.

Family of outsiders

The particular sense of identity as a 'family of outsiders' that shaped the realities of life for the missionary women at New Norcia, no less than for the Aboriginal children in their care, is an awkward theme. The affective, emotional relationship that affirmed a 'New Norcia family' might seem pathetic in a context where assimilation carried all the racist assumptions of removing children from Aboriginal family and culture 'for their own good'. What makes the theme so resonant for New Norcia, for the Aboriginal people in the town as well as for the missionaries who worked there, is the recognition that they were oriented together towards a frame of reference that put them all outside the standard assumptions of White 'success'. In a racist context, the concept of 'family', and particularly a family of outsiders, forged bonds among the town's communities that stretched across boundaries of ethnicity and culture. To put the metaphor of the St Joseph's 'family' in context, it is useful to look back briefly to the mission's foundation in the mid-nineteenth century.

---

38 Torres to Altimira, 29 January 1910, 24; *Torres Diaries*, 211.
39 On the accounts of her death, Katharine Massam, '"That There Was Love in This Home": The Benedictine Missionary Sisters at New Norcia', in *Evangelists of Empire? Missionaries in Colonial History*, ed. Amanda Barry, Joanna Cruickshank, Andrew Brown-May and Patricia Grimshaw (Melbourne: eScholarship Research Centre in collaboration with the School of Historical Studies, 2008), 201–14.

Early New Norcia and provision for families

New Norcia had been imagined from the beginning as a community and an extension of the Benedictine world rather than as an institution. New Norcia's nineteenth-century founder, Rosendo Salvado, has been celebrated as a compassionate champion of Aboriginal people, building cottages for male workers and their families, not dormitories for separated children; integrating Aboriginal men into the workforce alongside the lay brothers of the monastery; and promoting the employment of women against government scepticism.[40] The 'Girls House' and 'Boys House' with their dormitory accommodation had not been part of Salvado's original vision, but the monastic timetable reflected in the life at St Joseph's at the beginning of the twentieth century was probably established in Salvado's day. Théophile Bérengier, a monk of Solesmes Abbey and Salvado's agent in France, re-created the mission for French readers in 1879.[41] He reported that the children got up with the sun 'at the sound of the monastery bell'. Prayer and then breakfast in a common dining room were followed by routines of play, work, and study 'suitable to their age'. The ideal for Bérengier, and on into the twentieth century, was a formative lifestyle governed by monastic principles and structured according to a regular daily pattern of prayer and work.

New Norcia's reputation as the 'single success' of the Western Australian mission effort was affirmed by contemporaries and was credited to the particular dedication of the Benedictines. As Alexander Maitland, a missionary with the Church of England in India, told readers of the *Perth Gazette* after his visit in 1867, the monastery was the secret of the mission's success:

> The faith, patience and courage which have been enabled … to establish the monastery and Christian village of New Norcia, as we see it now, are beyond all praise. … The success obtained by the Benedictines of New Norcia shows us clearly the only means by which a happy result may be obtained. But for Protestants it will always be difficult to establish and maintain a similar institution

---

40 George Russo, *Lord Abbot of the Wilderness: The Life and Times of Bishop Salvado* (Melbourne: Polding Press, 1980); John Harris, *One Blood: 200 Years of Aboriginal Encounter with Christianity; A Story of Hope* (Sutherland, NSW: Albatross Books, 1990); Anna Haebich, 'No Man Is an Island: Bishop Salvado's Vision for Mission Work with the Aboriginal People of Western Australia', *New Norcia Studies* 9 (2001): 20–28.
41 Théophile Bérengier, *New Norcia: The History of a Benedictine Colony in Western Australia 1846–1878*, trans. Peter Gilet (Northcote Vic.: Abbey Press, 2014).

with our habits of comfort; and above all to find a like number of men so full of self-abnegation, patient and persevering and entirely devoted to this work of civilisation.[42]

The vision of an agrarian village of families surrounding a monastery did not survive the expansion of European settlement, especially not the rapid growth of the non-Aboriginal population following the discovery of gold in 1886. This transformed the struggling colony of fewer than 30,000 Europeans in 1880 into one of almost 300,000 by 1910.

As Salvado's successor, Abbot Torres has been identified with a change in policy away from the mission work, but the reality was more complex. Although Torres did not have the easy rapport with people that had served Salvado so well, he never repudiated the mission work or his own sense of missionary vocation.[43] The crucial difference was that Torres consistently underestimated the Aboriginal people at New Norcia. The Benedictine foundation at Drysdale River, still on the frontier of European contact, seemed to promise more than the complex interactions among people of mixed descent in the south. In the same way that he replaced the Aboriginal organist and choir director Paul Piramino with Fr Planas and offered Piramino a job as a shepherd, he could not see the role played by the Aboriginal women, Eliza Willaway among others, as matrons at St Joseph's and assumed he needed European missionaries.[44]

How much he was influenced in this by the now controversial ethnographer Daisy Bates, who visited New Norcia as Torres was settling in and who travelled with him to the north, is an interesting question. It is also intriguing to consider how much of the view of Torres as 'remote' from Aborigines has been influenced by the reports Daisy Bates published in the *Western Mail*.[45] Salvado himself had been forced to adapt as the colony grew. Although he maintained that the mission was for working families, by the 1880s the number of unaccompanied children was increasing, and Salvado was writing to the Chief Protector impatiently protesting that he did not know or care whether their parents were alive, only that they were children in need.[46]

---

42   Alexander Maitland, *Perth Gazette*, 1867, cited in H. N. Birt, *Benedictine Pioneers in Australia* (London: Polding Press, 1911), 487.
43   Katharine Massam, 'Cloistering the Mission: Abbot Torres and Changes at New Norcia 1901–1910', *Australasian Catholic Record* 89 (2012): 13–25.
44   Katharine Massam, 'The Spiritual and the Material: Women and Work at the New Norcia Mission 1860–1910', *New Norcia Studies* 29 (2015): 53–61.
45   Bob Reece, '"Killing with Kindness": Daisy Bates and New Norcia', *Aboriginal History* 32 (2008): 128–45.
46   Salvado to Aborigines Protection Board, 4 August 1896, cited in Russo, *Lord Abbot*, 253, and Harris, *One Blood*, 300.

Figure 3.3: A First Communion photo c. 1908 including the Aboriginal matrons in the main doorway of St Gertrude's College.
Source: NAA w7-a3-4-496.

Figure 3.4: The St Joseph's girls with Aboriginal matrons on the back verandah of St Gertrude's, c. 1908.
Source: Collection of the Royal Western Australian Historical Society, State Library of Western Australia, 021317PD.

Salvado maintained: 'This Benedictine mission of New Norcia was never intended to be, and it is not at all an orphanage',[47] and yet the institutions grew and monks were appointed as superintendents. Salvado's hope for the mission did not match the colonial reality; Aboriginal people probably saw the ambiguity in Salvado's day as they continued to experience it in the twentieth century. Greater numbers of immigrants, the spread of settlement, more intensive patterns of land use, increased competition for water and food as well as increased contact with Europeans put the Aboriginal people under pressure.[48] At the same time, the WA *Aborigine Act 1905* made the government's Chief Protector the legal guardian of all 'Aboriginal children' under 16 years of age, regardless of whether their parents were living or dead, and whatever their family circumstances. The government's powers to remove and relocate Aboriginal people were strengthened in 1911, and again in 1936, remaining effectively in place through minor repeal and adjustment until 1967 and 1972.[49] The decision to join this 'family' of outsiders at New Norcia was a choice for the missionary women, a decision they understood as a calling from God. For the children and their parents, however, St Joseph's was part of a network of compulsion. So, it is all the more striking when, within circumstances so narrowed by government regulation and community prejudice, Aboriginal girls made choices in their interactions with the missionary women. From early on, as the next section shows, St Joseph's was an ambivalent space 'between' sanctuary and coercion.

Choosing and not choosing New Norcia as home

New Norcia, in common with other missions, worked within government parameters and valued government approval, only occasionally protesting against government policy.[50] In her work on the Catholic missions in the far north of Western Australia, including the 1908 Benedictine

---

47   Salvado to Aborigines Protection Board, 4 August 1896.
48   On the impact of the *Aborigine Act 1905* (WA), see Anna Haebich, *For Their Own Good: Aborigines and Government in the South West of Western Australia 1900–1940* (Nedlands, WA: University of Western Australia Press for the Charles and Joy Staples South West Region Publications Fund, 1992); South West Aboriginal Land and Sea Council, John Host and Chris Owens, '*It Is Still in My Heart, This Is My Country': The Single Noongar Claim History* (Crawley, WA: UWA Press, 2009). On the economic and social changes in Western Australia: Penelope Hetherington, *Paupers, Poor Relief and Poor Houses in Western Australia 1829–1910* (Crawley, WA: University of Western Australia Publishing, 2009), 129–31.
49   'List of WA Legislation', Kaartidijin Noongar–Noongar Knowledge, South West Aboriginal Land & Sea Council, www.noongarculture.org.au/list-of-wa-legislation/; accessed 3 April 2018.
50   On Catholic mission policy nationally, see Stefano Girola, 'Rhetoric and Action: The Policies and Attitudes of the Catholic Church with Regard to Australia's Indigenous Peoples, 1885–1967' (PhD thesis, University of Queensland, 2007).

foundation at Drysdale River (from 1952, Kalumburu), Christine Choo argues that government policy to remove Aboriginal children from their families could not have been implemented 'without the encouragement and compliance of Church agencies'.[51] She also shows, however, that for 'many Aborigines ... there is an ambivalence in their attitude towards the missionaries and the Mission itself because for them it had become home'.[52] Peggy Brock chose the word 'ghetto' to convey the effect of the missions that 'simultaneously oppressed and nurtured the communities they confined'.[53] New Norcia was not unique in the cognitive dissonance that it both was and was not an orphanage, that it both encouraged family life and modelled monastic separation from it, but the choice to frame the experience of the mission as 'family' is striking in the records.

The institution as both 'ghetto' and 'home' is visible in two fragments of the *Chronicle* that concern the foundational phase of the work of missionary women at St Joseph's. Both point to the determining power of the relationships at St Joseph's to sustain or break the institution. They also show Aboriginal residents negotiating the boundaries of New Norcia, in one case choosing and in the other rejecting St Joseph's. Both cases make it clear that Aboriginal people expected (or hoped) to find safe haven and respect at the mission. Both are accounts of conflict, one at a distance, the other in the town itself. The accounts of the monastery's diary hint, however faintly, at an institution shaped partly by the choices of Aboriginal women, even as the same fragments highlight institutional control and narrowing options for Aboriginal people.

The first instance came to the diarist's attention in the cold, wet winter of 1907 when the Teresian community was still at full strength with seven members, among 30 other residents at St Joseph's.[54] The *Chronicle* records on 15 June that year:

> An Aboriginal girl (half-caste) 14 years old presented herself to the College when it was already night asking to be admitted. It is not known who her parents are, if they are still alive. She was in service

---

51   Christine Choo, 'The Role of the Catholic Missionaries at Beagle Bay in the Removal of Aboriginal Children from Their Families in the Kimberley Region from the 1890s', *Aboriginal History* 21 (1997): 14–29.
52   Choo, 'The Role of the Catholic Missionaries', 28. See also Christine Choo, *Mission Girls: Aboriginal Women on Catholic Missions in the Kimberley, Western Australia 1900–1950* (Crawley, WA: University of Western Australia Press, 2001).
53   Peggy Brock, *Outback Ghettos: A History of Aboriginal Institutionalisation and Survival* (Cambridge: Cambridge University Press, 1993), 1.
54   New Norcia's Annual Report to Chief Protector Prinsep, 10 September 1906, gave the number as 34 (NNA 05132).

far from here, and having escaped from the home of her masters, she arrived here with another half-caste Aborigine. This fellow was claiming her as his, but the girl refused to follow him.

It rained again in the afternoon.[55]

At one level, this diary entry tells a colonial story of resistance. The girl presented herself to the mission, choosing it as an alternative to other possibilities. Most immediately, she preferred New Norcia to the man who claimed her as a wife, but the *Chronicle* also accepted her 'escape' from the indentured labour covered by the WA *Masters and Servants Act 1892*, and her long journey to make sure of it. The account shows us her initiative to separate from the man she had travelled with, but we do not know the background or the reasons: whether this relationship had any traditional standing, whether there was a rift between them, whether she intended the separation as permanent or not, whether she made a pragmatic decision for dry shelter or was drawn by the network and the prospects at New Norcia.

The house of Catholic sisters in the mission context gave the girl an option to act against the cultural expectation of marriage or male supervision, common to both sides of the racial divide. The monks' *Chronicle* implied support for her choice. She approached 'the College' at night, making contact with strangers and imposing herself on their routine. The colonial context is clear in the English biological term 'half-caste' imported into the Spanish account as well as in the disruption to family and social networks that meant the mission had no prospect of finding her parents and that no one else, including the girl herself, was able (or willing) to connect with her relatives either. We do not know her name, and so far the records do not let us take the story further, but the vignette of her decision suggests a resourceful young woman who judged the sisters were her best bet.

Two years later another or, just possibly, this same girl was noticed by the *Chronicle*. She was '15 or 16 years old', from elsewhere, with no known relatives, and she chose to leave New Norcia rather than 'humble herself' after an angry encounter with one of the sisters, including more than one 'cuff on the ear'.[56] The sister is not named, but by 1909 there were three in the community: Maria, Teresa and Leonor. The *Chronicle* recounted the incident at some length, suggesting that it was unusual enough and

---

55   *Chronicle*, 15 June 1907.
56   *Chronicle*, 15 September 1909.

worrying enough to warrant careful attention, perhaps not least because it prompted other girls to leave. This account also points to the colonial context and shows the permeable boundary of St Joseph's as an institution. It shows the Aboriginal girl's reaction against what she clearly judged to be unjust treatment but also underlines the mission's expectations of conformity and the frightening choice the girl had to make when 'home' came at the price of 'humbling herself'.

The incident began on a Monday, 13 September 1909; it would have been a washing day and came after the busy period of preparing for the local Agricultural Show. The *Chronicle* did not note any pressures in the context, however, but focused on the girl's behaviour:

> 15 Sept 1909: The day before yesterday a girl from the Native College behaved badly, and on being corrected behaved worse; for this reason she received a cuff on the ear from the Sister who reprimanded her. As the girl wanted to retaliate, she received a second blow. This was enough for the annoyed girl to abandon the College, and she went to the bush, since she has neither friends, relatives nor acquaintances here. Neither has she parents living or known.[57]

It seemed that if she had had a network in New Norcia someone might have taken her in, but without that, her only refuge was the bush. She spent the Monday night away but returned to St Joseph's on Tuesday, tired and hungry, the *Chronicle* noted, but 'without humbling herself for her bad behaviour'. Even when the sisters involved Torres, she remained defiant and told him she would leave again. So, the *Chronicle* recorded verbatim, 'Fr Abbot answered, "she might do as she wished, but that if she went to the other side of the fence she would not be received back home"'.

The *Chronicle* did not pause to consider how consciously the abbot called St Joseph's her 'home', or what connotation the word might have had for this child. It did make clear the leaving was not easy. She went on Tuesday morning but came back that night and drew the sisters, perhaps other sisters from the one she was in conflict with, into the compromise of letting her eat supper separately and sleep in the bakery. If this signalled some give and take, it was ultimately still on condition that she apologise. On Wednesday morning 'as she persisted in not humbling herself, she was sent away'. The *Chronicle* does not say by whom. Neither does the entry end with her departure but goes on to say that in the afternoon

---

57   *Chronicle*, 15 September 1909.

the missionary women and the girls walked to the Agricultural Show at Yarawindah, 10 miles (or 16 kilometres) away, to see the displays. The house was still tense. That night two other girls left, one of them for the third time, expecting better prospects elsewhere. The *Chronicle* predicted this would be the last time she left with one of the neighbours, her 'boyfriend', but did not clarify whether this was because she had new plans or would not be allowed to return.

All in all, this is delicate and unstable material. The *Chronicle* gives us a privileged insight into how the mission authorities saw the situation. It is, so far as we know, the only surviving account. Created as an internal record to hold the memory of the monastic community, it is too far from the people to notice the names of the girls involved. Neither does it challenge the assumptions that a work supervisor or teacher could hit an apprentice or pupil. It does not critique the situation in which institutional conformity was the price of food and shelter. It is clear from the material that there was no room at New Norcia for girls who challenged authority or 'behaved badly'. If there was even a chance to state the case against the sister, no one found it persuasive. So, it is fair to see this incident as an example of the tightening of control and the disappearance of viable alternatives for Aboriginal people. But it is also fair to notice in the first incident that the 14-year-old actively sought and received help at St Joseph's, while in the second the girl of 15 or 16 negotiated with the institution over three days and then left rather than apologise or conform, perhaps spurring others to do the same. She did not find the relationships in the house that would have made it 'home', but the abbot's rhetoric and the sisters' efforts at compromise, as well as her own decision, backed up implicitly by the actions of two other residents, all agreed she was entitled to something better. The struggle to provide better, including the effort to resist the racist imagination that saw no future for Aboriginal people, was what had drawn Maria to New Norcia in the first place.

Maria Harispe Quilliri: 'That they may regard me as a native'

In the end we can piece together only a little of Maria's situation at St Joseph's when the Teresian community folded and guess at how successful or not she was at keeping open a space for something 'better'. She had been clear in her bid to stay at New Norcia that the monastery should 'regard me as a native'.⁵⁸ To be happy she asked only for recognition of her vocation and permission to spend her life among the Aboriginal people.⁵⁹ The *Notebooks* compiled and copied by later generations of Benedictine sisters preserve the difficulty of this time and affirm Maria's fidelity. Maria might have joined Mary MacKillop's Sisters if she could have been assured her work would be at St Joseph's; she was on the point of abandoning everything 'many times' but 'God preserved her spirit', 'her heroic temperament'.⁶⁰ What we know from her own words is her insistent choice of the life at St Joseph's.⁶¹ If she saw herself as alone, she was also remembered as speaking often 'of the kindness and assistance given her in that trying time'⁶² by the community at St Gertrude's College, especially by the sister whose name is lost to us who took on the teaching of reading and writing in the mornings, so that there was little change in the overall routine.

Whatever arrangements were in place, they ran smoothly and without controversy, and this in itself tells us something of Maria and her style. The 'dance of comings and goings' that Maria managed with the smallest children while the renovations at St Joseph's were underway has already been noted.⁶³ Then for over a year, from 8 August 1910, when work on the new building was completed, nothing at St Joseph's attracted the *Chronicle*'s notice until early November 1911. In that summer of drought the 'Sisters' pumped water from St Gertrude's to other tanks 'which the native girls use to wash the clothes'.⁶⁴ The entry does not name Maria, and characteristically she falls between the categories of the 'native girls' and the Josephite 'Sisters'. But the transfer of water signalled practical cooperation between the women's institutions. Perhaps Maria had a hand in this.

Work continued, and prayer continued; we can assume that much. A visitor to New Norcia's 'rising educational centre' in 1911 told readers of the *Western Mail* the 'broken clans' were 'practically extinct' but noted the church was 'full of aboriginal and half-caste girls singing clear responses'.⁶⁵

---

58   Maria Harispe to Henry Altimira, 6 June 1908, *Visitation*, 82.
59   Maria Harispe to Henry Altimira, 6 June 1908.
60   'Origen de la Congrecacion de las Hermanas Benedictinas Misioneras de New Norcia, Western Australia' unpublished typescript from the notebooks of Sister Felicitas Pampliega c. 1921–c. 1967, transcribed and edited by Sister Teresa González, Madrid c. 1980, Archives of the Benedictine Missionary Sisters of Tutzing (ABTM) (hereafter *Notebooks*, Madrid), 2–4.
61   Maria Harispe to Henry Altimira, 6 June 1908.
62   Obituary, Sr Maria Harispe, *St Ildephonsus College Magazine*, 1925, 57.
63   See Chapter 2; *Notebooks*, Madrid, 5.
64   *Chronicle*, 15 November 1911.
65   *Western Mail*, 18 February 1911, 44.

The unremarkable daily pattern included gathering in the church most evenings to pray the rosary. On Mondays and Thursdays as the girls from St Joseph's rolled through their responses to the rosary's 'joyful mysteries' they would have recalled the story of the Visitation, the feast on which Maria had made her Benedictine commitment. Most people attached particular intentions to the steady repetition of Our Fathers and Hail Marys. Probably Maria prayed frequently for the household and, knowing the abbot's concern for a teacher in the school, perhaps she was prompted sometimes to pray for companions.

The household of oblates expands

Through the years, when newspaper headlines covered the sinking of the *Titanic*, the battles of the First World War, the completion of the transcontinental railway from Perth to Sydney, and the development of psychological testing for children, three other women joined Maria Harispe in the work at St Joseph's. At New Norcia these years spanned the death of Abbot Torres and the election of Anselmo Catalan as the third abbot.

First, Elias Devine, born in Tipperary in 1839, made her way to New Norcia through an international network of Catholic connections in April 1912; then two of the Teresians returned, not as members of that community, but as laywomen acting on their own initiative: Maria Consuelo Batiz Abelleyra in August 1912 and Teresa Roca Lluch three years later in September 1915. These four women had each made extraordinary decisions to be nowhere else but New Norcia.

Like Maria, Consuelo and Teresa both made a commitment to New Norcia as Benedictine oblates, and on 8 December 1915, three weeks after Teresa formalised her new status, the *Chronicle* noted 'the Spanish Sisters appeared for the first time in public in the habit of Benedictine oblates'.[66] It was a feast day honouring the unique holiness of Mary the mother of Jesus under her title as Immaculate Conception, a great public holiday in Spain and a popular day for formal steps in religious communities. With three, and a mysterious fourth in the background, there was a new solidity to the small community.

---

66 *Chronicle*, 8 December 1915.

Figure 3.5: The Sisters, dressed in Benedictine habits with the St Joseph's girls, after December 1915.
The Benedictine sisters, from left to right, are Maria Harispe, Consuelo Batiz and Teresa Roca. The Drayton family recognises the baby to the left of Consuelo as Benedict Drayton, b. 1917.
Source: NNA 73745P.

The arrival of Mother Elias Devine, April 1912

The four women each brought distinct skills and qualities. Crucially for the future of the school at St Joseph's, Mother Elias Devine was an English-speaking teacher; she was also veteran of a distinctive missionary career. Elias was 73 when she arrived 'to teach the Aboriginal girls'[67] on 16 April 1912. It was the day after her birthday and a week since Easter. New Norcia made no fuss. The *Chronicle* noted she was 'a Carmelite' and simply recorded that she arrived with the intention of staying.[68] She remained at New Norcia until her death on 20 October 1933 and 'never renounced the Carmelite habit'.[69] There is a single photograph of her in an album in the Benedictine convent in Madrid. It shows her on the latticed verandah at St Joseph's,

---

67 *Chronicle*, 16 April 1912.
68 *Chronicle*, 16 April 1912.
69 Francisca Pardo, Interview, Madrid, May 1999, trans. Stuart Fenner. Transcript held by author.

aged 95, supporting herself against the railing with hands resting on her furled umbrella; her gaze is direct, her face soft. Her story had been muddled over the years: Sr Francisca reported Elias was French; the *Notebooks* recorded she had arrived in 1917. They remembered accurately that she was a teacher, an important mentor to the early Benedictine women, and that she was never in the community photos: a clever, humble, holy, if slightly eccentric, sister.

Figure 3.6: Mother Elias Devine, Easter 1933, aged 95, 'a woman of uncommon common sense'.
Source: ABTM.

At one level, Elias Devine is the most conventional of all the sisters who lived at St Joseph's. Christened Teresa in 1839, she came from a Tipperary family of 10 and was one of many Irish women who responded to the need for teachers in Catholic Australia. There is no doubt she had plenty in common with the Sisters of Mercy in Bunbury where she stayed when she first arrived in Western Australia. But there were more years and more steps to her journey than most; certainly none of the other sisters had been celebrated for missionary work in England's Catholic weekly the *Tablet*.

In 1900, Fr Metcalf, a priest in Pau, on the French side of the Pyrenees, had written to the *Tablet* to alert English readers to a new missionary college that was training candidates for India. Our Lady of the Missions at Ypres in Belgium was a 'new effort' of Mother Elias of Jesus. The work was flourishing and Metcalf saw the success as typical of Elias:

> All who come in contact with her fall under the charm of her sweetness and the magnetism of her spiritual zeal, and are struck by the uncommon common sense which directs her every undertaking.[70]

Elias was already well-known for her educational success in the south of India, and the *Tablet* carried the note to update her 'many friends' in England.

---

70   Theodore Metcalf, 'Carmel in India', *Tablet*, 2 October 1900, 20.

The backstory to Elias Devine's arrival at New Norcia was of an international missionary venture beginning in France in the 1850s, then centred on India, and a twentieth-century crisis that required a change in direction. As a child, Teresa Devine had been sent from Ireland to school in France and 'later' joined the Carmelites at Pau, taking the name Elias. In 1868 she was one of the two sisters who left Pau with Mother Veronica Leeves, an English woman raised in India, to found a new group at Bayonne. They wanted to draw on the Carmelite spirit for missionary work and to be 'contemplatives in action'.[71] With Mother Veronica and four others, Elias established the first house of the Apostolic Carmelites in 1870 in Mangalore, in the southern Indian kingdom of Travancore, and pioneered schools and training colleges, particularly for girls. The Carmelite houses spread steadily, with three new foundations over 15 years. In 1880 Elias was superior of the Holy Angels Convent at Trivandrum[72] and, with the local Carmelite bishop, co-founder of the Congregation of Carmelite Religious that developed from this house. It was recognised by Rome in 1892.[73] The associated school was highly regarded, being accredited as a matriculation college in 1885 and recognised as a college of the University of Madras in 1899. The work of education ranged from university preparation through practical skills to earn a livelihood as well as catechetical instruction. It came to wider attention through Mother Veronica's book, *Carmel in India*, published in London in 1895. A profile in Europe helped foster support for their missionary outreach, and, as the *Tablet* reported, the community opened a missionary college in Ypres in March 1900.[74]

Elias was superior of this training college and missionary novitiate from its foundation until 1905, when she made her own appeal to *Tablet* readers. New regulations in India had increased the training requirements for teachers, and Elias hoped for English speakers, 'earnest souls [to] share our labour of love'.[75] It is likely her colleges were under pressure at this point.

---

71 The Congregation of the Apostolic Carmel, www.apostolic-carmel.org/index.htm; accessed 14 March 2013. Carmelites of Trivandrum, goanchurches.info/orders/carmelites-of-trivandrum-c-c-r/; accessed 29 September 2020.
72 *Souvenir of the Centenary of Holy Angels* (Kerala, India: Congregation of the Carmelite Religious, n.d.), 106. I am indebted to Sr Phyllis and Sr Letty of the Carmelite Community who sent a copy of this work 7 May 2014.
73 All Saints College, Trivandrum, Golden Jubilee Year, www.allsaintscollege.in/allSaints/ccr.php; accessed 14 March 2013, domain expired; also Holy Angels Convent: Our History, www.holyangelstvm.org/history.aspx; accessed 29 September 2020.
74 *Souvenir of the Centenary*, 118.
75 *Tablet*, 23 September 1905, 21.

Indian government policies were centralising and regulating schools and requiring instruction in local languages so that many private institutions were closing.[76] At the same time, church authorities were promoting 'a line of action which, though most worthy in itself, did not win her commendation'.[77] The records are discreet, but the dates coincide with conflict within the church over the caste system as well as strategies to promote an indigenous leadership.[78] In any case, Elias resolved she should not return to India from Belgium.

Seeking advice and support, Elias heard from her friend, Fr Luigi Martelli, dean of Bunbury, that the Benedictines at New Norcia needed a teacher.[79] There is no trace of their correspondence, but it makes sense that they knew each other. Martelli had been born in Goa to Italian parents and educated in India. Arriving in Western Australia in 1881, he knew New Norcia well through his uncle Fr Raffaele Martelli, parish priest of Fremantle and later of Toodyay and a close friend of Salvado.[80] Thus, Mother Elias made her way to Western Australia. New Norcia would remember how she treasured the memories of India, how 'her face would glow with admiration of a noble people' as she told stories, but how she had 'sought another field of labour'.[81] Was it remarkable that the Teresa Devine of Tipperary, Trivandrum and Ypres joined the community at New Norcia? Or was this simply a predictable enough variation on the general theme of commitment that led Catholic women to missionary work and life in religious communities in far-flung countries?

For the community at St Joseph's there was nothing unusual in a journey across the globe, and all the signs are that Elias moved smoothly into the work of the mission. Perhaps the most intriguing aspect of the story is the strong, but misleading, tradition among the Benedictine women that she arrived in 1917. How did memory slip out of agreement with the *Chronicle* and other records by five years? The likely explanation is simple

---

76   'Introduction to Lord Curzon's Education Policy', Krishna Kanta Handiqui State Open University, kkhsou.in/main/education/education_policy.html; accessed 18 March 2014.
77   Brother Sebastian, 'Mother M. Elias', *St Ildephonsus College Magazine*, 1933, 47.
78   Paul Pallath, *The Catholic Church in India* (Kerala: Oriental Institute of Religious Studies, 2010), 165–69; Kenneth Ballhatchet, *Class, Caste and Catholicism in India, 1789–1914* (London: Curzon Press, 1998), 40–46.
79   Sebastian, 'Mother M. Elias', 47.
80   John Kinder, 'I'm Writing Simply to Say I Have Nothing to Write About: The Martelli Letters 1854–1864', *New Norcia Studies* 19 (2011): 19–33; John Kinder and Joshua Brown, *Canon Raffaele Martelli in Western Australia, 1853–1864: Life and Letters* (Northcote, Vic.: Abbey Press, 2014).
81   Sebastian, 'Mother M. Elias', 47.

enough and entwined with the story of Consuelo Batiz, also a teacher. It was Consuelo's story that shaped the popular understanding that New Norcia was without a teacher, not in 1912, but in 1917.

The return of Mary Consuelo Batiz Abelleyra, 1912

Mary Consuelo Batiz is an elusive and compelling figure. One of the original party of Teresians and widely respected as the 'director' of the school, her recall from the troubled Teresian community in 1907 struck everyone at New Norcia as a mistake.[82] We can only imagine the reactions of the people who had grieved Consuelo's departure when, five years later, on 5 September 1912, they assembled to welcome her back.

We do not know how contact was re-established. In the first phase of her recall to Valencia, the *Chronicle* surmised the Teresians were intercepting letters to her from New Norcia.[83] But within the small talk of the Spanish congregation the news that Maria Harispe had remained in Australia would certainly have reached her. It is tempting to speculate that somehow news of Elias encouraged her and that the promise of a new community prompted her move, but the records leave us guessing. Certainly, the monks at New Norcia had no warning.

The *Chronicle* was confused and surprised by news of her journey, thinking at first that her telegram was from Torres, but her arrival was recorded as a stately homecoming:

> At two in the afternoon there arrived from Spain, Sr Consuelo Batiz who five years before left the Mission recalled to Spain by her superiors; but today she returned, probably never to leave again as she is freed from her religious vows that bound her to the Congregation of the Company of St Teresa of Jesus.[84]

Consuelo's return was a powerful vindication of the glowing 1907 assessments of her love for the Aboriginal people and their regard for her. To make the journey from Spain to Australia a second time, and to return

---

82 See Chapter 2.
83 *Chronicle*, 8 November 1907.
84 *Chronicle*, 5 September 1912; that the monks thought her telegram announcing her return was from Torres. *Chronicle*, 27 August 1912.

as a single woman, formally separated from the missionary congregation that had sponsored her work, gave that work absolute priority. As the next chapter shows, her second sojourn ended badly, but it began in hope and confidence.

Acknowledging her new, more vulnerable status, Consuelo negotiated a contract with the abbot. Torres agreed the monastery would feed and clothe her while she was in residence. This was standard. But we have her later word that he also agreed that should she ever leave New Norcia he would pay her fare to Mexico or to Spain, as well as a retrospective wage of £1 per week. This was exactly half the basic wage of 8 shillings a day for men, and just under the average annual earnings of £56 for female factory hands in Western Australia in 1912.[85] According to evidence given at the Roth Royal Commission in 1905, wages paid to Aboriginal men working on the farm at New Norcia ranged from £1 a month up to £1 8s a week.[86] The verbal contract between Torres and Consuelo reflected the good working relationship they seem to have enjoyed. Consuelo was adamant the contract was agreed, but she had no cause to mention it while Torres was in charge.

Consuelo had never met Maria or Elias. When Maria first joined the Teresians, Consuelo was already at New Norcia, and when Maria arrived Consuelo had already been recalled. The two missionaries were of the same generation, Consuelo at 34 years to Maria's 31, they had both come from South America to Spain to join the Teresians, and both had stood out against the congregation's leadership. Elias was twice their age but shared the capacity for bold decisions and the priority of a missionary call. Perhaps they had corresponded. Undoubtedly, Consuelo's friends at the mission had talked about her.

---

85   Commonwealth Bureau of Census and Statistics, *Official Year Book of the Commonwealth of Australia Containing Authoritative Statistics for the Period 1901–1913*, no. 7 (Canberra: Government Printer, 1914), 469. On the contract, Catalan to Northmore and Hale, 17 November 1917, Catalan Correspondence 1917, NNA 01419/70.
86   Evidence of Fr Edmund McCormick, New Norcia, 'The Aborigines Question: Evidence Taken by Dr Roth', *Western Mail*, 20 February 1905, 19–20.

Figure 3.7: Consuelo (centre) with Teresa (left), Maria (right) and residents of St Joseph's, after September 1912 and before December 1915.
Source: NNA W7-a3-4-494.

Consuelo's role at the mission had already been contested once; her affirmation in the town had contrasted with tension in the Teresian community. How much that memory coloured her return and the subsequent record is impossible to say, but the *Notebooks* compiled without direct contact with Consuelo are against her. The view preserved among the Benedictine sisters was that Consuelo 'had exceptional talents for the leadership of the Orphanage',[87] but her style of religious life was out of order. We are not told how she offended, just that, in a phrase that echoes the Teresian complaints, 'her behavior as a religious sister was undesirable'.[88] Maria's initial joy in the arrival of another companion was short-lived. More than that, for Maria, working with Consuelo became 'a true Calvary'.[89] The word is stunning. Its heavy connotation of unjust suffering hangs in the air. It underlines the memory of Maria's holiness as it loads the dice against Consuelo. Perhaps the verdict in the *Notebooks* was misinformed; it was certainly retrospective.

---

87   *Notebooks*, Madrid, 6. '*Esta Hna de nacionalidad mixicana tenia dates extraordinarios para gabernar el Orfalinato que ya estaba casi constuido. No obstante su conducta como religiosa era indeseable. Con sus rechazos por parte de los Superiores y con su terco y destructivo teson permanecio en la Mision 5 años hasta 1917. Estos años fueron de verdadero calvario para Hna Maria.*'
88   *Notebooks*, Madrid, 6.
89   *Notebooks*, Madrid, 6.

3. BENEDICTINE OBLATES

On her return, Consuelo slipped back into her role as 'director' of the school, bringing the resources and education of a former choir sister to the work. The transition did not disturb the routine enough to cause the *Chronicle* to comment, so we have to surmise most of what it meant in the day-to-day. The elderly Elias was active in her support, and sometimes to the fore, as when she coached the girls in songs and dances for a concert with the French-speaking soprano Antonia Dolores Bettini in 1915 or when she engaged the English-speaking Travelling Inspector in 1913.[90] The report prepared by George S. Olivey of the state's Department of Aborigines and Fisheries gave a rare overview of the institution. He met and talked with the three sisters and affirmed enthusiastically that 'all were heart and soul in their work, taking the greatest interest in the welfare of their charges'.[91]

Before we turn to consider Olivey's report, there is one more sister to acknowledge in this first expansion of the community. Teresa Roca had spent six years at New Norcia before her departure 'under obedience' in 1910,[92] and at 47 years old she was a generation older than the other former Teresians, an experienced lay sister with some early training as a nurse.[93] The fact of her return in 1915 is almost all we know of her motivation, but it heralded a commitment that was to last four decades.

The return of Teresa Roca Lluch, September 1915

The story of Teresa Roca's journey underlines her determination as well as a fearless trust in God. She sailed out of Barcelona in 1915, undeterred by the difficulty of wartime travel as a single woman without proper papers. The sisters who knew her remembered that she insisted on sailing even though 'the superior had a headache and forgot to bring her passport to the ship'.[94] There were no formal passports at the time, but the memory enshrines an ongoing connection between Teresa and the congregation that had, perhaps reluctantly, released her from vows. It paints the superior as a little vapid, and it highlights Teresa's resolve.

---

90 See Chapter 4.
91 George S. Olivey, Travelling Inspector, 'Report on New Norcia Mission', State Records Office of Western Australia (SROWA) S1644 cons652 1913/0213.
92 *Notebooks*, Madrid, 2–3.
93 *Pax*, 3 February 1953, n.p. Newspaper clipping, ABTM.
94 Francisca Pardo, Interview, Madrid, 31 May 1999.

Figure 3.8: Teresa Roca, one of the original Teresian community, remembered in the *Notebooks* as setting out again in 1915 'without fear and with great confidence in God'.

Source: ABTM.

The community's *Notebooks* imply she had spent the five years of her absence seeking a dispensation from her vows and permission to travel. When finally she could make the journey, she felt the voyage nearly killed her. Ill with 'dizziness and fear' she haemorrhaged 'to the brink of death' as they arrived in Singapore.[95] Then, with no documents, a dubious nationality, and, the *Notebooks* record tellingly, not able to speak English, 'a language necessary for defending herself' (*idioma [im]presinible para su defensa*),[96] she was detained as a suspected German spy. An elegant black-and-white photograph taken as a memento for her family shows a serene face and graceful lace veil that might have evoked stereotypes of espionage more readily than missionary hopes. She was kept under surveillance at a convent. Eventually, the authorities made contact with New Norcia and Teresa was permitted to sail on.

With a firm emphasis on her missionary identity, she travelled as Sister T. Roca.[97] The cloud of police suspicion had not lifted, however, and when the *Charon* arrived at Fremantle on 15 September 1915, she was not permitted to leave the port unaccompanied.[98] There was no one to meet her, so a stewardess (*una azafata*) was assigned to take her to the address she pulled from her memory.[99] At the Benedictines' house in the city, 1 Murray Street,

---

95 *Notebooks*, Madrid, 7.
96 *Notebooks*, Madrid, 7.
97 *West Australian*, 15 September 1915, 6.
98 *Notebooks*, Madrid, 7.
99 Sr Francisca Pardo, Interview, Madrid, 31 May 1999; Sr Teresa González, Interview, Madrid, 10 July 2004.

West Perth, the monks vouched for her persuasively. Uncertain about the day of her arrival, they had nevertheless come from New Norcia to collect her. 'Finally', the *Notebooks* declare, 'she arrived at the Mission she so much desired'.[100] But the haemorrhages of the voyage returned, as severe as before. The timing suggests a difficult menopause. We hear nothing further and perhaps local knowledge came into play once she reached the community of women. The *Notebooks* made a different link, implying that New Norcia itself was the remedy. They preserved the memory of haemorrhage with an eye on God's Providence, explaining that Teresa 'skirted death for several days', until 'it was not her time and she was able to work in the Mission for 40 more years'.[101] The *Chronicle* had nothing to say about her return at all but noted carefully two months later: 'Sister Teresa Roca made her oblation at the hands of Father Prior Roberto Bas' on Sunday 14 November 1915.[102] The prior was deputising for the newly elected Abbot Catalan, still on his way to New Norcia from Manila.

Figure 3.9: Teresa Roca and Aboriginal girls working at embroidery and crochet in the sewing room.
Source: NNA w7-a3-4-495.

---

100 *Notebooks*, Madrid, 8.
101 *Notebooks*, Madrid, 8.
102 *Chronicle*, 4 November 1915.

Maria, Consuelo and Teresa as Benedictine oblates and Elias, the missionary Carmelite, had assembled as a community. Responsibilities were divided broadly. The monastery's summary of the leadership St Joseph's in 1913 noted 'three Sisters in charge'.[103] Torres does not tell us who did what but summarises 'one nun takes charge of school, another teaches needle and fancy work, and a third superintends all other work and directs the conduct of the girls in general'.[104] When a fourth arrived, gifted in handcraft and trained for domestic work, she added to the workforce outside the formal classroom. The sisters were all 'of good experience'.[105] Now they found themselves together in a shared commitment to St Joseph's. The complex of buildings that constituted St Joseph's at this time, newly renovated, enlarged and enclosed in the shadow of St Gertrude's, is almost another character in the story of the Benedictine sisters. The next chapter assembles a picture of the institution itself. St Joseph's was as much metaphor as it was location. On the edge of the mission town, St Joseph's helped shade emotional resonances and establish a pattern of life.

---

103 'New Norcia Mission. Annual Report for Year ending 30 June 1913', SROWA S1644 cons652 1913/1273.
104 'New Norcia Mission. Annual Report for Year ending 30 June 1913'.
105 'New Norcia Mission. Annual Report for Year ending 30 June 1913'.

4

St Joseph's Native School and Orphanage: Workers at the Edge of the Town

Sometime after 1910, a photographer recorded renovations at St Joseph's Native School and Orphanage, documenting the low buildings of the new laundry to the southeast of New Norcia's monastery. The image draws the viewer's eyes across the expanse of bare ground towards a woman dressed in a religious habit who stands with a toddler at her side between the camera and the new whitewashed walls; near her a group of children cluster around a sturdy swing.[1] Similarly robust posts support four neat washing lines in the foreground. At first glance in the grainy reproduction, the swing looks more like a gallows and the washing lines suggest barbwire fences.

Such stark realities fit our picture of Aboriginal Australia, and the first impression that this is an institutional photograph is accurate. But magnifying the image brings reassurance that this is also a domestic scene. In the deep verandah the camera has captured taller figures of the older girls and young women in long skirts. Enlarged further, a washing basket comes into focus, with some tubs, buckets, fine collars and cuffs, and the copper against the wall; a young woman at the far left attends to a cockatoo on her arm; on the right another veiled figure has turned towards the window. There are two children sitting on the swing. At several points the image blurs with movement: this photograph is only partly posed.

---

1   New Norcia Archives (NNA) 74622P.

There is no Sunday best: the children are in shapeless pinnies, barefoot, and no one is staying still for the occasion. The photographer intended that we would see the whole, the sweep of the scene, not scrutinise the parts. But as the magnification climbs, faces emerge in the group around the swing. Technology brings features to the woman's face: not European, not Aboriginal, perhaps reflecting Consuelo's Mexican village of Chalchicomula, but then higher resolution defines the eyeglasses that confirm her as Maria Harispe.[2] The children's different gazes come into focus—serious, alert, sombre, pained, curious, squinting. And then we can go no closer. The fine-grained image breaks apart, resolves into pixels, not reality. They are not there. It is the same with every photograph, every text: so far and no further.

Figure 4.1: Maria and children of St Joseph's near a swing, with laundry in the background, c. 1912.
Source: NNA 74622P.

---

2   Maria Ana Consuelo Cristiana Dolores Batiz Abelleyra, 15 December 1877, Baptismal Register, Archive of the Parish of San Andres Chalchicomula, familysearch.org; accessed 28 July 2012.

Figure 4.2: Detail of Maria and the children.
Source: NNA 74622P.

Figure 4.3: Detail of laundry work at St Joseph's, after 1910.
Source: NNA 74622P.

The site of St Joseph's itself holds fragments together across time. Just as surely as a written document, the buildings and the landscape they relate to are a text. We can trace the lives of the Benedictine sisters and the children at St Joseph's in the faint suggestions of the space just as we can catch their echo in the archival pages. In New Norcia today the swing and the clotheslines are gone, but visitors can still stand where that photographer stood and imagine the scene. The yard where Maria paced now hosts a barbeque when Aboriginal families gather for an annual reunion. There is a garden planted with succulents where the children once peered back into the camera, and we can still take our bearings from St Gertrude's and choose a spot within the frame. The reality of the township and its stories is reinforced by our experience of the place. Like the photographer, we are producing an image, creating a picture. We cannot see what they saw, or retrieve their experience—let's not imagine that. But we can pay attention. We are sifting and assembling fragments.

One fragment that takes on added dimensions when it is read 'in place' is the account left by G. S. Olivey who was charged by the Western Australian Government with inspecting the mission in May 1913. Olivey's report forms a spine for this chapter as we follow his progress around the site and pay attention to the physical realities of this space at the edge of the town. The picture it offers of the missionary women doing their best, 'heart and soul for their work',[3] is the administrator's extension of policies directed at Aboriginal people 'for their own good'. These are the years of Consuelo's influence. This chapter ranges over earlier sources, where we glimpse her impact in the years to 1907 as well as after her return in 1912. It builds a picture of the work of the community and the assumption that domestic work would define the women. Finally, gathering together the hints of Consuelo's story, it traces the tension between a monastic vision and missionary expectations.

Defining spaces: St Joseph's in a landscape

In the renovation of 1910, distinct zones of activity had become visible at St Joseph's. We have heard of the wall and how the Aboriginal people detested it.[4] But the structure that triggered the nickname Golden Gaol was not the only spatial reality to make an impact on the psyche of the town. Each of the carefully designated spaces at St Joseph's shaped experiences of the institution in patterns that endured through the decades: dormitories, laundry, kitchen and school rooms all resonated metaphorically. Overriding concerns for cleanliness, hard-working respectability and ordered seclusion

---

3   G. S. Olivey, Travelling Inspector, 'Report on New Norcia Mission', 7 May 1913, State Records Office of Western Australia (SROWA) S1644 cons652 1913/0213.
4   See Chapter 2.

were coded into the physical structure. There were also signs of what St Joseph's was not. Stretched out from the upright edge of St Gertrude's College and overlooked by its fairy-tale tower, St Joseph's was in contrast a modest and practical building with a utilitarian windmill as its highest peak. There was a hierarchy of aspiration here: St Joseph's knew its place.

Like most visitors, the travelling inspector Olivey was struck first by New Norcia's other buildings, especially the 'imposing … splendidly built' boarding schools, before he found the quadrangle of 'comparatively new brick buildings … surrounding a large square' that was St Joseph's. The 'fine and airy girls' quarters' compared more than favourably with St Mary's for the Aboriginal boys, where foundations had been laid to replace the original 'dilapidated' slab hut, and it also outshone the two-roomed cottages for families. In contrast to the domestic buildings, St Joseph's had a traditional monastic layout, centred on a 'work cloister'. We know that later this central area was busy enough as a playground, but the inspector did not comment on this. When he saw it, the space for play was divided again and again by the washing lines. The inspector noted the order of buildings (dormitories on the east side faced laundry on the west, kitchen on the north had a view of a school room in the south) and that there were 29 girls. The monastery's returns show that numbers increased through this decade, having more than tripled from 11 residents (aged from one to 26 years) recorded in the care of seven sisters in 1906 to 36 residents by the end of 1917, along with the four sisters.[5]

At this stage, there was no separate 'convent' for the missionary community.[6] Instead, one 'retiring room' near the classroom seems to have been the only communal living space for the sisters. Neither was there a separate chapel built into the structure. There were shared devotional images, and the painting of Mary the mother of Jesus in the dormitory was an important focus for prayer of the whole institution. Outside the patterns of domestic devotion, the sisters attended regular services in the church, joined by the girls on Sundays. Through their frequent appearances in church the Benedictine sisters were connected to the wider life of the town. The regular walk around the cottages to the church at the centre of the town also marked their style of religious life as 'apostolic', not so strictly 'monastic' as other Benedictines in Europe.

---

5   Torres to Chief Protector, 10 September 1913, SROWA S1644 cons652 1913/0213. See also Appendix 1.
6   See Sketch Plan, St Gertrude's and St Joseph's, NNA D7:89.

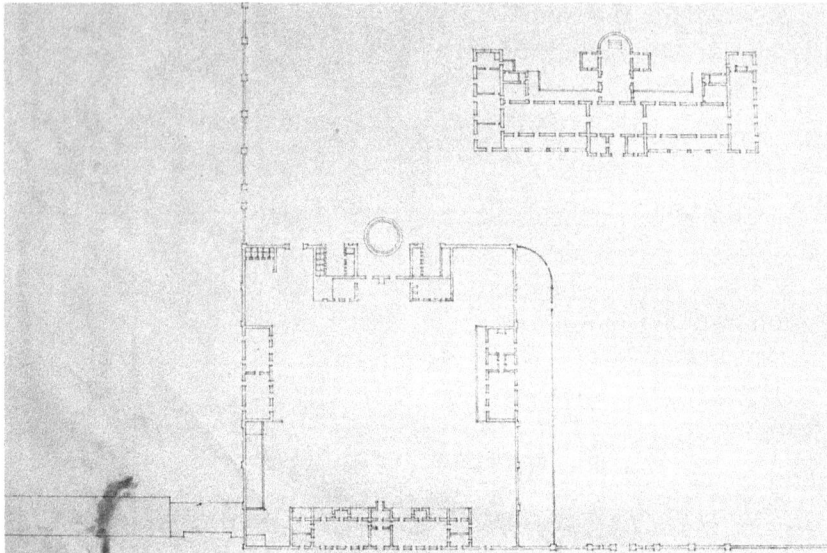

Figure 4.4: The drawings that guided the renovation at St Joseph's in 1910.
Source: NNA D7:89.

Their institution was not shuttered in the same way as traditional monastic communities of women, but nevertheless it was a distinct precinct and something of a borderland. For example, in one strange incident when rumours were flying in the middle of the First World War, word reached Consuelo at New Norcia that the Germans had invaded Geraldton, 390 kilometres north. Clearly, she was in a position to hear a rumour, true or not, and was expected to respond. Believing it to be true, she wrote an urgent letter and sent a messenger to the monastery. It is an action that shows the distance between the two institutions, on the one hand, and their interconnectedness, on the other. The report, though 'alarming to all',[7] proved to be only wild gossip. With the telegraph within their walls, the monks had access to official news, but the convent had heard the story first. Physically across the road and at the edge of the town, St Joseph's was metaphorically at a boundary linking the mission and the monastery, connecting the Benedictine and Aboriginal communities and also distinguishing between them. The sisters were focused on the work within their own quadrangular cloister, and the wall surrounding St Joseph's spoke strongly of confinement, but the township itself and particularly the cottages set their lives in a landscape that was not simply institutional.

---

7   'Chronicle of the Benedictine Community of New Norcia' (hereafter *Chronicle*), NNA, 20 February 1916.

Dormitories

Mission dormitories have become synonymous with the destruction of culture as institutional structures replaced other traditions. At New Norcia the surrounding 'village' of Aboriginal families, whose children lived in the 'Girls' House' or the 'Boys' House' but still had contact with their parents and networks, kept the cultural negotiation constantly in focus. But in the early twentieth century the improvement of dormitory facilities outweighed attention to housing for family groups. (Olivey thought these were 'good substantial huts … but very uncared for [in] appearance'.[8]) The common sleeping arrangements emphasised a shared life, with missionaries and the girls in close proximity. As Torres reported in 1911, the then newly completed dormitory measured 127 feet by 23 feet (or 39 m x 7 m).[9] There were two sections, both 'spotlessly clean and neat', with 14 beds in one and 15 in the other. Abbot Torres may have built with the future of the oblate community in mind, as the structure included eight small rooms for potential sisters (two at each end of each dormitory). Both dormitories also had common wardrobes: two small rooms, one at each end, for storing clothes, and there was more storage for boots and shoes, 'left by former inmates [and] repaired',[10] in the cellar below. The bulk storage of shoes and clothes, even more than eating and sleeping in large groups, marked the life definitively as communal.

According to the carefully lettered timetable for St Joseph's at the back of Olivey's report, the dormitories were the space where most time was spent: the girls went to bed at eight o'clock in the evening and began the day after nine and a half hours rest, at five thirty in the morning. Improbable as this pattern feels to us, it would have mirrored the daylight through most of the year and the monastic routine of the sisters. Like the rest of New Norcia, St Joseph's was lit by kerosene lamps at this time, and the town took its cue from the routine of the monks. Even in the 1960s the monks' office of Compline ended the day and the local generators were closed down religiously at nine o'clock.[11]

---

8   Olivey, Report, 1913.
9   Torres to Chief Protector, 'New Norcia Mission: Annual Report 12 months ended 30 June 1911', SROWA S1644 cons652 1911/1475.
10 Olivey, Report, 1913.
11 Sr Leonie Mayne RSJ, Telephone Interview, May 1999.

Each dormitory also had a 'lavatory' attached, facing the central square. There were three separate bathrooms near the enclosing wall, and each girl was 'compelled to take a bath … every Saturday'.[12] Adjoining these, Olivey reported a fowl house, pig-pen, dovecote and apiary, 'all attended by the children'.[13] Of these, the chickens and the sought-after freedoms of being a 'fowl-yard girl' are an especially strong tradition. The pigs, pigeons and bees are hardly remembered, but the general layout, with animals near the bathroom, mirrored many peasant farmhouses in Spain and Ireland.

The dormitories themselves broke down the village assumptions and enabled stronger and more constant oversight by the mission as an alternative to family life. Convinced that their influence would always run second to the impact of families and friends, the sisters 'deplore[d] … losing girls who were doing well'.[14] In words that ring with irony and pain for many Aboriginal families, they lobbied for increased protection against 'anyone taking them away'.[15] It was only 'orphans or others with no parents or friends in the vicinity'[16] who were likely to stay until they married, as the mission hoped:

> His Lordship Bishop Torres told me it is very hard to do much good for some of the children who attended the school as their parents come and remove them, often when they are just beginning to improve, those coming from afar have the best chance. … The Bishop would like to get absolute control of the children put under his care for some years, up to the age of 14 or 16, then he felt certain good results would follow.[17]

The hope was for 'absolute control'. The lament was that it was being resisted. The question was: who would arbitrate the meaning of 'good results'? For Olivey on his tour, the smooth running of the institution counted for a great deal; for the sisters and the girls, the routines he applauded depended on a commitment to shared and regular work, especially in the laundry but also in the kitchen.

---

12 Olivey, Report, 1913.
13 Olivey, Report, 1913.
14 Olivey, Report, 1913.
15 Olivey, Report, 1913.
16 Torres to Chief Protector, 'New Norcia Mission. Annual Report for Year ending 30 June 1913', SROWA S1644 cons652 1913/1273.
17 Olivey, Report, 1913.

4. ST JOSEPH'S NATIVE SCHOOL AND ORPHANAGE

Laundry and clothing

Across the square from the dormitories, there was the open side of the laundry, renewed in 1910 with running water, wash troughs and a built-in copper. We have seen how the laundry and washing day in particular could be a flash point for conflict. The records take the efficient running of the enterprise for granted in these years, however, probably in silent testament to good teamwork between the sisters and the young women at St Joseph's.

The hard work of washing efficiently for their own household, for some of the 26 families in cottages, as well as for the 'Boys' House', the 33 resident lay brother-labourers, and 18 other monks[18] relied on coordinated physical labour. It was no small task to tend the large coppers of boiling water, beat and lift the load with wooden sticks and paddles, scrub the dirty clothes with soap on the washboards, treat various stains, work the mangles, manage the 'blue' bleach and the starch, hang out the wet loads and bring in the dry. The household used some six cases of soap, worth £5 8s in a typical year.[19] The clotheslines stretched across the courtyard of the new St Joseph's buildings and defined the space.

Washing day on Monday was followed by ironing on Tuesday. In all weather, especially in the West Australian summer, this also was tiring work, involving underrated skills. Sister Maria, and the unspecified number of 'older girls', used flat irons heated on wood stoves to press the clothes, learning by experience when the irons were hot enough but not too hot and how to keep the heavy metal clean so that ash or caught starch would not mark the clothes.

Once washed and dried, clothes also required mending; this was Wednesday's task. There was a storeroom for clothes and linen alongside the laundry.[20] When Fr Edmund McCormick gave evidence on behalf of New Norcia at

---

18   Torres, 'New Norcia Mission – Annual Report for 1908', SROWA S1644 cons652 1909/0171; 'New Norcia Mission. Annual Report for Year ending 30 June 1913', SROWA S1644 cons652 1913/1273. Fr McCormick's evidence to the 1905 Roth Royal Commission gave the number of girls in the school as 39, the number of cottages as 26, and noted 39 lay brothers with six at outstations ('The Aborigines Question: Evidence Taken by Dr Roth', *Western Mail*, 20 February 1905, 19–20). The monastic community numbered 51 in total, P. Hocking, 'Benedictine Community 1900–1905', NNA 05517.
19   Torres, New Norcia's Annual Report to Chief Protector Prinsep, 10 September 1906, NNA 05132/96.
20   Olivey, Report, 1913.

the Roth Royal Commission in 1905 he highlighted 'a considerable amount of mending for the community' over 'their own cooking and washing under the superintendence of the sisters' and 'light' work gathering olives and helping to make the olive oil.[21] In the same year, the monastery purchased 40 yards (or about 36 metres) of material for dresses at 8 pence a yard, and spent £15 on 'underclothing, aprons and hoods'. Seventy pairs of shoes cost £24 10s and repairs to shoes, no doubt by the monastery's bootmaker, were priced at £14.[22] Inspector Olivey called on a Wednesday and saw how 'the elder girls make all their own clothes and do all the mending and repairing'. The sewing reached a high standard.[23]

St Joseph's had a well-established reputation for embroidered fancy work. In 1908 Lady Bedford visited with her husband, the governor of Western Australia, and was given 'some choice specimens of … work', presumably embroidery, by the sisters and 'one of the native girls'.[24] By 1914 it was the abbot's view that 'every year [they] gain prizes and certificates of merit at the local annual exhibition for their needlework'.[25] Travel either by coach or on foot for the 10 miles to the Yarawindah Hall to see the exhibits at the Victoria Plains Show had become a tradition.[26] The sewing in particular was a sign to the inspector of the careful training the girls were receiving. For the abbot, their practical domestic skills were 'so as to put them in a position to become useful in their future life',[27] equivalent to trade training and farm work for the boys. Perhaps the training bore fruit. At the start of the school year in 1913 Sr Ita from St Gertrude's wrote to Abbot Torres needing help with the separate laundry work there, hoping for 'some arrangement as to getting the native women to help us'.[28] If the girls who had refused to wash in the stand-off of 1908 were still in town they might have found something more like employment to fit their skills. Perhaps or perhaps not. The written records do not tell us, but later generations of Aboriginal women were paid for work at the colleges.[29]

---

21   'The Aborigines Question', *Western Mail*, 20 February 1905, 19–20.
22   Torres to Prinsep, 10 September 1906.
23   Olivey, Report, 1913.
24   *Western Mail*, 14 November 1908, 33.
25   Torres, 'New Norcia Mission. Annual Report for Year ending 30 June 1913', SROWA S1644 cons652 1913/1273. See also *Chronicle*, 12 September 1906.
26   *Chronicle*, 15 September 1909, 28 August 1907. See also *Western Mail*, 12 October 1907, 9.
27   New Norcia Mission Annual Report, 1911, SROWA S1644 cons652 1911/1475.
28   Sr Ita to Torres, 26 February 1913. Archives of the Sisters of St Joseph of the Sacred Heart, South Perth.
29   Veronica Willaway, Interview, Nebraska, June 2014.

4. ST JOSEPH'S NATIVE SCHOOL AND ORPHANAGE

Alongside the new laundry, the kitchen at St Joseph's had been renovated.[30] It was another site of practical training and opens out consideration of essential domestic work one step further.

Kitchen and food

Cooking was labour intensive. Olivey noted the cooperative work: 'two half-caste girls were doing the cooking under the supervision of a Sister'. Observing the work in progress, he found that the kitchen and dining room were 'perfectly clean and in order'.[31] Large cast-iron pots, pans and ladles testify to slow-cooking in bulk on the wood-fired stove, and occasional lists of supplies compiled for accounting purposes take us closer to the food that might have been on the table. Abbot Torres advised the Chief Protector Henry Prinsep of the cost and amount of food supplied 'for the native children of the colleges' in 1905.[32] Between the beginning of July 1914 and the end of June 1915, someone at the monastery was keeping a record of the meat, bread, milk and other produce supplied to all four of the schools across the road and making rough calculations about the value of what was provided or bought.

The lists are anything but a menu, but they suggest a diet in which meat and bread were staples, along with flour, sugar, rice, macaroni and tea. We know that in 1914 and 1915 this was supplemented by fruit, especially when the grapes and oranges were in season, milk (although none was supplied in March or April 1915), some vegetables, and other 'sundries', like the 140 pounds (64 kg) of garbanzo beans (or chickpeas) scratched at the bottom of the page as an afterthought and costing 12 shillings.[33] It seems that the community of about 30 at St Joseph's used an average of 278 pounds (126 kg) of meat each month. This averages out at nearly 2 pounds 10 ounces (1.2 kg) per person per week, with higher provision in winter than summer.[34] Bread from the bakery ran to 2,392 loaves for the period, or about two loaves each week for each St Joseph's resident. If the figures for St Gertrude's are averaged to take account of the lull in their kitchen during the school holidays, meals there involved comparably more meat each week, about 3 pounds (1.3 kg) per person, with half as

---

30 *Chronicle*, 3 April 1908.
31 Olivey, Report, 1913.
32 Torres to Prinsep, 10 September 1906.
33 Cashbook, 1914–1915, NNA 2969A/48, 86–93.
34 A total of 4lb 6oz (1.8 kg) per person each week in the winter of 1914 compared to just over 1lb a week, or about 60 g each, in the summer of 1915.

much bread. At the same time, the boys at St Mary's were eating more: each resident there accounted for something over 5 pounds (2.5 kg) of meat a week and a loaf and a bit of bread. Only bread and meat were allocated separately to the Aboriginal boys, but we know their meals were carried across town from St Joseph's kitchen, so it is possible that both institutions shared St Joseph's other stores: the 4 gallons (15 litres) of milk each week, the 10 dozen oranges for the season, some five dozen lemons, and the 304 pounds (138 kg) of grapes. There was also vinegar, olive oil, wine, £1 1s worth of macaroni, 'fowls' to the value of £3 1s and a turkey in May 1915. It is likely that St Joseph's own hens supplied eggs and perhaps other birds for the table. Certainly the fowl-yard girls in later generations trapped and tended wild ducks and pigeons.[35] Of the kitchens being supplied, it was only St Joseph's that drew an allocation of sheep's heads and livers, at an average of 15 of each, every week, and a record 81 for the month of January 1915. Consumption of other meat was at its lowest in this month. As it was summer perhaps the sisters used the offal to make brawn, but soup was a staple and more likely.

Sheep's head soup was a mainstay at St Joseph's through the years when the monastery did its own butchering, until the early 1960s. It features in oral accounts of St Joseph's as both a horror memory and a focus for cheerfully macabre stories of 'fighting for the eyes'.[36] Whether Maria Harispe drew on recipes from her home country of Paraguay where eyes of various animals were used in *tapas*, or whether the broth at St Joseph's followed the directions from classic British cookbooks that added 'forcemeat balls' of the tongue and brains baked in breadcrumbs as something like croutons,[37] the experience stayed with the Aboriginal girls as distinctive of their childhoods.

The *Golden Wattle Cookbook*, icon of housewifery in Western Australia through the twentieth century, set its sheep's head soup recipe between one for scotch broth and one for tomato soup.[38] It gave directions for cleaning the head and included carrots, turnips, onions and celery once the broth had simmered. In this version brains and tongue prepared with sage were chopped and served separately with a white sauce. From fresh ingredients to dishing up took somewhere between six and nine hours, depending on

---

35 Georgina and Mae Taylor, Interview, New Norcia, May 2017.
36 Mae Taylor, Interview, New Norcia, October 2001.
37 Mary Harrison, *The Skillful Cook: A Practical Manual of Modern Experience* (London: J. M. Dent and Sons, 1906), 85.
38 *Golden Wattle Cookery Book*, compiled by Margaret A. Wylie (Perth: E. S. Wigg and Son, 1924), 30.

how long the bones were simmered so as to soften. The whole thing turns stomachs in cultures that have lost the traditions of using the whole animal, but *powsowdie*, the Scottish sheep's head broth, and other similar dishes are enjoying a slow-food revival on gourmet and ecological grounds.[39] Such meals were promoted in British cookbooks at the turn of the century, especially during the First World War.[40] In these years the dish was a staple through the British Empire, including for breakfast.

For the other end of the day, and for celebrations, the Teresians had had a reputation for skilful baking. Whether the fine sponge cakes and *reposteria* sweets that so impressed the judges at the local show continued and whether the monks still received feast-day tubs of rich dessert *crema* is not certain.[41] We are sure, though, that Teresa Roca made the rich Spanish nougat, *turrón*, as a Christmas treat into the 1930s and probably beyond. (There was consternation when the new community at Drysdale River took the almond grinder with them for the same purpose and New Norcia's had to be replaced.[42]) As lay sisters, Maria and Teresa inherited the traditions of home-made confectionery that had supported friendship networks and income for Spanish convents since the sixteenth century.[43]

Cooking was not only fundamental in the daily routine of the town but also part of the domestic training featured at St Joseph's. One newspaper account in 1910 had noted the 'useful branches of civilised home-life' that the mysterious sisters, 'black-robed nuns', were teaching with 'exemplary patience' to pupils who seemed 'an exceptionally intelligent lot'.[44] That the girls' intelligence was directed to domestic training fitted with Salvado's principle of education for practical purposes, not roles that would be out of reach in a racist context, but there also was a classroom set aside for formal lessons.

---

39   See, for example, British Food in America, www.britishfoodinamerica.com/The-Hardship-War-Austerity-Number-Part-2/the-lyrical/An-Appreciation-of-the-sheep-s-head-both-at-the-table-and-on-the-page/#.X3QPeVllNTY; accessed 24 March 2014.
40   Nicola Humble, 'Little Swans with Luxette and Loved Boy Pudding: Changing Fashions in Cookery Books', *Women: A Cultural Review* 13 (2000): 322–38.
41   For affirmation of the Teresians' nougat, see *Chronicle*, 18 June 1905, 25 December 1906, 31 March 1907; for dessert cream, 14 July 1907.
42   Catalan to Benedictine Missionary Sisters at Drysdale River, 9 January 1933, NNA 01434 f.17.
43   Rachel Laudan, 'Convent Sweets', in *Oxford Companion to Sugar and Sweets*, ed. Darra Goldstein (Oxford: Oxford University Press, 2015); Eddy Stols, 'The Expansion of the Sugar Market in Western Europe', in *Tropical Babylons: Sugar and the Making of the Atlantic World, 1450–1680*, ed. Stuart B. Schwartz (Chapel Hill: University of North Carolina Press, 2011), 242–43.
44   James Thompson, 'Three Thousand Mile Trip', *Western Mail,* 5 November 1910, 44, 23.

Classroom

Five years after Torres abandoned hopes for the *colegia de nativas*, there were few signs of academic ambition at St Joseph's and no institutional memory of the hope for integrated education at St Gertrude's, but educational success was still measured in traditional European terms. In the single 'airy and well-ventilated' room on the south side of the quadrangle, Inspector Olivey reported some girls wrote, others sewed, while 'a few of the youngest [were] learning to keep quiet'.[45] The school program meant that 'most of them read and write fairly well … and they could count a little, but that is about all'.[46] The sister in charge, more likely to have been Elias than Consuelo, in conversation with the English-speaking inspector told him that she had little success in teaching geography or mathematics, but the report affirmed the children's 'intelligent interest in their work and play' and found they 'seemed perfectly happy and contented'.[47]

Whether we take the assessment of institutional happiness at face value or not, there were tensions between the mission and the children's families, with schooling as the touchstone. In these years, the conflict was not because children were being compelled to remain but because New Norcia did not have the power to overrule their parents. In the month following Olivey's visit, Abbot Torres urged the department to impose the requirements of the *Elementary Education Act* for compulsory schooling 'until 14 or 16', arguing 'it would not be doing any violence to Native parents to oblige them to send their boys and girls here to be trained and educated'.[48] Torres, who was apparently unaware of the Act's provisions to exclude Aboriginal children from state schools,[49] had also not modified his approach since the wholesale rejection of combined classes at St Gertrude's. If 'parents of our white children even at the furtherest end of the state don't look upon this [schooling at New Norcia] as any sacrifice',[50] why should Aboriginal families object? The Benedictine sisters did not propose a solution but 'admitted feeling much discouragement'[51] because promising pupils left.

---

45 Olivey, Report, 1913.
46 Olivey, Report, 1913.
47 Olivey, Report, 1913.
48 Torres, Annual Report to the Chief Protector, 1913.
49 Anna Haebich, *For Their Own Good: Aborigines and Government in the South West of Western Australia 1900–1940* (Nedlands, WA: University of Western Australia Press for the Charles and Joy Staples South West Region Publications Fund, 1992), 88–9, 133, 166–68.
50 Torres, Annual Report to the Chief Protector, 1913.
51 Olivey, Report, 1913.

As evidence of the work being done, the inspector attached samples of writing from five of the children, from 7 to 11 years old. Across town at the boys' school directed by Br Luis Arrufat the sense of disconnection between the school and its context is strong, even absurd. Nine-year-old Patrick Yapo Williams was working from a *Philips' Semi-Upright Copybook* on phrases concerning 'the four great bulwarks of English liberty' and the impact of the 'Great and Glorious Revolution'; Charles Sandstone's copybook showed a fine hand after two years at school. Placid Farrell's 'Story of Some Hot Water', featuring the Irish Marquis of Worcester in prison, was 'the most advanced'. At St Joseph's the focus was closer to home. Olivey filed work by Mary Stack, Louisa Ingram and Christine Picket, who had each written out the Lord's Prayer from memory and completed a dictation test. We can hope the gauche tribute to the sisters signals that it was worded by the inspector:

> Yesterday we went to the bush, and had a very nice time. Sister said she would take us again next week if we are good children. We will try our best and please the kind Sisters who are so good to us. They wish us to be not only good and obedient, but also *clever*. Friday will be our day for the bush.[52]

Two of the three writers capitalised 'Bush', hinting at the significance of this tradition of days out of town that dated back to Salvado and connected to life before the mission. Spelling 'obedient' was a challenge, but the virtue was taken more for granted in this system than the underlined quality of being 'clever'.

Transmitting a clear sense of Catholic values had been a priority outranking simple 'cleverness' since the time of Salvado. While shared values meant more than doctrine and a knowledge of Catholic observance, there was a sense in which the church at the centre of town was also an extension of the classroom. The daily routine copied carefully at the end of Olivey's report specified morning prayer and Mass at six o'clock in the morning, and evening prayer at six-thirty at night. Twice a week in the evenings from December 1906 there was a short sermon in the church in English, something of an innovation in the Spanish mission where most prayer was in Latin. The adult workers from the cottages were expected to attend this

---

52   Olivey, Report, 1913, appended, original emphasis.

weekday session, as well as Sunday Mass.[53] In 1913, the girls impressed Olivey with their 'devout attention' and the 'careful training' behind their capacity to sing hymns and part-songs and to recite well.[54]

The Benedictine focus on liturgical prayer meant music and singing was not a refinement so much as a practical skill for the life of the wider community. Expertise in domestic work counted for a lot in the regime at St Joseph's, as we have seen, but music also held a place in the timetable. New Norcia's tradition of congregational singing was flourishing, and the girls' choir as well as the boys' continued to give the liturgical responses. Both practices put New Norcia ahead of the changes that would come 50 years later at the Second Vatican Council.[55]

Music and ritual bridged the secular and sacred. The monastery recorded events that stood out of the normal liturgical round, from the stark vigils of prayer before major feasts[56] to the crashing noise at the end of Good Friday's *tenebrae*. This loud *fragor* was meant to evoke the earthquake of Christ's Passion for the monks, but the *Chronicle* admitted it was simply the 'best part of the entire Office for the children'.[57] Celebrations with a liturgical edge also included a 'vigil' held by a bonfire on the eve of Holy Trinity and the dancing which followed, probably led by Aboriginal musician Paul Piramino.[58] Visitors had long been impressed by the 'relish and artistry'[59] of the Aboriginal dances at New Norcia and joined in alongside women from neighbouring farms, so that 'they were dancing one European with one Aborigine'.[60] New Norcia's tradition of modesty set limits. When the girls were keen to 'match steps with the boys … the Sisters told them to pull back, as was fitting'.[61] Folk dancing could cross the racial line but it was only safe when it was single-sex. The gendered division of the town was second nature in a monastic environment, and increasingly New Norcia's authorities were concerned to maintain the boundary of the mission itself.

---

53 *Chronicle*, 7 December 1906.
54 Olivey, Report, 1913.
55 Eladio Ros, 'Music at New Norcia: A Historical Survey, First Period', unpublished manuscript, NNA S13.A3.4, 40.
56 *Chronicle*, 20 April 1905, 28 March 1907, 30 May 1907.
57 *Chronicle*, 27 March 1907.
58 For more on Paul Piramino, see Ros, 'Music at New Norcia', 67; Anna Haebich, *Dancing in Shadows: Histories of Nyungar Performance* (Crawley, WA: UWA Publishing, 2018), 123, 144–70.
59 Santos Salvado to Sr Gertrude, Compostella, describing a dance in 1878, cited in Ros, 'Music at New Norcia', 41.
60 *Chronicle*, 25 May 1907.
61 *Chronicle*, 25 May 1907.

4. ST JOSEPH'S NATIVE SCHOOL AND ORPHANAGE

This concern with the limits of influence pervades the monastery's reports in this decade. Alongside confidence in the work at St Joseph's, an anxiety that the mission would be undermined by influences outside its control was a steady theme. In the months after Olivey's visit in 1913 the abbot summarised that St Joseph's was 'happy and successful', the girls were hard-working, beautifully behaved, in good health and 'well worthy of their faithful teachers'. He maintained that 'they are not treated as orphans but more like the children of "the well-to-do"'.[62] And in that clanging phrase there is the rub.

The abbot and the sisters were increasingly conscious that the wider Aboriginal community was not 'well-to-do'. While they certainly knew some girls had families in town and elsewhere, they were keen to protect all the residents from influences beyond the mission. Abbot Torres wrote tellingly of 'our Natives' and the hope for segregation:

> On the whole we are very satisfied with the work we have done for our Native charges during the past year and we hope it may be productive of future good for all concerned, but we fear much of this good may be jeopardised when 'our Natives' hereafter get mixed up with their fellows outside of whom no care whatsoever is taken, and we regret many of these are growing up in the vicinity of New Norcia.[63]

The question of the limits of the mission underpins one case on the public record in which Consuelo played a key role as director at St Joseph's. It shows us the dynamics around St Joseph's as a site and the web of subtle and not so subtle assumptions in play as Consuelo interacted with an Aboriginal family.

In mid-January 1917 Sister Consuelo wrote to the state's Chief Protector of Aborigines to put the case of an Aboriginal woman; she is named in the record, but let us call her 'J.'[64] It was rare for anyone at New Norcia except the abbot or his deputy to write to the government, but Consuelo initiated this exchange. She chose to write to the government instead of consulting the monks, and she named herself superintendent of the institution. Heavily pregnant, J. had arrived at the mission sometime around

---

62 Torres, Annual Report to Chief Protector, 1913.
63 Torres, Annual Report to Chief Protector, 1913.
64 Consuelo to Office of the Chief Protector, 14 January 1917, 'Sr Consuelo. New Norcia. Reporting That Native Woman Recently Living with Indian John Michael Is in a Destitute Condition', SROWA S1644 cons652 1917/0331.

Christmas with her common-law husband, M., and their five-year-old daughter, D. According to the mission, they asked to place their daughter at St Joseph's but, after a few days, 'as the youngster was continually crying, the sister [Consuelo] advised the father to take her back'.[65] M. did this, but then he left New Norcia almost immediately, leaving D. with her mother 'in one of the cottages without food or clothing',[66] so that both came each day to St Joseph's for provisions.[67] The little girl would have been welcome to live in, and the abbot assumed she was already there, but when J. 'begged to be admitted also into the Orphanage',[68] she was refused because her pregnancy was, as the abbot put it later, 'not adifying [sic] to the larger girls'.[69] Consuelo arranged that another Aboriginal woman in another cottage would take them in, while the mission provided food and clothes.[70] Significantly for our understanding of the site, Consuelo enforced a boundary between St Joseph's and the cottages: first in response to D.'s crying distress, and then, more resolutely, to uphold a moral code against unmarried pregnancy.

Some two weeks passed with the mother and daughter in a cottage at New Norcia and the father somewhere else unspecified. Then, acting on J.'s request, Consuelo asked the Chief Protector for a train ticket to Guildford so that J. could go to the 'old women's shelter'[71] to give birth. Either informed by J. or drawing her own conclusions because, as she told the Chief Protector, 'his own wife is still living',[72] Consuelo assumed the man was not coming back. Consuelo put the case starkly to the Chief Protector:

> She is in a most destitute state: no one in the cottages around will give her shelter. We await your answer to see what can be done for her.[73]

The Chief Protector's office checked their files of 'personal particulars' but could find no information. They decided a ticket to Perth would be more appropriate and sent one, asking Consuelo to fill in the appropriate names.

---

65 Catalan to Chief Protector, 8 February 1917, NNA 01418/131.
66 Catalan to Chief Protector, 8 February 1917.
67 Consuelo to Office of the Chief Protector, 14 January 1917.
68 Catalan to Chief Protector, 8 February 1917.
69 Catalan to Chief Protector, 8 February 1917.
70 Catalan to Chief Protector, 8 February 1917.
71 Consuelo to Office of the Chief Protector, 14 January 1917.
72 Consuelo to Office of the Chief Protector, 14 January 1917.
73 Consuelo to Office of the Chief Protector, 14 January 1917.

Figure 4.5: Cottages for Aboriginal workers and families in front of St Gertrude's College; St Joseph's rear left.
Source: NNA 74433P.

If the story ended here, we would see Consuelo had intervened on behalf of J., perhaps to some good effect. But at the same time, J. received a letter from M. enclosing money for a fare to Guildford. Consuelo's advice was to travel on through Guildford to Perth. Perhaps she was being obedient to the Chief Protector, perhaps she was unpersuaded that a de facto relationship could be stable, perhaps she did not think M. would be there at all; J. disagreed and insisted she would go to join M. in Guildford. As the abbot reported it later, J. 'became insolent and abusive'[74] towards Consuelo. We do not know, however, whether this was before or after Consuelo took the decision that five-year-old D. would not travel with her mother.

It is not clear what form the confrontation took, or whether it happened at New Norcia or at the Mogumber station, but on the file copy of Consuelo's telegram advising the Chief Protector to 'please meet Aboriginal woman [J.] going train to Perth', there is a departmental note that 'arrangements have been made to stop the train at Guildford'.[75] Someone, perhaps in

---

74 Catalan to Chief Protector, 8 February 1917, NNA 00918.
75 Telegram, 26 January 1917, SROWA S1644 cons652 1917/0331.

the face of J.'s distraught insistence, overruled Consuelo on the matter of destination. This was on a Friday. An undated letter from M. to the Chief Protector, written within the week, protests that his wife is 'too much upset' and 'worrying and fretting night and day for her child'.[76] The following Friday, 2 February 1917, the Chief Protector wrote to Abbot Catalan, restating J.'s anxiety and the parents' hope to have D. sent to Guildford. He asked with bureaucratic flourish to hear 'the reasons which actuated you in retaining the child'.[77] The abbot replied with the details of the initial involvement of the mission, reiterating the parents were not married, noting that D. and her parents were all Catholics, by which he may have meant that the mission had some authority to judge in this matter. He reported that J. 'willingly left the child at the Orphanage' and that D., 'now accustomed to the other little ones', was 'still very happy' there.[78] The Chief Protector sent the police to ask M. to call in again and wrote to the abbot again on 20 February, advising that both parents 'appear to be emphatic in their desire to have the child returned to them'. The new baby had arrived, a son, and 'J. appears to be well able to look after the little girl'.[79] On Monday, 26 February, word was sent to M. that the abbot was sending his daughter, and on Thursday, 1 March 1917, her parents met D. from the morning train at Guildford. The Chief Protector wrote to thank the abbot.

In this one instance of church and state implementing provisions for the 'protection' of Aboriginal Australians, the determined struggle of the Aboriginal parents to keep their daughter is compelling. The role of the sisters and their institution is also striking. Turning the pages of the file, St Joseph's fills multiple roles: networked with the cottages, while answerable to both the government and the monastery; offering support, while also implementing racist and moralising policies. The conflict between Consuelo and J. also moved quickly to become a wider drama played on a masculine stage. As Consuelo overruled J. to keep the child at St Joseph's, so M. appealed to the Chief Protector, and the Chief Protector sought advice from the abbot and then overruled that advice on his own assessment of the situation. Perhaps as the situation played out Consuelo also began to advocate that the little girl should go to Guildford, but we do not hear her voice. Consuelo was in direct contact with J. before any other

---

76 'M' to Chief Protector, n.d. but probably 29 January 1917, SROWA S1644 cons652 1917/0331.
77 Chief Protector to Catalan, 2 February 1917, SROWA S1644 cons652 1917/0331.
78 Catalan to Chief Protector, 8 February 1917.
79 Chief Protector to Catalan, 20 February 1917, SROWA S1644 cons652 1917/0331.

figure of authority and could marshal resources for her as well as disrupt plans. She did not hesitate to intervene with the authority of the mission, but ultimately she did not determine events. For the Chief Protector and for the abbot, her role was entirely ancillary to theirs and would not determine policy. As this case shows, St Joseph's might have looked like a distinct institution at the edge of town but it was not autonomous.

Through 1917, tension deepened around Consuelo's role. Two issues mingle in the records: questions about the extent of her authority at St Joseph's merge with hints that her approach to religious life was out of step with the abbot and the other sisters. In the end, her decision that there was no space for her in New Norcia adds another layer to this chapter's spatial reading of St Joseph's. It points to ongoing tension between a vision for vowed obedience in the women's community, on the one hand, and aspirations for independent missionary work, on the other.

Consuelo and St Joseph's: No separate sphere

Consuelo's life was apparently increasingly fraught as she sought to protect a sphere of influence in a context where her loyalty was mistrusted. The warm regard she had enjoyed 10 years earlier had apparently faded, and there was scant respect for the missionary role she claimed for herself. The conflict also reflected dynamics within the monastic community itself where opinion was running against Consuelo's long-time supporter Fr Roberto Bas, and where Abbot Catalan himself was coming to grips with his new authority. In the midst of change, New Norcia was a quagmire of strong emotion. Consuelo found the ground slipping under her feet.

In March 1917, just one week after she had been overruled in her tussle with the Chief Protector and five-year-old D. had left New Norcia, Consuelo appealed to have St Joseph's exempted from the normal structure of monastic authority. Abbot Catalan was setting out for Europe, accompanied by Fr Roberto, and had left his prior, Fr Luis Tubau, in charge. Consuelo clearly felt she could not work with the young monk Tubau and wrote to propose an alternative. The note, sent 'in some distress'[80] to the abbot at the boat in Fremantle, shows her navigating

---

80   Consuelo to Catalan, 8 March 1917, NNA 00918.

awkward territory. She wanted permission to 'deal with Fr Castenares in everything that concerns the house and the girls with the exception of anything in which there is the intervention of the Chief Protector'.[81] She knew she risked confirming a reputation for being difficult and was at pains to reassure the abbot that the request was 'not made by one who has the intention of quarrelling with anyone'.[82] Rather, she framed her request to circumvent monastic authority in spiritual terms. Consuelo underscored her intention for *paz y caridad* and saw a divine test in the community's tensions: 'my resolutions are for *peace* and *charity* and to benefit greatly from this sacrifice that God asks in order to sanctify me'.[83] We do not know whether Abbot Catalan replied.

Conflict continued through 1917, apparently focused on the assumption that Consuelo's work was under the direction of the abbot and at the disposal of the monastery. At issue was the abbot's expectation and direction that Consuelo would sew for the monks. Consuelo found this 'unacceptable'.[84] She specifically refused to make new scapulars for a group of junior monks who made their profession on 6 November 1917. On the day of the profession Consuelo wrote to the abbot revealing their unresolved dispute about her role and responsibilities. She had been trying to speak to him since his own letter had affronted her in mid-October, but now she resorted to putting pen to paper:

> Although you have told me not to write I see I am obliged to do so, as it is three weeks since I indicated I needed to speak to you privately and you have not given me an audience.
>
> I suppose you remember that on 26 September last, my state, obligations and tasks at the Mission were under discussion, and the matter was pending, and so you will understand my wish to have things arranged soon. On 14 October I received a letter from you with such categorical phrases that surprised me very much, since I had not committed myself to anything and consequently Fr do not expect to make any further habits. If you would like a further verbal explanation, I will provide it.[85]

---

81 Consuelo to Catalan, 8 March 1917.
82 Consuelo to Catalan, 8 March 1917.
83 Consuelo to Catalan, 8 March 1917, original emphasis.
84 Consuelo to Catalan, 6 November 1917, NNA 00918.
85 Consuelo to Catalan, 6 November 1917.

Discussion did not resolve the matter. Four days later Consuelo wrote to advise the abbot that she would be leaving New Norcia; she reminded him of a financial contract agreed with Abbot Torres in 1912 that would come into effect.[86] Her claim for payment as a worker exercised Abbot Catalan, but he was even more clear that Consuelo could not leave town dressed as a sister, wearing the habit 'that distinguishes the other Sisters from the rest of the ladies of the world'.[87] He even apparently suggested that she should leave St Joseph's immediately and do the necessary dressmaking elsewhere, staying with Juan and Catalina Casellas. In the abbot's view, the household of the monastery's woodcarver was a better venue for secular dressmaking. But Consuelo assured him that plan would only draw more attention from the girls and that she could prepare discreetly enough at 'home', at St Joseph's.[88]

While Consuelo prepared to leave town, the abbot wrote to his lawyer about the monastery's financial obligations. Catalan later told the Apostolic Delegate that they found the record of her oblation, but they could not find a contract; none of the other sisters were contracted.[89] Negotiations took on an air of intrigue. A week after announcing Consuelo was to leave and reporting the advice that she should be paid £1 a week, the *Chronicle* noted the abbot was setting out to Perth to seek further information. The writer exploded and marked his text with exaggerated dots of ink to lament the absence of real information:

> And…Incombustible Reader! Here at this point…I am more convinced this 'chronicle' is full of nothing but nonsense and great trivialities. That someone comes, that another goes, that a frog fa[rts].[90]

By the following day, the diarist had recovered and announced that 'the disgraced Miss Consuelo' had been sent away. He recorded the venomous wish that Fr Bas, outspoken and opinionated, would meet this same fate as 'his prodigy', this 'pious penitent'.[91] But Fr Roberto remained, and it was in fact another 10 days before Consuelo left New Norcia.

---

86   Consuelo to Catalan, 10 November 1917, NNA 00918.
87   Catalan to Consuelo, 26 November 1917, NNA 01418/79.
88   Consuelo to Catalan, 10 November 1917.
89   Catalan to Cattaneo, 17 June 1921, NNA 01849.
90   *Chronicle*, 20 November 1917, original ellipses.
91   *Chronicle*, 21 November 1917.

While the furious negotiations about financial reparation for Consuelo's work continued, Maria Harispe made a rare intervention in writing. In an undated letter, she assessed the situation for the abbot in terms that disparaged Consuelo. Her focus is the dressmaking, but the implication is that Consuelo is, as usual, outside monastic norms. Maria reported that Consuelo was making not two but four dresses, and various blouses, and was altering a habit and using two lengths of fabric that had been bought for the girls. Maria thought all of this was improper but predicted that Consuelo would explain it away: 'you know how smoothly she talks'.[92] The letter suggests that opinion was united against Consuelo. Maria was frank about the relief she would feel when Consuelo was gone; her regret was only for what she saw as the loss of Consuelo's religious vocation:

> It seems to me Father, that if she goes and leaves us in peace she does us a great favour. … She is very content and I (although I want her to go, as it seems right to me) sometimes I am more sad than happy to think that after having left the world for so many years she is so content to return to it.[93]

Consuelo herself did not see her departure as repudiating a vocation. In her farewell letter to Catalan she first made her claim for a full £282, not the £250 he had furnished, and then asserted her conscience:

> I am sorry to have to take this step, but I am convinced that this is the will of God. Forgive me what has been lacking, and commend me well to God.[94]

Her motives are lost to us, and assessments of her are contested, but this could have been a declaration that God outranked the abbot and the expectations of the community.

Consuelo left New Norcia, but she did not return to Spain or Mexico. Instead, as Miss Batiz, she took a position as a 'sewing teacher' at Carrolup in the southwest of Western Australia, near Katanning, at a settlement run by the United Aborigines Mission. She applied for a certificate of naturalisation, declaring it was 'her intention to remain in Australia',[95] with references from Richard Lanigan, Jeremiah Clune and Charles

---

92 Maria Harispe to Catalan, n.d. but November 1917, NNA 00918.
93 Maria Harispe to Catalan, n.d. but November 1917.
94 Consuelo to Catalan, 26 November 1917, NNA 00918.
95 M. C. [Consuelo] Batiz to Secretary of Home and Territories Department, 24 June 1918, National Archives of Australia, NAA A1, 1919/1216 37354 f.20.

4. ST JOSEPH'S NATIVE SCHOOL AND ORPHANAGE

Davidson, all neighbours at New Norcia. This move to an evangelical Protestant mission station to work as a sewing teacher with Aboriginal people, rather than remain at New Norcia and sew at the abbot's direction for the monks, underlines Consuelo's conviction about the purpose of her return to Australia. Her sense of missionary identity that outweighed her original commitment to the Teresian sisters now enabled her to break her connection to New Norcia and probably to minimise, if not compromise, her commitment to Roman Catholicism.

Consuelo was still at Carrolup in 1921 when she reopened her claim for further funds from New Norcia through the Apostolic Delegate, the representative of the Vatican in Australia.[96] She may have been prompted by rumours that Carrolup was to be closed. When that proved true and most of the people were moved to the Moore River Settlement, a mere 6 miles (9.5 km) from New Norcia, Consuelo's nerve failed. By January 1922 she was in Mexico City. The Apostolic Delegate passed on her new address to Abbot Catalan, urging him to defray her travelling expenses.[97] The abbot wrote to Mary Consuelo Batiz the following day to close the matter, noting: 'already we have done more than charity requires'.[98] He wished her a prosperous New Year and 'goodbye'.

* * * * *

The community of Benedictine sisters probably never heard that Consuelo had been in touch with New Norcia. The tension of her time with them had eased, and attention had turned to the need for new members. In September 1918 Abbot Catalan wrote, at the suggestion of Teresa Roca, to one of her priest friends in Barcelona, to ask him to recommend other women, around 30 years old, 'who have a spirit of sacrifice and good will to live in the Orphanage with the native girls and work in this Mission for the Glory of God and the good of these poor souls'.[99] They hoped for up to six responses.

It was the first of many recruiting letters that Abbot Catalan would send on behalf of the sisters through his long tenure in office, and it sounded the domestic note that would inform them all: 'once in this Mission

---

96   Apostolic Delegation to Batiz, Ref 607/21, 23 July 1921. Copy at NNA 01849.
97   Apostolic Delegation to Abbot Catalan, Ref 1102/21, 17 January 1922. Copy at NNA 01849.
98   Catalan to Consuelo, 23 January 1922, NNA 01424/12.
99   Catalan to Rd. Sr. D. Luis Brugado, 27 September 1918, NNA 01418–01421/473.

[the sisters] will be considered like family'.[100] The mission would provide 'all the necessities of life'.[101] While Abbot Catalan was thinking in financial terms, the statement would prove to be true on other levels as well. As surely as any family, New Norcia would have the capacity to transform their lives, nurture their hopes, and break their hearts.

---

100 Catalan to Brugado, 27 September 1918.
101 Catalan to Brugado, 27 September 1918.

5

Agencia Benedictina: Burgos, Belgium and the Kimberley

Steadily, over a dozen years, women came to New Norcia to join the Benedictine sisters, travelling alone or in twos and threes among the parties of aspiring monks that left Spain with the abbot. By the early 1930s the community of women missionaries had grown to 14. As this chapter will show, more members enabled the abbot to send his 'oblate sisters' to open the long-awaited convent at Drysdale River in the Kimberley. In turn, the first branch house in the Kimberley reinforced the need for equally long-awaited formal structures, finally pursued in the mid-1930s through Benedictine networks in Belgium. Teresa Roca and Abbot Catalan had hoped new recruits would come from Barcelona. Certainly, their network of friends close to the international port gave them invaluable practical support as young missionaries prepared to leave Spain, but the heart of the effort was the inland city of Burgos. The medieval capital of Castile and its surrounding farming villages proved to be the hub of an informal *Agencia Benedictina* in these years.

Although the community's hopes were fixed on Spain, the first new arrivals came from Sydney. One, who was briefly known as Mechtilde, enquired about joining in June 1919 and evidently arrived in New Norcia only to be 'headed for the Good Shepherd Sisters in the suburbs'[1] on 7 October 1920 for reasons the *Chronicle* does not explain. The other, Nellie Banks,

---

1 'Chronicle of the Benedictine Community of New Norcia' (hereafter *Chronicle*), 7 October 1920, New Norcia Archives (NNA). See also Catalan to [Mechtilde], 10 June 1919, NNA 01421/95.

131

telegraphed that she was on her way a week later. She was a widow, aged 42, from Drummoyne in Sydney's inner west, born in Redfern.[2] There was no mention of the mission itself in her correspondence with Fr Rios, the monastery's prior, only the hope she had held for some nine years, 'to live and work for my God in the best manner He has chosen for me'.[3] Evidently warned about the rural focus of the community, she declared herself ready: 'I might mention I have never done heavy work in my life, but am afraid of nothing'.[4]

Nellie arrived in mid-October and everyone at New Norcia was keen to see whether she would 'persevere' as an Anglo-Australian in the community.[5] When she made her formal commitment as an oblate on the evening of 10 March 1921 the *Chronicle* lapsed into English to record her new name: Sister Mary Gertrude. The diary noted:

> This Lady has been in the Orphanage for our native girls since 16 October last year. She is happy with this kind of life, and the other Sisters are satisfied with her comportment. At the end of the ceremony [Abbot Catalan] preached on the monastic state, congratulating her on her good resolutions and commending them to perseverance.[6]

Among the community of sisters and monks assembled in the church to witness Gertrude's public commitment at St Benedict's altar were two young women who had been at the mission for just three weeks. They were the first of 11 from Burgos who came between 1921 and 1933 to spend the rest of their lives as Benedictine women.

Burgos and missionary tradition

The first two Spanish postulants, and all the sisters bar one who came in the years before the Spanish Civil War, were village girls from scattered farming settlements west of Burgos; their average age was 19. We can piece together a roll-call of their arrivals. Isobel Pampliega from the small village of Cañizar de los Ajos was 18 and Perpetua Perez Santamaria from the neighbouring

---

2   Copy of baptismal certificate, NNA 01365; 'Some History of Redfern', Creative Spirits, www.creativespirits.info/australia/new-south-wales/sydney/redfern; accessed 12 January 2008.
3   Ellen Banks to Fr Rios, 10 February 1920, NNA 01365.
4   Banks to Rios, 10 February 1920.
5   *Chronicle*, 16 October 1920.
6   *Chronicle*, 10 March 1921.

village of Palacios de Benaber was 21 when they sailed into Fremantle with the abbot and 11 young men for the monastery on the *Osterley* from London on 17 February 1921.[7] They made their commitment on 25 May 1921 at the same public altar in New Norcia's church, taking the names Sister Felicitas and Sister Margarita (quickly known mostly as Margaret). In 1925 Erestina Gozalo and Concepción Martinez, both teenagers from Cavia, came on the *Mooltan* to become Sister Benita and Sister Escolastica. Three more young women left villages near Burgos in 1928 to make their way by train to Barcelona and then Marseilles, sailing from there on the *Comorin*: Benilde Ruiz Bebere from Tapia de Villadiego was 19 years old when she became Sister Hildegard; 17-year-old Martina Cidad Simón from Sasamón became Sister Maria; and Carmen de la Fuente, aged 16, also from Tapia, became Sister Matilde. Aurora Marcos, who became Sister Ludivina, was born in the same year as Sister Margaret Perez and also came from Palacios de Benaber,[8] but she arrived a decade later, in April 1931, and so she was 31 when she joined the community. Ludivina came on the *Ormonde* with Trinidad Lopez, who was from the same village and who briefly took the name Sr Edita but did not continue with the community.[9] Felisa Ruiz de la Barga, who arrived in October 1933, was also older than usual: the future Sister Magdelena, from Cavia where her father was a miller, was 26. Her companions on the *Otranto*, however, were among the youngest. Andrea Pardo Lopez from the hamlet of Villorejo became Sister Francisca at 16, and Pilar Catalan was just 15 when she became Sister Placida. Pilar, daughter of Abbot Catalan's cousin and from the neighbouring province of Navarra, not Burgos, was the twelfth and last recruit before the Spanish Civil War. She arrived at Corella's railway station in pigtails and a child's short skirt but suddenly understood the journey differently when she met the others, 'so grown up' in skirts to their ankles and swept-up hair.[10]

Each of these young women had a personal account of their decision to join a Benedictine mission in Australia, a drama or romance, a story of faith, family tradition, pragmatism, intuition or decision. The personal stories were bound together by a common rural heritage in settlements no more than 30 kilometres apart and threaded into a whole by referrals that flowed to New Norcia's abbot as he travelled through parishes and convents in the province.

---

7   Incoming passenger list, *Osterley*, National Archives of Australia, NAA K269 (Barcode 30151233). See also *Chronicle*, 15 November 1920.
8   Sr Lorenza Diez to Abbot Catalan, 28 August 1948, NNA 01442–01456.
9   Maria Gratia Balagot, Visitación Cidad and Teresa González, email communication, 13 July 2014.
10 Pilar Catalan in conversation, Madrid, September 2010.

Figure 5.1: Home villages of the Benedictine sisters who arrived at New Norcia, 1921–33 (Cañizar de los Ajos, Cavia, Corella, Palacios de Benaver, Sasamón, Tapia de Villadiego and Villorejo).
Source: Map by Alejandro Polanco Masa.

Figure 5.2: The village of Tapia de Villadiego, Burgos.
Source: Archives of the Benedictine Missionary Sisters of Tutzing (ABTM).

Two communities of contemplative women in Burgos in particular were fundamental to the foundation of the community of missionary women at New Norcia. Both the Benedictine nuns at the monastery of San Salvador in the village of Palacios de Benaver and the Cistercian nuns at the Abbey of Santa Maria Real at Las Huelgas in the township of Burgos itself connected young women from their networks to New Norcia. The communities of Benedictine women at Estrella and Lumbier also played a role in raising awareness of New Norcia. At one level, it was a simple and obvious move on the part of Abbot Catalan to appeal to these nuns: the mission had shimmered on the horizon of Catholic life in Burgos since at least 1883 when Rosendo Salvado had forged a link with Fr Isidoro de Lope Moral.[11]

Fr Isidoro, the parish priest of Barbadillo del Mercado, a small wool-market town near the Benedictine monks at Silos, had been Salvado's agent and the heart of a network that sent brothers and priests to New Norcia in the late nineteenth century. Such a network could certainly locate potential missionary women too. Fr Isidoro had also become chaplain to the abbey at Las Huelgas in 1899 while he was still writing to Salvado.[12] Certainly his recruiting for the missions was well within living memory in 1915 when Perpetua Perez, the future Sr Margaret, connected with the Cistercian nuns to begin five years with them as a domestic worker.[13]

The networks of friendship and family that brought young missionaries to New Norcia are also evident in the sisters' early community. For example, Felisa Ruiz kept in touch with her friend Escolastica Martinez after Escolastica left Cavia in 1925. In 1931, at the last minute, Felisa backed out of the group Abbot Catalan had gathered. In 1933, she heard through Escolastica's mother that the abbot was recruiting again and wrote to him several times, persuading him that her vocation was now solid.[14] Families were reluctant to see two daughters go so far, but at various points the Martinez, Pardo and Cidad families were each expecting another sister

---

11   Fr David Barry, email correspondence to the author, 3 August 2002, 26 August 2002.
12   Teresa De Castro, 'New Norcia's Golden Decade: Rosendo Salvado's Correspondence in the Last Years of the 19th Century (1891–1900)', *New Norcia Studies* 14 (2006): 64–107.
13   Obituary of Sr Margarita Perez Santamaria, Archives of the Benedictine Missionary Sisters of Tutzing, Carabanchel, Madrid.
14   Catalan to Escolastica Martinez, 24 July 1933, NNA 01434/190. See also Lauren Mosso, '"Your Very Affectionate Father in the Lord": The Letters of Abbot Anselmo Catalan during His Visit to Spain, July–August 1933', *New Norcia Studies* 19 (2011): 53–62.

to join their daughters Escolastica, Francisca and Maria.[15] By 1952 three of Hildegard's nieces were professed at New Norcia.[16] Brothers and male cousins were also encouraged, including in this generation Augustine Gonzalo, Adalbert Perez, Abundio Pardo and Emiliano de la Fuente. More often than not in this chain of migration the men followed their sisters, and the women let it be known they were praying for more vocations from home.

The choices to come to New Norcia were all particular. Some women were propelled into the mission by limited opportunity and the economic hardship of large families; others were drawn by the promise of purposeful service, healthy living or the conviction that God willed this life for them. Abbot Catalan's journeys to 'meet the girls' (*encontrando las chicas*) are remembered as a significant missionary effort in Benedictine houses in Burgos today,[17] along with the half-joking sense he evoked among young women with sisters or friends in Australia that 'I would be next'.[18] Joining the mission was both high drama and yet predictable enough.

In contrast to the attention given to the education and training of young men who came to New Norcia, Abbot Catalan assumed the young women needed no formal preparation for the mission. While future lay brothers trained as shoemakers, bookbinders and carpenters and in gilding and motor mechanics, and while future priests as well as brothers came after some time in formation at a European monastery or even at the archabbey of St Vincent in Pennsylvania for the foundation in the English language it would provide,[19] the sisters came straight from the villages. Like most Spanish women at this time they had had a rudimentary primary education that equipped them best for the work of a household as 'members of the family'.[20] Literacy among Spanish women through the 1930s ran at about 68 per cent.[21] All the recruits for New Norcia could read and write, but a few struggled, and there was no priority given to scholarly types.

---

15   For example, Catalan to Cipriano Martinez (brother of Escolastica), 23 February 1928, NNA 01429/21; Catalan to chaplain at Monastery of San Salvador, Palacios de Beneber, 4 June 1948, regarding Vicenta, NNA 01452/69; Catalan to Maria Nieves Rojo (Cavia), 21 July 1931, NNA 01432/66; Catalan to Melquiades Pampliega, 17 October 1931, NNA 01432/114.
16   Sr Visitación Cidad, Sr Agnes Ruiz and Sr Matilda Arroyo.
17   Sr Catalina, in conversation, Monastery of San Salvador, Palacios de Beneber, September 2013.
18   Sr Josefina Diez in conversation, Benedictinas de San José, Burgos, July 2012.
19   See *Chronicle*, 18 October 1920, 15 November 1920.
20   Frances Lannon, 'Identity and Reform in the Second Republic', in *A Companion to Spanish Women's Studies*, ed. X. de Ros and G. Hazburn (Woodbridge, Suffolk: Tamesis, 2011), 275.
21   Lannon, 'Identity and Reform', 275.

They all prayed in Latin, but English was utterly mysterious. The abbot looked above all for 'good will and strong vocation';[22] it was 'being faithful to the call of God' that would fuel a sense of purpose in working hard 'for the missions'.[23]

Through this period Spain held strongly to an ideal of women as the 'angels of the hearth' (*angel del hogar*) at the heart of households headed by men: fathers, brothers, husbands. According to the Spanish Census of 1930, fewer than three out of every 10 single women earned an independent income; and of every three who did work outside the home, one was in domestic service.[24] Compared to these averages, it is interesting to notice that the first New Norcia sisters included a higher proportion in formal employment (five of the 11 so far as we know), all as domestics. What the abbot commended to them as their 'daring project'[25] traded the family home for a wider domestic sphere.

Overall, both church and culture endorsed the choices these young women were making. The institutional church was robust in the rural north of Spain; parishes and religious orders flourished in the peasant communities, and the Benedictine presence in the landscape went back centuries.[26] The anticlericalism that marked the cities and the subsistence farming of the south had not bitten so deeply in these areas where networks of community banks and agrarian co-operatives were fuelled by strands within Catholicism that were socially inclusive and economically alert, though not typical of the Spanish church.[27] The tradition of Spanish missionary endeavour and New Norcia's own particular history were both claimed in Burgos. It was a small step to include young women in the regular contingents of young monks who sailed for New Norcia.

---

22   Catalan to Rev. Mother Carmen Corral, affirming Andrea Pardo, 20 July 1933, NNA 01434/191.
23   Catalan to Matias Catalan, concerning Pilar, 18 and 21 July 1933, NNA 01434/171, NNA 01434/180.
24   Lannon, 'Identity and Reform', 275.
25   Catalan to Isidora Garcia, 15 July 1933, NNA 01434/170. (Garcia did not join the group.)
26   The first Benedictine community established outside Italy is said to be San Pedro de Cardeña near Burgos, with firm documentation from 902 and a tradition dating foundation in the sixth century. 'Monasterio de San Pedro de Cardeña: Historia', www.monasteriosanpedrodecardena.com/mspc-mon-historia.html; accessed 3 April 2018. See also Martial Besse, 'The Spanish Benedictines', *Downside Review* 16 (1897): 268–97.
27   William J. Callahan, 'The Spanish Parish Clergy, 1874–1930', *Catholic Historical Review* 75 (1989): 407, 417, 410. The *Record* reported on Spanish co-operatives approvingly; see, for example, the abbatoir in Salvado's home town of Tuy, *Record*, 14 November 1925, 7.

On the other hand, the assumptions built into Abbot Catalan's decision to recruit in Spain are also important to notice. The abbot looked for Spanish women to expand the numbers. He did not build on the Benedictine connection with the Sisters of the Good Samaritan who were active in the east of Australia, nor did he seek to extend the involvement of the Josephites who were already at New Norcia and in other schools through the territory of the abbey nullius. He also looked to the networks around Benedictine communities, not teaching or missionary congregations in Spain. Although there were some contacts at least as late as 1929 through Teresa Roca with the Teresians,[28] there was no question of reviving that connection or of establishing any link with another missionary teaching group. Officially, Abbot Catalan denied any familiarity with the Teresian history, reporting only 'it was said' that they had come and gone in the time of his predecessor.[29] The original decision taken at New Norcia under Torres had been for religious women who were Spanish and Benedictine. Those priorities were even firmer under Abbot Catalan.

The unresolved issue was around the status of the community the women were joining. The abbot's contacts in the convents reported that more than one potential member was confused about exactly what kind of group was at New Norcia. There were no clear answers to this question. The girls saw the symbols of traditional religious life, but New Norcia's structure for women was officially non-existent; essentially they were being asked to work informally alongside the missionary monks. Abbot Catalan required the hopeful new members to bring clothes that suited European postulants: two black dresses (one wool; one lighter, it could be silk), closed-toe black shoes with a small heel, stockings (not transparent ones), handkerchiefs and four changes of underwear. He would cover the cost of these clothes, alongside passports and documentation, if necessary.[30] Unlike the established congregations, he did not ask families for a dowry. But confessors reportedly advised against joining a community that was so hard to explain, and Catalan lost candidates whose resolve had seemed firm to more standard communities. He found it especially galling when one girl joined the Dominicans, whom she got to know while staying with their community in Barcelona waiting for the boat

---

28 Abbot Catalan to Reverend Mother, Teresian Convent, St Gervase, Barcelona 14 January 1929: 'I have your address from Sister Teresa Roca, Benedictine Oblate of this Mission long known to you', NNA 01430/5.
29 Catalan to Rvd M. Carmen Mascaró, 24 April 1930, NNA 01431/94.
30 Mosso, 'Your Very Affectionate Father', detailing, for example, Catalan correspondence 1920s, NNA 01341.

to New Norcia. While others who changed their mind received letters observing that a choice that was not God's will would have been a mistake all round, and wishing them well, in this case the abbot severed all ties. He returned her travel documents to her family through an intermediary, suggesting her father use them 'as he thinks fit'.[31] The stress of the international expeditions touched the abbot too.

At New Norcia, the *Chronicle*'s own confusion about how to refer to the new missionary women also points to the fragile status of the group. Through the decade, they were given various titles. They were sometimes absorbed into the community of Benedictine monks (as in September 1920, when the diarist reported good relationships between three, and only three, communities in town—Benedictine Fathers, Marists and Josephites[32]— or when a report of an invitation to *la Communidad*, 'the Benedictine Community', included 'Sister Maria (oblate) and the native girls'[33]). At other times they were variously referred to as *oblatas* or specifically female oblates, Oblate Sisters, oblates of (or in) our orphanage, Benedictine oblates, Oblates of New Norcia, girl oblates, sisters, *religiosas* or female religious, and Spanish sisters.[34] In correspondence, the abbot referred to them most often as 'Sisters' when writing of them to the monks and by name or as 'the little nuns' in letters to friends and supporters in Spain.[35] In response, the nuns in Spain who had set the process in motion for the young women asked for news of 'our oblates' and the *burgalesas*, the women or girls from Burgos.[36]

The single source from the Benedictine women themselves in these years is the heavily edited *Notebooks* of Sister Felicitas. The three versions of this account (two in English and one in Spanish) vary in subtle ways, especially between Spanish and English, but overall they share a concern for discretion. In the three sentences about Felicitas's own arrival in 1921, the *Notebooks* used the range of terms that appear in New Norcia's

---

31   Catalan to the Abbess of Estrella, 23 November 1925, concerning Deogracias Mangado, NNA 01358.
32   *Chronicle*, 30 September 1920.
33   *Chronicle*, 9 October 1920.
34   *Chronicle*, 15 November 1920, 19 February 1921: 'Oblatas Benedictinas'; 16 October 1920: 'Oblata de San Benito'; 10 September 1920: 'Hermanas Oblatas'; 25 January 1924: 'hermanas españolas'; 23 December 1925: 'Oblatas en nostra orfanata por las indigenas'; 15 August 1928: 'chicas oblatas'; 16 August 1928: 'oblatas de Nueva Nursia'.
35   Catalan to Salinas, 30 August 1921, NNA 01423/95; Catalan to Sosa, 17 March 1926, NNA 01427/21; Catalan to Felisa Escudero, 28 September 1922, NNA 01424/71; 25 January 1924, NNA 01426/17; 22 February 1924, NNA 01426/38; 10 October 1926, NNA 01427/121.
36   Calderón to Catalan, 19 July 1925, trans. David Barry, OSB, original NNA 01341, translation NNA 05496.

other sources to introduce the sisters. Tellingly, the later generation also preserved, in broken English, the shock that Felicitas felt on her arrival and her disappointment that the convent was so different from the large communities that had encouraged her to join the mission:

> In February 1921 Abbot Catalan was returning from Spain; with him were 11 young boys, students for the Benedictine community, and two young girls from Burgos, to join the small group of the Benedictine Oblates. They were Srs. Felicitas Pampliega and Margaret Perez. When they arrived at New Norcia and saw the small group they were discouraged as they thought to find a community.[37]

Girls, from Burgos, becoming oblates, sisters, with new names, and hoping for a community. The narrative of the *Notebooks* does not pause at the 'discouragement' evoked by New Norcia's fragile group but pushes on immediately to a statement of faith in the community they found and in the task they had already claimed as a godly calling by the journey they had made. Their decisions are attributed to the same twin love of God and the Aborigines that had drawn Maria Harispe.[38] A string of metaphors tries hard to cover the experience:

> But coming from far, their decision was to abandon the things of this world for God's love and the aborigines. They found many obstacles on their way. But with God's grace they triumphed. [The] example of the other Srs. before them like the star that shines in the darkness would be for them the guiders [sic]; and persevering on their footsteps one day will come when reaching to the submit [sic] god [sic] will reward according to their merits.[39]

God was at work, the *Notebooks* affirm, and things were not as they imagined. While the text rallies to insist that the community did enlighten and guide them to holy lives, the anxious question of what it was that they had really come to ran through the decade unresolved.

What was it that the 16-year-old Felicitas had expected? 'A bigger community, more nuns': the testimony of later sisters is adamant.[40] Felicitas, like Margaret, had been a domestic at the Cistercian community

---

37 'Benedictine Missionary Sisters: Foundation and Progress', unpublished typescript summary in English from the notebooks of Sister Felicitas Pampliega c.1921–c.1967, ABTM (hereafter *Notebooks in English*, Madrid).
38 See Maria Harispe's letter to Henry Altimira, 6 June 1908, NNA 01717/82, discussed in chapter 2.
39 *Notebooks in English*, Madrid, n.p.
40 Visitación Cidad, Teresa González, Interview, Madrid, 6 October 2010.

of Las Huelgas, and the ancient heritage there shaped her expectations. But none of the examples of religious life from around Burgos would have looked as idiosyncratic as the community at New Norcia. Six members were required before a community could be recognised officially by Rome, and New Norcia had not reached that minimum even with the new arrivals because Mother Elias was not technically a Benedictine, and, in any case, the community remained an informal house of oblates. In Spain the communities of nuns had been less affected by the anticlericalism of the nineteenth century that closed many houses of Benedictine men. Some had lost land and possessions, but their convents were seldom abandoned. The 1889 Spanish Civil Code, based on the Napoleonic Code of 1804 and only briefly repealed under the Second Republic (1931–36), defined citizenship as essentially masculine.[41] Nevertheless, women in religious communities had an institutional status in the church that stretched categories of family and state. The historic stone convents remained landmarks of stability and tradition and, to a certain extent, of women's agency and enterprise.

At Las Huelgas, founded by royal patrons in 1187,[42] Abbess Maria de la Gloria Calderón governed her Cistercian community in a tradition that gave her privileges akin to a diocesan bishop, including episcopal staff and mitre as symbols of authority. The opening out of the community beyond noble women, and the end of provisions that allowed personal maids for the choir sisters, still left family insignia in place over the prayer stalls, the twin tombs of Eleanor Plantagenet and Alfonso VIII in the chapel's central nave, and a long tradition of village girls who joined the community both as lay sisters and as domestics without vows to take the weight of the housework.[43] Five of the earliest of New Norcia's sisters made contact with the mission through the regal austerity of this community at Las Huelgas. In 1925 Benita and Escolastica were domestic workers 'within the enclosure'[44] like Felicitas and Margaret before them. In 1928 Maria Cidad was also working there,[45] and Hildegard and Matilde left their families in Tapia and stayed briefly at this monastery, too, before their journey to Australia.[46] The Cistercians were in the southwest corner of

---

41 Lannon, 'Identity and Reform', 275; Sarah Leggott, *The Workings of Memory: Life-Writing by Women in Twentieth-Century Spain* (Lewisburg, PA: Bucknell University Press, 2008), 35–37.
42 Valentin de la Cruz, *El Monasterio de Las Huelgas de Burgos* (Léon: Editorial Everest, 2005), 6.
43 de la Cruz, *Las Huelgas*, 30.
44 Calderón to Catalan, 19 July 1925, NNA 01341.
45 Sr Maria Gratia Balagot, email correspondence, 13 July 2014.
46 Catalan to Abbess Filomena, 1 July 1928, NNA 01429/66.

the town, near the railway station. Abbot Catalan arranged the departure of the trio in 1928 with the new Abbess Filomena and, with attention to both propriety and economy, reminded her that all three should set out for the station wearing veils, 'as this is the moment to recognise that they are like religious postulants, and also so they will not have to pay more than half-fare'.[47]

Las Huelgas had unique privileges, but it was not the only Spanish community to make solemn claims. Sister Lorenza Diez at Palacios de Benaber passed on news that the abbess at Catalayud had been invested with staff, ring, and pectoral cross.[48] At Palacios de Benaver itself, the Benedictine monastery of San Salvador had a history first documented in 1231.[49]

Over six centuries of tradition endorsed the community where Mother Josefa Ramos had gathered Felicitas and Margaret to 'their new life',[50] where Francisca heard about New Norcia from her Benedictine aunt, and whose abbess supported the 16-year-old's campaign for her father's consent to leave the country,[51] and where Sr Lorenza would assemble documents and coordinate the departure of later groups.[52] These Benedictines had weathered the attacks on monastic foundations with minimal disruption and ran a small school just within the walls. It is likely New Norcia's Sisters Margaret and Ludivina learnt to sew and to read there. Possibly Felicitas travelled the 7 kilometres from her village to attend as well, before she took the post as a domestic at Las Huelgas. All the women in farming families were familiar with hard work on the land as well as domestic work. But there was nothing that prepared Felicitas for the mute isolation and loss of identity she felt out in New Norcia's paddocks clearing the ground for ploughing. It was her record of tears in these early days at the mission, 'every day picking stone, every night crying, all the time crying',[53] that so embarrassed the later generation of sisters and led most directly to the destruction of the original *Notebooks*.

---

47   Catalan to Abbess Filomena, 1 July 1928. For the location of the train station, see Luis Santos y Ganges and José Luis Lalana Soto, 'La antigua estación de Burgos y el precario papel del patrimonio en los proyectos urbanos y arquitectónicos', arquitecturaviva.com; accessed 20 October 2019.
48   Lorenza Diez to Catalan, 5 and 16 November 1947, trans. David Barry, OSB, NNA 01341.
49   Luciano Serrano, *Una fundación medieval de la Casa de Lara el Monasterio de Palacios de Benaber*, Burgos, 1941, digital copy (Valladolid: Junta de Castilla y León, Consejería de Cultura y Turismo, 2009–10). See also Monasterio de San Salvador, www.benedictinaspalacios.com/.
50   Abbess Josefa Ramos to Catalan, April 1921, trans. David Barry, OSB, NNA 01341.
51   Catalan to Abbess Carmen Corral, 29 July 1933, NNA 01422–01436D/191.
52   Diez to Catalan, 16 November 1947, NNA 01341.
53   Teresa González, Interview, Madrid, May 1999.

Figure 5.3: Monastery of San Salvador, Palacios de Benaver, Burgos.
Source: Photo by John H. Smith. Author's collection.

'Just waiting … for our broken inglish'

The young woman's failure of courage was edited out, as 'anyone might read it [and misunderstand]',[54] but if we stay with the *Notebooks*' account of the 1920s we are jack-knifed through doubt towards security. Felicitas poured out the words we no longer have, but both the memory of the sisters who knew her and the remnant of her lament suggest that she wrote so much in Spanish chiefly because she was speechless in English.[55] As she found a voice in English, her trauma eased and her confidence in the community increased. Language was not simply acquisition of grammar and vocabulary but the foundation for rapport and authority.

The English versions of the *Notebooks* have been edited more firmly into an overview of this time. It is significant that even here the initial fear Felicitas felt for the Aboriginal girls at St Joseph's remained in the text. Generations of the sisters knew the shame of having only 'broken inglish' (sic). While we cannot know exactly what Felicitas wrote, the edited end-

---

54 Teresa González, Interview, Madrid, July 2002.
55 Teresa González and Visitación Cidad, Interview, Madrid, 30 September 2010.

product shows us clearly what the community thought it acceptable to retain. Weaving between the voice of Felicitas and a later narrator, the *Notebooks* vividly conveys her stress and alienation. As she and Margaret took over supervision of work in the sewing room, the class stared and waited for Felicitas to speak. The girls' fixed eyes were a strong Aboriginal challenge that even these newcomers knew how to read. It was a test of wills:

> Here the two young Sisters in charge of a group of aborigine girls, without knowing how to speak inglish, and how little they like on those days to be under supervision, and discipline; these girls then were waiting to hear some commands of the young Srs; some broken inglish, to have some fun of them perhaps. In the sewing room most of the time they would do nothing of their work, but with eyes fix on them just waiting now and then for our broken inglish. On those days jet [sic] their civilisation and manners still more or less wild, use to fight and quarrel among themselves terribly and useless saying it was a very difficult job to stop them.[56]

The Spanish *Notebooks* omitted the detail here and chose simply to say they were 'wrapped in countless difficulties with minds completely blank'.[57]

In contrast, Abbot Catalan was cheerful as he reported the progress of the new recruits in letters to Spain. Catalan wrote to Mother Josefa at San Salvador in April 1921, assuring her that the two had made the journey well, without any seasickness and embracing the adventure. He attributed the easy arrival to God and the prayers of the Benedictine sisters: 'How much we have to thank our Lord God for such grace! And our Sisters at Palacios, it is not for nothing that we are grateful to them!'[58] As the *Record* had told its readers in parishes around Western Australia, and as the *Chronicle* recorded for the monks, the abbot also reported overseas that the town had been decked out as for a major solemnity for their arrival,

---

56 'Benedictine Missionary Sisters', handwritten summary from the notebooks of Sister Felicitas Pampliega c. 1921–c. 1967, previously held at the convent of the Benedictine Missionary Sisters, Kalumburu (hereafter *Notebooks*, Kalumburu), n.p, NNA.
57 'Origen de la Congregacion de las Hermanas Benedictinas Misioneras de New Norcia, Western Australia' unpublished typescript from the notebooks of Sister Felicitas Pampliega c. 1921–c. 1967, transcribed and edited by Sister Teresa González, Madrid c. 1980, Archives of the Benedictine Missionary Sisters of Tutzing (ABTM) (hereafter *Notebooks*, Madrid), 9 (*envueltas en innumberable dificultados y con la mente complamente en blaco*).
58 Catalan to Josefa Ramos, 10 April 1921, NNA 01422/74; Catalan to Felisa Escudera, Barcelona, 28 September 1922, 25 January 1924, 22 February 1924, NNA 01436A/17-38-74.

with Australian, Spanish and Papal flags across the college buildings, cadets presenting arms, the pupils of the boarding schools lining the path from the monastery to the church, 'and behind these again the children of the native schools'.[59] The organist played them into the church with the royal march of Spain. After Solemn Benediction of the Blessed Sacrament in the church everyone celebrated with the new arrivals in the 'salon' at the centre of the monastery. The *Chronicle* remembered an excellent meal and judged 'a most sincere enthusiasm and a most complete happiness reigned'.[60]

In the sewing room and in the bush — tension and community

The St Joseph's girls had lined the way to the church for the newcomers, but in the sewing room, once the town's festival of welcome had ended,[61] trust and openness needed to be earned. Four of the 'girls' in the sewing room at St Joseph's in 1921 were young women in their twenties, 'tall, strong, physically big', the Spanish account reminds us,[62] older than either of the two sisters 'in charge', and connected through shared history and family to the dozen or so younger girls. In 'do[ing] nothing of their work'[63] but 'watching while the others did theirs',[64] these Aboriginal women had an effective means of protest. Withdrawing their labour was less public than the silence in church of 1907, and perhaps less effective while others (sisters or the younger girls) kept up the work; perhaps the protest was directed specifically to St Joseph's. But whether or not the Aboriginal anger was against the new sisters, the work itself, or their situation at the mission, the two new arrivals were intimidated.

Both the young sisters were good craftswomen. The school system in Spain encouraged handcraft for girls.[65] In later years, Felicitas organised formal dressmaking lessons, and girls knew they could rely on her talent to restyle

---

59 *Record*, 5 March 1921, 2.
60 *Chronicle*, 19 February 1921.
61 See below, 00.
62 *Notebooks*, Madrid, 9 (*eran altas, fuertes y de gran corpulencia física*).
63 *Notebooks*, Madrid, 10.
64 *Notebooks*, Madrid, 9.
65 José María Borrás Llop, *Historia de la infancia en la España contemporánea, 1834–1936* (Madrid: Ministerio de Trabajo y Asuntos Sociales, Fundación Germán Sánchez Ruipérez, 1996), 349; Consuelo Flecha Garcia, 'Education in Spain: Close-Up of Its History in the 20th Century', *Analytical Reports in International Education* 4 (2011): 17–42.

donated clothes;⁶⁶ Margaret's knitting extended to at least one full-length wedding dress and is still treasured.⁶⁷ They were very different: Felicitas the future superior and Margaret the group's longest-serving novice, but both were idealistic and apparently dumbfounded by their reception. The Spanish account described more of the conflict as the weeks wore on: the older girls used to run away and leave the work rather than take 'advice' from the sisters, these 'youngsters' (*jovencitas*);⁶⁸ the conflict between those younger Aboriginal girls who worked and the older ones who did not was physical—often there were fights the sisters could not stop, which left the young women (perhaps all of them?) 'useless and bleeding'.⁶⁹

Visitors who had seen St Joseph's residents as models of quiet good behaviour would have been shocked. Embroidery was already a speciality of the school, and accolades continued through the 1920s and 1930s for work so highly skilled that 'superlatives alone do justice to its excellence'.⁷⁰ It is hard to imagine the 'quantities of fine lace'⁷¹ and other delicate creations coming from anywhere except a peaceful workshop. Certainly the reports in the press implied this, and the traditions of collaboration and pride in good craft come through the oral record too.⁷² The guest from Government House in Perth who wrote in 1923 that she would treasure the tablecloth embroidered with black swans 'so quickly and so well' as a favour by someone 'kind and clever'⁷³ clearly had no idea. Perhaps it was all over by then, but a year earlier the sewing room was the setting for a power struggle made worse by a language barrier.

---

66 Mary Nannup (Philomena Drayton), Interview, Moora, March 1999; Anne Moynihan, Interview, North Perth, March 1999.
67 The dress was made for Rose Willaway, who wore it when she married Preston Narkle in 1974.
68 *Notebooks*, Madrid, 9 (*aconsejarlas se acababan mas y se largaban con todo el trabajo*).
69 *Notebooks*, Madrid, 9 (*con frecuencia … saliendo malparadas y sangrando unas y otras*).
70 *St Ildephonsus College Magazine*, 1929, 7; *Daily News*, 8 October 1929, 2; *Recorder* (Port Pirie), 14 February 1938, 3. On the work sent to the Missionary Exposition in Rome, Catalan to Abbot Romauldo Simo, 2 September 1924, NNA 01436A/125; Catalan to Fr Salinas, 10 September 1924, NNA 01436A/127; and high standards at Yarrawindah Show, *St Ildephonsus College Magazine*, 1927, 74.
71 M. Edward Dasey, *The Story of the Regional Missionary and Eucharistic Congress, Newcastle, NSW* (Newcastle: Specialty Publications, 1938), 59.
72 Mae Taylor, Interview, New Norcia, 2003; Sheila Humphries, Interview, New Norcia, May 1999; Veronica Willaway, Interview, Nebraska, 9 July 2013.
73 Katharine Campion to Sr Gertrude, 27 December 1923, NNA 01123.

Figure 5.4: Display of needlework by St Joseph's Girls, *St Ildephonsus College Magazine*, **1929, 7.**
Source: NNA.

We hear nothing of a resolution. The English version of the *Notebooks* pushes the narrative through the initial stand-off and on to better things. There is a leap forward to a picnic scene in the spring of 1924. Now the new missionaries are in charge of the excursion; symbolically, the land is blossoming and abundant. The account is alive to the traditions of the Aboriginal children, and the young sisters take their day in the bush with them 'joyfully' in stride. The Spanish summary of the *Notebooks* adds that the change was specifically because they could now chatter away enough in broken English (*chapurrear*) that they felt both comfortable and useful (*consoladora y provechosa*):[74]

> One of those days of spring in New Norcia's bush, we two were sent for a picnic with the children, and as usual this [sic] children spent their time picking wildflowers, cutting a tree with honey. On those days no one would have bee boxes. We pass the day joyfully in the bush with the children and came home that day about 8.30 in the evening, this our first picnic day, quite satisfied of the day.[75]

---

74   *Notebooks*, Madrid, 9–10.
75   *Notebooks*, Madrid, 7–8.

The institution had grown to include 45 girls. If the boys from St Mary's had joined the occasion there would have been 76 children with Felicitas and Margaret that day.[76] The regular outings in the bush are a recurring motif in the oral evidence. This is the only account of a picnic in the sisters' written narrative, but here as elsewhere it was an occasion of harmony and community.

Yet once again the *Notebooks* shifted gear quickly, replacing tranquillity with a sombre mood. Met on their return from the bush with news that Maria Harispe, 'the foundress', was grievously sick, the community faced the trial of her treatment for cancer ('an internal growth close to the heart'[77]) in Perth and the eventual loss of hope in her recovery. The *Chronicle* records her treatment in regular entries about her trips to hospital.[78] The Spanish *Notebooks* include Maria's 'unspeakable suffering' and an incident during her illness when a violent fight between the older girls made her cry out, 'I die without seeing any fruit!'[79] In the English version there is no such distress about the work. Instead, the focus is on the community's sorrow. Maria's illness left God as the only steady point: 'we were left like orphans, and we have to say now "My God and my all"'.[80] When Maria died the following spring, aged 44, the English account was precise and, for all its phonetic spelling and poor grammar, it gave details that disappeared in the Spanish copy about the time and the order in which the groups in the town came to mourn, before reiterating Maria's status as 'Mother':

> During this weeks, Sr got very sick and 10 [minutes] after receiving Holy Communion at 7.20 am died on the 16th of November 1925. As soon as possible three Benedictine Fathers came to say prayers for the death. They rung the church bells for the death, Masses were offered for her eternal rest. As soon as the natives knew Sr. pass away they all came around her remains praying to see her, that which had been a Mother to them for 15 years. The Josephine Sisters [from St Gertrude's] also came to pray around her remains.

---

76 New Norcia Annual Return, 24 September 1924, 'New Norcia Mission – Subsidy and General', State Records Office of Western Australia (SROWA) S2030 cons993 1926/0350. See also Appendix 1.
77 'Sister Mry [sic] Harispe', New Norcia *Sunday Leaf*, 18 October 1953.
78 *Chronicle*, 25 April 1925, 13 May 1925, 27 June 1925, 8 July 1925, 30 July 1925, 25 August 1925, 25 September 1925, 13 November 1925, 16 November 1925, 17 November 1925.
79 *Notebooks*, Madrid, 11 (*sufrido … indeciblemente*) (*muero sin ver ningun fruto*).
80 *Notebooks,* Kalumburu, n.p.

Her remains and her grave was covered with beautiful flowers. She was loved by everyone, as she was a Mother to everyone. So we were without a Mother.[81]

Of course, there were other mothers in town, Aboriginal women in the cottages and the surrounding bush and also white women on the surrounding farms. But in the English version the young sisters had lost the figure who had represented their particular brand of a shared public maternity lived in the name of the church. The Spanish account is briefer here, noting 'her death was felt deeply by all' and especially by the missionaries for whom Maria was 'a physical and spiritual force'.[82] In both languages, the relationship of spiritual motherhood, framed by assumptions of a shared Catholic culture, was used to identify the missionaries with the people, and the people with the missionaries.

The *Chronicle* also stressed the shared mourning for Maria. Her body was moved to the church and the 'native orphan girls' kept vigil through the afternoon and night. The funeral the next day saw the whole community turn out 'in full' (*en peso*, literally by weight in Spanish), all four schools, the Benedictine community, 'all the workers, and several of the neighbours nearby'.[83] Her obituary, published in the *Record* as well as in the magazine of St Ildephonsus' College, was in keeping with the tributes offered to nuns in other congregations,[84] honouring her simplicity, duty and sacrifice, 'in the carrying out of what was, humanly speaking, an almost impossible task … [that had] won her the love and admiration of all within the Mission'.[85] The *Record* gave her the title 'Friend of Native Orphan Girls' and stressed their need, showing the residents gathered around Maria, more informally than a decade earlier, still in boots and lace collars but in front of a broken wall. It was an image of sacrifice and hardship rather than triumph.

---

81 *Notebooks*, Kalumburu, n.p.
82 *Notebooks*, Madrid, 11 (*su muerte fue muy sentida por todas*) (*especialmente por los Hnas que perdian fuerza fisica y esperitual*).
83 *Chronicle*, 17 November 1925.
84 *Record*, 12 September 1925, 13 (Sr Marie de Chantal, Fremantle); 19 December 1925, 21 (Sr Marie Celestine, Albany).
85 *Record*, 19 December 1925, 11; *St Ildephonsus College Magazine*, 1925, 57.

Figure 5.5: Maria Harispe, c. 1925; the photograph that accompanied her obituary in the Perth *Record*.
Source: NNA W7-A3-4-498.

The *Notebooks,* however, concluded the account of her loss by focusing on the sisters. There is a hint of her suffering bearing fruit in the arrival of new members. In the 18 years since she had travelled from Spain with the Teresians, Maria Harispe had been a stable presence as the band of missionary women dispersed, reconfigured and endured. Hearing before her death that Benita and Escolastica would travel with the abbot to join the group and take the numbers above the canonical requirement of six, the *Notebooks* concluded Maria's life by recording her hope that: 'Now our desire will be realised to form a little community'.[86] Maria had wanted to pioneer the house in the Kimberley. It was therefore fitting that the future of canonical status she hoped for would be firmly linked to the need for Benedictine women at the Drysdale River Mission. Perhaps only at New Norcia would the decision have been taken to realise this hope through a link with Belgium.

---

86 *Notebooks,* Madrid, 11.

Made in Belgium: Spanish Benedictine Missionary Sisters for New Norcia and the Kimberley

It was no secret among the Benedictine sisters that a Kimberley mission was talked about, but it is only Abbot Catalan's letters to the missionary monks in the north that make it clear how seriously the sisters' presence was being sought in the early 1920s. Both the recruiting of new members and attention to the group's canonical status were given impetus by the need for the community to be large enough and secure enough to send sisters to join the monks in the north.

The plea for women to join the mission effort was prompted by the increasing number of children at the Kimberley mission and turned on assumptions about both race and gender. When the Benedictines first established a camp at Pago Pago near the Drysdale River in 1908, and through the first decade when tension between the local Gwini people and the monastics made the future of the mission doubtful, the monks puzzled that there were no children among the people and remarked on the small number of women.[87] As trust grew, and sporadic attacks ceased,[88] the concern to preserve the Aboriginal population and to see it increase was a mission priority. When the first baby, a girl named Mary Pandilow,[89] was born in the mission in 1918, the call went out for sisters to exercise a spiritual maternity. The monks' letters do not mention the Aboriginal mothers or wider family, although children were predominantly cared for in the Aboriginal camp, even after the arrival of the sisters when a dormitory and institutional care of the children developed.[90] As at New Norcia before the Teresians, Aboriginal women at the Kimberley mission exercised responsibility in relation to the dormitory, but the role of Matilda Morechi, and later Mary Pandilow herself, was a stopgap in the absence of the sisters.[91] Father Seraphim Sanz, the later and longest-serving Benedictine superior at Kalumburu, summarised the arrival

---

87 Christine Choo, *Mission Girls: Aboriginal Women on Catholic Missions in the Kimberley, Western Australia 1900–1950* (Crawley, WA: University of Western Australia Press, 2001), 72–73; Seraphim Sanz de Galdeano, *Memoirs of a Spanish Missionary Monk* (Carlisle, WA: Hesperian Press, 2006).
88 Ian Crawford, *We Won the Victory: Aborigines and Outsiders on the North-West Coast of the Kimberley* (Fremantle, WA: Fremantle Arts Centre Press, 2001), 182–86.
89 'Biographical Cuttings on Mary Pandilow, First Child to Be Born at the Old Pago Pago Mission', National Library of Australia, nla.gov.au/nla.cat-vn1991118; accessed 31 August 2019.
90 Choo, *Mission Girls*, 164–65.
91 Crawford, *We Won the Victory*, 58; Choo, *Mission Girls*, 166–67.

of the Benedictine women pithily: 'When there were no children in the Mission the Sisters would have been a burden; with children they were indispensible'.[92]

Recognising a new necessity, Abbot Catalan's negotiations with the monks in the Kimberley about when and under what conditions the sisters would be sent were also marked by assumptions about gender and race. On the one hand, the women were deemed essential for the outreach to children and, on the other, the conditions in the Kimberley would be a particular problem to the health of European women. Later, the record gives us glimpses of the sisters' own understanding of their role. At the outset we can see only the discussion between the monks.

Shortly after Felicitas and Margaret arrived in New Norcia in 1921, the abbot responded to a letter from Fr Raimundo Salinas at Drysdale River. Fr Raimundo had admitted that his happiness on account of these new Benedictine sisters was 'watered down'[93] because there was silence about sisters for the north. The abbot reassured him: 'I can see very well how useful it would be to have religious women there. … I haven't changed my mind, it is the same: to send the Sisters as soon as possible'.[94] But the possibility was itself watered down as the abbot gave instructions about conditions that needed to be met.

First, there must be enough sisters, and, second, the monks must prepare properly for them. The abbot required a convent to be built separate from the still-to-be-completed monastery, including at least three cells to accommodate at least three sisters, a refectory and 'one or two rooms more'.[95] Then they must also establish a herd of goats. As early as 1919, Catalan had asked advice on tropical goat-herding from the Durack family at Argyle Station.[96] He wanted these animals to safeguard the sisters' health as women were 'not so resilient as men, even less in the tropics'.[97] By providing red meat, the goats would prevent anemia. Probably the threat of the tropics to Europeans, including the Mediterranean Spanish, was a familiar enough idea,[98] but who among the local game hunters would

---

92 Seraphim Sanz, OSB, personal correspondence, June 2000.
93 Catalan to Salinas, 30 August 1921, NNA 01423/95, paraphrasing Salinas's letter, which is not extant.
94 Catalan to Salinas, 30 August 1921.
95 Catalan to Salinas, 30 August 1921.
96 M. Durack replied to Catalan, 20 November 1919, NNA 01441.
97 Catalan to Salinas, 30 August 1921.
98 See D. Arnold, 'The Place of "the Tropics" in Western Medical Ideas since 1750', *Tropical Medicine and International Health* 2 (1997): 303–13; Alison Bashford, *Imperial Hygiene: A Critical History of Colonialism, Nationalism and Public Health* (London: Palgrave McMillan, 2014).

not have wondered about the particular need for goats? (As it turned out the flock, once established, was valued more for its milk and cheese.[99]) Abbot Catalan invoked Sr Maria Harispe as the Reverend Mother to warn the monks she would 'investigate' to ensure that the sisters would live in 'some comfort and decency'.[100] Would she have been offended that he urged Fr Salinas to act 'before they can snub us' over a poor building?[101] Whether or not the abbot was entirely convinced of the conditions he set, he assured Fr Salinas that another year was all that it would take 'to do everything calmly, so it will be more perfect'.[102]

When four years had passed and Benita and Escolastica were being welcomed to New Norcia, it was a letter from Fr Rosendo Sosa that prompted further clarification from the abbot. Apparently Sosa suggested working with the Sisters of St John of God, who had been in Beagle Bay near Broome since 1907. The girls from Drysdale River were sent to their school, with significant trauma for the community at Pago Pago.[103] It made sense to suggest these sisters could be involved further north. But Abbot Catalan dismissed the idea as 'dreaming' and likely to undermine the Benedictine community.[104] The 'others that are not ours' would be 'quibbling' (*quisquillosa*) and lack self-denial. He had heard of trouble in the Broome and Beagle Bay communities and had been shocked by stories that 'these good Sisters asked the [Pallotine] Fathers for some sort of salary for their work'.[105] The Benedictine family of missionaries worked by different expectations. Catalan would not be paying wages.

In these letters of 1926, the abbot pointed out that Maria's recent death had 'left a big gap at the Orphanage',[106] but he held out the hope that the two young newcomers might be leaders among the sisters, 'when they have a few more years'.[107] It would 'not be too long'[108] and he would be able to divide the sisters between New Norcia and the Kimberley. The vague timeline reflected the fragility of the enterprise.

---

99   Maria Gratia Balagot, Visitación Cidad and Teresa González, email correspondence, 26 July 2014.
100 Catalan to Salinas, 30 August 1921, NNA 01423/95.
101 Catalan to Salinas, 30 August 1921.
102 Catalan to Salinas, 30 August 1921.
103 See Mary Pandilow's story in Crawford, *We Won the Victory*, 55–58.
104 Catalan to Sosa, 17 March 1926, NNA 01427/21.
105 Catalan to Sosa, 17 March 1926.
106 Catalan to Sosa, 17 March 1926.
107 Catalan to Sosa, 17 March 1926.
108 Catalan to Sosa, 17 March 1926 (*paréceme que no tardaremos en tener las suficientes para dividarlas*).

A month after Fr Rosendo proposed collaboration with the Sisters of St John of God, Abbot Catalan made enquiries to secure the future of the congregation as a specifically Benedictine venture. Catalan wrote (in Italian) to the Belgian abbot Theodore Neve to remind him that 'one day at the meeting at San Anselmo last autumn'[109] he had promised to send copies of the constitutions for some Benedictine oblate sisters. Abbot Catalan was vague. The group were 'Oblate Nuns of St Benedict or Missionary Sisters of the Order of St Benedict',[110] but to have copies of the constitutions would be a special favour. Neve's house of St André in Bruges had been founded by the Belgian Abbey of Maredsous as a training centre for the missions and was rather controversially designated a 'monastery for the missions' in its own right.[111] Abbot Neve in turn had founded the Benedictine Missionary Sisters, establishing them at nearby Bethanie in 1921.[112] These sisters were focused on assisting the work of missionary monks in the Belgian Congo. They would have been an interesting model for the New Norcia sisters, but it seems that Abbot Catalan never received or was not impressed by their constitutions. At least, nothing was done about the canonical status of the oblates at New Norcia until, in 1932, a three-page note at the back of the journal *Revue Liturgique et Monastique*, published by Maredsous, prompted the abbot to write again to Belgium. This time the author he contacted was Fr Andre Schyrgens, a monk at Maredsous itself, who had established a 'new institute' of women, formally professed as sisters, living the Benedictine spirit not as monastics but like oblates 'in the world'.[113] Abbot Catalan was keen to know more, as he told Schyrgens: 'I deduce from the details of the Sisters and their work, that this congregation of oblates is exactly what we need to have in New Norcia'.[114] Probably Abbot Catalan remembered his previous discussion about the Belgian missionary oblates at Bethanie, or possibly he confused this second congregation at Maredsous with the first, but Schyrgens's article made no mention of missionary work as such. The community at Emmaus House in the grounds of Maredsous was founded by the abbey as a 'practical response' to the need for manual workers in the

---

109 Catalan to Neve, 18 April 1926, NNA 01422–01436B/26.
110 Catalan to Neve, 18 April 1926.
111 St Andriesabdij Zevenkerken, www.abdijzevenkerken.be/abdij/geschiedenis/; accessed 27 July 2014. The foundation in Bruges was 70 km from Ypres, where Mother Elias had taught before her move to New Norcia.
112 'Theodore Neve OSB', ldysinger.stjohnsem.edu/@texts2/1910_neve/00a_start.htm; accessed 27 July 2014. See also 'De priorij Onze-Lieve-Vrouw van Bethanië', www.priorijbethanie.be/; accessed 27 July 2014.
113 Andre Schyrgens, 'Notes et Documents, Maredsous—Les soeurs bénédictine de la maison d'Emmaüs', *Revue Liturgique et Monastique* 17 (1931–32): 243–45; see also Daniel Misonne, *En parcourant l'historie de Maredsous* (Maredsous: Editions de Maredsous, 2005), 265–74.
114 Catalan to Schyrgens, 10 June 1932, NNA 01433/107.

kitchen and laundry of their boarding school, a community that would also foster an 'intense interior life' through simple, hidden labour.[115] Part of the refounding of European monasticism after the French Revolution, Maredsous was publisher of the influential *Revue Benedictine* from 1884 and founded communities in Brazil (1895) and Ireland (1927) as well as elsewhere in Europe. With memory of the saintly Abbot Marmion still strong, a School of Art as well as the boys' boarding college on site, alongside brewing and cheesemaking, Maredsous was a powerhouse of Benedictine life. Schyrgens foreshadowed the significance of the rich context for fostering 'contemplative, apostolic, liturgical, intellectual and artistic life',[116] but his new group remained essentially a community of lay sisters for a European monastery and quite different from the earlier group.

Nevertheless, Abbot Catalan proposed enthusiastically that training with this primarily domestic congregation would encompass all that the New Norcia sisters would need. He asked for a copy of the constitutions and proposed immediately that New Norcia might send two of the sisters to Maredsous for formal training with these 'Sisters of Emmaus'. Once formally professed, these two would return to Australia, to establish (in effect) a 'daughter house' of Maredsous but as an independent congregation, thus circumventing the long and difficult process of obtaining approval in Rome for a new foundation of women.[117] This was administrative thinking that was both extraordinarily convoluted and brilliantly simple—both daft and inspired.

There was no response to the proposal. Five months later, therefore, the abbot followed up his original Spanish letter with a Latin one, proposing the same thing. This time he received a reply. In January 1933 Fr Schyrgens sent not only the constitutions but also, apparently, a report of his discussions with four key players in Belgium. Schyrgens had consulted a canon lawyer (Fr Bastien), the Mother General of the Sisters of Mercy in Heverlé-Louvain who sponsored the community of Oblate Sisters at Emmaus House within the grounds of Maredsous, also the superior of that house itself, and the bishop of Namur. All parties were open to the proposal put by Abbot Catalan.[118] In March 1933 the abbot exchanged letters with Reverend Mother Marie Thérèse Hyernaux, speaking broadly about the good work she was doing for the missions in Australia and

---

115 Schyrgens, 'Notes et Documents, Maredsous', 243, 245.
116 Schyrgens, 'Notes et Documents, Maredsous', 245.
117 Catalan to Schyrgens, 10 June 1932, NNA 01433/107.
118 See Catalan's letter of thanks to Schyrgens, 20 February 1933, NNA 01436D/76.

sending Australian stamps as a favour; by 6 November 1933, Felicitas and Benita were sailing for Belgium. The *Notebooks* claimed the step as a commencement and identified the journey as central to the foundation of the New Norcia congregation of Benedictine Missionary Sisters. Dressed as postulants of the 'Benedictine Sisters of Mercy of Heverlé',[119] and destined to live with the community at Emmaus House in the grounds of Maredsous for the next two years, Felicitas and Benita left Australia to 'begin to form a congregation of Regular Oblates of New Norcia'.[120]

The whirlwind of activity that saw the connection with Belgium blossom from 1932 had intensified because in August 1931 the conditions the abbot had set for sending the Benedictine women north had been met. There had been a realistic prospect that the abbot would divide the sisters into two houses ever since August 1928 when Hildegard Ruiz, Maria Cidad and Matilde de la Fuente had arrived at New Norcia, and Catalan had met renewed requests from the monks in the north with a firm reminder 'not to insist'. On the other hand, he promised: 'Let us know that the convent is finished and soon you will see the veils'.[121]

Based at Pago Pago, where the water supply was uncertain, and looking to move the whole mission to a better site elsewhere, the monks nevertheless began gathering stone for a convent. The building was well underway by early 1930, but Abbot Catalan was concerned about the design. Safety was an issue. He forbad side doors 'to prevent trouble where we can'[122] and insisted on windows that would be protected but still allow airflow. Work continued. The abbot left for Europe in October 1930 and did not return until the last day of April 1931. His party included Ludivina Marcos, who brought the number of Benedictine oblate sisters to 10. The numbers in the south were sufficient; the convent in the north was complete. The abbot wrote to Fr Tomás Gil with a hint of triumph, announcing without further preliminary warning that he was keeping his promise and that the sisters would arrive on 18 or 19 August 1931.[123] He also wrote to Bishop Raible in Broome to say they would call in and collect the Aboriginal girls from the school run by the sisters of St John of God as they could now return to Drysdale River.[124]

---

119 *Notebooks*, Kalumburu, n.p.
120 *Notebooks*, Kalumburu, n.p.
121 Catalan to Gil, 12 March 1930, NNA 01422–01436B/57.
122 Catalan to Gil, 12 March 1930.
123 Catalan to Gil, 7 July 1931, NNA 01434/42.
124 Catalan to Raible, 5 July 1931, NNA 01434/47.

Figure 5.6: Emmaus House, Maredsous, Belgium, 2010.
Source: Author's collection.

Figure 5.7: Abbey church at the monastery of Maredsous, Belgium, 2010.
Source: Author's collection.

In May and June 1931, three Benedictine sisters answered the abbot's call for volunteers to join the mission in the north. The records do not show us the process, but Abbot Catalan's letter to Fr Tomás more than hints at the practicalities. In July he could not say whether there would be two or three sisters. Gertrude, the Australian, had made a firm offer and, although not young at 52 years of age, she would be an English-speaking teacher. Some other potential volunteers were taken aback. 'That's the way things are', the abbot remarked, 'or better to say, the people.'[125] It is an intriguing hint at the complexity the community confronted as the women made choices that were no longer 'theoretical'. We do not know who among the Spaniards was hesitating, but a month later three sisters set out with the abbot. Escolastica Martinez was the 23-year-old superior, with Hildegard Ruiz, aged 22, as cook, and Gertrude Banks as teacher.

The journey along the coast in the *Koolinda*, the motorised lugger run by the state shipping service, took more than a fortnight. The passengers turned out to include a party of 30 or more tourists, as well as the children returning from Broome. Their arrival at Drysdale River on 18 August 1931

---

125 Catalan to Gil, 7 July 1931.

was a 'red letter day'.[126] The community of four monks 'most sincerely welcomed all, and especially the Sisters whose aid had been so earnestly solicited'.[127] A group of 20 from the Aboriginal community (probably men, though the account does not say) met them with a 'typical and innocent'[128] dance while the tourists took photographs. The monastery's photographs stress the form of travel—boats, barges, luggers and carts— and the drama of distance and arrival again and again.

The abbot remained for four weeks, writing an account that became the basis of several articles and a radio talk. It stressed the missionary success. The new convent was blessed on 23 August 1931, after Mass sung to a setting by Dom Moreno and a procession of 120 Aboriginal people. On 7 September 1931 there was a baptism of eight Aboriginal converts and confirmation of 13 more, followed by a picnic to mark the festival. Ten days later the *Koolinda* returned by special arrangement, leaving six months worth of supplies and collecting the abbot. He was back at New Norcia by the end of September 1931. The arrival of the Benedictine women in the Kimberley was a major step and a sign to the Australian church and the wider community that the mission was secure into the future.

Figure 5.8: Arriving at Pago Pago Mission in the Kimberley, 18 August 1931. Benedictine sisters at right in shoes and stockings, possibly Abbot Catalan in bare feet.
Source: NNA 65179P.

---

126 Catalan, 'First Sisters at Drysdale River Mission', account filed with Catalan correspondence 1931, NNA 01422–01436D/133.
127 Catalan, 'First Sisters', 1931.
128 Catalan, 'First Sisters', 1931.

Figure 5.9: Transferring to Drysdale River site, 1932.
Source: NNA 65231P.

Figure 5.10: On the lugger *Koolinda*; Matilde, Escolastica and Hildegard with Fr Boniface and Aboriginal children.
Source: NNA 65218P.

But if the mission in the north was going to be permanent, and if the women were to remain, surely there had to be a more secure basis for their own community. Even before he left the Kimberley the abbot could see things would not last with Sr Gertrude,[129] and the durability of the new venture was tested when she took the first available boat out in January 1932. Fr Gil reported, using her English phrase, that she had told him, 'This Mission is very disappointing'.[130] She wrote to the abbot from Wyndham, the small port nearest Drysdale River, confessing she had fled.[131] Gertrude did not explain why she had left but presented what had happened as a 'failure' of her vocation. She proposed to go to Darwin instead.[132] Catalan wrote to her kindly, and directed her firmly to New Norcia. Given the canonical situation, his authority to do this was minimal, but he sent her £25 for the fare, via a letter entrusted to the captain of the *Koolinda*, her only means of transport.[133]

The abbot was concerned above all that Gertrude should not freelance as a missionary. He reassured her that the other sisters would welcome her 'with open arms'.[134] Actually, he now understood that her personality was a trial to the other sisters, and he had his own reservations. He identified the cause of her distress in the north as not being able to follow her 'whim' or provide as she chose for the Aborigines.[135] Abbot Catalan mused dispiritedly to Fr Tomás that some characters were able to convince everyone involved, including themselves, that they were martyrs.[136] But he did not want loose talk about the mission at Drysdale reaching Darwin or Beagle Bay or circulating at New Norcia. He advised Gertrude to explain only that 'to work with success in that Mission you had to learn the native language for which you are too old'.[137] Warning her against 'asking permission' for anything except a return to New Norcia, Abbot Catalan asserted the status of the group as strongly as he could. He urged Gertrude to 'straightway return to your own Home, New Norcia, and join

---

129 Catalan to Gertrude, 27 February 1932, NNA 01433/42; Catalan to Gil, 4 March 1932, NNA 01433/53.
130 Catalan to Gil, 4 March 1932, reporting Gil's phrase back to him.
131 Gertrude Banks to Catalan, 30 January 1932, NNA 01061; Catalan to Gertrude, 27 February 1932.
132 Gertrude Banks to Catalan, January 1931, NNA 01061.
133 Catalan to Captain of the *Koolinda*, 10 March 1932; Catalan to Gertrude, 27 February 1932; Catalan to Gil, 4 March 1932, NNA 01433.
134 Catalan to Gertrude, 27 February 1932.
135 Catalan to Gil, 4 March 1932 (*No podia disponer a su antojo, ni hacer lo que quiziera en curar a los nativos, proveerles de cosas*).
136 Catalan to Gil, 4 March 1932.
137 Catalan to Gertrude, 27 February 1932.

again to your Community and work in the Orphanage for the native girls in whatever you may be required'.[138] It could only be an exhortation. As it turned out, Gertrude was grateful and complied.

Figure 5.11: Gertrude, Escolastica and Hildegard with Aboriginal children on the steps of the first convent at Drysdale River, 1931.
Source: NNA 80487P.

138 Catalan to Gertrude, 27 February 1932.

The need for formal structures was urgent. Fr Tomás wrote from Drysdale to clarify the 'juridical status' of the two sisters who remained. Balancing limitations with commitments, the abbot replied that they were 'only' Benedictine oblates, although their status conformed to the statutes of Leo XIII. They had taken vows 'but' privately, although Escolastica's commitment was for life, and Hildegard would make a perpetual profession 'when the time comes'.[139] Moving swiftly from one unwieldy topic to another, the abbot lamented the failure of a recent attempt to establish mango trees at New Norcia. It was hardly surprising that Fr Schyrgens's article on organising an oblate community should arrest the abbot's attention a few weeks later and set in train the sisters' departure for canonical training. Abbot Catalan wrote to Escolastica at Drysdale River in July 1933, promising that 'by the time this letter reaches you, Sisters Felicitas and Benita will already be in Europe'[140] and that the canonical community, 'which you had all so longed for', would be underway. After a long search, he had found 'Benedictine nuns who would adapt to your way of life'.[141]

The abbot's two-way correspondence between the Kimberley and Belgium would continue through the 1930s. The two sets of letters are compelling both for the connections between them as well as for their contrast. Felicitas and Benita wrote from the novitiate in Belgium; they were learning to make nougat and starch lace, they cooked and cleaned for the school and the monks, while struggling along in French and nourishing their missionary calling with the tradition of a European monastery. In the Kimberley, Escolastica and Hildegard were joined by Matilde in September 1932,[142] returning the group to the trio of sisters first intended. They also wrote as directed in their own style without worrying about oratory.[143] They sent letters down the coast whenever a mail boat called, reporting on their hopes for the local people, their work in the vegetable garden and their conversations with the women. They washed the laundry, taking it to the river, and cooked, including sweets for special occasions, while also sampling crocodile and 'the first-class meal' of dugong.[144] They were anxious about the rains and the heat and assured the abbot they

---

139 Catalan to Gil, 5 March 1932.
140 Catalan to Escolastica, 24/26 July 1933, NNA 01434.
141 Catalan to Escolastica, 24/26 July 1933.
142 Matilde de la Fuente to Catalan, Broome, 15 September 1932, NNA 01061.
143 Catalan to Escolastica and Hildegard, 28 August 1932.
144 Escolastica to Catalan, NNA 01061, sweets: 6 July 1934, 8 February 1935; crocodile: 30 September 1934; dugong: 9 October 1936, trans. Kerry Mullan.

were healthy. These letters might well be the only common link between Belgium and the Kimberley. But both from Europe and from the north, a shared conviction governed the sisters' writing. How simple it seemed to these women that they should be worlds away from the villages of Burgos and how much they prized their new identities as missionaries and as Benedictines.

6

Monastic and Missionary Sisters: 'Their Currency and Savings Were the Work'

In the 1930s and 1940s the Spanish women embraced their status not only as active missionaries in the remote Kimberley but also as 'true and authentic Benedictines'.[1] The intertwined monastic and missionary dimensions of their life had been a fault line since the time of the Teresians. Over these years, when the church recognised their community life, the work done by the 'Benedictine Missionary Oblate Sisters' became the bridge that connected monastic principles to their tasks as missionary women. The Rule of St Benedict in the sixth century had identified manual work as part of monastic spirituality. This chapter begins by exploring the place of work in the long history of Benedictine life, especially as it had been interpreted in the traditions of the mission at New Norcia. Then, by gathering together fragments from the sisters' writing and their recollections, it will trace the intertwined themes of work and prayer as the sisters shaped their new community in three vastly different locations: in Belgium and in the tropical Kimberley, as well as in the original house at New Norcia.

---

1   Abbot Catalan to Escolastica Martinez, 28 April 1937, New Norcia Archive (NNA) 01438/125.

Figure 6.1: Benedictine Oblate Sisters of New Norcia early 1931.
Left to right: Hildegard Ruiz, Escolastica Martinez, Gertrude Banks, Benita Gozalo, Mary Cidad, Margaret Perez, Felicitas Pampliega and Teresa Roca.
Source: NNA W6-B3-4-108.

The equivalent status of manual work, formal study and prayer within Benedictine life paradoxically gave hard work dominance over both study and prayer as the preferred currency of religious commitment in the lives of these Benedictine sisters. Their work was part of their commitment to poverty: a giving over of their time and energy to be deployed as directed. Within a strong hierarchy that reserved many decisions to the monks, they gave their labour to the institution without expecting to influence that institution. As the Spanish *Notebooks* commented ruefully after detailing the heavy load of allotted tasks: 'The Sisters did not have anything; absolutely everything was provided to them by the Monastery, even down to the stamps for writing letters. Their currency and savings were the work'.[2] How poignant that the letters they sent with precious 'provided' stamps now play such a valuable role in piecing together their lives, and how telling that stamps were remembered as essential to life, a staple that they were not quite able to take for granted.

---

2   'Origen de la Congregacion de las Hermanas Benedictinas Misioneras de New Norcia, Western Australia', unpublished typescript from the notebooks of Sister Felicitas Pampliega, c.1921–c. 1967. Transcribed and edited by Sister Teresa González, Madrid c. 1980 (*Notebooks*, Madrid). Literally, *Sus moneda y ahorro er[a] el trabajo*.

Gathered on the bridge

At the start of a decade when 'work' was the metaphorical bridge connecting the monastic and missionary aspects of life in the New Norcia convent, eight sisters from the small community had their photo taken on a literal bridge. Sometime early in 1931 as the moves to regularise the community were brewing, they gathered on the high wooden walkway above the Moore River that linked the monastery's orchard and the apiary, near the waterhole the Yued people call *booradjin*. The bridge has no railings, and the drop of 6 feet (2 m) to the water below them is arresting. We don't know who chose this quirky place to have a photo taken, but the daring location is symbolic. Standing between earth and sky, the Benedictine Oblate Sisters were also standing between phases in their history.

The other bridge across the Moore, the one where there was often an Aboriginal camp,[3] was at the edge of town on the road to Perth. It had brought the women to the mission, and, from the time of this photo through another dozen years until the end of the Second World War, most of the Benedictine sisters crossed it again, leaving town for a time to implement the decisions detailed in the previous chapter. As the informal community expanded and evolved into a diocesan congregation, overseen by Rome through the abbot at New Norcia, six of the eight women pictured here, and three of the four others who joined them in this decade, were away from New Norcia for up to seven years at a stretch in other houses, most often for stints at their own branch house in the Kimberley.

Perhaps it was the foundation of the Kimberley house that prompted the photo. Certainly the three 'pioneer sisters', Hildegard, Escolastica and Gertrude, whether by dint of their new assignment or an accident of height, had led the line out onto the bridge. As the Spanish *Notebooks* affirm, the New Norcia sisters were 'already a community, although they had no constitutions, no statutes or anything at all'.[4] They were 'guided only by good will',[5] but they appear here as a collective, steady with each other above the water, uniform as daughters of the church in black serge, starched collars and regulation shoes. Elias Devine, the Carmelite, now aged 92, is absent as usual from the community photo, as is 16-year-old Matilde de la Fuente. When Elias had arrived in 1912 she found

---

3   Veronica Willaway in conversation at New Norcia, September 2015.
4   *Notebooks*, Madrid, 12.
5   *Notebooks*, Madrid, 12.

a class of eight girls under the age of 12.⁶ But increasingly active policies of 'Protection' for Aboriginal people as well as the economic pressure of the Great Depression made for a different picture. Now, instead of the neat rows of a 'whole school' photo with the teachers as in the years before the First World War, numbers in the institution had more than tripled. On this occasion when the photograph was being taken the oldest and the youngest of the sisters remained at home with the 51 girls of St Joseph's, while the rest of the community assembled for the record.

The camera has captured small distinctions in stance and style that help us sense something of their life together. Teresa Roca, aged 64, stands closest to the bank. After 27 years at New Norcia, she meets the camera with a direct gaze and a warm half smile; her feet are planted firmly on uneven planks, and her hands rest outside her scapular. Felicitas Pampliega is beside Teresa and also looks gently at the camera, her face shadowed by her veil, her hands tucked away in the demure stance of the cloister. With a decade of service in town, she is already a senior in these ranks and looks older here than her 28 years, ready to set out for Belgium before she turns 30. On her right, her contemporary in the community, Margaret Perez, is less composed and seems about to shift her feet from the awkward edges of the board. With Teresa Roca, Margaret is one of the two who will remain at New Norcia throughout this decade of travel, but the camera has caught her, here in her early thirties, not quite settled. In contrast 19-year-old Maria Cidad on Margaret's right appears in perfect symmetry, immediately recognisable to those who knew her 'always with her veil far forward',⁷ the sun just catching the gleam of her polished shoe. Teaching alongside Felicitas under the tutelage of Elias, she is now more often 'Sister Mary' at school, and in 1938 she will become the new superior of the house in the Kimberley, returning to New Norcia dramatically from hospital in Darwin in 1942 ahead of the Japanese bombing in the Second World War. For Benita Gozalo, standing beside Mary, a different war will make the most impact. She was honoured to be the standard bearer of the new congregation with Felicitas in Belgium but was overwhelmed with a lasting grief. The Spanish Civil War that broke out in 1936 meant she could not visit her dying father in Burgos despite

---

6   Numbers at St Joseph's are recorded in 'Returns of Children at New Norcia Mission', 31 March 1912, State Records Office of Western Australia (SROWA) S116 cons652 1916/1592, also 1 August 1930; Abbot Catalan's Ad Limina Report to Rome, Catalan Correspondence 1930, NNA 01436. See also Appendix 1.
7   Scholastica Carrillo, Interview, Madrid, 7 June 1999.

being 'close enough'.⁸ Here she has tucked not only her hands but also her arms behind the scapular. She seems to stand with her weight on her heels as some soldiers do, her young face almost entirely blinkered by her veil.

The Australian Gertrude Banks is in her early fifties and stands ready, too, her steady regard framed by the same veil, her scapular outlining her hands folded classically beneath. Her journey through this decade moves from the mission in the north, back to New Norcia, and then, independently of the community, to the Aboriginal mission at Lake Menindee near Broken Hill, before joining the Carmelites in Adelaide as Sister Gertrude once again. Thirty years Gertrude's junior, Escolastica Martinez is next: at ease and unselfconscious, one hand free and her sleeve rolled up a little, her belt buckled to the side. Like Benita, she is a veteran of five years at New Norcia, and she will soon lead the new community in the Kimberley. On her right, Hildegard Ruiz, who will travel north with Escolastica and Gertrude, is more sombre here as a 20-year-old than memories of her 'infectious laugh and energy'⁹ suggest. She is turned towards the photographer on the shore, rounding the line of companions into a group, the breeze wrapping her veil back like a villager's scarf. Their habits were simple and less confining than other nuns of the era. Their veils and skirts were long, but above their starched collars there was no enclosing coif to cover the neck or sides of the head. These assembled sisters were workers too; everyone knew that.

When the later Benedictine sisters reflect on the founding generation of their community they affirm hard work and a positive spirit above all. 'She was a good worker … very cheerful … a good and holy nun.'¹⁰ The unofficial Benedictine motto, *ora et labora*, drew attention not only to the two poles of the community's life but to the balance between prayer and work that was the ideal: 'She was a good sister, a good worker. Work is good, but to be with the Spirit is much better, you have to join the two'.¹¹ Benedict's Rule explicitly instructs his followers to value the cooking pots and kitchen utensils as highly as the 'sacred vessels of the altar'.¹² The Rule creates a climate where humble tasks are not ancillary but valid spiritual tools in themselves, a response made in faith to God's call.

---

8   Catalan to Benita and Felicitas, Maison d'Emmaus, Maredsous, 15 November 1935, NNA 01436/345.
9   *Pax*, November 1966.
10   Visitación Cidad and Scholastica Carrillo, Interview, Kalumburu, May 1999.
11   Teresa González, Interview, Madrid, 17 May 1999.
12   *The Rule of St Benedict in Latin and English with Notes*, ed. Timothy Fry (Collegeville, MN: Liturgical Press, 1980), 31.10 (hereafter *RB*); Terrence Kardong, *Benedict's Rule: A Translation and Commentary* (Collegeville, MN: Liturgical Press, 1996), 271–72.

Abbot Catalan's decision, explored in the previous chapter, to establish the missionary congregation through links with a Belgian house committed to the domestic care of monks gave implicit priority to the monks themselves and underlined a practical rather than intellectual or spiritual calling for the sisters. Again and again in letters to Felicitas and Benita as they trained in Belgium, the abbot reported the sisters at New Norcia were 'going well and full of work as always', 'healthy and working a lot as is the custom',[13] with a focus on their capacity for physical labour. But for the sisters concerned, all facets were linked by their understanding of work as a central element of Benedictine life, and all tasks were equal. As the wider literature on monasticism is showing, the Rule of Benedict freed the women and men of the monasteries to claim manual and domestic work as central to their religious vocation and, in the case of New Norcia, to the wider purpose of the mission as well. While the priests were the decision makers, the women were essential to the mission's enterprise.[14] Their specific and constant domestic tasks, their particular role with the Aboriginal women and girls and their contradictory status as informally professed but still vowed monastics put them 'between' and at the intersection of categories in the mission town.

Work and the body in monastic history: From Michel Foucault to Pierre Hadot

New Norcia's sisters understood their commitment to hard work as part of living prayerfully. The place of work as an embodied expression of prayer in monastic life has attracted scholarly attention since the 1980s, and that discussion helps us see the reality of the Benedictine sisters. In the first phases of the conversation in the mid-1980s the political philosopher Michel Foucault argued that ancient philosophical schools of thought promoted particular physical disciplines.[15] His work raised awareness of the bodily dimensions of the history of ideas and of monastic history. Essentially, the Rule of Benedict is not a set of beliefs that are assented to but a set of practices that are embodied: monasticism is enacted; it is a way of life that is followed (or not). So, the day-to-day realities of

---

13 For example, Catalan to Benita, 26 September 1935, NNA 01436/320; Catalan to Felicitas and Benita, 15 November 1935, NNA 01436/345.
14 Katharine Massam, 'Missionary Women and Holy Work: Benedictine Women in Western Australia', *Journal of Australian Studies* 39 (2015), 44–53.
15 Especially Michel Foucault, *Histoire de la sexualité*, vol. 3: *Le souci de soi* (Paris: Gallimand, 1984), in English as *The History of Sexuality*, vol. 3: *The Care of the Self* (New York: Vintage Books, 1986).

cooking, washing, sewing, teaching and meeting for prayer are validly what Foucault might call 'technologies of the self', at the core of the creation of a monastic and missionary person. Later, in response to Foucault, Pierre Hadot offered important and insightful clarifications. He argued that the endpoint of these technologies of belief is not in the fashioning of the person but in taking the person involved beyond the self and, by extension, taking communities beyond themselves.[16] The goal of the disciplined physical life is not discipline for its own sake. Spiritual disciplines, such as work, fasting and practices of prayer, are tools to reach beyond and engage the mystery of the universal. For Christian monastics, like the women committed to the mission at New Norcia, the goal was holiness, salvation, God. So the physical practices of the Rule should not be seen so much as technologies of the self but as strategies for going beyond the self. Work, like prayer, is a tool for living faithfully. The purpose of work was not production but rather to enable people to take their place in a community of commitment. To be a Benedictine was not to hold a set of precepts but to live a way of life.

The monastery was a community, not a factory or a work camp. Here is a vital nuance in the Benedictine understanding of labour as it was inherited at New Norcia. Alongside the affirmation of work without any hierarchy of tasks, Benedict also insisted the members of the community needed to be seen clearly as individuals, not as cogs in a machine. Pithily, he insists that talent has a role to play in determining tasks, that 'brothers should read and sing, not according to rank, but according to their ability to benefit their hearers'.[17] Artisans with particular skills were to 'practice their craft with all humility' for its own sake and the sake of their souls, not with the conceited sense of 'conferring something on the monastery'.[18] Members were given particular roles, as prior, as cellarer, in counselling the wayward, in answering the door to visitors and as abbot with responsibility over all, according to the qualities they possessed.[19]

---

16   Pierre Hadot, 'Reflections on the Idea of the "Cultivation of Self"', in *Philosophy as a Way of Life: Spiritual Exercises from Socrates to Foucault*, trans. M. Chase (Oxford and New York: Blackwell, 1995), 206–13. For the connections between Foucault and Hadot and their distinct views, see Cory Wimberly, 'The Joy of Difference: Foucault and Hadot on the Aesthetic and the Universal in Philosophy', *Philosophy Today* 53 (2009): 191–202; Orazio Irrera, 'Pleasure and Transcendence of the Self: Notes on "a Dialogue Too Soon Interrupted" between Michel Foucault and Pierre Hadot', *Philosophy and Social Criticism* 36 (2010): 995–1017.
17   *RB* 38.12.
18   *RB* 57.2.
19   On the cellarer, *RB* 65; prior, *RB* 31; counsellors for the wayward, *RB* 27; doorkeeper, *RB* 66; abbot, *RB* 2, 64.

All through the Rule, Benedict insists the monastic leaders should pay attention to specific needs of individuals in making sure they have clothes that fit, sufficient food, appropriate tools, and also the opportunity to negotiate 'impossible tasks'.[20] The watchword of the entire document is 'listen' so that authority is exercised in light of the experience of the whole.[21] A Benedictine eye would see the people involved in the work and their particular talents and needs, as well as the tasks that require attention. The Rule was a manifesto for clear-eyed discernment of ability and guidelines aimed not at the production of goods but solely at bringing the community closer to God.

In the context of Benedictine life, the point of work is not the task itself or the achievement of the person but rather the refinement of the soul. The overarching focus in the Benedictine framework was 'elsewhere', and the stock in trade of the lifestyle of the monks and for the sisters, as well as the girls in their care, was a commitment to technologies of godly living.

Spiritual disciplines cannot be imposed. There is a vast difference between hard work, poverty and obedience chosen within a commitment to ultimate values and that same regime being lived through force of circumstances. For the Benedictines, the Rule was to ensure prospective members understood the life on offer and to provide ample opportunity for the community and the applicant to assess each other. For the Aboriginal people at New Norcia, the choice about how closely they associated with the mission enterprise was much more constrained. Adults were not compelled to stay in town, but if they stayed they were expected to work for modest wages and goods in kind. The mission cottages were reserved for employees, almost always men with families. Unsatisfactory workers were dismissed and expected to leave town.[22] The collaborative manual work between the hardy Spaniards and the local people was an enduring hallmark of New Norcia's culture and at its best underpinned relationships of trust and respect. Even so, the most devout Aboriginal Catholics were not monks and were not bound to the monastery except as employees. On one occasion in the 1930s Abbot Catalan also spoke out against the government's increasing surveillance of Aboriginal people.

---

20 On individuals having what they 'need', *RB* 33, 34; provision of adequate food and drink, *RB* 39, 40; clothes and shoes, *RB* 55; impossible tasks, *RB* 68.
21 The entry for 'listening' in the thematic index to *RB 1980* makes the network of mutual listening clear, with the primary need for the whole community to listen for the divine voice.
22 Paul Willaway and Veronica Willaway in conversation, Perth, November 2014. Veronica's parents, Harold and Philomena, were sent away when Veronica was a sickly child because Harold missed days at work to care for her and her mother.

In a rare protest against government policy Abbot Catalan objected to 1936 amendments to the 1905 *Aborigines Act* that in his view made the people 'slaves'. The proposed legislation extended the powers of the state's Commissioner for Native Affairs, making him the legal guardian of all Aboriginal people under 21. Anyone who had more than one Aboriginal grandparent came under the Act and could be moved by the government not just to or from a 'reserve' as in the earlier laws of 1905 but also from any 'district, institution, or hospital'.[23] New provisions tightened requirements for a permit to work and required all marriages to be approved by the commissioner.[24] There were exceptions for men and boys under 21 with one or two Aboriginal grandparents 'where such person does not live after the manner of original full-blood inhabitants',[25] but no exceptions were made for girls and young women. In keeping with the recognised disproportionate impact on Aboriginal women and girls,[26] the numbers at St Joseph's grew steadily and more quickly than St Mary's, with more girls being placed by parents from outside the mission itself. The government was overruling the mission in Abbot Catalan's view. Freedom of decision making, mostly for the mission but also for the Aborigines, was at the heart of his complaint.

Some Aboriginal parents saw New Norcia's institutions as a lesser evil when the state threatened to remove their children. For example, one mother sent an urgent letter from Toodyay after a visit from the Chief Protector early in 1937. Writing as she spoke and with emphatic capitals for the official and the child, she asked permission to bring her daughter to New Norcia, explaining the threat of removal:

> I suppose you have heard by Mr Nevell the Proctor. He is taking every girl that is fair from their mothers. He Has taken several now and He came to my place to see my Daughter. … He doesn't want them to reconize their mother any more and I don't recond that's fair for Him to do that to my Daughter.[27]

---

23 *Aborigines Act Amendment Act 1936* (WA), sections 9 and 12, www.slp.wa.gov.au/pco/prod/FileStore.nsf/Documents/MRDocument:12388P/$FILE/AborgnActAmAct1936_00-00; accessed 19 January 2016 (site discontinued).
24 *Aborigines Act Amendment Act 1936* (WA), sections 13 and 25.
25 The phrase recurs through the Act; for example, *Aborigines Act Amendment Act 1936* (WA), sections 8, 13, 17.
26 Fiona Paisley, *Loving Protection? Australian Feminism and Aboriginal Women's Rights 1919–1939* (Carlton, Vic.: Melbourne University Press, 2000); Marilyn Lake, 'Feminism and the Gendered Politics of Antiracism, Australia 1927–1957', *Australian Historical Studies* 29 (1998): 91; Alison Holland, '"Wives and Mothers Like Ourselves"? Exploring White Women's Intervention in the Politics of Race, 1920s–1940s', *Australian Historical Studies* 32 (2001): 292–310; Alison Holland, 'Mary Bennett and the Feminists: A Response', *Australian Historical Studies* 33 (2002): 398–400.
27 Mrs J. Gillespie to Catalan, 16 March 1937, NNA 05120/5.

She made the case that her daughter was a Catholic and would be able to go to church at New Norcia. The Sisters of Mercy at the Toodyay school thought New Norcia was a good solution. 'Please send me a wire at once because I want to take her over on Sunday', the mother pleaded, 'Hoping the Lord will Help me.'[28] The girl and also her sister were admitted to St Joseph's within five days.[29] They were removed six weeks later, following a flurry of letters from the Commissioner Francis Bray: 'taken by the Protector', the record noted grimly.[30]

By July 1938, when the regulations to implement the full force of the Act were to be debated in parliament, Abbot Catalan was sufficiently alarmed to slip a complaint into the final paragraph of a letter to Aubrey Coverley, the long-serving member for Kimberley. Writing to thank the Catholic parliamentarian for sensible advice on a funding request that was turning controversial, the abbot took the opportunity to ask him to speak against the regulations.[31] They were 'ignoring entirely the descretion [sic] of the Missionaries and their Superiors'[32] and effectively binding Aboriginal people so firmly to the department 'that they become … slaves'.[33] He had long held the view that the power of the commissioner as a single authority, 'absolute Monarch and Pope of the Natives',[34] was a menace.

Mr Coverley did speak out but the overall thrust of the Act for more control remained in place.[35] Enforced obedience and governance by fear was at odds with Benedictine principles. New Norcia hoped to be admired by the government but on this occasion, at least, the abbot took issue with official policy.

---

28   Gillespie to Catalan, 16 March 1937.
29   Aboriginal Families Index (NNA), 203, 204 (with thanks to Peter Hocking for these details).
30   Bray to Catalan, 20 April 1937, 23 April 1937, 24 April 1937, NNA 05120.
31   Catalan to Coverley, 1 July 1938, NNA 01437/187. See also Catalan to Coverley, 1 November 1927, NNA 10425/137.
32   Catalan to Coverley, 1 July 1938.
33   Catalan to Coverley, 1 July 1938.
34   Catalan to Coverley, 1 July 1938.
35   Western Australia, Parliament, Legislative Assembly, Hansard Archive, 27 October 1938 (p. 1701), 16 November 1938 (p. 2152), 15 December 1938 (p. 3202), www.parliament.wa.gov.au/hansard/hansard1870to1995.nsf/screen1930s; accessed 19 January 2016.

Binding prayer and work together at New Norcia

Through the development of the community in the 1930s, prayer and work melded together. The Spanish *Notebooks* preserved the memory of back-breaking work in the late 1920s that almost eclipsed everything else. Alongside the St Joseph's girls, whose story as workers deserves separate attention, and picking up English from the girls as best they could, the missionary sisters worked as farmhands, until 'finally', at the end of crowded days, they gathered exhausted for prayer in the church. The produce of the 5,000 acres (2,023 hectares) then under cultivation was itself directed not only to the immediate practical needs of St Joseph's, St Mary's and Drysdale River but also to underwriting fees at the boarding colleges and to longer term investment in the Benedictine life of the town so as 'to form and educate our Missionaries'.[36] The work served all purposes and, as the *Notebooks* show, governed their lives:

> The Sisters and the girls went to the field and gathered grain, cleared small stones, collected gum from the trees, pulled weeds where they got above the wheat, picked fruit from a big orchard, harvested grapes and olives. The days were very busy and there was little time left for spiritual or cultural formation. Nevertheless the Sisters learnt English on the strength of parroting the girls. In spite of so much hard work they finally said their prayers with the fathers from one side of the Church.[37]

The spatial distinction from the monks in the church gave the sisters a clear place and a separate role in the prayer. The monks were on one side of the choir screen, and the sisters were on the other. Both gathered as religious communities, but it was the men, not the women, who occupied the monastic zone while the sisters shared the public space with any of the lay workers who came along. As numbers at St Joseph's grew, the sisters led separate devotions with the girls at home in the evening focused on the recitation of the rosary. Felicitas and her editors have left the challenge of the work and the sisters' ambivalence in these years intact: 'As the years ran on these young sisters were sometimes lively and other times longing to return to Spain'.[38]

---

36   Catalan to Chief Protector, 28 September 1928, NNA 01429/86.
37   *Notebooks*, Madrid, 12.
38   *Notebooks*, Madrid, 12.

It was looking back on this situation in August 1928 when Mary, Hildegard and Matilde joined the community that the Spanish *Notebooks* introduced the powerful economic metaphor of work as vocational 'currency' that gives this chapter its title. The arrival of three teenagers lowered the average age of the community to 28 years, with half not yet 21. All 10 sisters were responsible for the 42 girls at St Joseph's as well as cooking, cleaning, laundry and farm work together with the small school. The *Notebooks* affirm the community was forged in work, leading into the sentences we have already seen above that affirm their dependence on the monks:

> The work made them happy and already they were making a life as a community. The Sisters had taken private vows before the Abbot who was Superior, Administrator and teacher. The Sisters did not have anything nor had they means to provide anything; absolutely everything was provided to them by the Monastery, even down to the stamps for writing letters. Their currency and savings were the work.[39]

That there was pleasure in purposeful work was one thing; that it was their sole asset, the only 'currency and savings' they had to trade,[40] is another.

What stock were they building, using this currency of work? It depends on how they understood the transaction. Spiritually, with God as the focus, their lives were defined as offerings, literally 'oblations', and they had vowed 'not to count the cost' of their commitment. The economic metaphor made their material dependence clear and, in the reciprocal arrangement with the monks, their work bought them livelihood and institutional identity. But as the letters of the foundational sisters sent from Belgium and the Kimberley make clear, they had high aspirations for the new congregation and saw the daily work of the mission kitchen and laundry, in the garden in the north and on the farm at New Norcia, as part of a quest for sanctity. The connection with Belgium would underpin a formal status as 'brides of Christ'.

---

39 *Notebooks*, Madrid, 12–13.
40 Literally, *Sus moneda y ahorro er[a] el trabajo*.

6. MONASTIC AND MISSIONARY SISTERS

Emmaus House, Maredsous, Belgium

Felicitas and Benita left Australia on 6 November 1933 on the *Otranto*, dressed as postulants for the Benedictine Oblate Sisters in Maredsous. Accompanied by Fr Paul Arza, who was setting out to begin a doctorate in canon law at the Benedictine Academy of Sant'Anselmo in Rome, they travelled under their legal names as Isobel Pampliega and Ernestine Gozalo, although the passenger list acknowledged their years in community with the courtesy title 'Reverend Sister'.[41]

Much had changed in the month before they left: Magdalena, Francisca and Placida arrived from Spain, young and able to pull their weight in the community that was about to be reduced by two; and Mother Elias had died. Honoured by the *Notebooks* as 'unique among women',[42] Elias was buried with quiet ceremony after her death on 20 October.[43] She had come from running a Belgian missionary training college but there had been no opportunity for them to learn from her fluent French. They would therefore meet their new community in that mute state familiar to New Norcia's sisters, 'able only to smile since they did not speak a word'.[44]

Figure 6.2: Benita and Felicitas en route to Belgium with Fr Paul Arza.
Source: NNA W6-B4-1-023.

---

41   *West Australian*, 7 November 1933, 15.
42   *Notebooks*, Madrid, 17.
43   'Mother M. Elias', *St Ildephonsus College Magazine*, 1933, 47.
44   *Notebooks*, Madrid, 16.

The departure of the two founding sisters added to the flux of endings and beginnings. They sailed for Naples and spent a fortnight in Rome. An audience with Pope Pius XI was eclipsed by being part of the canonisation of Bernadette of Lourdes on 8 December. Then on 12 December 1933 they made the journey from Rome to Belgium, accompanied by the abbot of Montserrat, Benito Lopez. There was confusion about the need for meals. The *Notebooks* enshrine the memory of one small cup of coffee that saw them through a night and a day. At the town centre of Namur, near the monastery, communication failed again and they waited at the station in the dark. The young women in quaint clothes felt they attracted too much attention on the platform. Finally, well over 24 hours after they left Rome, one of the monks arrived to collect them, 'bringing blankets but nothing to eat'.[45] Once introduced to the community, language difficulties notwithstanding, there was at last a warm meal. The following day they were admitted formally as postulants, and on 15 July 1934 they took the habit and white veil of novices.[46]

They fell into the order of a 'proper' religious house with gusto, keen to learn all they could of work and prayer from this community of women 'oblate sisters' so they could translate it to New Norcia in the future. Of course, they had both been domestics at Las Huelgas in Burgos, but now they wrote with excitement and pride about their growing confidence in the Benedictine life. They mixed the learning of the Latin Office with the making of lace and the routine of the laundry with the pattern of prayer. The Abbey of Maredsous was a large, busy community with a residential school. The small group of sisters at Emmaus had responsibility for the washing and the cooking for both establishments. In so far as that arrangement matched New Norcia's exactly, Abbot Catalan had chosen well. If they regretted the narrow focus, Felicitas and Benita did not complain to him, although later Felicitas confided to the sisters that if they had to train in Belgium she would have chosen the motherhouse at Heverlé or the monastery of Benedictine women in Maredret ahead of Emmaus. At the time she gave the abbot no sign of any misgiving. Writing of their progress, both Felicitas and Benita assumed a link between learning the technicalities of monastic prayer and acquiring new domestic skills.

The interconnections between mundane work and the ultimate horizons of prayer are nowhere clearer than in the letters that the two novices sent to Abbot Catalan late in 1935 when they were waiting to hear the date of their profession as the first members of the new congregation. Felicitas and Benita

---

45 *Notebooks*, Madrid, 16.
46 *Notebooks*, Madrid, 17.

had hoped they would take formal vows on 1 November, the feast of All Saints, with two members of the Belgian community. The Mother Superior at Emmaus had offered to cut through the legal complexity by incorporating the New Norcia house into that congregation, but Abbot Catalan preferred to delay until Rome approved the 'new' foundation.[47] He had already firmly shut down proposals that they would adopt the habit of the sisters who had hosted them: because of the climate and 'other differences between there and here' they would stay in the simpler habit 'of New Norcia'.[48] A new and distinct congregation in the abbey nullius was the best hope to maintain the existing clear lines of authority.

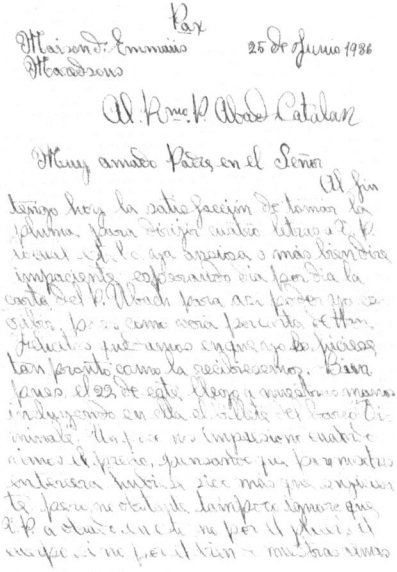

Figure 6.3: Benita Gozalo to Abbot Catalan, June 1936.
Source: NNA 01047.

Plans were in place for the profession at Maredsous, but still the paperwork to officially establish the congregation of the Benedictine Oblate Sisters of New Norcia was running behind. As Benita reported: 'The day finally arrived and the telegram did not, so the two Sisters made their profession and we were left with our desires'.[49] She consoled herself with a motto of Teresa of Avila, 'Patience wins all', and the conviction that God sees beyond the immediate to 'what most benefits souls'.[50] As urgent letters went from the Congregation for the Propagation of the Faith in Rome to New Norcia and back, Felicitas saw a comparison with the parable of the wise and foolish bridesmaids: 'four of us had heard the invitation, but only two were admitted to the wedding feast, those who were well-prepared'.[51] The legal preparation was not theirs to make, but she assured Abbot Catalan she would 'remain knocking at the door without ceasing to call

---

47 Catalan to Schyrgens, 16 July 1935, NNA 01436/229. See also Catalan to Bastien, Sant'Anselmo Rome, 18 July 1935, NNA 01436/231.
48 Catalan to Felicitas, 26 September 1935, NNA 01436/224.
49 Benita to Catalan, n.d. but clearly November 1935, trans. David Barry, OSB, NNA 01061.
50 Benita to Catalan, November 1935.
51 Felicitas to Catalan, 4 November 1935, trans. David Barry, OSB, NNA 01061.

out, showing ever greater fidelity until the beloved has compassion'.[52] She pressed the traditional allusions to the 'divine espousal' of her religious vocation in one paragraph, and in another gave details of the whirlwind of practical work the delay made possible:

> For some days now we have had almost all the Sisters busy working for us, I have never seen such charity. We hardly finish saying that we would like to know how to do something or other when they are already trying to satisfy our wishes. So one is copying kitchen recipes for us, others recipes for pastries, conserves of every kind of fruit etc. One day I happened to say that I would like to know how to make men's clothing, and the next day they sent me to the tailor who comes here. ... [H]e will give us patterns for trousers and jackets in different sizes. We have also had some lessons in the cut of women's clothing and as many patterns as we want.[53]

The letter that began with assurances of her constancy as an aspiring bride of Christ ended by asking permission to buy kitchen thermometers and for the abbot's prayers.

With a new possible profession date approaching on 8 December, the feast of the Immaculate Conception, the two women took confidence and 'placed ourselves under the direction of the Most Holy Virgin'.[54] For Felicitas the preparation for her vows drew sewing and biblical allusion figuratively together: 'with great care we began to put in place the rich ornaments that were still lacking to the beautiful wedding dress which was already made long before. ... We were convinced that no one could be as capable as she [the Blessed Virgin Mary] of perfecting this work'.[55] Around them members of the Belgian community all had various views about whether the permissions for canonical profession would arrive in time, but the New Norcia sisters apparently shared a serene conviction that Mary would see their prayers answered. With time running out on 3 December, Fr Schyrgens, whose correspondence with Abbot Catalan had been so crucial to this formal novitiate,[56] came to find them 'when we were both busy ironing ... asking us again how long it took for letters from Rome'.[57] They told him 10 days by ordinary mail and that they would not lose hope, but 'his only answer to this was a gesture of diffidence'.[58]

---

52 Felicitas to Catalan, 4 November 1935.
53 Felicitas to Catalan, 4 November 1935.
54 Felicitas to Catalan, 8 December 1935, trans. David Barry, OSB, NNA 01061.
55 Felicitas to Catalan, 8 December 1935.
56 See Chapter 5.
57 Felicitas to Catalan, 8 December 1935.
58 Felicitas to Catalan, 8 December 1935.

Two days passed with no news. Then on 5 December when the community gathered for the regular Wednesday conference the director announced a letter from Australia. Felicitas remembered: 'All the Sisters then bowed in our direction and gave us a big smile, and just as impatient as we were, wanted to know the contents'.[59] Benita reminded herself: 'Patience! Let us first say the Hail Mary because everything will come in due time'.[60] The letter was the one required from Abbot Catalan thanking the host community and completing the paperwork with his 'consent to our consecrating ourselves to God by means of canonical profession, and directly for the Mission of New Norcia'.[61] Although 8 December was a Sunday, a major festival, and not an easy day for extra events at the monastery, Abbot Lopez had already agreed to hold the profession for them at four o'clock in the morning if need be. But, 'it wasn't necessary', Felicitas wrote, 'and he presided for us at 6am'.[62] In a simple ceremony after the Offertory at morning Mass they made their public vows. They were the first women to take that formal canonical step with the community at New Norcia.

The rush and then the occasion itself had a touch of transnational eccentricity. The Spanish sisters destined for Australia prayed with incomprehensible accents, as Benita relayed home, 'The formula we read in French, or rather it was written in French, because the Fr R[ector] told us later than none of those present had understood anything, only he himself, so that was enough'.[63] Felicitas told Abbot Catalan she did not need to give him details as he would see the documents. If she had blamed him for the administrative delay that made her the 'foolish virgin locked out of the wedding', she took the opportunity to thank him for work on behalf of the new congregation. They had heard by accident through a visitor about efforts he had made to move things forward before the profession. She did not gild her hurt but acknowledged she did not know the whole story: 'although you had shown us an external indifference to our prayers and urgent requests, secretly you had been quite preoccupied, and with just as ardent desires as ours, or greater, to find what we were looking for'.[64] On the day when she had 'the peerless

---

59 Felicitas to Catalan, 8 December 1935.
60 Benita to Catalan, 9 December 1935, trans. David Barry, OSB, NNA 01061.
61 Benita to Catalan, 9 December 1935. Also Catalan to Schyrgens, 14 November 1935, sent after he received a cablegram from Fr Bastien in Rome, NNA 01436/344.
62 Felicitas to Catalan, 8 December 1935.
63 Benita to Catalan, 9 December 1935, NNA 01061.
64 Felicitas to Catalan, 8 December 1935.

grace … the happiness of being counted in the number of the spouses of Jesus', she wrote 'renewing in complete truth my gratitude, [to] thank you most sincerely for all your paternal solicitude directed to our spiritual good'. The same letter, so full of emotion, ends with an apology that she will not have time to write to the sisters but sending them regards. At the last the practical concerns of work flood back in. She assures him she has 'the machine that Sr Theresa asked us for' as a generous unlooked-for gift from Emmaus House, and records that the open-handedness of Maredsous in general means that 'they do nothing but give us things'. Their gifts included not only the preparation for monastic profession but also the tools of trade for a missionary life.

The history of the Benedictine women at New Norcia is full of false starts and amendments. The feast of the Immaculate Conception was a deeply appropriate date, for, as Felicitas with her awareness of records would have surely known, 20 years earlier the missionary women at New Norcia had first appeared in Benedictine habits on that day. Given her sense of history perhaps Felicitas was also not surprised when it turned out that there had been an administrative glitch despite the frantic flow of letters: they had made promises to an entity five days before it had been formally created.[65] Abbot Catalan wrote to them through January stubbornly insisting their title 'Reverend Sisters' was already formal, even though he was busy at the same time repairing gaps in the official record in Rome.[66] Once the Benedictine Oblate Sisters of New Norcia actually existed as a formal congregation, the two public members had to make their vows again on 28 February 1936.[67] Similarly, Felicitas has been remembered as the founding superior of the new congregation (although 'she never wanted to be a foundress, rather to be somewhere established'),[68] but Abbot Catalan's initial appointments made Benita superior while Felicitas (on advice from Emmaus) was given 'the most delicate responsibility'[69] as mistress of novices. They served in those roles for six years until August 1942, when the abbot announced a swap.[70]

---

65   Catalan to Schyrgens, 3 January 1936, reporting his Decree of Erection of the Congregation cabled to Rome on 13 December 1935, NNA 01437/4.
66   Catalan to Felicitas, 8 January 1936, NNA 01437/10.
67   Catalan to Schyrgens, 1 January 1936, NNA 01437/4.
68   Teresa González, Visitación Cidad and Pilar Catalan, Interview, Madrid, 4 October 2010.
69   Catalan to Felicitas and Benita, 20 July 1936, NNA 01437/96. Catalan acknowledges the advice in his letter to Schyrgens and the Mother Prioress of Emmaus, both 22 August 1936, NNA 01437/160-161.
70   *Notebooks*, Madrid.

Their shared task was to introduce the community into the monastic pattern of life they had learnt in Belgium. The practical skills of missionary life were taken for granted but Abbot Catalan exulted that they were 'returning clothed as true brides of Christ'.[71] Formal status as religious would bring a new phase for the missionary community:

> [Canonical profession] is a great consolation, consolation to yourselves, to your Sisters, and also to me. What can I say? This time your profession has been accepted by the church, your vows are public and you are truly Religious 'Oblatas Regulares de San Benito'. You will be the beginning of a new congregation, whose mother-house will be New Norcia.[72]

The abbot also warned them in a joint letter that there could be trouble because 'the Sisters [are] already veterans in the house and more or less accustomed to their ways, since naturally it was not possible in the past to demand the regularity that will be possible now'.[73] As it turned out, the transition was smooth.

Implementing the new congregation

On 22 July 1936 Abbot Catalan gave an informal talk to the sisters at New Norcia, announcing their new status, and on 23 August, four days after Felicitas and Benita returned to Australia on the *Viminale*, the seven in the New Norcia house were received as postulants of their new congregation. Did it make Sr Teresa Roca smile to do this again, 34 years after she had first arrived at New Norcia already fully professed as a Teresian? She was being replaced as superior of the oblate group. Perhaps the abbot had her in mind when he told Fr Tomás in the Kimberley that 'some of the changes in office have dented some individuals, but this is a natural aberration not supernatural. … [T]hough they have felt it perhaps, they have been able to overcome it'.[74] The formal status of the community gathered momentum and shifted the structures of the group. Catalan told a potential recruit, an Australian from Brunswick in Melbourne, there

---

71 Catalan to Felicitas and Benita, 20 July 1936.
72 Catalan to Felicitas and Benita, 20 July 1936.
73 Catalan to Felicitas and Benita, 20 July 1936.
74 Catalan to Gil, 18 September 1936, NNA 01437.

would be no new members for some time, 'not until the new convent is built and other circumstances are conveniently settled'.[75] He signed himself 'For Sister Teresa'.

The older sisters, Margaret and Gertrude, had known the group before talk of regularisation had begun, but in April 1937 Felicitas told them that Abbot Catalan intended they should remain oblates rather than become members of the new foundation.[76] Although we can speculate, the reasons are lost to us. Both accepted the decision, but their reactions diverged. Gertrude acknowledged that her path was elsewhere and made an energetic exit. While her first letters from Perth were signed 'the faithless one',[77] she also sent love to the sisters and asked them as well as the girls and the abbot for prayers as she tested a hope that the archbishop would support her to work with 'thousands of children' near Wagin in the southwest.[78] When that came to nothing, she gravitated east, seeking the support of Bishop Fox of the diocese of Wilcannia-Forbes for work near Broken Hill. Four years later, when the Carmelites in South Australia approached Abbot Catalan about her wish to join them, he responded promptly with the necessary reference, wishing her well as an extern sister.[79]

Margaret, on the other hand, remained at New Norcia even though classified as a novice in the new community.[80] With limited English, she had far fewer options in Australia than Gertrude, and perhaps after 20 years at the mission her connections in Spain were limited too, but there is nothing to indicate she wanted to leave or even took the slight to heart. Established as a favourite among the girls, and respected for that by the sisters even as they tolerated what sounds like mild kleptomania,[81] her strange status as permanent novice was no more odd than her previous situation as a private oblate. It continued for 17 years before she made her first profession under a new abbot in January 1953, 'assisted by only some of the Sisters'.[82] Whether that was a protest or an attempt to limit speculation on the long novitiate we can only guess.

---

75 Catalan to Miss Florence Jones, 24 June 1935, NNA 01436/207.
76 Gertrude Banks, 262 Fitzgerald St, Perth, to Catalan, 14 April 1937, NNA 01365.
77 Gertrude Banks to Catalan, 14 April 1937.
78 Banks to Catalan, 14 April 1937.
79 Catalan to the Prioress of the Carmelite Community, Glen Osmond, 20 May 1941, NNA 01444/233; Catalan to Gertrude Banks, 21 May 1941, NNA 01444/246.
80 *Notebooks*, Madrid, 26.
81 Teresa González, Interview, Madrid, May 1999.
82 *Notebooks*, Madrid, 26.

The new routines were welcomed by the other younger sisters at New Norcia. Francisca was impressed by the faithful observance, 'very prayerful, very reverent' even in the mission,[83] and recalled that with Mary, Magdalena, Ludivina and Placida she embraced the new, authentically monastic routines. But Edita, who had arrived as a 16-year-old with Ludivina in 1931 and been with the community when Felicitas and Benita set out for Belgium in November 1933, had already left on her own journey back to Spain in September 1934.[84] Listed without a surname or given the wrong one in various versions of the Spanish *Notebooks*, the shipping records tell us she was Trinidad López, and the correspondence shows that she, too, came from Tapia.

There is just the faintest outline in the records of this young woman's decision to return to her home town. Apparently she made the choice, supported by her family, with her father giving the abbot assurances he would accept responsibility for putting the 19-year-old on a boat alone.[85] Evidently with a clear conviction that she had made a mistake, and with resources at home, this sister was able to leave the mission. There had been unspecified failings, 'four times she repented, but without amendment',[86] so that in the end the sisters noted simply: 'This was not her call'.[87] The abbot seemed to think she might still have made a nun but, as he put it to her parish priest, she was just not sufficiently grateful to God for her vocation.[88] Catalan wrote careful instructions to Trinidad herself, explaining the month-long journey from Fremantle to Gibraltar and the boat trip of half an hour that would take her from Gibraltar to the Spanish town of Algeciras to catch a train to Madrid and Burgos. He said nothing of her vocation or the hopes that had brought her to Australia, just assured her that if she did as he said 'you will arrive happily at your destination, which is what you wish'.[89] She made it home safely and spoke well of the mission to the parish priest. We have no record of her own sense of the events. The abbot assured his colleague in Tapia he should not be 'ashamed' that one of the parishioners had 'failed' as those who remained were 'worth a dozen each'.[90]

---

83   Francisca Pardo, Interview, Madrid, May 1999.
84   Catalan to Victoriano López, Tapia, 25 September 1934, NNA 01434/296.
85   Catalan thanks Victoriano López for the assurances, 15 September 1934, NNA 01434/282.
86   Visitación Cidad, Interview, Madrid, 23 October 2013; Catalan to Pio Palacios, 15 September 1934, NNA 01434/283.
87   *Notebooks*, Madrid, 13.
88   Catalan to Pio Palacios, 15 September 1934.
89   Catalan, 'Instrucciones para Trinidad Lopez que va en Fremantle Australia Occ a Burgos en España', filed with correspondence 1934, NNA 01434/284.
90   Catalan to Pio Palacios, 28 December 1934, NNA 01435/358.

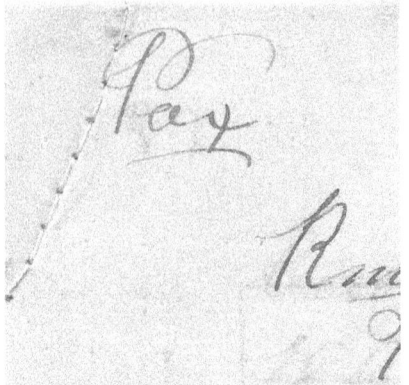

Figure 6.4: Escolastica's sewing machine put to another good use, 1937.
Source: NNA 01061.

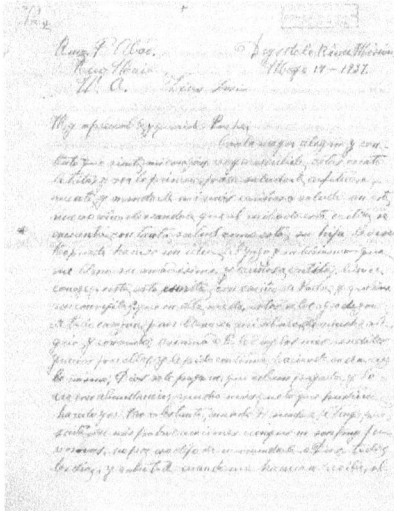

Figure 6.5: Escolastica Martinez to Abbot Catalan, 1937.
Source: NNA 01061.

In the north, the highly valued duo from Tapia, Hildegard and Matilde, along with Escolastica welcomed news of the monastic changes they would find when they came to undertake their own novitiate. 'I think we were all sighing waiting for them', Escolastica wrote.[91] Essentially there would be a new timetable with more emphasis on monastic practices. The changes were made possible because the new convent at New Norcia, built with some urgency and dedicated on 5 January 1936,[92] created spaces for the sisters as a community that were separate from the work areas they shared with the girls. There was a chapter room for meetings and a chapel upstairs with fine pieces of devotional art shipped from Valencia[93] and where the Blessed Sacrament was now permanently reserved. This, the abbot told Escolastica, 'supports the devotion a lot and helps them continue in their fervour'.[94] Escolastica shared that fervour. At Drysdale River the convent was much closer to the mission church than at New Norcia, and she found it easy 'to go and visit Jesus my sweet love'[95] in the tabernacle, 'the nest of our

---

91 Escolastica Martinez to Catalan, 17 May 1937, trans. Kerry Mullan, NNA 01061.
92 Catalan to Gil, 10 January 1936, NNA 01437/12.
93 Catalan to Benita, on the Stations of the Cross in particular, 26 September 1935, NNA 0136E/305.
94 Catalan to Escolastica Martinez, 28 April 1937, NNA 01438/125.
95 Escolastica to Catalan, n.d. but by internal evidence c. June 1932, NNA 01061.

love'.[96] Such prayer was already at the centre of her commitment, 'Oh! I can tell you truly that the time spent in front of the Holy One, life of our love, is so beautiful'.[97]

Figure 6.6: Interior of the church at Drysdale River c. 1947, Sister Magdalena Ruiz with a First Communicant.
Source: NNA 65851P.

---

96 Escolastica to Catalan, 6 July 1934, NNA 01061.
97 Escolastica to Catalan, n.d. but by internal evidence c. June 1932.

Figure 6.7: Interior of the church at Drysdale River c. 1947, sanctuary and two side altars, St Joseph and St Thérèse, patron of missions.
Source: Archives of the Benedictine Missionary Sisters of Tutzing (ABTM).

What she had been doing informally was now more prescribed at New Norcia, along with other practices from traditional convents. The abbot told the Kimberley sisters that Benita, who 'carries herself as a real superior',[98] had introduced reading in the refectory while they took two of the meals each day in silence, so that 'in this they are equal to the monks'.[99] They prayed the psalms in common, not only in the early morning, at sunrise, and in the evening, but also at three other points in the working day, as 'authentic Benedictine women [who] have the Rule as their foundation'.[100] Their place in the church remained in the public pews, but on Sundays they stayed after Mass to pray the offices of the middle of the day, while the monks prayed too, behind the choir screen. They also came to the church on Sunday evenings, sitting in the public pews while the monks sang Vespers.[101]

---

98 Catalan to Escolastica, 28 April 1937, NNA 01438/125.
99 Catalan to Escolastica, Hildegard and Matilde, 19 September 1936, NNA 01437/193.
100 Catalan to Escolastica, Hildegard and Matilde, 19 September 1936, NNA 01437/193.
101 Catalan to Escolastica, 28 April 1937, NNA 01438/125.

There was so little change to the work itself that the abbot saw no need to mention it. We catch glimpses of the tasks continuing unabated in other letters of the time. During the grape harvest, the abbot heard one of the monks stationed nearby at Goomalling was planning to bring visitors to the vineyard at Wyening. Catalan sent a telegram to forbid the visit. He explained later by letter that the work made decent appearances impossible: 'our Sisters who are working with the girls in the vineyard have their own pride and they do not like to appear before the people dirty or in an inconvenient way. This cannot be avoided while they are picking up the grapes'.[102] He underlined the primitive conditions to insist that ordinary hospitality would be impossible: 'our Sisters would be terribly disgusted if they were unable to prepare a decent meal to [sic] the visitors and at Wyening there is not abundance of means to satisfy even the most humble ambitions'.[103] Essentially they camped in the simple house on site, sleeping and eating in common, and taking in the harvest by hand.[104] Whether or not the sisters and the girls shared the sense of social decency the abbot claimed for them, it is clear their role was demanding, not decorative. Around the same time, another letter pointed to the financial significance of work at St Joseph's. Continuing the long tradition of controversy over laundry, Abbot Catalan wrote to the Provincial of the Marist Brothers who staffed St Ildephonsus' School, restating a claim for £331 for the school's washing. He asserted the monopoly of the laundry at St Joseph's, emphasising that the washing should be done in town, not sent elsewhere, and certainly not in the monastery's truck.[105] And just as the monastery, not the Marists, oversaw the school finances, so the monastery and not St Joseph's collected the laundry fees, set by the monks at an annual £4 per student.[106]

In the frontier environment of the Kimberley, the demand of the work continued while the significance of the sisters' presence as women was even more marked. Women working with women conformed closely with Aboriginal as well as Benedictine traditions.[107] The appointment of one of the sisters as 'practical infirmarian' and midwife was therefore an obvious move if the work of Fr Tomás Gil as doctor and pharmacist was going to continue. The sisters were certainly visiting the sick before

---

102 Catalan to Gregory, 22 February 1936, NNA 01437/52.
103 Catalan to Gregory, 22 February 1936, NNA 01437/52.
104 Francisca Pardo, Interview, Madrid, 31 May 1999.
105 Catalan to the Provincial, Marist Brothers, 28 February 1936, NNA 01437.
106 Catalan to Suñol, 13 May 1935, giving the fees for college students, NNA 01436.
107 See the description of four generations of childbearing in the East Kimberley in Catherine Bridge, 'Midwifery Care for Australian Aboriginal Women', *Australian College of Midwives Incorporated Journal* 12 (1999): 7–11.

Abbot Catalan wrote in September 1936 to insist Fr Tomás nominate an assistant 'when it comes to attending women and more particularly in illnesses and necessities appropriate to their sex … to wash and do the other things the case requires'.[108] Perhaps aware that midwifery was still controversial work for women religious, or perhaps acknowledging the sisters' lack of training, he commented that while they were 'not entitled to carry out the office alone … under your direction they will do well, and it is more fitting'.[109] Encouraging marriage and families had been a particular goal since the first missionaries in 1908 had been alarmed to find so few children among the local people. The presence of the sisters as nurses made contact with the women more normal and extended the mission's influence.

Roman authorities were against the involvement of vowed women in childbirth.[110] Although there was an exemption made for missionary congregations in the very month of these letters (following steady lobbying by nursing congregations in particular), Catalan was cautious not to compromise the hard-won canonical status of the new congregation. In commentary that betrays the abbot's own assumptions, he observed that 'some will find it more disgusting that others, even morally disgusting',[111] and then advised, following Benedict's precepts that the superior should assign work according to capacity, that the appointment could either rotate or be given permanently to the one most suited: 'perhaps not all are called to this. … [Y]ou must judge this for yourself and decide accordingly for the spiritual and bodily health of the Sisters'.[112]

In the sisters' own letters there are hints of both more contact and a closer relationship with the local women. Tasks such as dressmaking were shared equally and the sisters' skills were apparently appreciated and copied quickly by the Aboriginal women. There were regular occasions picking peanuts and joking with the women in the garden.[113] Escolastica assured the abbot, 'We communicate a lot with the natives, the children of course'.[114] But the strangeness of local customs and the role of the mission played on her mind too. Describing a visit of a group of Aborigines in 1934,

---

108 Catalan to Gil, 19 September 1936, NNA 01437/191.
109 Catalan to Gil, 19 September 1936.
110 Carmen Mangion, '"To Console, to Nurse, to Prepare for Eternity": The Catholic Sickroom in Late Nineteenth-Century England', *Women's History Review* 21 (2012): 657–78.
111 Catalan to Gil, 19 September 1936.
112 Catalan to Gil, 19 September 1936.
113 Escolastica to Catalan, 6 July 1934, trans. Kerry Mullan, NNA 01061.
114 Escolastica to Catalan, 8 February 1932 [1933], trans. Kerry Mullan, NNA 01061.

she was struck by both the impact of the mission and the resilience of Aboriginal customs. On the one hand, small children were left behind by the families; on the other, young sisters already committed in polygamous marriage left, and happily:

> The women also came [to the mission], with their beautiful children, but to me they seem too small for them to want to leave them here, and what's more, they are from very far away. They say yes, but I don't believe it, because they always say yes, and later they escape. There were also another two—one of ten and one of fifteen, the poor things—we were upset to see them placed between these such brutal customs that they have, but these ones didn't leave them, because they are already with a husband who could almost be their grandfather, and they are so happy, and the two are sisters and with the same man.[115]

Exuberant about her own faith, Escolastica did not dispute the girls' happiness. She saw it as clearly as she saw 'brutal customs' and felt the dissonance as children were left behind.

Escolastica remained realistic about the degree of change the abbot should expect from the mission. Although her 'greatest wishes are none other than speaking to them of the great love that we should have for Our Lord',[116] she was taken aback when the abbot suggested she keep a lookout for Benedictine vocations in the small school. She put more modest missionary goals in God's hands:

> I would be satisfied if God gives them the grace to be good Christians; I think this would already be a lot, but as for becoming nuns, I doubt it. But in the end God and Our Mother know what's best for them.[117]

If there were vocations among the girls she would be delighted, but did not think it very likely, 'because they are very difficult to crack'.[118]

As the sisters took on monastic practices there was some acknowledgment that the intensity of their work, almost literally burning candles at both ends, would sometimes create friction in the community. The abbot was especially pleased that shared recreation was compulsory in the official

---

115 Escolastica to Catalan, 6 July 1934.
116 Escolastica to Catalan, 8 February 1932 [1933].
117 Escolastica to Catalan, 14 September 1934, trans. Kerry Mullan, NNA 01061.
118 Escolastica to Catalan, 14 September 1934.

timetable as 'an opportunity for peace' if the working day threw up 'stress due to personality or faults in humility'.[119] He held up common leisure time and careful attention to the Rule in general as an 'impenetrable wall'. It would protect the community against quarrels and the murmuring of complaints so it could 'grow in virtue and merit'. Murmuring about the circumstances or the other members was a classic monastic ailment, expressly forbidden in the sixth-century document as corrosive of community.[120] Unity between the sisters was a key sign of good formation, and the abbot urged the Kimberley group to 'be full of the good spirit that should exist between religious sisters and those of the same habit [at New Norcia]'.[121] In the same week as this admonition the abbot purchased a Singer sewing machine for Drysdale River and told the sisters, playfully or not, it was a concession to 'the wishes of you three' so that 'murmuring' against their work should stop.[122] Escolastica used the Singer to treadle stitch across the corners of her longer letters. Her immediate reply was brief and written to catch the mail boat by stealing time from sleep.[123] Touched, Catalan acknowledged the grind of the life: 'I know how much appeal there is in sleeping after many hours of continuous and heavy work'.[124] When Escolastica did comment on the machine directly, it was to link the work with God in the Benedictine spirit: she was 'enormously grateful' for it, and for the irons he'd also sent 'because now at least we can iron with pleasure and without anybody grumbling. So our work will be more pleasing to God; don't you think it is better like that?'[125]

In public statements Abbot Catalan maintained that experience at New Norcia had prepared the Kimberley sisters for their work in the north. He told the Melbourne Eucharistic Congress in 1934 that 'their life is a life of work and prayer' so that they 'found themselves quite at home'.[126] Certainly there were continuities between what they had done at New Norcia and work in the new environment. Some were predictable and

---

119 Catalan to Escolastica, Hildegard and Matilde, 19 September 1936, NNA 01437/193.
120 *RB* 40. See John H. Smith, 'Grace and Grumbling: With Reference to the Rule of St Benedict', in *Immense, Unfathomed, Unconfined: Essays in Honour of Norman Young*, ed. Sean Winter (Melbourne: Uniting Academic Press, 2013), 309–21.
121 Catalan to Escolastica, Hildegard and Matilde, 19 September 1936, NNA 01437/193.
122 Catalan to Escolastica, Hildegard and Matilde, 25 September 1936, NNA 01437/203.
123 Escolastica to Catalan, 9 October 1936, trans. Kerry Mullan, NNA 01061.
124 Catalan to Escolastica, 28 April 1937, NNA 01444.
125 Escolastica to Catalan, 15 May 1937, trans. Kerry Mullan, NNA 01061.
126 Catalan, 'Drysdale River Mission', in *The National Eucharistic Congress, Melbourne, Australia, December 2nd–9th, 1934*, ed. J. M Murphy and R. F. Moynihan (Melbourne: Advocate Press, 1936), 188.

already published widely: 'teaching and instructing [the children] in the truths of religion', as well as 'cooking and sewing and other occupations so indispensible to the Mission'.[127] Others were more surprising and tucked into the detail of letters: nougat at Christmas made with the almond grinder they brought from the kitchen at St Joseph's, regular production of 80 bottles of tomato conserve, devotional reading for an hour before lunch (Escolastica asked the abbot to send a biography of St Francis, a collection of his letters, and the letters of St Teresa), walks in the New Norcia tradition on Sunday and Thursday.[128]

There were the perpetual language difficulties. 'Don't worry,' the abbot tried to reassure Matilde as she took her turn at the school of 10 pupils at Drysdale River, 'soon you will know how to tell them the most important things and they will understand the catechism'.[129] From afar, Escolastica encouraged the idea that the new novices, Magdalena, Francisca and Placida, should have lessons in English at St Gertrude's when they arrived at New Norcia in 1934, 'because that's what we need [to speak] in this country, and then they will be able to teach those who don't go out, like myself'.[130] But 'bored in a bad way and growing sad because it seemed they were not teaching them as they hoped',[131] the newcomers left the college and began lessons with Mary, by then in charge of the school at St Joseph's, on the strength of the English she had learnt from Mother Elias. In the abbot's eyes this 'concession to human weakness' put Matilde in the north at the forefront of studies: 'How are you going with English?' he asked her. 'I understand you like it a lot, and have regular lessons [from the monks] and read a lot in this language. Good, so it will be more useful every day.'[132] She was also learning to sing the psalms: 'Well done', the abbot affirmed. 'When you come back to New Norcia you will be ahead of everything.'[133] Escolastica reminded the abbot that with English they could be 'more useful' to the mission.[134] It was obvious to everyone that without a proper grounding in the language the sisters were reliant

---

127 Catalan, 'Drysale River Mission', 188.
128 Catalan to Benedictine Missionary Sisters, 9 January 1933, NNA 01434/17; Escolastica to Catalan, 30 September 1934, NNA 01061; Catalan to Escolastica, 24–26 July 1933; Escolastica to Catalan, 6 July 1934, NNA 01061.
129 Catalan to Matilde, 5 March 1934, NNA 01435/100; numbers in the school from Escolastica to Catalan, 8 February 193[3], NNA 01061.
130 Escolastica to Catalan, 6 July 1934, trans. Kerry Mullan, NNA 01061.
131 Catalan to Matilde, 2 May 1935, NNA 01436/143.
132 Catalan to Matilde, 2 May 1935.
133 Catalan to Matilde, 2 May 1935.
134 Escolastica to Catalan, 6 July 1934, NNA 01061.

on others in all their contacts with the Australian community. In the Benedictine scheme of prayer and work, however, language skills were not a priority. Or to put it another way, the impracticality of not speaking the language did not impact on their capacity to pray or to work.

The rhythm of prayer and work framed the Benedictine life wherever the sisters were, but there was also plenty that was unfamiliar at the isolated tropical mission. Their correspondence picks up newsworthy differences against a background of unquestioned monastic observance: Easter marked with all-day singing and interrupted by the mission bell only 'because when they start to dance they don't know when to stop', the 'Purgatory' of ground so hot they could not stand on it despite shoes wrapped in four other layers of covering, the itch of *zarpullido* or prickly heat under regulation black serge clothing, the relief of the river where (against the abbot's concern for propriety) they could swim in their expansive pinafores, 'nice' photographs where they wore their collars so the abbot could 'show them to anyone', and other photographs so 'mixed with natives' that the abbot could not tell who was who.[135]

There was the walk of over five hours through head-high grasses, between the Drysdale River Mission station and the new convent and mission settlement with a reliable water supply at Kalumburu; a real danger that without flour they would become a 'house without bread'; and crocodile, mangoes, dugong and other unfamiliar food so that the intrepid Escolastica could declare: 'What doesn't poison you makes you fatter'.[136] The *Notebooks*, compiled at a distance and later, stress the community's hardship especially in relation to cooking. Supplies came in by barge every six months, but most familiar food could not be stored; 'therefore', Felicitas or her editors recorded crisply, 'it was not sent'.[137] Flour was a mainstay, lasting three months before what remained was 'fermented' with moths and other insects. The sisters made bread notwithstanding and added it to great pots of soup as both breakfast and supper for all at the mission 'unless', the *Notebooks* concede without telling us how often, 'one of the Aboriginal women brought some fish or kangaroo tail'. The heat of the oven and the kneading of the bread was 'unimaginable'.[138]

---

135 Escolastica to Catalan, 6 July 1934, 8 February 1935, trans. Kerry Mullan, NNA 01061; Catalan to Matilde, 7 August 1934, NNA 01434/238.
136 Escolastica to Catalan, 6 July 1934, 17 May 1937, 30 September 1934, trans. Kerry Mullan, NNA 01061.
137 *Notebooks*, Madrid, 15.
138 *Notebooks*, Madrid, 15.

6. MONASTIC AND MISSIONARY SISTERS

Figure 6.8: Washing in the river, but wearing collars.
Source: NNA W7-A5-180-1.

Figure 6.9: Washing as it was more usually done, without collars and with helpers.
Source: ABTM.

Figure 6.10: Magdalena (seated), Ludivina and Maria (in apron) on a picnic at Drysdale River, c. 1939.
Source: NNA 65318P.

Figure 6.11: Escolastica with her class at Drysdale River, 1932.
Source: NNA 65312P.

Figure 6.12: Fr Boniface Cubero with a camp oven on a picnic, 1930s.
Source: NNA 80499P.

In the tropical wet season, and also in the dry, the sisters kept the conventions of the convent as the norm: routines of prayer and work and even standard habits designed for Europe's climate remained. The small community of between four and six monks also continued to work hard in practical as well as pastoral tasks, but with the arrival of the sisters they were freed from routines of domestic work. Asked to comment on a photograph of Fr Boniface Cubero baking bread in a camp oven around this time, Scholastica Carrillo, the later namesake of Escolastica Martinez smiled mischievously. '*This* …', she announced with all her dramatic flair, '*This* … was for a picnic'.[139]

---

139 Scholastica Carrillo, Interview, Kalumburu, May 1999.

Figure 6.13: Posing for a photo on an excursion, 1930s: Hildegard (left), Escolastica (right), Matilde in front, local 'bush' men, woman in mission dress, and Benedictine monk with rifle.
Source: NNA 90509P.

Through the decades, the photographs tell a story of a more relaxed community than at New Norcia. The sisters socialised with the monks and shared recreation with the people, especially on Sundays at the beach.

6. MONASTIC AND MISSIONARY SISTERS

Figure 6.14: Josephine and Visitación with fishing nets at the beach, 1970s.
Source: ABTM.

The dual identity of the sisters as hard-working missionaries and faithful monastics was a matter of pride in Spain among their family and friends, as well as at New Norcia. Abbot Catalan's letter to the parish priest of Tapia, the village that was home to Hildegard and Matilde, was typical. He included a photograph to add to the reality of their reputation as heroines of the community:

> I show you this interesting photograph of the little nuns so you can see those you've heard talk of so many times and always with great praise, bursting with joy since they have gone to the mission at Drysdale: your former parishioners, today daughters of St Benedict and most fervent missionaries.[140]

---

140 Catalan to Pio Palacios, 28 December 1934.

The two from Tapia and Escolastica from Cavia returned to New Norcia in June 1938, six years and nine months after the foundation of their house in the north.[141] A second trio of sisters had joined them in May and stayed on to continue the work.[142] Magdalena replaced Matilde as the teacher, while Mary took over as superior and Ludivina as the cook.

Escolastica feared that the missionary life might have made the Drysdale sisters wilder than the rest of the community. As she returned to the motherhouse to begin the novitiate, she drew a distinction between herself and the sisters who had trained at Maredsous, 'who had the true spirit of true Benedictines', and was concerned 'in case I offend my beloved Sisters when I am in their company'.[143] Although she regarded her vows as an oblate as already fully binding, Escolastica also faced a reality that monastic discipline was in contrast to the freer forms of life in the Kimberley:

> [Perhaps] the mistress of the novices will find it a bit hard to get us professed ... I say this for myself because after spending so many years in this wild bush, there's no doubt it will be more difficult for us.[144]

But in the event it was a physical challenge rather than a spiritual one that she faced.

On their return Hildegard, Matilde and Escolastica took their places in the normal rosters at New Norcia, but Escolastica could not shake a persistent cough. It did not seem serious until 'one day working outdoors she was caught by a sudden heavy rain ... [and] her breathing became so difficult that she had to be rushed to Perth'.[145] Dr Lucraft at St John of God Hospital in Subiaco recognised tuberculosis. Treatment for TB promised little in the years before the mass production of penicillin or the development of the antibiotic streptomycin. Escolastica was in hospital for over a year as Lucraft operated twice without success. Friends in Perth, supporters of the mission in the north, wrote to enquire. The abbot thanked them for their concern but reported 'she does not improve

---

141 *West Australian*, 18 June 1938, 15; *Northern Times* (Carnarvon), 24 June 1938, 1; 'Pioneer Nuns of Drysdale River Mission', *West Australian Catholic Record*, 23 July 1938, 14.
142 'Chronicle of the Benedictine Community of New Norcia' (hereafter *Chronicle*), 10 May 1934, NNA.
143 Escolastica to Catalan, 17 May 1937, trans. Kerry Mullan, NNA 01061.
144 Escolastica to Catalan, 17 May 1937.
145 'Sister Mary Scholastica OSB', New Norcia *Sunday Leaf,* 29 November 1953, 2.

much'.[146] To Sr Gertrude, now in the Carmelite convent in Adelaide, he confided: 'it seems there is no human remedy for her. She can do nothing except praying, and that she does'.[147] Over the next two years of illness some weeks were better than others, but hope of recovery had faded. It seemed she had been ill almost since she left Perth and had probably caught tuberculosis from one of the friends of New Norcia who had come to see the pioneer group off on their way to the Kimberley. 'Among the Natives of the North this sickness is not to be found', the New Norcia news-sheet, *Sunday Leaf*, claimed.[148] Escolastica prepared for the end with Fr Boniface, also a veteran of Drysdale River and a friend of her family in Cavia, with 'exemplary resignation and patience'.[149] Defying pious platitudes she told her young nurse Francisca Pardo often enough that, 'When I am dead, I will come to pull your nose.'[150] Ardent and clear-sighted, Escolastica resisted stereotypes but she had long had a holy death in mind.

Work and prayer and salvation

From the beginning of her time in the Kimberley, Escolastica Martinez had been writing of her spiritual ambition to be 'a real saint, whatever the cost'.[151] She saw a direct connection between her work, whatever the tasks, and the merit God would find behind her effort to pave the way to heaven. In Catholic thinking of the 1930s, unchallenged since the Council of Trent, work undertaken graciously would not only find favour with God but warrant eternal life. Her work in the north was her response to a divine command, and she asked the abbot to pray 'strongly' that she would 'carry out [her] missionary duties well', because 'otherwise I will answer to God'.[152] Answering to a loving God still included the possibility of being found wanting. Escolastica relished the life of the mission and the natural beauty of its setting. She gave thanks to God she was 'very happy and content with my little blacks',[153] but she also wrote of suffering as a gift. She recast hardship as an invitation to trust God more:

---

146 Catalan to Catherine Herlihy, North Perth, 29 March 1941, NNA 01444/458.
147 Catalan to Gertrude Banks, 21 May 1941, NNA 01444/246.
148 'Sister Mary Scholastica OSB', New Norcia *Sunday Leaf*, 29 November 1953, 2.
149 'Sister Mary Scholastica OSB', New Norcia *Sunday Leaf*, 29 November 1953, 2.
150 Francisca Pardo, Interview, Madrid, 31 May 1999.
151 Escolastica to Catalan, 13 September 1932, 8 February 1933, trans. Kerry Mullan, NNA 01061.
152 Escolastica to Catalan, 13 September 1932.
153 Escolastica to Catalan, 30 September 1934.

> It is very difficult (but what is difficult is valuable) but I think that … a voice inside my soul says to me[:] Onwards daughter, onwards; even when you have to cross a mountain of pain, walk up this Calvary and embrace the cross through my love, then life is short and glory is eternal.[154]

Like the famous young Carmelite (and victim of tuberculosis) Thérèse of Lisieux, whose statue the missionary women crowned with roses and whose patronage was invoked in the name of the vital mission motorboat, the *Teresita*,[155] Escolastica was playing out a hidden, but divinely inspired, personal drama.[156]

Escolastica aspired to heaven for herself and also for the Aboriginal people she had come north to serve and 'save' if she could. At New Norcia, Aboriginal involvement in the church often stretched four generations and the drama of conversion was rare, but in the Kimberley of the 1930s Christianity had not overtaken Aboriginal tradition.

Conversion from being 'bush-y' was a priority for the Benedictines. 'God wanted us all to have the same right', Escolastica told the abbot: 'Pray for them'.[157] She envied the simple road to eternal life that Aboriginal converts enjoyed if they were baptised close to death. The 'cheap' and 'easy' road to heaven was one of Escolastica's themes. She put it to the abbot: 'This is truly happiness don't you think Father?', that the Aborigines 'enjoy themselves in this world, and then they enjoy the savannah forever in the next'.[158]

Escolastica's appreciation of the happiness among the people before conversion was unusual; even Salvado had stressed the misery of Aboriginal Australians before their contact with the mission.[159] The 'savannah' of heaven was also an image that linked eternity with the bush of the north and echoed the Spanish *selva*, the forest or jungle, that most missionary Spanish speakers hoped the Aborigines would leave. The echo continued in Escolastica's use of *salvaje* to refer to the people coming to

---

154 Escolastica to Catalan, n.d. but June 1932, trans. Kerry Mullan, NNA 01061.
155 Escolastica to Catalan on the gift of the statue (from the governor or from the Benedictines in Sydney), 8 February 1932; on the motorboat, 14 August 1934, NNA 01061.
156 On the significance of Thérèse, see Katharine Massam, *Sacred Threads: Catholic Spirituality in Australia, 1922–1962* (Sydney: University of New South Wales Press, 1996), 127–52.
157 Escolastica to Catalan, 14 August 1934.
158 Escolastica to Catalan, 9 October 1936, trans. Kerry Mullan, NNA 01061.
159 Work on Salvado's Spanish writing continues but Frederica Verdina has found no positive adjectives associated with Aborigines in a sample of his Italian discussion. See Frederica Verdina, 'The Depiction of Indigenous Australians in Catholic Missionary Epistolarity', Paper presented at the Eighth Biennial Conference of the Australasian Centre for Italian Studies (ACIS), Sydney, 1–4 July 2015.

and going from the mission or in the camp across the river. Literally, they were 'savage' in English, more evocatively, 'uncivilised', as in outside the settlement, and still in Escolastica's estimation 'fortunate':

> This is how to win Heaven easily, and what's more is that after being created in and enjoying this life, they are going to enjoy themselves in the next, so you see Father, how fortunate these semi-savages are. Oh God, that we might have the same pleasure of sending everyone to their heavenly home with such a good ticket!.[160]

She saw her own path as narrower because she might not live up to the ideals she had taken on. She also knew the abbot's estimation of contemporary Western politics, and probably shared the view he put to her and to Hildegard in late 1932 that, 'today in Europe and also in America there are people incomparably more savage than the Australian Aborigines'.[161] He saw a disdain for faith, or at least a stance against the church, in the Spanish Republic of the 1930s and condemned it also as uncivilised: 'among the hordes of savages we have to count a large number of our Spaniards, who don't care about justice and claim also to put God below their feet'.[162] In the abbot's estimation, Europe was in the grip of 'prejudice, anti-religion, in sum hell'.[163] It stood in contrast to the heaven the missionaries would enable for the people of the north. Making a bleak connection between the natural and supernatural world, Abbot Catalan suggested the frequent thunder and lightning should remind them 'that God is near … and that he is witness to all the work that you do for Him and through Him'.[164] He urged the missionary women to see this as 'a great consolation for the souls who for the love of God live a life overflowing with humiliation, which is usually the case for Missionary Sisters'.[165]

Escolastica was confident each deathbed baptism in the Kimberley secured eternal happiness as 'one more angel in heaven',[166] but she was also close enough to the people to recognise the fear among some who stayed away 'because they think that if they come to the Mission, we will make them Christians straight away and then they will die'.[167] She saw a clear division

---

160 Escolastica to Catalan, 14 September 1934.
161 Catalan to Escolastica and Hildegard, 28 August 1932, NNA 01433/185.
162 Catalan to Escolastica and Hildegard, 28 August 1932.
163 Catalan to Escolastica and Hildegard, 28 August 1932.
164 Catalan to Escolastica and Hildegard, 28 August 1932.
165 Catalan to Escolastica and Hildegard, 28 August 1932.
166 Escolastica to Catalan, 8 February 1935, trans. Kerry Mullan, NNA 01061.
167 Escolastica to Catalan, 9 October 1936, trans. Kerry Mullan, NNA 01061.

between missionaries and people, secure in the superiority of her faith and way of life, but, like Maria Harispe before her, Escolastica was committed to the Aboriginal people. Her faith suggested that the world's dismissal of them was not God's: 'I feel a special happiness in my heart when I visit them because I see that they are so looked down on by everyone, but at the same time it seems to me that Our Lord loves them very much'.[168] Linking herself with the people, she asked the abbot's prayers, 'For me and for these natives I love so tenderly'.[169]

Just as heavenly and earthly realms were paradoxically interconnected, Escolastica also saw a reciprocity between her effort on behalf of others and the vitality of her own spirit. She wanted the abbot's prayers to 'win many souls for my spouse Jesus, which is what he asks of me, and at the same time that he can save my soul, which, as you tell me, is the most important thing to us'.[170] The flow of grace between her faithful attention to her missionary tasks, the example she set and the quality of the explanations she offered the women and children of 'what our holy religion is, and at the same time the great love we must have for God Our Lord',[171] bore fruit in ways she could not predict. Only God knew what her work might yield: 'sometimes they don't pay much attention to what we say, but in the end God will be glorified in everything'.[172] The work of the Benedictine women in the north covered a spectrum of apparently mundane tasks valued for its practical contribution to the mission, but from Escolastica's point of view there was a divine scheme in motion.

From the outset, Escolastica had given her private commitment as an oblate the same significance as a formal religious profession. She celebrated 'the great grace [by which God] conceded to consecrate me to Him with the three precious nails: Poverty, Chastity and Obedience'.[173] She spoke of the mission as a cloistered world, and asked the abbot to pray that she would 'be grateful to my sweet Jesus for having taken me out of the world and brought me to the holy ark of religion, where, away from so many dangers, I can save my soul more easily'.[174] In a high-spirited flourish that calls on the motifs of religious women as 'brides of Christ', Escolastica

---

168 Escolastica to Catalan, 6 July 1934, trans. Kerry Mullan, NNA 01061.
169 Escolastica to Catalan, 14 September 1934.
170 Escolastica to Catalan, 14 September 1934.
171 Escolastica to Catalan, 14 September 1934.
172 Escolastica to Catalan, 14 September 1934.
173 Escolastica to Catalan, 29 October 1935, trans. Kerry Mullan, NNA 01061.
174 Escolastica to Catalan, 29 October 1935.

echoed Thérèse of Lisieux once again, stressing profound commitment and holiness through service in small things and offering the abbot a manifesto of her dedication:

> Yes I am loyal to what I promised Him on the day of my betrothal with the Heavenly spouse. Oh, how he obliges me to be a generous soul and at the same time, with a heart that never says enough and which links itself with all manner of hardship and sacrifice with a smile, for the good of such a good God who has done so much for this unworthy daughter of His.[175]

Perhaps most simply and significantly of all, she signed herself using her full religious name, Hermana Maria Escolastica, and included the initials of her Benedictine identity: OSB.

Poignantly, although predictably, it was Escolastica's status as a Benedictine that the abbot stressed when he wrote to her mother in early December 1941 after her long illness ended. His letter offered formal condolences on the death of 'your daughter, our most beloved Sr Escolastica OSB who worked with so much zeal in the missions of New Norcia and Drysdale'.[176] The early summer was already hot and in the last week of her life a bushfire had roared through 10,000 acres (4,000 hectares) of paddock nearby.[177] The abbot described only the classic monastic scene of the young nun's death for her family. She had prepared carefully, receiving communion all but daily through her final six months; there had been good days and bad days, but now the sisters gathered in her room, singing and praying, as the final hours lengthened out. They sent for the abbot about six o'clock in the evening, and they waited with Fr Boniface, still chanting quietly, until the end came about eleven o'clock. Escolastica herself was fully conscious until 'almost the last moment', her family heard, and 'completely resigned to the will of God' so that 'her death was most happy and worthy of a daughter of Saint Benedict'.[178] There was a solemn requiem Mass at nine o'clock the next morning, and the abbot penned his letter. Promising that Fr Boniface would write with more detail, Abbot Catalan hoped the family would find some comfort as they grieved in knowing the community had done all they could for her, 'everything, spiritually as temporally'.[179]

---

175 Escolastica to Catalan, 29 October 1935.
176 Catalan to Señora Nieves Rojo Martinez, 5 December 1941, NNA 01444/444.
177 *Daily News*, 27 November 1941, 1; *West Australian*, 28 November 1941, 9.
178 Catalan to Rojo Martinez, 5 December 1941.
179 Catalan to Rojo Martinez, 5 December 1941.

Echoing Escolastica's own sense of the interconnection of work and divine reward, the abbot assured her mother: 'It has ended then her happy path, and now she only rests in God who must reward with the glory of Heaven she who worked so for the glory of God and the salvation of souls'.[180] Then as the temperature climbed to 99 degrees Fahrenheit (37 degrees Celsius), they brought forward the funeral planned for the following day. In the early dusk as the heat waned, 'all' in the town gathered in the small cemetery for her burial.[181]

Grief and pragmatic attention to the mechanics of the afterlife mingled in the other reports of the death of 'a little saint'.[182] The community at Drysdale River got the news by radio-telegraph sometime on Saturday 6 December, and the monks recorded her role as 'foundress' of the sisters' community in their *Chronicle* and sent 'feelingly worded' messages of condolence to the community.[183]

Less than a week later the Kimberley community in turn sent news to New Norcia by telegram that Mary had been evacuated by air to hospital in Darwin with pernicious anaemia. The abbot decided the sisters at St Joseph's would be alarmed and 'feel it'[184] too much if he told them so soon that another of their community needed hospital treatment, but he wrote directing Mary to come home to recover. He also elaborated for her on Escolastica's death with light-hearted banter built on shared assumptions about the process of moving between this world and the next. If Mary had flown to Darwin, Escolastica had 'flown further than you'.[185] Furthermore, the timing suited her baptismal name Conceptiòn perfectly. The abbot observed she 'went to Heaven a few days before her nameday feast of the Immaculate Conception [8 December] in order to toast herself a little in Purgatory ... so be purified to enter Heaven on this extraordinary feast'.[186] Liturgically, the feast day, as with all the church's prayer, brought the worlds together, and the community was confident their dead were not far away.

---

180 Catalan to Rojo Martinez, 5 December 1941.
181 *Chronicle*, 5 December 1941.
182 Catalan to Maria Cidad, 11 December 1941, NNA 01444/231.
183 Chronicle of the Benedictine Community of Kalumburu (*Chronicle*, Kalumburu), 6 December 1941, NNA; 'Obituary of the Late Sister Mary Scholastica', *Record*, 18 December 1941, 7.
184 Catalan to Maria, 11 December 1941.
185 Catalan to Maria, 11 December 1941.
186 Catalan to Maria, 11 December 1941.

The realities of physical distance and an increasingly active war zone in the north of Australia remained for the Kimberley sisters. Following the attack on Pearl Harbor on 7 December 1941, there were fears that Darwin and surrounding areas were also likely targets. The monks painted the word 'Mission' on the roof of their main building on 9 December 1941.[187] As part of a government evacuation of women and children from Darwin, Sister Mary was airlifted out and transferred to St John's in Subiaco on 18 December 1941, much to the astonishment of the abbot who really did not like planes.[188] Darwin, 400 kilometres east of the Drysdale River Mission by air, was bombed on 18 and 19 February, and Broome, some 600 kilometres south, on 3 March 1942. Up to 1,100 people died in these attacks.[189] Despite the large sign on the roof, or perhaps because it was assumed to be a deliberate decoy, the Benedictine mission itself was targeted on 27 September 1943. Six people were killed: Fr Tomás Gil; an Aboriginal mother, Veronica Cheinmora; and four boys whose family names were not recorded, Sylvester, Dominic, Benedict and Jeremy.[190] Many mission buildings were also badly damaged, and the convent was levelled completely. By this time, Magdalena and Ludivina had been evacuated and were safely at New Norcia, but not before they had been held at a Catholic hospital in North Adelaide on suspicion of espionage, or at least claiming a false identity.

The misunderstanding underlined the marginal status of the small community. Two women in unconventional faded black habits had arrived late at night and were met by a priest who had never heard of Spanish sisters in the Kimberley or even 'such a place' as New Norcia.[191] If they spoke so little English and in such strange accents they were surely German, or worse, as the Spanish *Notebooks* record it: Protestants. It was after midnight on a long day, but they declined food so they could keep the fast and receive communion the next day and so inadvertently established some confidence among the observers that they really were Catholic. Then in daylight Archbishop Beovich, who had visited New Norcia, 'ended all suspicions',[192] though the arrangements for their onward travel still took

---

187 *Chronicle*, Kalumburu, 9 December 1941.
188 Catalan to Maria, 19 December 1941, NNA 01444/231.
189 'Japanese Bombing of Darwin, Broome and Northern Australia', Australia.gov.au, Australian Government, www.australia.gov.au/about-australia/australian-story/japanese-bombing-of-darwin; accessed 25 January 2017 (site discontinued).
190 'The Bombing of Kalumburu', Kalumburu Mission, www.kalumburumission.org.au/main/bombing.html; accessed 31 December 2015.
191 *Notebooks*, Madrid, 21.
192 *Notebooks*, Madrid, 21.

several days. Back at New Norcia neither their arrival nor the drama of the journey rated a mention in the monks' *Chronicle*, but they had a story to compete with Sister Teresa Roca's account of being taken into custody and held at a convent in Singapore on similar suspicions in 1915. Apparently little in the sisters' situation had changed in the 30 years that separated the two spying incidents.

It must have felt dangerously familiar too when Matilde de la Fuente fell ill early in 1944. She had gone to help with the vintage at Wyening for a 'change of air' despite not feeling well,[193] but suddenly she was vomiting blood. By the time she reached the hospital in Subiaco she needed transfusions before first one and then a second and third operation in a period of five weeks.[194] This time, the threatening illness was not tuberculosis but cancer. News from St John's of the potential need for a fourth operation prompted the community to enlist the whole town in a novena invoking the prayers of Rosendo Salvado as the founder of the mission for her recovery. Matilde remained in hospital through the following four months, but there was no further surgery, and the community welcomed her home to New Norcia in May 1944. She was not as well as she appeared, but an apparent cure secured by prayer would surely have buoyed everyone's confidence in the importance of her future at the mission. She had always been trusted and respected, as the abbot would recall, 'So energetic, so good, so missionary!'[195] Now perhaps she had been spared for a reason.

Matilde had taken her turn as infirmarian at Drysdale River with the other sisters in the original community there. She returned from hospital committed to the idea of taking up that post again. Indeed the *Notebooks* record that she hid signs of her ongoing illness because she was focused on completing an accelerated course in midwifery at the St John of God hospital in Geraldton.[196] Before this proposal for intensive training in nursing there had been no thought of providing the Benedictine sisters with education for more than domestic work. Almost certainly Matilde herself came up with the plan as she got to know the St John of God Sisters who nursed her. The records do not help us see how events unfolded, but undoubtedly the training would help her work on the mission. Disregarding her own health, she risked a great deal to undertake

---

193   *Notebooks*, Madrid, 23.
194   *Notebooks*, Madrid, 23.
195   Catalan to Boniface, 22 April 1948, NNA 01458/40.
196   *Notebooks*, Madrid, 23.

it, actions remembered as typical of 'the humble Spanish nuns who … find their happiness in spending themselves in the service of others'.[197] Clever, competent and patient, she completed the program with aplomb, and when the community returned to Drysdale in May 1946, Matilde took charge of the small mud hut that was the hospital. It gave her a great deal of satisfaction. Her community praised her 'uncommon intelligence, constant cheerfulness and amazing capacity for work'.[198] A few months of training was nothing in the scheme of things really, but it was an important innovation for the community in preparing the sisters for work that they saw as fundamental to their vocation.

In years when work remained a constant for the Benedictine women, there had been changes in their context. Aboriginal people found their lives increasingly scrutinised and regulated, so that institutional life became more than ever the norm for Aboriginal children.

The coercive *Aborigines Act* of 1905 and the amendments of 1936 were intensified with further laws in 1941 and 1944 that began to focus on cultural assimilation as well as race.[199] Overall, the climate of duress and surveillance meant Aboriginal families increasingly took the option, with varying degrees of freedom and consent, to 'place' their children with the Benedictines, especially when there was a family history at New Norcia. Numbers at St Joseph's grew steadily with more and more girls coming from families outside the mission. Relatively few were sent by the government. The Chief Protector, A. O. Neville, wanted to build the state institutions at Moore River and Carrolup, not foster church missions. The Benedictines argued at least annually that more of the children on their lists deserved government support and their institutions were growing. The ratio of children to adults at St Joseph's increased dramatically from two-to-one before the First World War, to five girls for every sister at New Norcia

---

197 'The Late Sister Matilda OSB', *Record*, 31 May 1948, n.p., copy in the Archives of the Benedictine Missionary Sisters of Tutzing, Carabanchel, Madrid.
198 'The Late Sister Matilda OSB', *Record*.
199 Peter Biskup, *Not Slaves, Not Citizens: The Aboriginal Problem in Western Australia 1898–1954* (St Lucia, Qld: University of Queensland Press, 1973); Anna Haebich, *Broken Circles: Fragmenting Indigenous Families 1800–2000* (Fremantle, WA: Fremantle Arts Centre Press, 2000). See also Derrick Tomlinson, 'Too White to Be Regarded as Aborigines: An Historical Analysis of the Policies for the Protection of Aborigines and the Assimilation of Aborigines of Mixed Descent and the Role of Chief Protectors of Aborigines in the Formulation of these Policies in Western Australia from 1898 to 1940' (PhD thesis, University of Notre Dame, 2008).

in the 1940s.²⁰⁰ Only five out of 94 residents at both of New Norcia's institutions in the first half of 1931 were on the government subsidy list, 12 out of 79 in 1941,²⁰¹ and the payment rose only slightly by May 1946, when overall numbers had reached 95, before dropping back to 45 the following year.²⁰² The mission administrators valued government approval rather than Aboriginal opinion and rarely spoke against the policy regimes of segregation and assimilation. Instead, the mission focused on Catholic identity as shared and overriding all other categories.

Most energy at St Joseph's was still directed to the routines of cooking and washing, mending and cleaning that had served the town since the 1860s. There was little time to spare for reflection on immediate problems, let alone to consider wider policy reported in newspapers that the sisters did not see and could not read. There was no incentive to change arrangements that met immediate needs. There was every indication that the institution was sorely required and that the work would continue and increase. But there were also some nagging questions about how the women could sustain the effort.

When the Benedictine sisters reopened the Drysdale River house in 1946, Sr Teresa Roca was 80. Aching with arthritis, she climbed the spiral staircase to the chapel by sitting on the stairs and easing herself slowly from one step to the next. Even the youngest in the community, Placida Catalan at 28, had spent 13 years following the rigorous schedule of days and weeks that depended primarily on the energy of the women. When Matilde's health began to fail again and someone was needed to replace her in the Kimberley, the abbot worried about the numbers needed to carry on the work: 'they are not very numerous even at New Norcia'.²⁰³ There was pressure from the archdiocese of Perth and the Christian Brothers to establish another branch house at Bindoon that would split the numbers again.²⁰⁴ For individual sisters who found their footsteps flagging as they made their way to chapel, fatigue had a deeper purpose and could be redeemed in prayer. But, as a whole, 'their currency and savings' were still the work, and the community needed more and younger members.

---

200 Fr Maur to the Commissioner of Native Affairs, 23 October 1950, 'New Norcia Mission – Subsidy and General', SROWA S2030 cons993 1926/0350; Catalan to the Commissioner of Native Affairs, 28 May 1947, NNA 01450/104, and 30 September 1941, NNA 01444/306. See also Appendix 1. (The subsidy increased from £15 in 1931 to £16 in 1947, although the abbot proposed the real amount should have been closer to £22; the correspondence trail shows discussion of 12 blankets but no cash amount in 1950.)
201 Placid Spearritt, Submission to the National Inquiry into the Separation of Aboriginal and Torres Strait Islander Children from Their Families, 17 July 1996, NNA 04583.
202 See Appendix 1.
203 Catalan to Boniface, 22 April 1948.
204 See Chapter 8.

7

Gathering New Energy: Abbot Catalan Recruiting in Spain, 1947–48

In July 1947 Anselm Catalan took a one-way ticket to Europe on the first stage of a journey that sought new life and energy for New Norcia. For 12 years safe travel between Australia and Spain had been restricted, limited first by unrest and civil war in Spain and then prevented by the Second World War. But now, as the Australian Government actively sought immigrants to boost agriculture, establish industries and build population for national security, there would be new arrivals again at New Norcia. Unable to find a return berth on any boat, the abbot left his travel plans open; in any case, he did not know for sure how many new members would be making the return journey with him. This time he was looking for at least a dozen young people: six men for the monastery and at least six new members, perhaps more, to join New Norcia's missionary women. It was imperative that the group gathered new energy.

Like a photographic negative, the carbon copies of Anselm Catalan's correspondence, so diligently kept, invite us to imagine the subtle colours of the wider missionary enterprise. This chapter draws on the abbot's letters as the key surviving source for the dynamics of recruiting new members. We can trace his continuing preoccupations with good health and simple holiness as requirements for a life of hard work at the mission. Even without the replies we catch glimpses of what it meant to receive his letters, and, in faint outline, we can follow other characters in the drama. As his replies mirror back the personalities of the young women interested in his work, we can also sense in this correspondence assumptions that do not quite mesh and the potential for challenges and conflict at the mission. Moving into the postwar period there was a mood for rebuilding at New Norcia. As the abbot gathered his party he brought together young women who would provide the foundation for new work in the school, a branch house at Bindoon, and the continuing work in the Kimberley, as well as for fresh energy in the laundry and kitchen. It was Abbot Catalan's intention that there would be change, but many of the new sisters would be shocked by the conditions they found at New Norcia. Their group was buoyed by the expectation that they would make a difference.

Catholic missions continued to be a matter of national pride. Idealistic young people were regularly invited to consider emigration to serve the church as missionaries. Most travelled to former Spanish colonies in Central and South America, Africa and China. Australia was an unusual destination but clearly recognised as a part of the broader mission enterprise, especially in the network of villages in the north of Spain where New Norcia was well-known.

In the 1940s the local paper in Burgos gave full coverage to events such as an annual 'Mission Week' and regularly featured both the Benedictine tradition and the significance of missionaries for the church. It reported proudly on the Spanish commitment to the church overseas, in keeping with the tenor of General Franco's Nationalist Government in which Spain was identified with Catholicism. Missionary work was affirmed as a heroic and also realistic choice in these reports. The public face of missionary life was always male. But young women read the papers too, heard the admiring stories, and were moved by the hope that they could save souls, work for God, and live a good and meaningful life.[1] It was, as Scholastica Carrillo would recall, 'a missionary time in my place'.[2]

Scholastica, whose baptismal name was Josefina, remembered telling her mother that she wanted to be a missionary. It was an early memory, firmly dated from before her father died when she was six years old. It was the same kind of childhood ambition that might have seen her older brothers hope to be businessmen or teachers, but it came to have much greater significance for her. The general talk about overseas church work in the parish and in her family's fish shop that had so inspired her as a child

---

1 For example, *Diario de Burgos*, 29 March 1948, 25 May 1948, 12 August 1948, 19 August 1948.
2 Scholastica Carrillo, Interview, Kalumburu, 1 May 1999.

reassured her as an adult that her vocation was real. The memory of how specific she had been in the childhood conversation with her mother kept her confident in later life of her decision to join the Benedictine community at New Norcia and especially nourished her conviction that her home was in the mission in the Kimberley. Six-year-old Josefina Carrillo was probably not the only child to announce one day to her mother that she would be a missionary, but as an adult she remained surprised at what her child-self seemed to have known:

> I was not yet seven years of age. … [M]y father died on 20 February [1924] and I make seven on the 15th March, … and I told my mother before my father died, so I was not yet seven: 'When I am older, I will go far away from here (I couldn't go further!) and I will be dressed in white and I will be in a very hot place.' All that I told my mother when I was not yet seven.[3]

Her early hope of being a missionary encouraged the young woman through loss and hardship in her twenties as she nursed in war-torn San Sebastian and wrestled with saving up a dowry to join the Sisters of Charity who ran the city's hospital. When she heard that a friend's visiting uncle was an abbot recruiting for New Norcia's convent and would not ask for a dowry, her childhood dream was all the explanation she needed.[4]

Abbot Catalan's journey of 16 months in 1947 and 1948 stretched across a wide canvas of international Catholicism. It connected him to celebrations marking 14 centuries since the death of St Benedict, to meetings in Rome to elect a new abbot primate, to the inner-city youth networks of Catholic Action, and to small Spanish farms where children heard stories of the missions. As he travelled through the north of Spain in the second half of the trip, drawing on some 30 years of experience to assess potential new workers for the mission, Abbot Catalan had a certain public standing as well as private connections. He was listed among the dignitaries of both church and state whose presence to honour Benedict at the famous monastery of Silos was reported by the *Diario de Burgos* in May.[5] He was one of a number of Spanish priests from far-flung dioceses in South Africa, Brazil and Mexico at that occasion who exemplified the wide reach of Spanish Catholicism. As the church in Burgos sponsored

---

3   Scholastica Carrillo, Interview, Kalumburu, 1 May 1999.
4   Scholastica Carrillo, Interview, Kalumburu, 1 May 1999; Visitación Cidad in conversation, Madrid, 2 August 2010.
5   *Diario de Burgos*, 25 May 1948, 1.

charlas misionales or 'missionary chats' to inspire support during the Mission Week in August, the Australian missionary travelled in the wake of other Spanish priests—Jesuits from India, Oblates of Mary Immaculate from Canada, Dominicans from Japan—as well as presentations on the sixteenth-century 'missionary giant' Zumárraga, the first bishop of Mexico.[6] In the months that Abbot Catalan was in his home region, the significance of Catholic missionary life for Spain was taken for granted in the press.[7]

In the villages near Burgos, where families already had ties to New Norcia, support for overseas missionary work had long been part of the Catholic culture. Once again, the abbot peppered the parishes with letters to likely candidates and their sponsors, by turns cajoling and cautioning, sifting and assessing the responses, referring them to government officials or his own agents. He was part administrative tour leader and part physician of souls. He also tapped out a steady stream of correspondence to New Norcia on his portable typewriter, ultimately sorting his copies by clerical status and gender. He wrote most often to the prior and other monks at New Norcia, to other abbots and to the superiors of women's communities in Spain, but he also kept individual Benedictine sisters at New Norcia and in the Kimberley up to date on his progress in recruiting, giving them news of Spain and their families, offering direction and commenting on what they had told him.

One letter gives a particularly compelling insight into how he saw the context at St Joseph's in which the sisters worked. Close to the mid-point of his journey, in March 1948, he wrote in accented English to the Aboriginal girls themselves at St Joseph's.[8] Sent in response to a collective greeting from the girls in February, the letter stands out for intriguing clues about the pattern of relationships in the town. Like the abbot's letters to the missionary women themselves, this single letter to the Aboriginal girls reflected not only his understanding of the work the Benedictine women were doing, and an alert sense of the interactions that made up the life of the institution, but also a warm regard for the children. He wrote to them sounding like a concerned and pious parent who knew the life of St Joseph's well enough to joke about it. Perhaps he imagined Felicitas Pampliega or Mary Cidad reading the letter aloud in English to them all,

---

6   *Diario de Burgos*, 19 August 1948, 12 August 1948.
7   For example, the 1948 Mission Week featured in *Diario de Burgos*, 12 August 1948.
8   Catalan to St Joseph's Orphanage, 27 March 1948, New Norcia Archives (NNA) 01451/112.

perhaps after breakfast before the work of the day, perhaps before prayers in the dormitories at night. It was a rare example of his interaction with the children and gave a picture of the community of sisters he imagined around them. The letter outlined Abbot Catalan's sense of their shared world at St Joseph's:

> My dear children,
>
> I do appreciate your nice letter of 23rd February. I was indeed anxious to know about you all, and your letter gave me indeed a great relief, for I know that you are keeping in good health and contented. It is true that some of the big girls have already left the Orphanage, but other girls younger came to take the place of those who left, and you are there, I understand more than ever. You are 57, and as you are all so young, you will be alright and no mischief among you. I suppose there will be plenty of noice [sic] there being so many and so young, I am afraid that some times [sic] you will cause headache to the Sisters. Am I mistaken?[9]

Abbot Catalan saw the children as a group, cared for in turn by the group of sisters; both groups kept busy with shared tasks and taking a collective place in the work of the mission town. Writing himself into their midst, he was concerned to reassure the children they were part of a secure ongoing institution. He asked them to 'insist in [their] prayers' that he would find transport for the new missionaries who would secure the future, and gave them a sense of his connection with Spain in the process. Unless they found a boat soon, it would 'be too hard to pull me out of this beautiful Country, which suits my health so well'. In 1948 Catalan's capital C for his homeland 'country' was almost certainly not connected with any awareness of the significance of land for Aboriginal Australians. Perhaps he wrote that sentence expecting that the sisters would understand; being uprooted and transplanted was a metaphor used by Thérèse of Lisieux the patron of missionaries and one of Catalan's favourite saints.[10] Perhaps some of the children also caught an echo of their own experience of disruption and loss in his phrase.

The abbot did not elaborate. He moved on to discuss the practicalities of the laundry, reading 'the tune of your letter' to reflect back to the children (and no doubt to the sisters who had helped them in the drafting), collective

---

9   Catalan to St Joseph's, 27 March 1948.
10 [Thérèse Martin,] *Soeur Thérèse of Lisieux* (London: Burns, Oates and Washbourne, 1908), Chapters 1 and 7.

gratitude for the labour-saving washing machines bought secondhand in the neighbouring town of Northam.[11] The abbot echoed popular piety (or had his tongue in his cheek) suggesting that 'now that you will finish your work quicker, you will have more time to pray'.[12] Achieving holiness through ordinary domestic work was a hallmark of the Benedictine sisters, as the previous chapter shows. It also sat well with the spirituality of St Thérèse as patron of missions. Her spirit of selflessness seemed strong in the passages of the abbot's letter in which he commended the girls for what they had written to him about doing all things well for the glory of God.[13] He also warned about the need to be careful and wary of the machines that were indeed industrial units that 'don't care whether they wash the clothes or smash the arm of a girl'.[14] Catalan told the children, reinforcing what he had told the sisters already,[15] that it was dangerous to try to manage the washing machines without training: 'So, you should not interfere with them unless you are appointed for that'.[16] The arrival of the new machines and a concern about the workload in the laundry were recurring themes in the letters he sent to the missionaries too, women and men.

After the domestic work, the abbot dealt with farm work. In decades when winemaking was a cottage industry in Western Australia, the routines of the vintage were one of the strands of cultural life that marked off New Norcia from mainstream Australia and potentially formed part of the distinct collective identity that the Aboriginal children shared with the sisters and the monks. Catalan presented it as a happy time that he was sorry to have missed. The sisters recall the harvest as hard work, especially in years that were 'a taste of purgatory',[17] some of the children do not remember having any fruit for themselves,[18] and Felicitas was pleased the newcomers would not arrive until those tiring days were over.[19] The abbot's

---

11   Catalan to Chick, The Laundry Service, Northam, 29 April 1947, NNA 01450/143.
12   Catalan to St Joseph's, 27 March 1948.
13   On devotion to Thérèse in Australia, see Katharine Massam, *Sacred Threads: Catholic Spirituality in Australia, 1922–1962* (Sydney: University of New South Wales Press, 1996), 127–54.
14   Catalan to St Joseph's, 27 March 1948.
15   Catalan to Felicitas, 18 March 1948, NNA 01451/94.
16   Catalan to St Joseph's, 27 March 1948.
17   On the hard work: Francisca Pardo, Interview, Madrid, 31 May 1999; Pilar Catalan, Interview, Madrid, 1999. On heat: Catalan to Matilde, 5 February 1947, NNA 01450/154.
18   Abbot John Herbert, in conversation, 27 April 2010.
19   Catalan to Felicitas, 27 March 1948, NNA 01451/93.

assumptions about the work meant he teased the girls about eating the grapes, while he also passed on some praise from the winemaker, Felix, and affirmed their 'behaviour' with a more formal tone:

> Have you finish [sic] to pick [sic] the grapes? What a pity that I missed the vintage this year! … Did you eat many grapes? I presume you did eat as many as you could, as usual. Is Fr Felix satisfied with the quantity of wine he made this year? Perhaps he expected some gallons more wine, but he forgot that you like the grapes too much, and that many of the grapes instead of going into the bucket go somewhere else, and you know it better. One thing I know, and it is that Fr Felix is always delighted to see you at the vineyard, whether it be to pick the grapes or to put together the cuttings after the pruning. The reason is because he thinks that you do your work quickly and well. This speaks highly of your behaviour, at least in this respect.[20]

This discussion of work and behaviour led the abbot immediately to name and praise three young women who continued to live at 'the Orphanage' and share in the work of the sisters, although they were over 17.[21] The abbot affirmed this 'safer' and (by implication) holier choice in contrast to those who were anxious to leave. His picture of St Joseph's as a safe haven against the dangers of the world drew on traditional understandings of the cloistered monastic life. Staying on at St Joseph's was an option for otherworldly success that would be good for the soul. For Abbot Catalan this was the only success worth validating:

> I am glad to hear that Rosie and Grace and Angelina are still with you at the Orphanage. They care not for the things outside the Orphanage, as they know that in the Orphanage their souls will be safer than in the world where God is so often offended. You will not hear of any miracle of the girls who are too anxious to leave the Orphanage even when they are less than 17 years of age.

The moralising tone of this section gave way to more gentle teasing about a recent picnic, before the abbot concluded his letter. He repeated his thanks for their prayers, reminded them to be good, and assured them of his blessing:

> You say that you had a lovely picnic. Of course, provided you go in the lorry all picnics are good. I know that you enjoy it much better when Fr Peter takes you far away, like this time when he took you

---

20 Catalan to St Joseph's, 27 March 1948.
21 Rosie Finucaine, Grace Williams and Angelina Moody.

> to the lakes of Wannamal. Did you catch many gilgies? Did you offer them to the Sisters? Or were you too greedy and kept them all for yourselves?
>
> Thanks for your prayers that I and my big party may arrive there soon. I expect that on arriving there the Sisters will give me a good news [sic] of every one of you. I am sending you my blessings from the famous shrine of Our Blessed Lady of Montserrat where I am spending the Holy Week, and where I am listening to beautiful music every day in the church.
>
> Wishing you all heavenly blessings and asking you to pray for me, I remain, my dear children, sincerely in Jesus Christ, Abbot of New Norcia.[22]

The ending recalled them to the hierarchy of the town. His carbon copy left a space between 'sincerely' and his title where he would have signed 'Anselmo', but the children never called him that, nor did the sisters. He was 'the Abbot Catalan', and 'Father Abbot', and 'My Lord'. He knew their names but probably not so well. The abbot's letter shows his view of their life was shaped by the mission's concern for the laundry and the farm but not limited only to work. It extended to a sense of the good times on the picnics and even in the harvesting, and it was governed by an ambition for their holiness. He was genuinely interested in life at St Joseph's, but in the end he was in Catalonia, or remote within the monastery; he was not part of the everyday. As always too, the silences are telling: for instance, the abbot did not think to ask the children about school.

At the same time, in his exchange of letters with the young women who were weighing their decision to join the New Norcia enterprise, the abbot found himself drawn into discussions of education and training. Practical domestic training had been the focus of education at St Joseph's from the outset, and academic aspirations were nowhere on the horizon for either the sisters or the students. In December 1947, however, both Angelina Cerezo of Tordómar, in the small town of Lerma near Burgos, and Amalia González of Villaquirán, also near Burgos, enquired about New Norcia's missionary Benedictines. Neither of them was connected to the families already represented at the mission, but the qualities and capacities of these two gradually brought the needs of the mission school into focus for the abbot. For these young women, the school at St Joseph's shaped the hope of their vocation.

---

22   Catalan to St Joseph's, 27 March 1948.

Angelina Cerezo wrote first, apparently asking for information before offering herself as a candidate. Abbot Catalan responded respectfully and at greater length than to the daughters of the village families he knew well. Angelina impressed him not only for good qualities that she shared with others who had already signed on but also because she had finished the high school *bachillerato* and wrote 'elegant' prose, 'very much to the point'.[23] She was 18, and the abbot's response suggests a careful, focused, perhaps rather serious young woman. He encouraged her to treasure her missionary vocation if she had one and indicated that teaching could well be part of her future:

> I received your letter and was filled with joy to see your outstanding humility and sincerity, two virtues that honour everyone who possesses them. Your letter, notwithstanding the low opinion it has of itself, is very good and very much to the point in what you want to know.
>
> There are nine girls who have offered to come with me. They are apparently very good but they have no more instruction than they have received in their villages. There are certainly none among them who have completed the studies you said you have done, and that show in your letter which though short, is elegant, simple and well-written. I am very happy you have written and I would say something about your good hopes.
>
> If God gives [you] the vocation of missionary religious life, do not despise the favour that God does. It could be a mark of predestination.
>
> You are young, and perhaps you have not realised how difficult it is to lead a devout life in the world, even though you have noticed the frivolity that dominates the youth of today. Courage then. If you feel moved by God, co-operate with all your strength for what God wants of you. And even if you cannot come to Australia do not be discouraged as perhaps God wants you for another religious congregation dedicated to teaching.[24]

The abbot could not have claimed that New Norcia's sisters were themselves dedicated to teaching, and certainly not as their main work.

---

23 Catalan to Angelina, 6 December 1947, NNA 01451/65; on her *bachillerato*, Catalan to Felicitas, 30 July 1948, NNA 01451/98.
24 Catalan to Angelina, 6 December 1947.

Rather than focus on the school, the picture of the sisters' life that the abbot sketched for Angelina was of a farm run by a flourishing, hard-working, closely networked Spanish community. First, he warned Angelina that 'several of these girls who are going to Australia soon have relatives already in the mission, some have brothers, others aunts or family friends'.[25] Then he clarified that the missionaries were not cloistered but prayed together 'more briefly than ... enclosed Benedictines who cannot be a missionary by spending hours in choir'.[26] New Norcia's sisters were dedicated to God but were specifically called 'oblates' to mark their offering to the work of New Norcia itself. He offered a picture of their focused obedience: 'they do what they are told to do as is necessary or useful to the Mission'.[27] Then, within this frame of devotion and utility, the abbot explained the school. He set the lessons of an undifferentiated curriculum as additional to a long list of practical tasks, and implied a moral training in the example of the sisters:

> Our Benedictine Oblates are in charge of a school for Aboriginal girls. They teach these girls primary school curriculum and also domestic work, washing, ironing, sewing, darning, mending, cooking and all classes of work compatible with their sex and strength. Our Benedictine Sisters always are an example to their former students and advance the Mission.[28]

He told Angelina about the town, pointing out that 24 Spanish priests provided for the spiritual needs of the community and that the farm furnished everything else. Perhaps Angelina had asked for details of this, as the abbot specified 'huge quantities of wheat', 'great herds of cows, pigs, chickens and bees', 'all kinds of fruit—grapes, olives and oil', and noted the mission had its own flour mill, bakery and electricity generators.[29] He concluded with a promise to help if she believed God had called her and a subtle invitation to heroism, 'entrusting your case to God and asking him to strengthen your vocation if not for Australia then for another community that does not ask the sacrifices that are needed for overseas missions'.[30]

---

25 Catalan to Angelina, 6 December 1947.
26 Catalan to Angelina, 6 December 1947.
27 Catalan to Angelina, 6 December 1947.
28 Catalan to Angelina, 6 December 1947.
29 Catalan to Angelina, 6 December 1947.
30 Catalan to Angelina, 6 December 1947.

Events were moving quickly: Angelina would have received his letter on 7 December; she replied with a clear request to be admitted as a postulant no more than five days later, so that the abbot certainly had her letter by 18 December. But in the intervening time the abbot had reached and exceeded his upper limit of 12 postulants for the sisters. He replied to Angelina promptly, acknowledging that she was a more suitable candidate on account of her age and her studies, as well as her sincerity, than some of the younger women whom he had accepted. He assured her that she would have first preference if any of the others pulled out. While he could not say this was likely, it was not impossible.[31]

There had been no hint of urgency in the abbot's first letter to Angelina and much encouragement. In the second letter he did not seem to think she would be shocked by his decisions. Perhaps he simply assumed she shared his view that God guided the speed of letters and that this was as good a tool of discernment as any, or perhaps he consciously made room for doubt about this clever, cautious girl in New Norcia's bush and left her 'knocking at the gate' for a while, as the Rule required.[32] He did remind her that God was in charge, as he gave her his own address to write to over Christmas: 'Do not be sad if this reply is not what you wanted, if God wants you to come to Australia He will arrange everything in the way that will fulfil his divine will'.[33] Ten days later he wrote again in response to new letters from her. He welcomed her willingness to conform to God's will, her growing appreciation of the privilege of being the 'bride of Christ', and assured her she would be just that in time, if she continued to model such openness to God. Hoping that there would be a place for her, while promising nothing, he asked her to collect the documentation she would need to be ready to leave if a place came up.[34]

Anselm Catalan did not tell the aspiring missionary Angelina that she was being put through this edifying trial of waiting because he had replied immediately to a straightforward offer hand-delivered on 16 December 1947. Amalia González sent her application through the Benedictine convent in Barcelona; she was as unknown to the abbot as Angelina Cerezo, but in this case he did not hesitate. Slightly older, at 24, she had also completed her schooling and had written to the abbot after she read

---

31   Catalan to Angelina, 6 December 1947.
32   *RB* 58.
33   Catalan to Angelina, 18 December 1947, NNA 01451/201.
34   Catalan to Angelina, 28 December 1947, NNA 01451/202.

an announcement in her local paper, the *Diario di Burgos*, that New Norcia needed young women to work as missionaries. The notice was so small that it seems that it will be lost to researchers until *Diario de Burgos* is digitised, but it caught Amalia's eye and prompted her letter.[35] She was also a keen member of the Falangist youth movement, with its emphasis on social action and Spanish national destiny. Pushing the boundaries of their expectations for women, she had begun to think of a career. Law attracted her, but teaching seemed her greater gift. She had trained formally and informally as a primary school teacher; she had been to workshops with Maria Montessori when the Italian pioneer of child-centred learning visited Spain.[36] She had taught with the followers of Andrés Manjón in Zaragoza, learning firsthand from the innovative educational theoretician and practitioner as he worked with Romany children. Whether or not Amalia made all this clear to the abbot we do not know. We do know that he found her 'vehement and holy desire to be a Benedictine missionary and before too long'[37] compelling. He wrote to her on 17 December to let her know she had made him change his plans:

> Your letter has my admiration, and it has made me think, as I see in it a decision that can only be attributed to a strong divine vocation. I had intended not to accept any more candidates as missionary Benedictines for our Missions in Australia but if God wants you how can I leave this vocation to rot? What a pity that we did not meet in Burgos and I could have given you some idea of the sacrifices required in a missionary life.[38]

It was a robust reply to what was probably a similarly forthright offer. He went on to give in half a paragraph what he had told Angelina in two pages, reserving in this case most of the space to information about the school. He explained the focus on domestic work specifically as preparation for motherhood and made no mention of a formal primary curriculum at all. Perhaps, in writing to Amalia, it was the older girls who came to mind:

---

35 Teresa [Amalia] González, Interview, Madrid, 22 May 1999.
36 Maria Montessori, *The Child in the Church: Essays on the Religious Education of Children and the Training of Character*, ed. Mortimer Standing (London: Sands and Co., 1930); Barbara de Serio, 'The Profile of the Montessori Assistant: Historical Paths and New Education Projects', *Studi sulla Formazione* 19 (2006): 171–85.
37 Catalan to Teresa (Amalia), 17 December 1947, NNA 01451/68.
38 Catalan to Teresa (Amalia), 17 December 1947.

> Our Benedictines in Australia are not enclosed and much of their work is outside the convent. They are in charge of an orphanage of Aboriginal girls and to these they must teach theoretically and practically all the work that a household needs so that when they leave the Orphanage they will know all for the house and be good mothers of families.[39]

Four days after Christmas he received from Amalia the photographs and documentation he needed to begin her passport application. He had also sought and received assurances from her parish priest and the Benedictine community of San José, Burgos, that she was healthy, physically normal and 'likely to succeed' as a missionary.[40] He told the referees he was confident he had 'with this last girl twelve who are willing to come to Australia',[41] and he told Amalia it seemed as if at Christmas 'the Child Jesus … has given you the present of an easy path towards your ardent desire to be a missionary'.[42] He prayed that the Divine Child would give her 'perseverance'.[43]

Something like pride as well as perseverance kept Amalia on track as weeks and months went by, waiting for a firm departure date. Over the months of negotiations through the immigration process the small photographs attached to her travel documents show an increasingly wan, strained face as the reality of her decision sank in. Her family found the decision of this youngest daughter incredible. Envelopes bearing New Norcia's insignia arrived. Handing them over, her father announced with questioning pride, 'an Abbot is writing to you!'[44] Her brothers told her she should not go, as they did not believe she would stay. They told her particularly that going so far was a mistake because it would be a long journey home when, inevitably, she 'failed'. She had not settled to anything so far, and therefore she would not settle in Australia, her father maintained. In any case, her mother asked, why could she not find a religious community at home if she had to be a nun? She needed permission from her father, at least, in order to leave the country, and it did not take long. Abbot Catalan did not write directly to her father, but he did put Amalia in

---

39 Catalan to Teresa (Amalia), 17 December 1947.
40 Catalan to Rev. Mother, Benedictinas de S. José, 17 December 1947, NNA 01451/89; Catalan to Rev. Pedro Martinez Garcia, Villaquirán, 17 December 1947, NNA 01451/58, 25 December 1947, NNA 01451/59.
41 Catalan to Rev. Mother, Benedictinas de S. José, 17 December 1947.
42 Catalan to Teresa (Amalia), 30 December 1947, NNA 01451/69.
43 Catalan to Teresa (Amalia), 30 December 1947.
44 Interviews with Teresa González, her sister and nephews, Villaquirán, Burgos, 30 May 1999.

contact with the network of New Norcia families nearby, in particular the uncle of Matilde de la Fuente. Although in late 1947 Matilde was losing the battle to recover her health and also praying she would die young,[45] she was a practical model of missionary heroism. Above all, her family was proud she been among the first Benedictine women in the Kimberley.[46] In mid-January 1948 Abbot Catalan thanked Amalia for sending him greetings from Matilde's mother, younger sisters and brother. In the same letter he rejoiced with her that both her parents, 'wanting her happiness', had given permission for her 'to follow the vocation God had given'.[47] In each of his letters to Amalia after that date, whether administrative or pastoral in tone, the abbot unfailingly signed off with greetings to her parents, sometimes to the whole family, and praying 'all the blessings of heaven' or a similar benediction on them all.[48] A missionary vocation had social implications.

In March, after the Holy Week he described to the St Joseph's girls, Abbot Catalan travelled to Burgos and Corella again, and then, if not before, he met the new members of the party in person.[49] Amalia recalled she travelled backwards and forwards to Burgos from her village of Villaquirán alone by train, as she often did, for interviews with the abbot and to make arrangements over a few days.[50] She met the abbot at the hotel he nominated: Hotel España, on the tree-lined Paseo Espalon by the river, close to the cathedral and the town administration. In person she found him serious and a little severe, but she knew that she should not be daunted if she wanted to be a missionary. Approaching 70, and perhaps a little shocked to meet a fashionable daughter of postwar Spain, or now remembering the Rule's precepts to warn and discourage newcomers, Catalan told her bluntly that if she wanted to be a missionary she would 'have to clean the make-up off [her] face'.[51] He appreciated that she was 'valiant' and not afraid to travel alone, but mostly, she recalled, he wanted her to understand that the life required sacrifices and that she would not

---

45   'The Late Sister Matilde OSB', *Record,* 31 May 1948, n.p., Archive of the Benedictine Missionary Sisters of Tutzing, Madrid (ABTM).
46   Catalan to Paula Amo de la Fuente, NNA 01451/162–5, Emiliano de la Fuente, NNA 01451/132–3, Teófil Rojo, NNA 01451/113–120.
47   Catalan to Teresa (Amalia), 16 January 1948, NNA 01451/204.
48   For example, Catalan to Teresa (Amalia), 7 June 1948, 22 June 1948, 5 August 1948, NNA 01451/204–210.
49   Catalan to Felicitas, 18 March 1948.
50   Teresa González, Interview, Madrid, 22 May 1999; New Norcia, 30 August 2000, 17 October 2001.
51   Teresa González, Interview, Madrid, 25 May 1999.

be able to change her clothes so often.⁵² Specifically, she remembered she would not be able to bring any of the many fashionable outfits she wore to her interviews. This did not surprise her. It was heroism that drew her. Amalia told him simply, '*Claro*'.⁵³ She felt she was rising to a challenge.

If the strained dynamics of the interviews contributed to her tense-looking photographs, Amalia continued to imagine her work as a teacher in Australia and felt free to make plans that she put to the abbot in regular letters. In response to her suggestion that she might be placed with some nuns to learn 'something useful', Abbot Catalan sympathised that it was indeed 'too hard to wait in the village'.⁵⁴ He told her he was gathering the postulants together in the Dominican convent in Montserrat so they could get used to community life and 'learn the household skills that are used so much on the missions'.⁵⁵ Two letters in June 1948 made the same point, that she should join the other New Norcia postulants in learning domestic work. At Montserrat, the haphazard interim arrangement took a toll: at least two candidates thought better of their choice and returned to the villages. Illuminada Perez remained but did not see the relevance of days spent sewing, especially when she did so much of it that the cotton wore a path through the needle of her sewing machine and she could no longer thread it.⁵⁶

Amalia remained in Burgos. Whether the post did not arrive in time or whether she just did not turn up to join the group of five other postulants who left Burgos for Montserrat on 11 June in the care of Señor Don Teofilo Rojo is not quite clear. But evidently doubting, if not ignoring, the abbot's advice, she proposed an alternative plan to him. Catalan responded patiently to this 'much appreciated daughter in the Lord', pleased rather than perturbed as she pursued her own sense of what a teacher in New Norcia would need. Her focus was music.

Amalia followed her interest and, supported financially by her father, shaped a different view of what would serve her well at the school. Impressed by Amalia's 'strong vocation', the abbot encouraged her 'to go ahead in music as much as possible' while she had free time.⁵⁷ At New Norcia, Felicitas

---

52 Catalan to Teresa (Amalia), 21 August 1948, NNA 01451/208.
53 Teresa González, Interview, Madrid, 25 May 1999.
54 Catalan to Teresa (Amalia), 7 June 1948, NNA 01451/206.
55 Catalan to Teresa (Amalia), 7 June 1948.
56 Illuminada Perez [Sr Florentina], Interview, Burgos, September 2010.
57 Catalan to Teresa (Amalia), 21 August 1948.

was hoping for a musician among the newcomers.[58] Music was part of New Norcia's heritage: in Salvado's day the Aboriginal boys had formed a brass band and the girls sang to the accompaniment of violin and double bass. Catalan was abbot to the composer Fr Stephen Moreno, and the children sang his impressive harmonies on Sundays. The abbot wrote to Amalia that lessons in *solfa* musical theory were indeed part of 'preparing … to be in the Mission as God has destined for you'.[59] He could see no point in starting piano, although if she had the opportunity in her village or in Burgos 'to catch the handling of the keyboard' she should not ignore the chance.[60] But when she pressed him, and apparently suggested that, as she was not afraid of travelling alone, she might well meet up with the group now at the Dominican convent in Barcelona and learn piano there, he drew the line, reminding her the schools were closed and teachers deserved their holiday. Besides, the Dominicans did not have a piano and he expected by mid-October they would have 'one foot in the stirrup for our trip'.[61]

As the abbot drew Amalia into the shared vision of the group that would journey together to 'our beloved Mission',[62] he had no doubt about where she was headed, or how much the destination might mean to her. Living by faith, his nerves honed by previous recruiting trips, he knew to watch for 'God's will above all'[63] as names and travel documents fell into line. He could assure Amalia that 'we have to take it all as Providential'[64] that two 14-year-olds had withdrawn and their places had been filled by others. He knew, as Amalia did not, that one of those newcomers was Angelina Cerezo and the other was Josefina Carrillo, now in her early thirties and able to fulfil the missionary dream she had shared with her mother as a child. What the abbot did not know, even in the first week of September 1948, was how he was going to get the party home.

---

58 Catalan to Felicitas, 27 March 1948, NNA 01451/93.
59 Catalan to Teresa (Amalia), 21 August 1948.
60 Catalan to Teresa (Amalia), 21 August 1948.
61 Catalan to Teresa (Amalia), 21 August 1948.
62 Catalan to Teresa (Amalia), 21 August 1948.
63 Catalan to Teresa (Amalia), 26 September 1948, NNA 01451/210.
64 Catalan to Teresa (Amalia), 6 September 1948, NNA 01451/209.

Travel funds from America, paid off in prayer

With shipping and international currency both disrupted by the Second World War, transport between Europe and Australia was hard to find and harder to finance. Abbot Catalan was rallying help on all sides when, in a process running from February through to November 1948, the international Benedictine network found him a solution. In the end, his missionary party of 1948 was able to travel to New Norcia because Benedictines in the United States provided a loan in American dollars that was secured by the monks at Montserrat and paid off at New Norcia in Mass stipends. This currency conversion combined Catholic tradition with American practicality, both mediated by Benedictine community. The correspondence travelled from Catalonia to Collegeville in Minnesota, through New York and back, with reference to precedents in Manila and with New Norcia informed at last. First, Catalan wrote from his base at the monastery of Montserrat to Abbot Celestine Gusi in Manila, and then a week later he sent much the same letter, this time in English, to Abbot Alcuin Deutsch of Saint John's Abbey in Collegeville, Minnesota. He outlined his problem and made his request.

Already absent too long from New Norcia, he could not get home with his new recruits because the English ships were full of government-sponsored migrants, and non-British companies would not accept payment in English pounds, stretched to the limit by the war. He knew of berths on a French steamer but he needed to pay for the entire party in American dollars. Suggesting that Abbot Deutsch might appeal to other American communities to help as well, Abbot Catalan named the sum, and proposed a solution:

> What I ask you for is to deposit at the Cook's agency in New York the amount of 12000 (twelve thousand) dillars [sic] to pay our 19 passages from Marseilles to Fremantle in Australia. To repay you this money I will open an account in the name of your abbey in Australia for the equivalent money in pounds. ... Please consider my proposition. ... [W]e shall be very obliged to you and your community for ever.[65]

---

65   Catalan to Alcuin Deutsch, Collegeville, 15 February 1948, NAA 01451/7.

The community at Montserrat, and Catalan himself, would have known that Collegeville had already helped missionary houses in the Philippines and elsewhere. Perhaps they all knew how other groups of missionary priests used stipends more conveniently than local currency for international transactions. But even Abbot Alcuin Deutsch, known in his Collegeville community for 'no request refused',[66] was facing a rejection from his council until Abbot Aurelius Escarré of Montserrat swung in behind Catalan with added security. The Spanish underwriting enabled Deutsch to bypass the dubious British currency and to counter with a different scheme. Deutsch wrote to Escarré in April to explain the deal:

> My chapter refused to accept Abbot Catalan's proposition. … The reason for our refusal is the present condition of the British Empire and the uncertainty of its monetary values. My Chapter would have refused the loan if you had not assured us, by your cablegram, that you will accept Mass intentions to guarantee the loan to Abbot Catalan. We are not so well situated financially that we can afford to lose the money; in fact we need money badly as we ought to build, for we are badly overcrowded.[67]

What Collegeville proposed, and what Montserrat accepted as go-between for New Norcia, was that $12,000 (USD) would be loaned to the Spanish community. The Spanish monks would work off the debt by celebrating Mass for the intentions that the Collegeville community had been asked to remember in their prayers. The stipend of a dollar a Mass that American Catholics sent to Collegeville with their prayer requests would stay in Collegeville and gradually liquidate the debt. The Americans noted that Montserrat could also contract New Norcia's priests to help with this prayerful labour, but the loan was essentially to the Spanish house.[68]

It was a practical offer, promptly accepted by Escarré. Abbot Catalan was also enthusiastic and wrote to the Americans saying New Norcia would take care of 6,000 Masses and could accommodate between 400 and 800 additional Mass intentions each month. Up to this point the abbots might have been trading contract work in baking or shoemaking. When Abbot Catalan proposed they would begin 'three weeks from now',[69] however, Abbot Deutsch wrote quickly to remind him of the requirements of canon law. He emphasised the need for order, literally and metaphorically:

---

66   Fr Columba Stewart, OSB, in conversation, New Norcia, July 2009.
67   Deutsch to Aurelius Escarré, 3 April 1948, copy at NNA 01451/10.
68   Deutsch to Aurelius Escarré, 3 April 1948.
69   Catalan to Deutsch, 27 April 1948, NNA 01451/13.

> Since the Code of Canon Law prescribes that he who sends Mass intentions to others is still bound by the obligation *until he has received an acknowledgement that they have been received* may I beg you to be very careful in sending to me each time a letter of acknowledgement of receipt of Masses, giving me the date when I sent the Masses, and the number of intentions sent—then I will be able to keep exact account in our Mass records.[70]

Deutsch also sent firm instructions via the abbot of Montserrat, reminding Escarré that the system could not be allowed to fall apart as it had done once before, that time in relation to Manila during the war.[71] Nevertheless, for all their practical and even monetary purpose, these transactions were shifted around the globe as part of a divine economy, and the abbots shared the role of accountant as part of a sacred trust.

With the fares secured, Abbot Catalan still needed to find space on a passenger ship. In February 1948 he sought help in London, appealing to John Beasley, the former Commonwealth Minister for Supply and Shipping who was now the Australian High Commissioner in London, as well as to the Western Australian Agent-General William Kitson. The abbot stressed the good service the missionaries would offer the state and his own need to return promptly to the diocese.[72] London offered a plane to fly the party to Australia, if New Norcia would foot the bill. The flight would have cost three times as much as a steamer and also meant paying for the plane to return to Europe.[73] Catalan frankly did not trust air travel and thought 'it would not be too poetic to see us falling out of the sky'.[74] He dismissed the idea as way beyond his budget; it was suited only, he joked, to the pocket of Melbourne's Archbishop Mannix.[75]

The abbot prayed for something more practical and routinely enlisted others to petition God and St Joseph to send a boat while he continued his earthly lobbying.[76] He urged English-speaking friends in London to

---

70 Deutsch to Catalan, 3 May 1948, NNA 01451/11.
71 Deutsch to Escarré, 2 May 1948, NNA 01451/10.
72 Catalan to Kitson, 8 February 1948, NNA 01451/34; Catalan to Beasley, 10 February 1948, NNA 01451/38.
73 Catalan to Ubach, 16 April 1948, NNA 01451/33.
74 Catalan to New Norcia, 23 March 1948, NNA 01451/49.
75 Catalan to New Norcia, 23 March 1948.
76 Catalan to Ubach, 21 May 1948, NNA 01451/34; also to Isodore, 17 February 1948, NNA 01451/39; to the monks of the juniorate, 17 February 1948, NNA 01451/51; to Sr Benita, 3 February 1948, NNA 01451/99; to Sr Felicitas, 18 March 1948, 28 April 1948, 3 June 1948, NNA 01451/91–3; to the girls of St Joseph's, 27 March 1948, NNA 01451/112; to Boniface, 29 April 1948, NNA 01451/40; to Gabayo, 22 May 1948, NNA 01451/41; to Sr Hildegard, 12 September 1948, NNA 01451/105.

go to the steamer companies and explain in person.[77] He imagined the community at New Norcia would 'form a chorus' to enlist the help of Arthur Calwell, Commonwealth Minister for Immigration, if his rumoured visit to New Norcia took place in March.[78] In July, while the Australian Prime Minister, Ben Chifley, was visiting London, Catalan wrote to him twice requesting help.[79] The abbot argued that, although his group did not qualify for Commonwealth assistance, they deserved some help as 'future missionaries in WA constitute the best sort of immigrants and cost nothing to the government'.[80] A possible solution fell through in August when the Abbot of Genoa recommended they cancel arrangements with a French steamer that seemed unlikely to last the distance to Australia.[81] It was the second week in September before Abbot Catalan advised the Department of Immigration that they had found berths on the familiar Italian steamer the *Toscana*, now resuming regular voyages after the war.[82]

Until the last, the abbot was sorting immigration documents with Mrs Clark at the Australian consulate in Barcelona, begging billets for the large group of 18 young people, including six young men for the monastery, dealing with Spanish authorities, and complaining to Fr Wilfred that 'these offices are models of delay'.[83] But finally the young men and women gathered with the abbot in Barcelona and began the long train journey through France and Italy to Genoa. On 19 October 1948 they were on board the *Toscana* and ready to sail. Remembering a promise to Felicitas in New Norcia to send a photo for the sisters,[84] Abbot Catalan assembled the 12 new postulants on deck.

77 Catalan to Anderson, 11 February 1948, NNA 01458/x.
78 Catalan to Gabriel, 24 March 1948, NNA 01451/52; also to Gozalo, 14 April 1948, NNA 01451/80.
79 Catalan to Chifley, n.d. but in context 14 July 1948, and 28 July 1948, NNA 01451/28–9.
80 Catalan to Chifley, n.d. but in context 14 July 1948, and 28 July 1948.
81 Catalan to Escarré, 3 August 1948.
82 Catalan to Secretary, Office of the Minister for Immigration, Canberra, 9 September 1948, NNA 01451.
83 Catalan to Wilfred Sanz, 4 October 1948. In Barcelona the young women stayed with the Oblates of the Holy Redeemer, founded by Joseph Serra in 1862 after his return to Spain. Catalan to Mrs Clark, British Consulate General, October 1948, NNA 01451/161. Five of the group had been boarding with the Dominican sisters in the same city for some months, Catalan to Reverend Mother, Dominican Convent, Montserrat, 10 August 1948, NNA 01452/88.
84 Catalan to Felicitas, 30 July 1948, NNA 01451/98.

The wind was strong, whipping their hair and skirts, and they stood, mostly smiling, beside the deck chairs. Angelina at the far right held a book; in the top row Josefina had not yet found her black dress, and Amalia balanced with the rigging across her shoulder. Amalia stood between Marina Diez, 19, from Villasilos, and Josefa Liroz, 25, whose brother Antonio was also travelling; both were from Corella, the abbot's home town in Navarra. At the other end of the row 15-year-old Josefa Rubio, from Sotopalacios near Burgos, tried to keep the wind from her hair and, in front of her, Francisca Alfarao, aged 19, from Corella, carried a gently bulging briefcase. Alongside in the front were four who all came from hamlets near Tapia Villadiego: Milagros Ruiz Nodal, 24, knelt alone, while Otilia Cidad, 20, smiled and looked away. Carmen Ruiz Ruiz resolutely met the camera's gaze as a nervous hand checked her belt. She was 15 and had joined the group at the urging of her brother Anastasio, 10 years her senior and also one of the postulants for the monastery. Their aunt was Hildegard, who had left Spain for New Norcia 20 years before. Tapia was also home to the family of Matilde de la Fuente. They were grieving for their daughter who had died of the cancer she had tried to ignore in April. ('*Qué lastima!* How much that hurts!' the abbot had confessed to Fr Boniface.[85]) She had inspired her brother Emiliano to join the abbot, and his neighbour Jesus Vallejo was also on board. Yet another Tapia family, the Arroyos, had given permission for their daughter, 18-year-old Florencia, to travel. She stood second from the right at the end. Beside Florencia and directly behind Milagros, 15-year-old Illuminada Perez had volunteered from Villorejo, home town also of the Pardo family, including Francisca, who was already at New Norcia, Vincenta, who until her health failed in August had hoped to join her sister, and their brother Abundio who remained part of the group. The networks of village and family life meant some in this missionary expedition had grown up together, others had spent the months waiting for a passage together in Barcelona, while some had barely met. However well or little they knew each other in October 1948, they were leaving port together on a journey that would change them all and would continue for some for more than 60 years.

---

85   Catalan to Boniface, 29 April 1948.

Figure 7.1: The 12 who arrived at New Norcia in November 1948 on deck of the *Toscana*.
Source: Archives of the Benedictine Missionary Sisters of Tutzing (ABTM).

The arrival of the 12

It was a peaceful voyage in the 'floating palace'[86] of the *Toscana*, with only one day of rough weather that made a few of the 12 young women seasick. They sailed slowly through the Suez Canal to Ceylon. They saw the sights over two days in Colombo and then steamed on for 11 long days across the Indian Ocean without land in sight.[87] The group was hopeful about their new life and had found an easy harmony.[88] On 22 November 1948 they arrived in Fremantle and docked in Gage Roads D Shed by about eight o'clock in the morning.[89] It was a hot Monday, and an easterly wind from the inland fanned grass fires to the north. Thunderstorms were forecast

---

86   Catalan to Miguel Catalan, 23 January 1949, NNA 01453/170.
87   Catalan to Miguel Catalan, 23 January 1949.
88   Catalan to Miguel Catalan, 23 January 1949; interviews with Teresa González, Madrid, 21 May 1999, and Scholastica Carrillo, Kalumburu, 1 May 1999.
89   *West Australian*, 22 November 1948, 12.

for the wheatbelt where the harvest was underway, but it did not rain, and Perth 'sweltered' without a sea breeze in 88 degrees Fahrenheit.[90] From the port, the Benedictine party travelled into the heat of the city. The group divided. The abbot and the six young men probably fitted comfortably enough into the monastery's house in West Perth. The larger group of 12 girls found themselves at the convent of the Sisters of St Joseph in South Perth, on the opposite side of the river. It should have been an easy visit full of shared assumptions, but without the abbot, or any other interpreter, the simplest conversation was impossible.

Australians spoke English, not Spanish. This was not new information, but the Spanish girls were shocked, especially those who had imagined themselves communicating beyond the small group. Knowing in theory that most Australians spoke only English felt very different from being misunderstood in practice. Fifty years later, Amalia recalled her stunned horror that her language was not just different but useless. The sheer wall of kind incomprehension daunted her as they all nodded and smiled in the parlour. Again and again as the hot day wore on she confronted the stark reality: 'I could not speak! How could I teach? How could I teach if I could not speak?'[91] The girls in the parlour were thirsty, and Angelina Cerezo tried to use the English she thought she had learnt to ask for plain water when they were offered cups of tea. Amalia watched with increasing dismay as Angelina's request for 'Watcha?' or '*Agua! Agua!*' yielded nothing. 'Only tea!' remembered Amalia, 'and in Spain tea is only for when you are sick.' They asked again, and were given more tea. As their distress increased they were shown to the bathrooms.[92]

The misunderstanding humiliated the young women who had travelled without difficulty in first-class, enjoying the Italian meals and the adventure of shipboard life. Suddenly, they were being treated as children. Amalia thought regretfully of the young man, now sailing on to Tasmania, who had hoped she might join him on his farm, her black dress and the warnings from the abbot, and Josefina Carrillo, notwithstanding. At least they had been able to speak to each other. Now, 'I could not speak! How could I have anything left to do?'[93] It was when they were on the road again the following afternoon, and their procession of cars stopped at Bindoon, that gentle Sister Francisca Pardo was there to meet them and

---

90 *West Australian*, 23 November 1948, 6.
91 Teresa González, Interview, Madrid, 21 May 1999.
92 Teresa González, Interview, Madrid, 22 May 1999.
93 Teresa González, Interview, Madrid, 22 May 1999.

give them plain *agua*. Perhaps, even 15 years after she had been sent to English lessons with the schoolgirls at St Gertrude's, Francisca not only remembered the culture that drank plain water but also understood the fatiguing reality of not being able to ask for it.

From Bindoon, the last stage of the journey to New Norcia wound on. The shadows were stretched and the sun sinking when they finally met the traditional guard of honour. As Abbot Catalan invited the assembled community to pray for the new postulants he reminded them all that it was 'an act of heroism to leave home and homeland for such a distant country and Mission, with little prospect of ever returning'.[94] Perhaps he spoke in Spanish, perhaps also in English, and certainly the *Record* in Perth reported him in English. Whatever the language, for Amalia the celebration of her arrival as an act of heroism merged into accusation: she should not have come; she wanted to return; she had made a mistake; she could not speak. The abbot 'vested immediately for the Liturgical reception',[95] and the new recruits processed into the mission church. As the young people filed in from the roadway the monks sang the *Te Deum*, the ancient Latin hymn of praise and thanksgiving. Amalia recalled that 'it was very deep and low and as in Spain', and it was too much. She bit her lip and tried to hide the tears. She was weeping for her family, her father, her mother, her older brothers and her sisters; for her studies as a teacher; for what else she might have done; and for Spain: 'Oh my Spain'.[96] She knew there were traditions for her to uphold: Spanish ideals of courage and daring adventure, Catholic aspirations to self-sacrifice and bravery sufficient even for martyrdom. The familiar hymn swept her up and confronted her with those expectations, but she could not conquer the homesickness and the doubt. Her swallowed sobs startled Josefina Carrillo.

Josefina was in high spirits with none of Amalia's anxious questioning. The two were already firm friends, linked together on the boat as lively personalities who were older than the rest, but their first reactions to New Norcia were completely different. Josefina was not daunted by subtleties of communication. It seemed to Josefina that they had done simply what missionaries did: they had left Spain, and they had arrived elsewhere. She tried to share her pragmatic zest for whatever came next in whispered advice: 'Don't worry. Be brave. Be a missionary!' She squared her shoulders and stared resolutely ahead: 'Be like me!' Defiance against adversity was already

---

94 *Record*, 2 December 1948, 5.
95 *Record*, 2 December 1948, 5.
96 Teresa González, Interview, Madrid, 21 May 1999.

her trademark. Through the next days she encouraged her friend: 'Be brave!' But advice did not help. Every morning Amalia put her boiled egg in her pocket because she could not eat and every night she cried herself to sleep.

Figure 7.2: Postulants on a picnic, 1949: Josefina Carrillo (standing left) and Amalia González (standing right).
Source: ABTM.

Amalia would recall that 'when we twelve arrived, we asked very often: "Why?"' Perhaps Amalia was most anxious of all. She put a brave face on it. A photograph of the postulants on a picnic in those early days shows her arms akimbo at the edge of the group, a pair for Josefina on the other side, but she continued to worry that her coming to Australia without any knowledge of English was a waste of time. She felt she should leave.

The abbot was clear she should stay. She petitioned him often but he insisted in return that she would find a way to teach and that it was too soon to turn around and sail back to Spain. It was a spiritual contest as she pleaded the need to be useful, but Abbot Catalan held out the holiness of the life she had chosen and more than hinted she would be in moral danger outside the convent. He joked she had too much energy for just one man, or even two, but the task of keeping three men happy would be a terrible choice and not to be compared to the holy life she could lead at New Norcia.[97] At one level, Amalia knew this was an unjustifiable ploy to get her to stay. Trained

---

97   Teresa González, Interview, Madrid, 3 June 1999.

to take the prelate seriously, however, she felt nevertheless that perhaps he spoke truly: she did face a moral choice. Looking at the community so strained by work, with Felicitas and Mary and Benita competing with each other, and with 'many of the sisters very strange',[98] she wondered if she could make the heroic decision she so admired in Teresa Roca and commit herself to this odd group, despite it all.

In the end, it was not the abbot's persuasion or the example of the earlier sisters that gave Amalia a sense of belonging at New Norcia; it was the children. The St Joseph's girls themselves built a bridge for her and gave her a forum as a teacher although 'I had no words'.[99] In those early days of summer 1948, the postulants had the job of combing the hair of the youngest children in the morning, looking for lice, and tying their ponytails: 'It was horrible', Amalia would remember.[100] But they would sit on the verandah, on the steps and on the ground, and gradually the 12 began to sing folksongs as they combed. This was to cure their own homesickness, to cover the absence of conversation, to share some sense of being a group, to keep the children settled and quiet as was the custom in their own villages. No one bothered to justify or explain the new routine; they just began and kept it up.

Folksongs accompany folkdances. In Spain, Pilar Primo de Rivera, leader of the Women's Section of the Falange party, had encouraged women to teach children Christmas carols to sing around the crib and to show them regional dances from other parts of Spain to enhance national unity.[101] Australia would have called the policy 'assimilation'. Whether consciously or not, the 12 all knew that dances carried meaning and identity. Nuns do not dance; even postulants and novices do not dance.[102] Sharing the Spanish folkdances with small children, however, was different.

Amalia began to teach the girls how to dance the *hortas* she knew from childhood: the 12 would sing the accompaniment and the children would follow the patterns they showed them. Suddenly, Amalia realised, 'I could not speak, but I could dance!' She could not speak, and she would not really learn English until she went to study with the Sisters of Mercy in

---

98 Teresa González, Interview, Madrid, 3 June 1999.
99 Teresa González, Interview, Madrid, 10 July 2004.
100 Teresa González, Interview, Madrid, 22 May 1999.
101 Frances Lannon, 'Women and Images of Women in the Spanish Civil War', *Transactions of the Royal Historical Society,* 6th series, 1 (1991): 224–25.
102 Isolina Ruiz in conversation at New Norcia, October 2001.

Perth more than a year later. But she could dance, and the children were responding. In the interviews that trace her memories of New Norcia, she repeated the phrase as the key to all the work that followed in the classrooms: 'I could not speak, but I could dance!'

Amalia began to feel she could stay at the mission. The girls gave her the courage to choose a new name for her new identity as a nun. Her choice went to the heart of the mission enterprise. She would be Sister Marie-Therese after the French patron of missions and after Mary, Our Lady Help of Christians, the patron of Australia. St Thérèse of Lisieux, the 'Little Flower' was strong in the missionary culture of the sisters already, a favourite of the abbot, and a patron of children too; she had died at age 24, Amalia's own age as she made life-changing choices. Amalia was drawn to the Spanish name Teresa as well, but that was not a real option, both in deference to Teresa Roca and to avoid the confusion of two sisters being named for the foundress of Avila. Later, some years after Sister Roca died, Marie-Therese claimed the other Teresa, for the 'bigger' patron and honouring Teresa Roca too.

In those first months, as the singing grew and the dancing practice continued, the relationship with the children opened up further possibilities. Marie-Therese started to pay attention to the mission with the eyes of her training as a Montessori teacher. One morning, she noticed one of the smallest girls not just singing with them but pretending she was playing the piano too, miming with an imaginary keyboard on the floorboards of the verandah. Alert to the Montessori principle of following the 'natural inclination', Marie-Therese decided she had to work with this little girl and teach her to play. There was a piano in the schoolroom, and Marie-Therese began to get up early and practise with a book before prayers. The lessons in *solfa* had gone only so far. She could not read music, let alone translate it to the keyboard, but she would sit with the little girl and sing to her, and together they would try to find the notes. It was a painstaking process, and some of the other girls who thought they might learn too lost interest quickly. Glenys Benjamin was patient and keen. The tune would emerge slowly. Marie-Therese would say often: 'No, not that note, another note, try another note', until eventually they had picked out enough of the tune that seemed right. They could ask Fr Eliado Ros to show Glenys some left-hand accompaniment when he came across to lead choir practice for the sisters.

For that first hot Christmas there was a concert, with the postulants singing in Spanish and the children dancing in Spanish costumes. They were just the kind of thing Felicitas would have delighted to create at short notice out of 'ladies' scraps' donated to the sewing room. The Aboriginal children in 1948 did not have other dances to offer in return, and the postulants would not have been allowed to learn them in any case. The concert was as confused and poignant an example of cultural mismatch as any that New Norcia offered, but it was a lifeline for the young missionary.

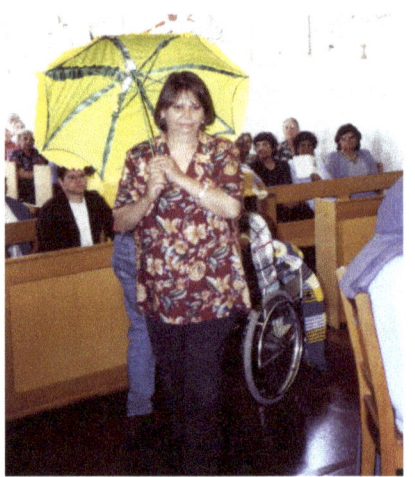

Figure 7.3: Fatima Drayton brings a crêpe paper parasol from the school concerts forward at the reunion liturgy, 2001.
Source: NNA W7-A5-3-119-1.

Perhaps it was a lifeline for some of the children too. When the women who had been the children in those Spanish folkdances were rummaging in the museum storeroom with Teresa and Visitación during the reunion of 2001, there was a whoop of recognition as a yellow crêpe paper parasol, long unexplained, emerged from the compactus. All of a sudden Martha and Mae and Fatima and Gloria were singing an old nursery song with Teresa: 'When I was la-dy, a la-dy, a la-dy', and re-creating a stately dance of curtseys and bows from a school concert some 50 years before, when English had succeeded Spanish and the costumes had extended to props. There was no question but the yellow parasol would be included in the liturgical display at the centre of the reunion, summing up the school years for many in the crowd. It stood not so much for the teachers' assimilationist hopes, or for attempts to mould the school days to the interests of the children, or for policies that aimed to 'discipline and refine' their manners, though it could have spoken for all of these. Instead, like so much else, it stood without irony for the relationship that the women found at the core of it all. There had been no triumphalism in those first attempts to share the Spanish dances. In the end, though there were many tears, there was no shame in claiming the connection they represented.

8

Triggering the 'Second Part': Old School Patterns, a New Bindoon Community and Visiting the Villages Again

In the *Notebooks* kept and edited by the Benedictine Missionary Sisters, the end of 1948 began the 'Second Part' of their history. A confident narrator announced a refounding after all that had gone before. Behind that new beginning, and important for understanding it, lay the foundation of another house at Bindoon and the continuing hope for a bigger, younger community. If the late 1930s and 1940s at New Norcia were marked by continuity or even stasis as buildings aged and the community tired, the verve of the newcomers challenged assumptions, setting the scene for change.

'Our Sisters may go to Bindoon'

Even before the party of 12 postulants arrived at New Norcia in 1948, it was clear that the branch house at Bindoon would demand more able-bodied workers than the congregation had to spare. The monastery had been under pressure from a powerful Catholic lobby in Perth to support the Christian Brothers at Bindoon in what seemed at the time to be a flagship innovation in social welfare and Catholic immigration. Now, after allegations in the late 1980s began a long process of former residents seeking justice and healing, the Bindoon Farm School, at the heart of 'the scheme' to bring British boys to Western Australia, is a focus within Case Study 11 of the Royal Commission into Institutional Responses to Child Sexual Abuse. The statue of the founder who pressed New Norcia for help has been removed at the request of former residents who suffered at his hands and those of 15 other men on the staff.[1] But in postwar Perth, Bindoon was lauded as a social justice innovation that would see boys in need trained as farmers and given land. It echoed the hopes that the mission's founder, Rosendo Salvado, had held for Aboriginal men at New Norcia in the 1860s.

In March 1948, however, New Norcia saw Bindoon as a large Catholic development on the Benedictine doorstep and something of a risk to the monastery's independence. When Bindoon's founder, Brother Keaney, called with a senator and four 'big men' (*prohombres*),[2] influential backers of the scheme in Perth, to put their case for domestic help, Abbot Catalan knew he did not have enough sisters to establish another branch house, not really: 'How are we going to charge our Sisters with more work when they are so few?' he asked his prior, Fr Wilfrid Saenz, in January 1948. 'Maybe when we have professed some of the postulants I am bringing with me, God willing, [but] there will be great difficulties if we try to increase the work without increasing the number of Sisters'.[3] While he could see the Benedictine women would be overstretched, he knew some other group would accept the invitation if he refused. Preserving the Benedictine character of the missionary work and his diocese had prompted other decisions on behalf of the missionary women in the past, and now Catalan observed to his prior that 'if we let other Sisters into Bindoon nobody will remove them'.[4] It could not be a matter of waiting until numbers were healthier.

---

1   Royal Commission into Institutional Responses into Child Sexual Abuse, *Report of Case Study Number 11, Congregation of the Christian Brothers in Western Australia Response to Child Sexual Abuse at Castledare Junior Orphanage, St Vincent's Orphanage Clontarf, St Mary's Agricultural School and Bindoon Farm School*, (Sydney: Commonwealth of Australia, December 2014).
2   Abbot Catalan to Fr Wildrid Saenz, 17 March 1948, New Norcia Archives (NNA) 01451/15.
3   Catalan to Saenz, 19 January 1948, NNA 01451/18.
4   Catalan to Saenz, 17 March 1948.

After some two months of deliberation, during which Sr Felicitas also led him to think that 'they will all like to have this new foundation',[5] Catalan sent a cablegram to the Christian Brothers announcing, 'Our Sisters may go to Bindoon'.[6] The way forward would be 'based on a number of girls living with the Sisters'[7] and sharing in the work. The work was apparently to be done on the same basis as at New Norcia and Kalumburu, with no separate payment to the monastery, the sisters or the Aboriginal women involved, beyond the food and lodging of the workers. Unsurprisingly, this is one of the causes of deep resentment against both Bindoon and New Norcia among some of the Aboriginal women and one of the issues raised regularly in conversations about the need for reconciliation and healing. The sisters are also frank about the level of exhaustion they experienced at Bindoon. Their community was responsible for the domestic support of the institution that included 12 Christian Brothers and almost 100 boys.

At the time, there was no discussion of conditions or remuneration. The abbot did, however, extract a candid promise from the Brothers to provide and pay for new washing machines. 'Have you still not asked?', he prompted his prior, urging him not to hesitate as prospects seemed bright, 'With the price of wool there's money, right?'[8] Sr Felicitas sent the clipping from the *Record* announcing the new foundation.[9] The abbot commented to Fr Ubach, 'Brother Keaney must be over the moon content to have achieved what they so earnestly desired'.[10] In marked contrast with the opening of the house at Drysdale River more than 25 years earlier, there was no satisfaction on his own account but rather foreboding at stretching the resources so thinly.

On 19 March 1948, appropriately the feast day of St Joseph, the sisters took possession of a pleasant, purpose-built convent they shared with the Aboriginal girls rostered to help. On 14 April there was High Mass in the chapel at Bindoon, followed by the formal blessing of the convent building.[11] Sr Benita and Sr Francisca were the steady founding members of the house. Benita, now 41, had been superior at New Norcia after her experience in Belgium. She had a reputation for being strict and unyielding

---

5   Catalan to Saenz, 17 March 1948.
6   Catalan to Saenz, 17 March 1948, reporting he sent this 'yesterday', presumably to Keaney.
7   Catalan to Saenz, 19 January 1948.
8   Catalan to Saenz, 17 March 1948.
9   'Sisters of St Benedict Come to Bindoon', *Record*, 1 April 22 1948.
10 Catalan to Ubach, 21 May 1948.
11 *Pax*, 28 October 1956, 2.

with the girls, especially as nurse in charge of treatment for stone bruises on bare feet; her hallmark method of discipline was to pull a child into line by the earlobe. Severe and sincere, she was not a lateral thinker, but she was practical and dedicated. Francisca was 30 years old and already had the reputation for amenable adaptability and kindheartedness that would see perplexed superiors request her presence in a community when there were tensions: 'If she will not be sympathetic ... send Francisca only on this occasion'. And still decades later: 'The time has come for Sr Francisca to return'.[12] Both sisters were hard workers, good plain cooks, ready to mend and make clothes.

Sharing the household with the sisters until the postulants were ready to take their place on the rosters were Rosie Finucane, Pearl Cameron and Phillis Stack. Rosie brought more experience than either of the sisters: now 52, she had first been admitted to St Joseph's in 1899. She had worked alongside Grace Williams with Maria Harispe and Teresa Roca and had returned in 1941 after an unknown number of years away.[13] Pearl and Phillis, 15 and 13 years old, respectively,[14] were also known as trustworthy and competent and similarly brought skills to the laundry, sewing room and kitchen. The next year, Vera Farrell, also steady and capable at 13 years of age, came to share the workload. The photograph of the community on the steps of the college echoes images from the turn of the century: Aboriginal and Spanish workers together outside a grand institution.

The Spanish *Notebooks* rang a familiar note: 'Hard were the beginnings and great the sacrifices of the first Sisters. Also at New Norcia the sisters were overwhelmed by ongoing work that was enough, and more than enough'.[15] In the six months before the new recruits arrived from Spain, a community of six (or five workers, allowing for Teresa Roca's age and arthritis) kept New Norcia running, while two sisters continued in the Kimberley and two established Bindoon.

---

12 Catalan to Wilfrid Saenz re Kalumburu, 19 January 1948, NNA 01458; Seraphim Sanz to Mary, 1970, Archives of the Benedictine Missionary Sisters of Tutzing (ABTM).
13 Peter Hocking, New Norcia, personal communication, 15 February 2016; 'New Norcia Mission – Subsidy and General', State Records Office of Western Australia (SROWA) S2030 cons993 1926/0350, 31 December 1917, 31 December 1918.
14 Aboriginal Families Index (NNA), Peter Hocking, New Norcia, personal communication, 21 January 2016.
15 'Origen de la Congrecacion de las Hermanas Benedictinas Misioneras de New Norcia, Western Australia' unpublished typescript from the notebooks of Sister Felicitas Pampliega c. 1921–c. 1967, transcribed and edited by Sister Teresa González, Madrid c. 1980, Archives of the Benedictine Missionary Sisters of Tutzing (ABTM) (hereafter *Notebooks*, Madrid), 22.

8. TRIGGERING THE 'SECOND PART'

Figure 8.1: First Community at Bindoon, c. 1949.
Source: ABTM.

Figure 8.2: A studio portrait to send to their families was a thank-you gift to the Benedictine sisters at Bindoon in the 1950s (Hildegard, Visitación, Florentina and Lucia).
Source: ABTM.

The first community at Bindoon followed the patterns of work at New Norcia but more intensely. There were two sisters with limited English running the domestic arrangements for a busy institution, assisted by older Aboriginal women who had trained at New Norcia too. The rosters were more rigorous because the tasks in the bigger institution were shared among fewer women. The conditions were demanding, even for women used to hard domestic work. Francisca recalled, 'Ah! At first! Ah! We did not know how to manage'.[16] The badly nourished boys she saw on her arrival shocked her; they seemed much worse off than the Aboriginal people:

> *Paubre*, poor things, poor things! And some of them had no hair at all. Brother Keaney said to give them lots of honey. Honey, always honey. And at first we used to peel the apples and put the scraps in the bin, and they would go for that, because that was how it had been when they were starving.[17]

---

16 Francisca Pardo, Interview, Madrid, 4 June 1999.
17 Francisca Pardo, Interview, Madrid, 4 June 1999.

On evidence of the residents, they still were starving.[18] But Francisca remembered improvement and progress: 'After a few months—oh different boys. They had a lot of cows there so always plenty of milk, and honey from the boxes'.[19] Did they see anything, hear anything that seemed wrong? 'About?' Francisca asks. I clarify: 'About the boys being treated badly'. 'No, no I didn't hear anything about that.'[20] They saw the boys who were rostered to help in the kitchen and serve in the dining room but had little interaction with them. The royal commission remarks on the Spanish sisters' lack of English and speculates that a stronger feminine presence in the institution might have helped.[21] The Benedictine Missionary Sisters interacted even less with the Christian Brothers. The work overwhelmed all:

> Sometimes [the brother in charge] was sorry we were working so hard, and he would say to us: 'You Sisters are working very hard, no time for prayer, no time for anything. You must come and see a picture with us.' Because, you know, they had films on Saturdays. He would tell us it would be *Our Lady of Fatima* or *The Story of the Little Flower* and I would think, '*ahhhh*'.

Francisca sighs and opens her hands in a gesture of helpless regret, 'I did not want to go'.[22] A film in English, even a religious film, was just another pressure when there was so much to do and rest was so rare.

When the postulants arrived they were rostered through Bindoon to help with the volume of urgent sewing as well as other tasks. 'They put me in the tower', Scholastica Carrillo remembers:

> and out of big military garments I was making smaller garments for the migrant boys. I didn't know any English and I was all day sewing and cutting and sewing and cutting. ... I think they did stop [for prayers], but I was a postulant, so not really bound by them. So I was in the tower, sewing and cutting.[23]

---

18   For example, Royal Commision, *Report of Case Study Number 11*, Transcript, WA15: 1694; on the role of the Benedictine sisters, Transcript, Day WA14: WA1620, WA1621; Day WA15: WA1705; Day WA19: WA2136.
19   Francisca Pardo, Interview, Madrid, 4 June 1999.
20   Francisca Pardo, Interview, Madrid, 4 June 1999.
21   Royal Commision, *Report of Case Study Number 11*, Transcript, Day WA19: WA2136.
22   Francisca Pardo, Interview, Madrid, 4 June 1999.
23   Scholastica Carrillo, Interview, Madrid, 7 June 1999.

But it was clear that the community needed more workers. Mary Cidad, newly appointed as novice mistress, was emerging as a strong advocate among the sisters; she wanted to see branch houses with the canonical six members, not fewer. Everyone agreed that two in a house was not enough. Francisca was needed at Drysdale River to make three there. Hildegard replaced her at Bindoon, leaving only four professed sisters at New Norcia.

Less than two weeks after the 12 postulants made their formal commitment to the Benedictine community as novices on 1 July 1949, Abbot Catalan embarked again for Europe with letters from the Immigration Department to enable him to bring more young women to the mission. The newcomers would be drawn into a heritage of 40 years of convent life at New Norcia, as well as into another round of negotiation between the sisters and the wider church about the collective identity of the missionary women.

Recruiting, again: 'The strongest vocations, best suited to the circumstances'

In July 1949 Fr Tubau took a photograph of the novices, nervously telling them they could burn it if they did not want to keep it.[24] 'It seems they all must have liked it', Abbot Catalan reassured Tubau from Spain in September. As he travelled around the villages of Burgos he found that photograph circulating too: 'I don't know of any who did not send it to her family'.[25] Sister Felicitas sent the abbot another copy, and he likewise showed it around 'with much pride',[26] promoting New Norcia as a place where the village girls were 'getting fat'[27] and flourishing. He told Felicitas that 'all who see them and know the young people are amazed at seeing them so full of health'.[28] For families in Spain's 'hungry years', a daughter gaining weight was a definite bonus to her missionary vocation.

The abbot took every opportunity to emphasise that the group was thriving. When he unexpectedly passed through Marie-Therese's home town of Villaquirán, he and his prior, Fr Wilfrid, took the opportunity to speak to a crowd of young women at the train station, hoping these

---

24 Catalan to Tubau, recalling this, 4 December 1949, NNA 01454/43.
25 Catalan to Tubau, 4 December 1949.
26 Catalan to Felicitas, 12 September 1949, NNA 01454/128.
27 Catalan to Vistación, February 1949.
28 Catalan to Felicitas, 12 September 1949.

locals knew her. They were in luck. The monks asked the girls specifically 'to inform the family that Sr Marie-Therese had stayed in Australia full of health and satisfaction'.[29] The friends promised to give the messages. The abbot was keen to reassure, but did he protest too much?

There had been some disquiet in the network of New Norcia families in the north of Spain, so the abbot was also armed with a letter from Sr Felicitas, 'To Whom It May Concern', defending him against charges of neglecting the community of missionary women. She referred to 'one or other of our religious, carried away by exaggerated zeal',[30] who may have been unhappy that the constitutions from Maredsous had been modified and to 'some Sister disgruntled because the Superioress [sic] was not appointed by election',[31] and she answered both complaints. The constitutions would soon be ready, and she wrote as the elected, not appointed, 'Prioress General' of the group. She assured readers the abbot provided 'everything'. She emphasised his spiritual oversight in particular. The monastery ensured they had confessors, celebrants for daily Mass, a chapel with the Sacrament, regular preaching, and now, with so many new novices, a reinstituted weekly conference. While the letter aimed to quell any anxiety about the status of the community and its integration into the monastic town, the simple fact that there was apparently a need to write it invites interpretation.

Although Felicitas meant what she said, when we read her testimonial in light of another letter she had written earlier in the year, preserved not at New Norcia but in the archives of the sisters in Madrid, it is clear that the nagging issue of the status of the community was still not resolved.

Waiting for the constitutions

Sister Felicitas had drafted constitutions for New Norcia's missionary sisters soon after her return from Belgium in 1936, using the documents of the Benedictine Sisters of Mercy of Heverlé in Maredsous as a template, but after 13 years they had not been confirmed. In January 1949 Felicitas lost patience with Abbot Catalan's delays. She wrote a frank letter threatening him with the community's 'discouragement' and loss of 'vigour' if he did

---

29 Catalan to Felicitas, 12 September 1949.
30 Felicitas, 'To Whom It May Concern', 10 July 1949, trans. Fr David Barry, OSB, NNA 01451/196.
31 Felicitas, 'To Whom It May Concern', 10 July 1949.

not attend to the legalities of the group that had just accepted an influx of new members. There was none of the deferential girlishness that marked so many of the sisters' letters to their abbot. She argued that her work did not need further review. It is hard to imagine that the monks would have tolerated confusion about their own constitutions for so long. In any case, the men would not have been dependent on another community for a decision.

Felicitas was a leader under pressure. She was less dynamic than Mary, less authoritative than Benita. The power struggle between the three was obvious to the novices. Magdalena was steadier and more perceptive but had hardly grasped English and excluded herself from the leadership battle except as a counsellor to Felicitas. The younger sisters felt that Felicitas 'did not think about the overall good of the situation'.[32] She has critics among the past students too: 'She had favourites among the girls and she was always for the underdog. If you had parents she was not for you'.[33] Emotion could cloud her judgement and some memories are bitter. She would 'take over' for 'her' girls, judging parents harshly and dismissing their claims for access on the grounds their daughters were 'better off without them'.[34] There was no questioning her commitment though, even when her benevolence was so misdirected: 'She was a very good person. She loved the girls, the natives, very much and wanted them to have everything they wanted. But she was not very strong, not very forceful'.[35] She valued a strong institution.

The unresolved constitutions weighed on Felicitas, but she could not end the impasse. If Abbot Catalan responded to her at all it was not in any way that left a documentary trace. The constitutions do not surface again directly in the sources at New Norcia. The archives of the sisters in Madrid, however, reveal that the formal confirmation was signed six years later by Catalan's successor, Abbot Gregory Gomez, on 22 August 1954. The sisters were told he affirmed the document 'gladly' and urged them to observe it 'solicitously and faithfully'.[36]

---

32 Teresa González, Interview, Madrid, 27 May 1999.
33 Veronica Willaway, Interview, Nebraska, 7 July 2012.
34 Sheila Humphreys in conversation, New Norcia, May 1999.
35 Teresa González, Interview, Madrid, 27 May 1999.
36 Gomez to Felicitas, 22 August 1954, ABTM.

Was it only the pressure of other things, including his own ill health, that kept Anselm Catalan from signing off on the foundation he had aimed at since 1921 and acted to establish in 1933, or was he actively withholding approval of something in the constitutions—something that Gregory Gomez was more willing to slide over? It seems the negotiation was around the familiar fault line of how (or whether) the sisters would manage a life that was both monastic and missionary. The changes Felicitas made in her translation of the Maresdous material, and then the variations that were finally approved, are explored in the final chapter.[37] For now, it is enough to note they all point to a community still struggling to fit its collective vocation into a recognisable framework.

No wonder, then, that Abbot Catalan thought he might need a pre-emptive 'To Whom It May Concern' in 1949. There was in fact a significant gap in the status of his diocesan community. As it turned out, however, apparently no one thought to press the point. Instead, he found more willing applicants than he had permission from Australian immigration to bring. '[T]his is better for me', Catalan observed as he asked a colleague to assess the candidates in the neighbouring province, 'as I can choose the strongest vocation and those who suit other circumstances best.'[38]

Four candidates were already waiting, all with ties to the group: Visitación Cidad had been born in the year her aunt Sr Hildegard went to the Kimberley and was cousin to two others in the group of 12, all from Tapia Villadiego. From the same village, Clementina Vallejo had been too young to travel with her older brother, Jésus, when he left with the group in 1948, but now she was 15, tall, mature for her years, and still keen. At 16 Julia Rubio from Sotopalacios was joining her sister Josefa, now the new Sister Edita. Twenty-one-year-old Maria Villaño, born and raised in Burgos, worked for a family in San Sebastian where she had known Josefina Carrillo, the new Sister Scholastica. The abbot also accepted two from the historic hamlet of Callohora, near Fr Wilfrid's home town: Maria Carmen Ruiz Besti, 26, who had found Australia could replace her dream of missionary work in China now that those borders were closed, and 15-year-old Ines Herce, who had been training as a seamstress.[39] On 6 March 1950 they arrived at New Norcia.

---

37 See Chapter 10.
38 Catalan to P. Valero Lopez, OSA, 9 September 1949, NNA 01454/21.
39 Carmen Ruiz Besti, with Sr Hilda Scott and Katharine Massam, Interview, New Norcia, 28 July 1999.

Figure 8.3: Home villages of the Benedictine sisters to 1950, still focused on Burgos.
Source: Map by Alejandro Polanco Masa.

If this recruiting journey seemed a simpler process, with awareness of New Norcia high in the wake of the 1948 departures, there was still plenty of drama, and perhaps none so telling as the tension the abbot provoked in the Cidad family during his visit to Tapia. The abbot's letter to Sr Hildegard, describing his confrontation with her sister Crispina, casts light on the place of New Norcia in the spiritual landscape, as well as taking us close to the dynamics of recruiting. Hildegard's own letters to her family played a role in the eventual decision too, we know, but the only account that has survived is the abbot's report, perhaps as close as he ever came to debriefing.

Tapia, 1949

Abbot Catalan's visit to Tapia late in 1949 had not been announced, 'but I had not been there two minutes when all the families interested in my visit were in commotion'.[40] The Vallejo, Ruiz, Arroyo, Amo and de la Fuente families already with sons and daughters at New Norcia all flocked

---

40   Catalan to Hildegard, 14 December 1949, NNA 01454/131.

to the parish house, determined to greet the distinguished guest. But not Crispina Cidad, 'not at all', the abbot wrote to Hildegard.[41] Instead, 'What did your sister do? Immediately, she went to do the washing in a neighbouring village and did not return until nightfall'.[42] Her daughter, Visitación, had always wanted to be a nun, and she had been interested in New Norcia for years. Her aunt had sent her photos. She had wanted to go last time, but her parents refused permission. Visitación had written to greet the abbot for his feast day earlier in the year and received a gracious reply telling her about the new novices, all well and happy and 'fattening up'.[43] He noted pointedly that it was 'too bad that instead of sending me this [holy card of a] dove to bring these good wishes you had not come yourself, as you wanted to when I was there'.[44] Now he had returned and he knew Crispina 'feared … Visitacion would insist again that she wants to be a missionary in Australia'.[45] Crispina would not join the festive welcome to the recruiting abbot. Laundry in another place was a responsibility that better suited her mood.

Visitación took the initiative. She was 'most animated in carrying out her project'.[46] Her father, Gregorio, and her older brother were persuaded that her wish to be a Benedictine missionary was the will of God. The day passed. Her mother returned. The Cidad family still did not call on the abbot, but well after sundown Visitación came with her father and two youngest sisters. The abbot suggested a return delegation: 'Seeing that the mother did not come, I proposed to your brother-in-law Gregorio to go to his house so that he would interview me with his wife, which seemed very good to him'.[47]

They all set off immediately. Crispina had been home late, and the house was not far, but they were surprised to find that in the time they had been away Crispina had gone to bed. Clearly she had expected no news worth waiting for to emerge from the visit to the presbytery. But the abbot had come to her. The family 'made her get up', but she did not feel obliged to be polite. She had said goodbye to Hildegard in 1928 when she was just Visitación's age, she had lived next door to the heroic heartbreak of

---

41   Catalan to Hildegard, 14 December 1949, NNA 01454/131.
42   Catalan to Hildegard, 14 December 1949.
43   Catalan to Visitación, 1 April 1949, NNA 01453/192.
44   Catalan to Hildegard, 14 December 1949.
45   Catalan to Hildegard, 14 December 1949.
46   Catalan to Hildegard, 14 December 1949.
47   Catalan to Hildegard, 14 December 1949.

Matilde de la Fuente's family, and she had heard how Escolastica, six years in the Kimberley with Hildegard, had died slowly from consumption and overwork. Perhaps she had also heard the claims that had prompted the letter of reassurance from Felicitas. In any case, Crispina felt no need to learn any more about New Norcia from the abbot. The interview did not go as the others hoped: 'she was in a very bad humour and said I don't know how many things to me that were not very pleasant'.[48] She stormed against her daughter having any part of this mission, and Abbot Catalan retreated, hastily formulating a different plan:

> I tried to calm her and left her, saying to her and to the others, that if in the end she changed her mind and gave permission to her daughter, that they should let me know quickly at Corella so that I do not take another girl, and that I would give preference to Visitación because she had kept her vocation to be a Benedictine missionary in Australia for some years.[49]

Crispina's gestures of resistance and the abbot's need to give an account to her sister make this letter a compelling archival nugget. But 60 years later Visitación does not want to hear; it is still fresh enough: 'You don't have to tell me. I was there'.[50]

In the event, her mother's opposition softened. Hildegard wrote from the mission itself to persuade her sister to moderate her views, and her neighbour Paula, Matilde's mother, also talked it through.[51] (Paula's voice would have carried weight: not only had she farewelled Matilde in 1928 but also her son Emiliano in 1948.) The mission's network encouraged Crispina to give her consent. Visitación and her father could advise the abbot she would make the journey.

Maria Villaño also encountered resistance. She too was drawn to New Norcia through a personal connection. Initially, following Scholastica Carrillo's swift departure for Australia in 1948, Maria had written to her friend in the new year of 1949, sharing her hopes of joining the mission herself. Scholastica shared the letter with the abbot, and three months later Catalan followed up with a letter to Maria. He was encouraging but asked her to consider her priorities clearly. Wanting to join her 'former

---

48   Catalan to Hildegard, 14 December 1949.
49   Catalan to Hildegard, 14 December 1949.
50   Visitación Cidad, Interview, Madrid, 26 October 2013.
51   Catalan to Hildegard, 14 December 1949; see also Catalan to Paula Amo, 13 January 1951, NNA 01456/86/118.

good companion' would not be sufficient: 'your main motive … must be to have time with the Benedictine Missionary Sisters for the good of souls and to help in all you can at the Mission. Look then at how much you really feel a vocation to be a religious and a missionary religious'.[52]

Maria was already in serious conversation about the prospect of missionary work. She had answered concerns of her family that Australia was too far away with practical information supplied by the abbot: there was no rationing in Australia, and the novices were 'healthy and have a lot to eat'.[53] There were advisors in San Sebastian suggesting she should do a novitiate in Spain and then offer for the missions, but Catalan scoffed: 'life in the missions is so different you would be in danger of losing your vocation. … [T]hey have no idea in San Sebastian about the Australian missions'.[54] Instead, he suggested she visit the network in Burgos where New Norcia was well-known. Call on the Cistercians at Las Huelgas, Abbot Catalan advised, or the Benedictines of San José near the cathedral or the community at Palacios de Beneber. The abbot was pleased with her letter to Scholastica, 'I see a strong heart eager to do good according to the will of God', and told Maria to 'write to me quickly not worrying about expression, so that I may know if I may count on your vocation'.[55]

By the end of the year Maria had left her job as a domestic in the fine house in San Sebastian, and the abbot was sending a parcel of fabric by registered mail to reach her in the village of Blandeande near Burgos so she could make the pleated black dress she needed (but could not otherwise afford) to travel as a postulant.[56] In Maria's case, it was a relationship with someone who had already taken the step that made the difference; as the abbot observed: '[Scholastica], your good friend, has undoubtedly been the means God has used to prompt you to do the same thing'.[57]

This time, in good time, the abbot sent a photograph of the six to Sr Felicitas, 'good looking and I think of good spirit too',[58] mixed in with details of finding the instruction book for the Alfa sewing machines that she had requested and the prospect of buying better fringing for

---

52   Catalan to Lucia (Maria) Villaño, 3 April 1949, NNA 01453/193.
53   Catalan to Lucia (Maria) Villaño, 3 April 1949.
54   Catalan to Lucia (Maria) Villaño, 3 April 1949.
55   Catalan to Lucia (Maria) Villaño, 3 April 1949.
56   Catalan to Teofilo Rojo, 12 December 1949, NNA 01453/87.
57   Catalan to Maria Villaño, 15 May 1949, NNA 10453/194.
58   Catalan to Felicitas, 23 November 1949, NNA 01453/127.

a processional canopy once they got to Barcelona. The abbot told Hildegard the passports had been finalised; they would catch the Italian steamer *Napoli* from Genoa. He signed off cheerfully, sending equal 'greetings to Rosie and to all'[59] at Bindoon, promising to call in to see them on their way to the mission. In his mind the journey was complete.

For the young women, the process of leaving with no intention to return was more taxing. There had been plenty to do in preparation, including a last-minute requirement for chest X-rays from an Australia fearful of tuberculosis, but Visitación was probably not the only daughter who knew her family still felt her leaving 'was like to bury me alive'.[60] On the train to Barcelona they stopped themselves crying by singing, although 'we were still very sad and worried about our families'.[61] In Barcelona they threw themselves into games with the children in the convent school where they stayed and then followed a whirlwind of sightseeing before travelling on to Genoa.

The departure from Italy was marked by confusion. Carmen Ruiz Besti remembers it as a frightening ordeal. Somehow, in the walk to the port the six were separated from the rest of the party.[62] By the time they caught up, the others were on board, the passenger gangplank had been taken up, and the young women faced a ladder up the side of the ship. The water was a long way below the deck they had to climb to, and there was a crowd looking on. They were told the passenger door could not be opened again. Perhaps some in the party had been half-hoping they would miss the boat. Carmen, however, intended to sail:

> Somebody had to go first. ... We saw the ladder, this is true, and one to another said, 'What! Oh no!' [It was] frightening to look at the water and to see ... fish jumping. We had to go up but [we said], 'You don't push me, because if you push me I'll drop in the water!' So one to another, the five of us, six of us, we go up. ... [T]hey follow[ed] me.[63]

---

59   Catalan to Hildegard, 14 December 1949.
60   Visitación Cidad, Interview, Kalumburu, 24 April 1999.
61   Carmen Ruiz Besti, Interview, New Norcia, 28 July 1999.
62   Carmen Ruiz Besti, Interview, New Norcia, 28 July 1999.
63   Carmen Ruiz Besti, Interview, New Norcia, 28 July 1999.

No one knows what the abbot and Fr Wilfrid had been thinking. As Carmen recalled it, once on board the women were allocated to their rooms and found the others on the deck. The rest of the journey was uneventful by comparison. They docked at Fremantle on Saturday 4 March and made their way to the monastery's house in Perth.[64]

The generous fig tree in the garden was the perfect backdrop for photographs to be taken for the families in Spain.

Figure 8.4: Visitación Cidad under the fig tree, Murray Street, Perth, 1950.
Source: ABTM.

Reflecting on the snapshot of her as a 19-year-old, Visitación mused on the mystery of a vocation: 'It is as Jesus said to Nathaniel, "Before another came to call you, I saw you under the fig tree"'.[65] The biblical story speaks of the insight of Jesus and his capacity to see the truth of his disciples. It is a story that affirms the hallowed nature of a call: 'No, I did not think of it at the time, but I have often thought of it since'.[66] In 1950, as they too were sung into the church at New Norcia in solemn procession, there was a new life to weave together with the hope or conviction that their choices were part of a deep and divine plan.

---

64 *Sunday Times*, 5 March 1950, 7, 24.
65 Visitación Cidad, Interview, Madrid, October 2013.
66 Visitación Cidad, Interview, Madrid, October 2013. For Nathaniel's call, see John 1:45–51.

9
Winding Together: 'The Grace of God Is Not Tied to Any Colour, Race or Nationality'

Across Australia, religion boomed in the 1950s. The phenomenon of flourishing youth groups and public demonstration of commitment touched the expanding suburbs of Australian cities as postwar prosperity created leisure and space for Sunday observance on a scale not seen here before.[1] The Billy Graham Crusade among Protestants, the Family Rosary Crusade among Catholics, and the Cold War hope that a third world war would be averted by prayer and action against 'atheistic materialism' gave this decade a feverish anxiety for something better.[2] Around the globe, Catholic convents and seminaries were bursting with new recruits drawn by hope for a new reality. Christian Europe's confidence in progress had been shattered by war and shamed by Auschwitz; in the quest for a new world of peace and justice, churches were anxious for spiritual rearmament at home, in former colonies and mission countries.

---

1   David Hilliard, 'God in the Suburbs: The Religious Culture of Australian Cities in the 1950s', *Australian Historical* Studies 24 (1991): 399–419; David Hilliard, 'Church, Family and Sexuality in Australia in the 1950s', *Australian Historical Studies* 27 (1997): 133–46; Anne O'Brien, *God's Willing Workers: Women and Religion in Australia* (Sydney: University of New South Wales Press, 2005).
2   Katharine Massam, 'The Blue Army and the Cold War: Anti-Communist Devotion to the Blessed Virgin Mary in Australia', *Australian Historical Studies* 24 (1991): 420–28; Judith Smart, 'The Evangelist as Star: The Billy Graham Crusade in Australia, 1959', *Journal of Popular Culture* 33 (1999): 165–75.

Secular powers shared similar hopes for change. The newly formed United Nations adopted the Universal Declaration of Human Rights in December 1948 with Australia among the initial signatories. The document signalled a growing awareness of the realities of discrimination, as it also provided a potential lever for change in the treatment of First Nations people and increased interest in missionary work.[3] By the middle of the decade, the Western Australian Parliament heard a ringing endorsement of missions like New Norcia as 'the organisations most likely to achieve the greatest good in uplifting the native population and particularly in training native children to become good citizens'.[4] Within the hope for 'citizenship' lay the old assumption that individuals should, in the words of the now retired Commissioner for Native Affairs, A. O. Neville, 'be advanced to white status'.[5]

Cultural assimilation of First Nations people had been championed by humanitarian advocates opposed to the biological regimes since the late 1930s.[6] Principles of assimilation would dominate official thinking not only on Aboriginal Australians but also on immigration until the 1970s. In both instances, it upheld the language and lifestyle of 'British Australians' as the goal to be reached by new arrivals and the original inhabitants, both racially by intermarriage and culturally by eliminating difference.

The irony of 'Mediterranean' women being agents of this policy was not lost on some of the Spanish Benedictine women: 'we were more brown than many of the children', Teresa observed.[7] In practice, however, the sisters' status as Catholic missionaries merged them with the mainstream effectively enough. Assimilationist policies sounded less patronising and more inclusive of Aboriginal Australians than the policies of protection

---

3   Stefano Girola, 'Rhetoric and Action: The Policies and Attitudes of the Catholic Church with Regard to Australia's Indigenous Peoples, 1885–1967' (PhD thesis, University of Queensland, 2006), 191.
4   The Treasurer, A. R. G. Hawke, member for Northam, Western Australia, Legislative Assembly, *Hansard*, 23 September 1954, 1826–27, www.parliament.wa.gov.au/hansard/hansard1870to1995.nsf/0/353772eedff490ac48257a41000ffbb3/$FILE/19540923_Assembly.pdf; accessed 22 January 2016.
5   A. Neville, *Australia's Coloured Minority: Its Place in the Community* (Sydney: Currawong, 1947), 56, cited in John Harris, *One Blood: 200 Years of Aboriginal Encounter with Christianity; A Story of Hope* (Sutherland, NSW: Albatross Books, 1990), 577.
6   Charlie Fox, 'The Fourteen Powers Referendum of 1944 and the Federalisation of Aboriginal Affairs', *Aboriginal History* 32 (2008): 27–48.
7   Teresa González, Interview, Madrid, 26 October 2013.

and 'breeding out the black' that had dominated the first half of the century, even though they were built on the same blindness to the merits of Aboriginal society. As it had been since the foundation of the mission, Catholicism was the cultural norm at New Norcia; it had long dominated Aboriginal custom and it refracted Spanish tradition into patterns mainstream Australia recognised.

Internationally in the decade after the Second World War, Catholic thought was moving towards greater awareness of racism and the challenges of decolonisation. Local churches were particularly encouraged to move beyond charity into social reform, 'for in the first place there must be justice which should prevail and be put into practice'.[8] The Vatican promotion of justice through missionary work, however, was linked to the 'supreme crisis' of the Cold War that had divided the world into 'two opposing camps, for Christ or against Christ'.[9] In Australian Catholicism this concern to protect the church against Communism overshadowed everything. The annual Social Justice Statements issued by the Australian Catholic bishops, from the first in 1940, were silent about Aboriginal Australia or missionary work until 1978.[10] In effect, this meant the mission at New Norcia and the Benedictines at St Joseph's were part of another world. While the sisters at New Norcia shared the overall buoyancy of the period, with new buildings and new members, they were on the far periphery of Catholic imagination in Australia.

Just as the novitiates of other religious communities expanded in the 1950s, drawing keen recruits from their schools, now at New Norcia there were promising former students from St Joseph's who joined the Benedictine Missionary Sisters. That Vera Farrell and Marie Willaway became the first Aboriginal Australians to take perpetual vows as religious was a momentous first. There was rejoicing and hope that Sr Cecilia and Sr Veronica Therese would be followed by others from St Joseph's. But not as Aborigines: 'nobody talked about Aboriginality', Veronica recalled, 'nobody used that word'.[11] As the final section of this chapter will

---

8   Pius XII, *Evangelii Praecones*, 51; see also sections 21, 46–47, 49, w2.vatican.va/content/pius-xii/en/encyclicals/documents/hf_p-xii_enc_02061951_evangelii-praecones.html, accessed 3 April 2018.
9   Pius XII, *Evangelii Praecones*, 70.
10 Catholic Commission for Justice and Peace for the Catholic Bishops of Australia, *Aborigines: A Statement of Concern* (Sydney: E. J. Dwyer, 1978).
11 Veronica Willaway, Interview, Nebraska, 9 July 2012.

show, it was significant and celebrated that two former pupils joined the community, but their decision was not understood as a new step towards an Aboriginal Catholicism. Instead, the new Aboriginal sisters were seen as exercising their overriding citizenship of heaven. As Abbot Catalan declared when Vera became a novice, here was proof if anyone needed it that 'the grace of God is not tied to any colour, race or nationality'.[12] The reality of cultural difference rested alongside a theology of overriding unity. Belief in a common God-given humanity sought to encompass a community that had been defined as Spanish from the outset, that took pride in their work with Aboriginal people, but that nevertheless shared many assumptions of White Australian society.

The Benedictine Missionary Sisters welcomed the commitment of the Aboriginal women but remained convinced that, to be secure, the community needed vocations among non-Aboriginal Australians. Through the decade, there was a concerted effort to raise awareness of the sisters and their work in parishes in Perth. The promotional material has left us the highest quality photographs in the history of the community, but there was no great influx of vocations from Irish-Australian parishes as a result. Anne Moynihan, who became Sr Pius in 1959, had grown up in East Perth. She had always known Aboriginal people and felt especially drawn to be among them.[13] Three others from Perth also entered through personal connections: Barbara Allen, a trained teacher from Dalkeith who had been employed by the Education Department at Kalumburu, and Carolyn Gould, from the Nedlands parish, both joined in 1964, and Philomena Roche, a New Zealander, transferred from the contemplative Benedictine community at Pennant Hills in 1971. But there was no wave of interest in Perth to compete with the pull towards the mission that Abbot Catalan had found on his recruiting trips in the north of Spain.

---

12   Abbot Catalan, address at Vera Farrell's reception as a novice, quoted by New Norcia *Sunday Leaf*, 15 October 1953.
13   Anne Moynihan, Interview, North Perth, 19 March 1999.

Figure 9.1: Back left to right: Cecilia Farrell, Ludivina Marcos and Mary Cidad. Front left to right: Angelina Cerezo, Dolores Vallejo, Magdelena Ruiz and Benita Gozalo, c. 1960.
Source: Archives of the Benedictine Missionary Sisters of Tutzing (ABTM).

Figure 9.2: Veronica Therese Willaway, Pius Moynihan, c. 1962.
Source: ABTM.

The sisters continued to pray and hope for Australian vocations while also actively seeking members in Spain. After the wave of commitment in 1948 and 1950, the arrivals came only in twos or threes: Spain was changing. Fewer young women from the villages saw the missions as their destiny. The last to make her profession in Australia was Natividad Montero, who arrived with Isolina Ruiz in 1958. In an effort to make Australia more accessible to likely candidates, in July 1959 the sisters established a permanent house of formation in Spain. It created few ripples at New Norcia at the time. In retrospect, however, it laid the foundation for the transfer of the motherhouse from Australia to Madrid. The decisions that would spin the New Norcia community apart were finally taken in the 1970s, but the seeds were sown in the midst of the renewal and hope of the postwar decades.

* * * * *

The dramatic new start or 'Second Part' announced by the Spanish *Notebooks* from the arrival of the 12 in November 1948 was at one level simply a shift in demographics. As the new recruits set sail, there were 10 sisters in the Benedictine community: their average age was 43. Perhaps more significantly, they had been together in the mission for at least 15 and generally well over 20 years. Suddenly this group of women, middle-aged or no longer young, found themselves in a crowd of 15 teenagers from farming villages, together with two in their mid-twenties (one with some teacher training) and a 31-year-old nurse's aide. By the middle of 1950 the average age was just over 28, and the median age had fallen to 25 years in a group that now had 28 members. There were three communities: St Joseph's was always the largest, while up to six sisters were stationed at Bindoon and three or sometimes four were at the Drysdale River Mission. It was still a tiny congregation by international and Australian standards, but all of a sudden there was energy and critical mass.

The convent at New Norcia was overcrowded. An asbestos and weatherboard dormitory-style extension accommodated the new group of 12 and then 18. There were curtains to separate their iron-frame beds, and only water jugs on stands to wash their faces. Some were shocked: Carmen's family had hot and cold running water at home, but others, like Illuminada, came from farmhouses where there was no bathroom as such, just the animal yard.[14] There was little privacy, 'no room at all to move',[15] and rosters covered everything.

---

14   Illuminada Perez, Interview, Burgos, September 2010.
15   Carmen Ruiz Besti, Interview, New Norcia, 14 October 2001.

The transition into the community was easiest for those who expected an isolated mission and the domestic work of a farm. Anyone who hoped for a quiet life of prayer, or a place to study, or a pathway into decision making and responsibility had much more to confront and dreams to abandon. Everyone was busy, and even those who prided themselves on stamina were stretched by the demands of St Joseph's. As Teresa González reflects:

> My energy was given away at New Norcia. I am very busy now [in retirement in Spain], but busy in my head, thinking. … At New Norcia I was busy in a different way: doing things, making things. My energy was given away.[16]

Twinned with prayer, work remained a pillar of the group. 'We prayed the monastic office; that was something I always appreciated,' Visitación recalls, 'in English with the books they got from Maredsous.'[17] At home in the contemplation of the liturgy, Visitación nevertheless found the intense work of the monastic town dominated life, especially at Bindoon, where there was 'no time even to scratch my ear'.[18] The young sisters mostly learnt on the job. 'I was kicked into the ocean and it was swim or drown in the kitchen', Scholastica observes. 'I swam. I did my best. I worked hard alright.'[19] She developed a routine early on that involved getting up before the first prayers of the day to get the stove going and then perfected a method for cutting the sides of lamb into chops and other portions. She mimes her capable action with the cleaver moving along the kitchen table as she remembers, proud of her efficiency and energy.[20] In 1950 the kitchen catered for 37 children across the two institutions, in 1952 there were 70, and in 1959 numbers peaked at 217 children at St Joseph's and St Mary's.[21]

---

16 Teresa González, Interview, Madrid, 17 May 1999.
17 Visitación Cidad, Interview, Madrid, 3 August 2010.
18 Visitación Cidad, Interview, Kalumburu, 3 May 1999.
19 Scholastica Carrillo, Interview, Madrid, 7 June 1999.
20 Scholastica Carrillo, Interview, Kalumburu, 1 May 1999.
21 See Appendix 1.

Figure 9.3: Scholastica Carrillo, making cheese in the 1960s.
Source: ABTM.

The rosters were unrelenting, but the work was linked to God and to a sense of purpose, as Carmen maintains: 'But God helps. I have God's help. And [I was] very happy; hurry hurry all the time'.[22] The work they were to do was the focus of their arrival in Australia. The *Record* reported they had come 'to engage in the various works of the diocese, both for whites and the natives, as obedience should ordain'.[23] Hard work in response to spiritual authority was a familiar and trusted formula to achieve holiness. There were no details, simply an expectation that, like earlier sisters, they would undertake practical tasks as the mission required.

Figure 9.4: Scholastica with cooking pots at Kalumburu, 1970s.
Source: ABTM.

---

22 Carmen Ruiz Besti, Interview, New Norcia, 14 October 2001.
23 *Record*, 2 December 1948, 5.

By weight of numbers the new arrivals had a separate collective identity, but the counterweight of monastic tradition began to integrate them into the community. The new names that most chose echoed Benedictine tradition and filled the place of sisters who had gone before. Already hoping fervently she would be sent to the Kimberley, Scholastica Carrillo was clear her choice was to remember Escolastica Martinez as well as to add a Benedictine patron:

> They put the names there for each to choose, if you wanted. … [Interviewer: *Why did you choose Scholastica?*] Well, for the other one that died before us, and as nobody wanted to pick Scholastica. I felt it is a great name and some Benedictine Sister's doing. That was the reason and I am very proud of it. I have one more advocate: Raiminda Juliana Josefina (always called Josefina) and now Scholastica! Four names! Four helping me![24]

Angelina Cerezo, Carmen Ruiz Besti and Visitación Cidad kept their baptismal names. This was a small gesture Visitación was glad to make for the sake of her mother: 'to keep the name she gave me'.[25] Her cousin Florencia Arroyo Ruiz chose Matilda, keeping alive the memory of their neighbour in Tapia, Matilde de la Fuente. Her other cousin, Hildegard's niece, 15-year-old Carmen Ruiz Ruiz, took the name of the young martyr and patron of girls, Agnes. Milagros Ruiz, already pale and ill but confiding in no one, chose another martyr: Cecilia. Maria Villaño chose a third: Lucia. Marina Diez became a new Sister Gertrude, though little was said about her Australian predecessor. Josefina Liroz became Sister Gema, and Illuminada Perez was Sister Florentina. Clementina Vallejo became Sister Dolores, and Ines Herce was first Bernarda and later Araceli, before reclaiming Inès in the 1970s when stationed in Spain. Four of the newcomers tried their new identities more briefly: after 18 months Casilda found she did not have a vocation and returned to Spain, 'many are called, but few are chosen', judged the *Notebooks*.[26] Isabel and Edita did not renew their temporary vows and also left the mission in 1954. Josefina was warned early that 'exaggerated piety is visious [sic]'[27] but an early

---

24   Scholastica Carrillo, Interview, Kalumburu, 25 April 1999.
25   Visitación Cidad, Interview, Kalumburu, 24 April 1999.
26   'Origen de la Congrecacion de las Hermanas Benedictinas Misioneras de New Norcia, Western Australia' unpublished typescript from the notebooks of Sister Felicitas Pampliega c. 1921–c. 1967, transcribed and edited by Sister Teresa González, Madrid c. 1980, Archives of the Benedictine Missionary Sisters of Tutzing (ABTM) (hereafter *Notebooks*, Madrid).
27   Catalan to Josefina, 23 November 1949, New Norcia Archives (NNA) 01454/137.

posting to the Kimberley did nothing for her hyper-religiosity. She was recalled after only seven months from Kalumburu, finally to make her way to Spain in 1957.

For those who stayed, the children supplied nicknames. Scholastica firmly discouraged the tempting rhymes 'plastica' and 'elastica' and embraced 'Schollie', as Visitación became Visi. Marie-Therese became 'Cowboy' because of the polished heels of her shoes. The children noticed other things too: 'You're too pretty to be a nun', they would comment to their lively teacher. 'I chose this way', Marie-Therese would reply.[28] The new names, the nicknames and the banter that affirmed decisions were all part of living into a new identity and negotiating the boundary between then and now, Spain and Australia, world and church, prospect and reality.

Schooling

On 10 September 1950, five weeks after they had made their first profession as Benedictines and on the day they saw the six new postulants received as novices, three of the sisters who would soon have responsibility for St Joseph's School went to Perth to learn English and prepare for teaching. While they were away, plans for new buildings at St Joseph's were put into effect with the help of funds from the state Lotteries Commission. There was a need for change.

Education had never been an end in itself at New Norcia, but by the mid-twentieth century the attention to individual capacity that had marked some memorable successes in Salvado's time had gone.[29] There was one small classroom with one small window at St Joseph's, literally relegated to a corner. As Marie-Therese remembers, it became the focus for the new sisters' most forceful questions.[30] They insisted on improvements: the larger dining room was converted into a new schoolroom, and a dormitory became the dining room. Beds were rearranged to make room for more in the dormitories.[31] Giving more space to the classrooms was not just a practical necessity as numbers increased; it also spoke of a new emphasis on schoolwork and the value of the teachers.

---

28 Mary Nannup, Fatima Drayton and Gloria Drayton, Interview, Moora, February 1999.
29 Katharine Massam, 'Work in the Benedictine Monastery of New Norcia 1860–1910', *Tjurunga: An Australasian Benedictine Review* 87 (2015): 33–47.
30 Teresa González, Interview, Madrid, 21 May 1999.
31 Teresa González, Interview, Madrid, 21 May 1999.

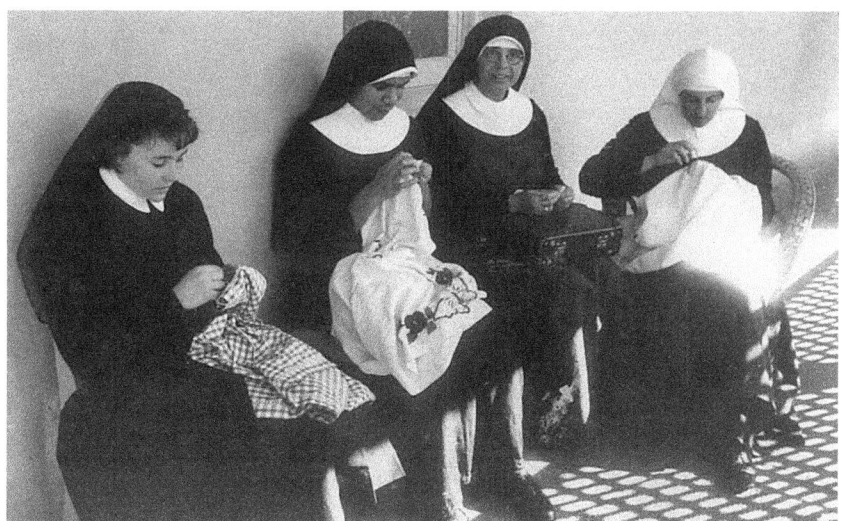

Figure 9.5: Needlework was a sustaining tradition in the convent and at the school.
Source: ABTM.

There had been trouble brewing at the school through the 1940s. Mary and Felicitas presided in turn over a single class, while the youngest children played in the space under the desk: 'we used to be *in* the table, there was an archway underneath, and Sr Mary used to put Glenys, Mae and myself in there with toys while she taught the big ones'.[32] An inspector's report in 1940 concluded New Norcia was doing 'very satisfactory work', but the detail revealed a patchy approach.[33] The children were 'well-kept, clean and healthy in appearance … [with] a very satisfactory training in regard to correct attitudes',[34] but Inspector Radbourn could see that they were 'behind what would be expected of white children of the corresponding age'.[35] English (especially reading) and arithmetic needed attention, although writing, drawing and 'expressional work' (choral singing, the set recitation of poetry and drama) was strong, 'particularly in the girls'.[36] The

---

32 Georgina Taylor in conversation, Old Convent, New Norcia, 17 October 2001.
33 Inspector Radbourn report on the New Norcia Mission School, 2 October 1940, 'New Norcia Mission – Education of Natives', State Records Office of Western Australia (SROWA) S2030 cons993 1940/0904; Commissioner Bray to Catalan, 28 April 1941, 'New Norcia Mission – Education of Natives', SROWA S2030 cons993 1940/0904.
34 Radbourn, report, 2 October 1940.
35 Radbourn, report, 2 October 1940.
36 Radbourn, report, 2 October 1940.

needlework too continued a tradition 'of outstanding merit'.[37] The inspector made suggestions to the sisters and left a copy of the syllabus, but 'attitudes', not curriculum, were the main concern for the Department of Native Affairs, as they were for the mission itself.

Despite the government policy of 'absorption' of First Nations people into White Australia, separate education at mission schools remained the norm. The absence of educational focus was one of the reasons, together with finance, that oversight of mission schools passed to the Department of Education early in 1944,[38] although schooling did not become compulsory for Aboriginal children in Western Australia until 1948.[39] Even after that, a provision in the state's *Elementary Education Act 1893* could be invoked against any child deemed to have infectious diseases or to be 'injurious to the health or welfare of other children' so that Aboriginal children were routinely excluded from state schools.[40] New Norcia was applauded for the practical training it offered. One local parliamentarian lamented the futility of other institutions where 'they are attending school and receiving instruction in reading and writing'.[41] The member for the Central district apparently saw no contradiction, in 1941, between his advocacy for Aboriginal people and his assumption they would not need to be literate. Ironically, while catechism, needlework and choral singing had more emphasis at St Joseph's than in most schools, the Spanish-speaking sisters knew firsthand that literacy in English should not be a luxury.

Nevertheless, the Benedictines assumed school prepared the girls for motherhood and domestic work and the boys for farm labour. Consequently, some Aboriginal parents 'expressed dissatisfaction with the standard of education at the Native School' when the department compelled them to return their children to the mission in August 1945.[42] Alerting the abbot,

---

37   Radbourn, report, 2 October 1940.
38   Minister for Education in the course of the debate on 'Natives (Citizenship Rights)', Western Australia, Legislative Assembly, *Hansard*, 10 October 1944, 1015, www.parliament.wa.gov.au/hansard/hansard1870to1995.nsf/vwMainBackground/19441010_Assembly.pdf/$File/19441010_Assembly.pdf; accessed 3 April 2018.
39   Sally Hodson, 'Making a Rural Labour Force: The Intervention of the State in the Working Lives of Nyungars in the Great Southern, 1936/1948', 'Historical Refractions', ed. Charlie Fox, special issue, *Studies in Western Australian History* 14 (1993): 26–41.
40   *The Elementary Education Act 1871, Amendment Act 1893*, section 22(4), www.legislation.wa.gov.au/legislation/statutes.nsf/law_a3146.html; accessed 3 April 2018.
41   E. H. H. Hall, Western Australia, Legislative Council, *Hansard*, 12 August 1941, 117, parliament.wa.gov.au/Hansard/hansard1870to1995.nsf/83cc4ce93b5d4e0b48257b33001cfef6/FCB617E07C72F0CE48257A4E0010ECA0/$File/19410812_Council.pdf; accessed 3 April 2018.
42   Bray to Catalan, 29 August 1945, 'New Norcia Mission – Education of Natives', SROWA S2030 cons993 1940/0904.

9. WINDING TOGETHER

Commissioner Bray made no secret of his view that parents wanted only to claim the Commonwealth Child Endowment allowance, extended to Aboriginal mothers in 1944. New Norcia knew that extra financial support meant parents did indeed have more options. While the abbot complained but could do nothing when families took children home or placed them with relatives in the cottages rather than St Joseph's,[43] there are hints that the criticism of the school hit home. The idea of mixed classes at St Gertrude's had been shelved long ago, but Catalan tried to recruit new staff for St Joseph's. Perhaps the Good Samaritan Sisters would help? He put the question to their provincial, Sr Oliveria. In 1947 she wrote to report that they did not have sisters to spare for a community in the west.[44] (Part of the reluctance, discussed among the sisters in Sydney, was the realisation that their teachers would be expected to answer to the abbot.[45])

In the meantime, New Norcia's stated priority was for Catholic education. Catholic Aboriginal parents who enquired were generally, though not always, told there were vacancies for their children.[46] Space was made to accommodate children at government request, especially if they were Catholics. The claims of religion and the mission's view of the best interests of the children always trumped the rights and requests of parents. For example, the abbot had thought one mother was motivated by Catholic faith when she 'left no stone unturned'[47] for her son to be transferred to New Norcia from Moore River. But when she asked the department to return the 12-year-old to her three years later, Catalan saw it differently: 'she endeavoured to place her son in a private institution to have a better chance to take the boy with her when she would like'.[48] Rather than claiming any credit for an institution that worked more in tandem with families, the abbot thought the mother had no claim to disrupt the mission's work. If the (clever and promising) boy left, he 'would never look at a book again'.[49] In a stunning turn of phrase, Catalan acknowledged the mother's feelings but discredited them as primitive:

---

43 For example, correspondence of Abbot Catalan, 18 September 1941, NNA 01444/306; 24 November 1941 NNA 01444/162; 22 August 1946, NNA 01449/225; 2 July 1946, NNA 01449/221; 24 August 1946, NNA 01449/224; 8 January 1951, NNA 01456/149; 14 July 1951, NNA 01456/162.
44 Sr Oliveria, St Scholastica's Glebe Point, to Abbot Catalan, 4 March 1947, NNA 01341.
45 Margaret Malone, SGS, in conversation at New Norcia, 18 February 2016.
46 For example, Catalan to Mr Peter Jackson of Moora, 9 August 1946, 'as soon as we have a vacancy'; and undated letter from the same year, 'the room for the three girls will be reserved for two weeks', NNA 01449/347; Mrs Eillen Farrell of Summers Hill, 23 July 1946, 'there is at present room', NNA 01449/375.
47 Catalan to Commissioner, 13 April 1947, NNA 01450/101.
48 Catalan to Commissioner, 13 April 1947.
49 Catalan to Commissioner, 13 April 1947.

> Mrs [L.] shows what she really is: a mother with plenty of love for her children, but a love of natural instinct rather than a love guided by reason. Her love may be compared to the love of a lioness for her cubs.[50]

The Commissioner was persuaded: the boy remained until he turned 14.[51]

Similarly, when Mrs Starr from Carnarvon arrived to collect her son and two daughters in April 1949, Catalan wrote warmly to her husband at home, to congratulate him on the older children and to put a case for the youngest daughter, aged 13, to remain. Schooling was one reason: 'I would advise you to allow her to stay with the Sisters here a little longer in order to give her the chance to be well educated and instructed'.[52] A second concern were the potential distractions, perhaps the moral threat, of life outside St Joseph's, even with a stable home:

> Once she leaves here she will have no chance to continue her formation as a good and practical catholic girl, and not because you will not look after her properly, but because she will always be occupied in so many things that she will have no time for her own personal affairs.[53]

He closed with the punchline of the girl's best interest: 'So please let the girl remain where she is at present for her own benefit'. We do not know what the parents thought and said, but their daughter did not leave.[54]

The government had the power to direct the movements of all Aboriginal people, but New Norcia could put an alternative view. When one 14-year-old was directed to the East Perth Girls' Home for further training, the sisters reported she 'objects to leave the Orphanage and naturally we are not going to force her to leave'.[55] Moreover, she was 'too simple [a] girl yet to clear her from the watchfulness of the Sisters'.[56] Some negotiations were on behalf of the children themselves: one 'full-blood' 16-year-old girl who had been 'restless' at St Joseph's was 'allowed to go with her family'. When the abbot heard she had found things 'not so bright',[57] he wrote to

---

50   Catalan to Commissioner, 13 April 1947.
51   Peter Hocking, personal communication, 21 January 2016.
52   Catalan to Mr J. Starr, 28 April 1949, NNA 01453/159.
53   Catalan to Mr J. Starr, 28 April 1949.
54   Peter Hocking, personal communication, 21 January 2016.
55   Catalan to Commissioner, 24 March 1949, NNA 01453/115.
56   Catalan to Commissioner, 24 March 1949.
57   Catalan to Commissioner, 17 March 1947, NNA 01453/99.

advise the Commissioner, hoping he might help to find domestic work for this girl, who was 'clever and in good health'.[58] New Norcia itself had been placing girls in domestic service at surrounding farms for decades, but the abbot was not above stretching the truth to dismiss requests from outside the mission's network:

> I am sorry to have to tell you that all girls here are of schooling age, and they return to their own relatives as soon as they are ever [sic] 16 years of age. This explanation will show you that we are unable to oblige you.[59]

The abbot made choices, but the children and their parents had few options. Harrowing stories of welfare officers and the police delivering children to St Joseph's or removing them to foster homes continue into the late 1960s.[60]

Families sometimes took action nevertheless. In one instance in April 1950, two sisters aged eight and 10 were removed from New Norcia by their father because, the abbot told the department, the sister teaching one of the daughters 'had punished' her three weeks earlier. The girls' removal coincided with the sudden departure of an Australian novice who had been helping at the school since July 1949. As the *Notebooks* record it, she had endeared herself to the girls,[61] but soon after her profession in March 1950 the mood changed. When the new sister was left in charge of a class while Felicitas went to Perth, her erratic anger shocked the girls. Holding books or bricks at arm's length as punishment took on a vindictive edge. When the two girls were removed by their father, the classroom events became public. The new recruit left, or was sent away, a bare month after profession because, in the stock phrase of the *Notebooks*, 'her vocation was not solid'.[62] The department issued a warrant for the girls, and they were returned from Moora by the police eight weeks later, in June 1950. The incident still resonates in the memories of those on the sidelines as well as those involved. The young Australian had come 'after many prayers and years of hoping for Australian vocations' but had proved a disaster. Instead, it was the new sisters from Spain who promised the way forward.

---

58   Catalan to Commissioner, 17 March 1947.
59   Catalan to Mrs Crothwaite, 6 April 1949, NNA 01453/178.
60   For example, Celine Kickett in *Many Voices: Reflections on Experience of Indigenous Child Separation*, ed. Doreen Mellor and Anna Haebich (Canberra: National Library of Australia, 2002), 44; Anne Moynihan, Interview, North Perth, 19 March 1999.
61   *Notebooks*, Madrid, 28. Literally, *se hizo querer por ellas*.
62   *Notebooks*, Madrid, 28.

Teachers for the school

The process of accrediting new teachers for New Norcia would take several years. It was made possible through the practical support of the Sisters of Mercy at Victoria Square in Perth. Matilde de la Fuente's 1944 initiative in linking with the St John of God Sisters to secure some training in nursing had paved a way for others. The arrangements for Marie-Therese and Agnes to join the community close to the cathedral and the mission's house at 1 Murray Street, for Angelina to go to St Brigid's in Lesmurdie on Perth's rural fringe, and for Scholastica to briefly 'collect ideas'[63] at St Anne's, the maternity hospital close to the city in Mount Lawley, also run by the Sisters of Mercy, would have been made by Abbot Catalan. All the memories of the later Benedictines underline the significance of his newfound commitment to the school. In the crucible of New Norcia's anxiety about the practical workload, it was an investment by everyone to send three of the sisters for longer-term study. It was another sign that the school was in focus and a priority.

While they were away, new red-brick buildings replaced the original cottage where Brother Miro and the Aboriginal matrons had presided, extending the facilities built in 1910. In 1952 a spacious school hall (60ft x 22ft, or 18 m x 6 m) and a wider dormitory (50ft x 28ft, or 15 m x 8.5 m) ran down the north of the site, and in 1956 a two-storey wing to the south of the convent added dormitories with 110 beds, a dining room, an upgraded kitchen and new bathrooms for the children and the sisters. The renovations came at a cost of £28,000, supported by the Lotteries Commission and the mission itself.[64]

Smaller contributions also made an impact. In January 1957 the sisters thanked 19 donors for a total of £32 towards the cost of a statue of St Joseph that had been blessed and installed above the doorway facing the road. Past pupils played a prominent part in meeting the 'overdue' need.[65] The names and amounts were a roll-call of New Norcia families. All the supporters except perhaps one were Aboriginal, and all but two of them were women.

---

63 *Notebooks*, Madrid, 28.
64 'Land, Melbourne Loc1, historical notes', NNA 01159; 'Lands, surveys and leases', NNA 01144.
65 *Pax*, 17 January 1956, 3. The donors were Mrs Louisa Starr £5, Miss Rosie Finucaine £5, Mrs Phil. Williway £3, Miss Doris Moody £3, Mrs Eileen Farrell £2, Mrs Lena Narrier £2, Mrs Mary Lawson £2, Mrs Agnes Taylor £1, Miss A. Moody £1, Miss Pauline Taylor £1, Miss Norma Stack £1, Mrs Lena Jose £1, Miss Lucy Paterson £1, Miss Frances Indich £1, Mrs Julia Maher 10s, Miss A. Cameron 10s, Mr Paddy Taylor 10s, Mr Thomas Taylor 10s and Mrs Laws (Vic) 10s.

Figure 9.6: New dining room at St Joseph's, 1956.
Source: NAA W6-B5-338.

Between these projects, in 1953, a concrete water tank with capacity for 50,000 gallons (190,000 litres) was installed on the western boundary to improve the water supply.[66] At the same time, the 'mission cottages' that had been a hallmark of the town were demolished. The bigger houses on the hill to the north of the monastery that accommodated eight employees of the mission and their families were renovated, and six new, two-bedroom 'monocrete houses' were also built to the north.

---

66   NNA 01159; NNA 01144.

David Brand, the member for Geraldton and future state premier, called attention to the additions as parliament debated the *Native Welfare Act* in 1954, calling them a hopeful experiment 'being watched with interest'.[67] The Act itself aimed to undo many of the restrictions imposed on Aboriginal people in 1905 and 1936. In keeping with prevailing policies for cultural assimilation, provisions for education, health, housing and welfare of Aboriginal Australians would be administered by the relevant departments within those budgets, rather than being overseen by the Department of Native Affairs. Oversight of the mission schools was part of that integration. In April 1952 Stanley Middleton, who had succeeded Auber Neville as Commissioner for Native Affairs, wrote to Thomas Robertson, Director of Education, to alert him to a request from New Norcia.

Middleton advised that the Benedictines had sought help 'to establish an educational standard comparable at least to the State Primary Schools'.[68] The Education Department arranged for G. F. Thornbury, soon to become the new Superintendent of Native Education, to visit New Norcia.[69] The department had also recently undertaken to staff mission schools, although none of the Catholic missions had taken up this offer. The prospect of alternative teachers surely added impetus to New Norcia's plan to train the sisters for this work. As it turned out, Marie-Therese would be called to assist earlier than planned.

When the younger sisters were sent out to study in 1950 the dispersal of the group helped to relieve pressure on the accommodation at New Norcia and gave those sent to the other communities a chance to see Australian convent life in action. Scholastica spent less than a month at the maternity hospital in Perth, before she and Matilda Arroyo went north in October to join the community at Drysdale River.[70] Early in 1953 Florentina and Bernada Araceli were 'already making progress'[71] in a full course of two years studying nursing with the Sisters of St John of God in

---

67   David Brand, Western Australia, Legislative Assembly, *Hansard*, 5 October 1954, 1968, www.parliament.wa.gov.au/hansard/hansard1870to1995.nsf/vwMainBackground/19541005_Assembly.pdf/$File/19541005_Assembly.pdf. The new buildings were also announced in the *West Australian*, 7 February 1953, 26.
68   Middleton to Robertson, 7 April 1952, 'Native Education – Reports from Officers of Native Welfare Department', SROWA S24 cons1497 1951/0953.
69   Robertson to Middleton, 18 April 1952, SROWA S24 cons1497 1951/0953.
70   They left on 8 October 1950. *Notebooks*, Madrid, 29.
71   Catalan to Francesca, 2 February 1953, NNA 01457; Catalan to Florentina, 3 April 1955, NNA 01457.

Perth, also with an eye on the mission in the north. At Victoria Square, Marie-Therese found a warm and welcoming group. She was soon part of the community with friends she could rely on.[72] 'She was very loyal to Agnes', one of the Mercy cohort remembered,[73] hinting the younger sister was less easy in the group. At Lesmurdie, Angelina was challenged by the unfamiliar food and routines. '[I]n a little time', she realised 'she could not adapt to the Australian community's customs'.[74] She returned to New Norcia and studied at St Gertrude's instead,[75] with strong results.

All three had set out on a path to teacher training, taking advantage of the measure introduced by the state Department of Education in 1951 to address a chronic teacher shortage by opening Claremont Teachers' College to mature-age students with a junior certificate (awarded after three years of high school).[76] To qualify, or to take the steadier route with a leaving certificate, they needed five junior subjects from various categories, including English.[77] Angelina passed eight subjects. There was a blitz of five languages (English, Latin, French, Italian and Spanish) as well as arithmetic and algebra, geometry, and art.[78] In the leaving certificate two years later she secured a distinction in Spanish besides three other languages (Latin, Italian and French, not English) and art.[79] Agnes also had strong results with six subjects in the junior: two languages (English and Spanish), two social studies subjects (geography and history), with physiology and art.[80] She sat and passed the same six leaving subjects three years later in 1956 from a country centre, probably St Gertrude's at New Norcia, with a distinction in Spanish,[81] and followed Angelina to Claremont Teachers' College. Marie-Therese passed a modest four subjects in the junior with Spanish, geography, physiology and art.[82]

---

72 Teresa González, Interview, Madrid, 31 May 1999; Sr Theophane, RSM, Interview, Perth, April 1999.
73 Sr Theophane, RSM, Interview, Perth, April 1999.
74 *Notebooks*, Madrid, 29.
75 Catalan to Sr Francisca at Kalumburu, reporting on the junior results, 2 February 1953, NNA 01457.
76 Kaye Tully, 'State Secondary Education in Western Australia, 1912–1972', *Education Research and Perspectives* 29 (2002): 81.
77 Tully, 'State Secondary Education', 46.
78 *West Australian*, 21 January 1953, 8.
79 *West Australian*, 11 January 1955, 8.
80 *West Australian*, 21 January 1953, 7.
81 *West Australian*, 9 January 1957, 13.
82 *West Australian*, 21 January 1953, 6.

It must have been a bitter disappointment to everyone that Marie-Therese missed English, and so did not qualify for the certificate. That had been so much the point of the exercise, and she was so at home in the classroom. But 'she had other gifts', as Visitación observed, including vast reserves of creative flair, the capacity to communicate with the children and to organise. Marie-Therese began a new year as a student at Victoria Square. The intention, the abbot confided to Francesca in the north, was to try again for the junior certificate,[83] but then plans changed.

While Angelina and Agnes pursued formal qualifications, Marie-Therese returned to New Norcia at the end of the first term of 1953 to play a key role in the school. The need for a teacher had become urgent, not so much at St Joseph's as for the 10 boys then resident at St Mary's.[84] Marie-Therese's availability cut through the conversations that had begun with the government in 1952 when New Norcia sought advice about the school.[85]

When the newly elected Abbot Gregory Gomez picked up discussion with the Department of Education in late March 1953, the Director-General Robertson pledged to help 'in any way'. Gomez took up the offer in mid-May: 'I will be obliged if you have one teacher ready for me'.[86] Non-Aboriginal lay staff, whether men or women, always stretched New Norcia, and a government employee in the boys' school would have been a significant innovation. A week later, on 25 May 1953, Gomez had reconsidered and wrote again advising that a teacher was not required. 'I am pleased to inform you that our Benedictine Sisters from the girls' Orphanage have today taken charge of the school.'[87] The department would register the new coeducational arrangement.

The new role for the sisters was announced to the Sunday congregation at New Norcia, and soon classes were combined with both boys and girls at St Joseph's.[88] Sister Marie-Therese had plenty of ideas, and Sister Felicitas was ready to listen if action promised improvement. It is unlikely that anyone at New Norcia studied the Education Department's 1953 curriculum for 'Coloured Pupils', but its tone and recommendations

---

83 Catalan to Francesca, 2 February 1953.
84 See Appendix 1.
85 B. A. McLarty, District Officer Central District, report 7 April 1952, SROWA S24 cons1497 1951/0953.
86 Gomez to Robertson, 18 May 1954, SROWA S24 cons1497 1951/0953.
87 Gomez to Robertson, 25 May 1954, SROWA S24 cons1497 1951/0953.
88 New Norcia *Sunday Leaf*, 31 May 1953.

matched the approach Marie-Therese advocated. The 'educational potentialities, interests and desires' of the children were 'inadequately known'.[89] Teachers should experiment, 'adapt any suggestions to fit the needs, interests and special conditions of their pupils', and expect their own observation and reflection to lead to 'continuous revision'.[90]

Marie-Therese took the need for change for granted and was deeply engaged by the challenges in the school. New Norcia was frustratingly isolated. It was hard even to get cardboard and ink to make a chart, let alone more elaborate teaching aids, but she agreed 'methods will need to make the fullest use of the concrete and the visual rather than the verbal "chalk and talk" technique'.[91] The department reminded teachers to watch for those 'who could profit from a more advanced education, technical, clerical, nursing or otherwise'.[92] Marie-Therese was alive to the possibilities that education offered:

> We know most of the sisters who came here ... the only thing they taught the girls was to do washing and work. Well, alright. I agree with that [summary]. But I have to say that when I came to Australia I had done something in Spain. I had my studies. So I tried to teach the girls not *only that*. Not only to dress 'as a native', [but] to dress as really going outside and doing something else.[93]

She brought the expectation that St Joseph's girls could and should match the outside world.

Her hopes were about more than simple appearances, but in a sense Marie-Therese's revolution in the school was led from the sewing room. The new uniforms for weekdays and for sport, with other clothes for after school and Sunday-best, broke away from the heavy mission dresses that had been deemed appropriate at some stage by the Josephites at St Gertrude's. No one remembers when or how:

> When I came to Australia and I saw the girls with those dresses there? *Oh!* Fire was inside of me. How could I bear to have the girls like that? I told the sisters: 'You have to take all this away, and do this a different way!' And the sisters answered me: 'No, we are not

---

89   *Provisional Curriculum for Coloured Pupils in Caste Schools* (Perth: Education Department of Western Australia, 1953).
90   *Provisional Curriculum.*
91   *Provisional Curriculum.*
92   *Provisional Curriculum.*
93   Teresa González, Interview, New Norcia, October 2001, original emphasis.

allowed to change their dresses and things because we have to ask permission to [sic] the sisters there in St Gertrude's.' So! Nobody was going to tell me what I had to do with the girls! They are not the teachers!⁹⁴

Marie-Therese had confidence in her own trained judgement. Change was also more possible as war-time restrictions were lifted and Australian manufacturing began to supply cloth to the local market again.

Veronica Willaway remembers pestering her mother that she wanted to start school at St Joseph's as the 'new look' at the school unfolded. Her mother, Philomena Nettles, who had grown up with the sisters and was still close to the community, would not let her go alone. 'If you're going in, your sister's going too'. So the two Willaway girls left the family cottage for the 'orphanage': Veronica, quiet, sensitive and just turned five, with Rose her younger but much feistier sister, aged four. They were together as their mother insisted—two among a group of 33 girls at that time.⁹⁵ 'Rosie's never forgiven me', but Veronica was not to be deterred. Living-in with the sisters appealed. 'I thought orphanage kids were spoilt: 2 weeks holiday at Dongarra every year, and nice things at Christmas, and all these clothes. You know, the grass is always greener.'⁹⁶ The new Alfa sewing machines (brought from Spain without their cases to save freight) were treadled into action for new clothes.

Marie-Therese was clear her role as a teacher was the main expression of her vocation, and she gave priority to the demands of the school over the convent. 'Everything was upside down', she chuckled to remember.⁹⁷ 'I was very much with the children. If I went to Moora with the children for sport or sports practice, I couldn't go to prayer. Sr Mary said I had to be on time for prayer. I told her this was impossible.'⁹⁸ As a novice, Marie-Therese had been befriended and encouraged by Teresa Roca, who, 'not knowing what it was to be idle' herself,⁹⁹ respected the younger woman's verve and capacity to relate to the children. When in 1950 the St Joseph's girls gave Teresa Roca a crucifix to mark 40 years at New Norcia, she earmarked the deeply symbolic gift, anointing Marie-Therese

---

94 Teresa González, Interview, New Norcia, 17 October 2001, original emphasis.
95 See Appendix 1.
96 Veronica Willaway, Interview, Nebraska, 7 July 2012.
97 Teresa González, Interview, New Norcia, October 2001.
98 Teresa González, Interview, Madrid, 25 May 1999. A photograph of the post-war sewing room is NNA 74205P.
99 *Pax*, 3 February 1953, newspaper clipping, n.p., 'Las Necrologias', ABTM.

as a worthy successor at the mission and announcing to the community: 'When I die this is for you, for you Sister Marie-Therese'.[100] It seemed to Marie-Therese, 'they were very few sisters and they were frightened to do anything by their own decision', but she felt confident.[101] The rest of the community gave her freedom from the other rosters, never expecting her to clean or cook or wash as they did, while she challenged the assumptions of several decades and saw herself as one against the crowd:

> Yes, well. My way of thinking was so different to the sisters. So different. But what was I to do? What the other person tells me to do? It is better to put my ideas into practice. Really.[102]

A public identity for St Joseph's began to emerge in coverage of sport, concerts and annual reports that was a step removed from the traditional 'training' offered by the mission.

At last the classrooms were a hub equal to the church and the laundry and the sewing room in the life of St Joseph's, not an afterthought. Even so, the Benedictine affirmation of menial work, of all work as equal for all disciples, as well as the expectation that most boys would take up farm work and most girls would become homemakers for their own or other families, made the assumptions of what was appropriate hard to shift. The older girls, sometimes including everyone over eight, still washed and ironed for the monastery and the boys' schools with the sisters rostered in the laundry. There were updated (or at least Army disposal) washing machines just as there was updated equipment for the farm, but there was no question that the women might train for other work. Veronica Willaway took it for granted:

> You mean Mondays? Mondays you washed the whole thing for the boys, everybody had to go to do that.
>
> [Interviewer: *No school at all?*]
>
> No, Monday you did all the washing. At least the bigger kids, maybe the younger kids went to school.[103]

---

100 Teresa González, Interview, Madrid, 25 May 1999.
101 Teresa González, Interview, New Norcia, 17 October 2001.
102 Teresa González, Interview, New Norcia, October 2001. A photograph of Marie-Therese in the co-ed classroom is NNA 74236P.
103 Veronica Willaway, Interview, Nebraska, 7 July 2012.

The goal for the school defined by the Education Department was 'bridging the gap between coloured and white'.[104] Training in domestic work provided useful skills, but enshrining laundry in the curriculum met practical needs in the town first and foremost and obviously reinforced rather than questioned the expectation of menial work.

For the government's policy makers, the emphasis of Aboriginal education was on gearing up for 'the greatest fight … against the tendency to drift so quickly into the camp atmosphere of illiteracy and apathy'.[105] At New Norcia the camp at the edge of town cast the mission into relief. It was distinct from the cottages and even more separate from the 'native school'. Some children, like Rose Willaway, would conclude later that 'we thought we were white',[106] but the division was not simple. Veronica remembers realising around the age of 10 that she and Rose had connections to the camp:

> One day with [my half-brother] Peter, I saw one of the old ladies from over near the river, and I was laughing at her and I said to Peter, 'Look at Old [Lady] down there, drunk.' Peter told me: 'That's my aunty.' So I said to him, 'Oh! I'm sorry. I didn't know.' That's when I thought. I hadn't thought before about the people there being his relatives.[107]

The camp was a threat. They had been taught that St Joseph's would ward it off. At 10, Veronica could barely comprehend that if Peter had family there then she was connected too.

The same instinct to protect St Joseph's girls from 'uncivilised', or 'bushie', influences extended to judging their families. If parents called to visit but had been drinking (perhaps, Sr Teresa speculates, finding some Dutch courage to face the stern expectations of 'the nuns'), they were sent away. The children would wait on the bench around the water tank on Sunday afternoons, calling out family names to summon others as visitors arrived.[108] If they were allowed to meet their children (and the sisters insist that family visits were usually welcomed), it is memories of mothers being made ashamed by the nuns and of daughters not recognising their families and not knowing how to interact that are among the deepest wounds.

---

104 *Provisional Curriculum*, 1953.
105 *Provisional Curriculum*, 1953.
106 Rose Narkle, Interview, Langford, 2001.
107 Veronica Willaway, Interview, Nebraska, 7 July 2012.
108 Mae Taylor and Georgina Taylor in conversation, New Norcia, May 2017.

The danger of 'outside' was also reinforced in language where 'blackfella' was an insult. 'Blackfellas until die! Never changing!' Ludivina would hurl her angry accusation if she thought the garden was being raided. 'She didn't normally say it, not all the time,' Veronica explains, 'just in that instance … to tell them that they should not steal, that they were kind of like black people who never change. You know, she was trying to lift their standards up in her own way, which was broken English'.[109] The defence is on shaky ground. Even if they laughed at Ludivina, the children heard the accusation that wrongdoing was somehow 'black' and innate. Only in the very last years at St Joseph's had Cecilia found a way to bring in visitors to talk about traditional culture and introduce some songs with clapping sticks.[110] Until the 1970s the school shared the assimilationist hope for honorary whites who could take their place (a subordinate one) in 'respectable' society. That hope was in tension with the appreciation that Marie-Therese and others had for the heritage of talent across the group for music, dance, drawing and handcraft as well as the recognition of widespread ability to go beyond basic education if only the school could encourage it.

The school defined Marie-Therese. Teaching also came to define Angelina, who returned with her teacher's certificate from Claremont Teachers' College in 1958 and a prize for her history essay on New Norcia.[111] The classrooms were the focus for their talents and their sense of call. They hoped their pupils would become 'good people' within white Australia but, better yet, that they would be good Catholics and therefore equal citizens of heaven.

In practice, in the junior grades, where Marie-Therese excelled, this meant a curriculum strongly focused on religious instruction and a program that reflected the teachers' strengths as well as students' perceived natural abilities. School days began with prayers and singing, catechism, maths and spelling, reading using the standard issue *Happy Venture* books with stories of Dick and Dora, Nip the dog and Fluff the cat, and then afternoons of nature study, verse speaking, drawing in the service of social studies or other subjects, drama and sport. There were long walks on Thursday afternoons, inherited from the monastic pattern of Salvado's day. It was 'in a way', as Veronica Willaway recalls, 'like big families, the

---

109 Veronica Willaway, Interview, Nebraska, 7 July 2012.
110 Anne Moynihan, Interview, North Perth, 19 March 1999.
111 *Pax*, 22 December 1957, 7. Angelina tied for first place in the Lee Steere awards for historical essays with her thesis 'An Historical Outline of New Norcia Mission'.

little girls always had a big girl to take care of you'.[112] There was sewing and other housework after school, the rosary to conclude the day in the dormitories, and certainly Mass every Sunday, where choral singing by the children, both boys and girls, featured strongly. As numbers increased from the late 1950s, however, the daily Mass in the chapel was no longer compulsory for the children.[113] The culture of saints and sacramental life was woven through it all, underpinned by daily devotion and the presence of the Benedictines themselves.

Celebrations for feast days, First Communion and confirmation were occasions for the school as well as the convent. They depended fundamentally on the work of the sisters in the kitchen and the sewing room who saw to special meals, a feast-day cake, while the children wore their best clothes. For First Communion and confirmation the sewing room excelled again with new outfits for the children involved: suits for the boys and white dresses for the girls, well-fitted, 'not dowdy';[114] short lace veils, good shoes, sometimes woven handbags and even bought underwear to replace the homemade pants and singlets that served on normal occasions. Preparation for the sacraments happened at school, but the occasion involved the whole community far beyond the teachers: 'Sister Felicitas, Sister Lucy, Sister Carmen, and others really did their best for their First Communion and their Confirmation. … [T]hey really put their heart and soul into it'.[115]

The school also held to standard educational outcomes. 'No-one left that room unless they knew how to read and write',[116] recalled Pius Moynihan who inherited the junior class in the 1960s with the system that Marie-Therese had established. Older girls would come in to hear reading or to coach phonics and printing for a range of abilities. Glenys Benjamin often helped out in this way. Clear goals and flexibility made the system work:

> [Sometimes] they would spend three years between grades one and two. … [If] they were malnourished, let's be blunt, by the time you had got them built up again half the year was gone and then no-one left that room unless they knew how to read and write.

---

112 Veronica Willaway, Interview, Nebraska, 7 July 2012.
113 Anne Moynihan, Interview, North Perth, 19 March 1999.
114 Anne Moynihan, Interview, North Perth, 19 March 1999.
115 Anne Moynihan, Interview, North Perth, 19 March 1999. Photographs of post-war First Communion groups at New Norcia have not been released for publication but see for example, NNA W7 A3-4-472.
116 Anne Moynihan, Interview, North Perth, 19 March 1999.

They used to be able to just pass through the system after that. Then you'd get the ones who were as bright as tuppence and just went straight through … just whizzed through school.[117]

The reports from government inspectors who called annually (and also unannounced) on their way through to Geraldton affirmed the approach.[118]

By 1959 results were up and *Pax* proudly detailed a glowing report from the visiting superintendent that 'testifies to the conscientious and capable work of the Benedictine Sisters'.[119] There was a wider horizon of both policy and practice being implied. St Joseph's had been judged to compare 'very favourably with any normal school in the district',[120] and there was confidence among the Benedictines that this was work of 'national importance'.[121]

In that year St Joseph's had three classes. In the junior room there were 60 students in Grades 1 and 2, then 33 'intermediate' pupils in a combined Grade 3 and 4 class, and a senior room of 44 in Grades 5, 6 and 7, for a total of 137 pupils, expected to increase to 180 the following year. St Joseph's was working to its traditional strengths: excelling in art and craft, doing 'fine work' in singing and choral speaking as well as outstanding 'voice modulation' in public reading in Grades 3 and 4, and the 'choral accompaniment to folk-dancing in the senior room showed precision and skill'. The superintendent had noted it was 'policy … at all levels to develop such cultural fields'. Other subjects were strong as well: 'reading is in a very healthy condition. … [M]any rate as very good indeed'. Results in written expression were across a 'wider range', with limitations in grammar and vocabulary, but the children were 'developing confidence and a willingness to express themselves'. Handwriting, spelling and dictation were all very good, with few exceptions. Arithmetic was 'well to standard'. There were 14 of the 60 students in Grade 1 who were 'still immature' and would repeat but the majority had reached 'good to very good' standard, while in the senior class 'care has been taken to ensure that all have the opportunity to succeed'. Overall, the inspector congratulated the sisters 'on the success they are achieving'.[122]

---

117 Anne Moynihan, Interview, North Perth, 19 March 1999.
118 Anne Moynihan, Interview, North Perth, 19 March 1999.
119 *Pax*, December 1959, 2.
120 *Pax*, December 1959, 2.
121 *Pax*, December 1959, 2.
122 All quotations in this paragraph from *Pax*, December 1959, 2.

Marie-Therese threw herself into the extracurricular dimensions of music and sport and the building of social skills. The tiny music room, one of the original sisters' cells from 1910 between the dormitories, was her particular domain at first. Building on the singing and dancing that had forged a sense of purpose for her as a postulant and some lessons at Victoria Square in Perth,[123] she was delighted that some of the children were interested and clearly talented. The retired abbot was also persuaded. Writing a warm letter to Dolores, who had gone north to run the school at Kalumburu in May 1955, aged 20,[124] he encouraged her to keep practising herself. He told her of the two little girls, aged six and eight, still being taught by Marie-Therese, who was 'very proud of her two disciples'.[125] Yvonne Anderson and Glenys Benjamin impressed an inspector from Native Affairs with their ability 'to manage a keyboard'.[126] The abbot's assumptions had been confounded too when he happened to see one of the students practising intently. 'It truly caught my attention that these little girls, so diminutive and native as well, can focus themselves on both lines on the page.'[127] Marie-Therese had never questioned their 'native' capacity but had simply followed the lead of the girls' own interest. She had been vindicated. As Glenys recalled, her encouragement continued to make the difference through several years that followed. Glenys passed formal exams of the Australian Music Examinations Board with flying colours, through to Grade 7, and shone at school concerts.

For others the music room had a primary role as the lolly shop. Minties, Fantales and Jaffas were made up into packets that Marie-Therese sold from a cupboard near the piano, first for 11 pence each and then for a shilling and threepence. The former teacher has forgotten, but in the banter of the reunion some details emerge clearly: 'They went up, and we used to all pitch in our money and save up and go buy a packet'.[128] Pocket money was not a great feature of life at St Joseph's. But 'different ones that had family come and visit them and what change they had left over, we'd all pitch in'.[129] Now the former teacher picks up the memory. Her younger self had encouraged an experience of shopping that she hoped was worthwhile:

---

123 See Chapter 7.
124 Dolores was sent to Kalumburu in May 1955 to replace Florentina, who had developed a kidney infection by October 1954 and was being treated in hospital in Perth.
125 Catalan to Dolores, Kimberley, 5 December 1955, NNA 01457.
126 Catalan to Dolores, Kimberley, 5 December 1955.
127 Catalan to Dolores, Kimberley, 5 December 1955.
128 Georgina Taylor, Interview in the Old Convent, New Norcia, October 2001.
129 Georgina Taylor, Interview in the Old Convent, New Norcia, October 2001.

'The important thing was how to handle money, how to spend the money, how to save the money. That's the important thing.'

'*We* thought it was the lollies.'

'Yes, yes, I know! Still the most important thing is not the lollies. After all, you had lollies.'

'Yes, they always had a pocket full of lollies for us.'[130]

The poignant undertow to the childhood significance of sugar is palpable. Later, for Teresa, the memory serves 'at least to show that we taught different things that were not picking olives and working'.[131] Talented teachers in Perth's schools had a simpler task.

Sport at New Norcia had meant cricket and football, both played with distinction for generations. From the 1950s there was formal team sport for the girls, too, with the introduction of hockey and basketball to St Joseph's. In 1954 a group from the Young Christian Students at St Gertrude's 'kindly undertook ... to teach the native girls of St Joseph's Orphanage to play basketball, with very good results'.[132] Sport provided a link between the separate schools, perhaps easing the way for some older girls from St Joseph's to move to full-time boarding in the high school when federal funding came through to support that in the late 1960s.[133]

Along with team sport at school came marching. With fond memories of her own experience of military drills in Falangist youth groups in Spain, Marie-Therese was an enthusiastic coach, assisted in time by Angelina and the monks from St Mary's. As the annual interschool Central Midland Sports Day approached, marching consumed the out-of-school hours: 'you would see the little ones walking around the school practising: "left, left, left, left"',[134] Pius recalled. There were in-house competitions at New Norcia with a well-drilled march past, and then in 1957 the combined team of boys and girls from St Joseph's began a run of success with the 'most coveted of trophies' at the Central Midland Interschool Sports meeting. The precision of their teamwork and their 'dignified'[135] easy style won admiration.

---

130 Reunion Group, Interview in the Old Convent, New Norcia, October 2001, original emphasis.
131 Reunion Group, Interview in the Old Convent, New Norcia, October 2001.
132 *Pax*, 24 October 1954, 3. A photograph of basketball practice c.1954 is with the Storylines project at the State Library of Western Australia.
133 Anne Moynihan, Interview, North Perth, 19 March 1999.
134 Anne Moynihan, Interview, North Perth, 19 March 1999.
135 *Pax*, December 1959, 2.

Figure 9.7: St Joseph's marching team at rest, New Norcia sports day, 1960s.
Source: ABTM.

Pax praised a 'truly remarkable performance', drawing attention to the children's elegance. Here the stereotyping was positive. Dignity seemed innate:

> [A] graceful walk and carriage are natural to the native children. It is this natural ability that gives a graceful poise to marching. Marching is so often marked by military stiffness, St Joseph's pupils retained the military precision but expelled the military stiffness and thus were worthy winners of the marching shield.[136]

St Joseph's won the 'march past' for six years in a row, from 1957 to 1962, and in four of those years (1958, 1959, 1960, 1962) they won the Moora Road Board trophy for overall sports as well. As Veronica Willaway recalls, preparation was purposeful and exhilarating:

> Come that time you're out there practising, every day practising. … It was an exciting time because you got to go out, down to that football oval down there, and so you were out there, running and doing all sorts of things. Then you got dressed up, getting ready … and then you came back with little ribbons, shields, all that kind of stuff. It was an exciting time.[137]

---

136 *Pax*, December 1959, 2.
137 Veronica Willaway, Interview, Nebraska, 7 July 2012.

Even a change in the rules to require everyone in the school to be in the march did not daunt St Joseph's, although it might have been intended to loosen their hold on the trophy. Efforts simply intensified: 'we had the devil's time trying to teach little six-year-olds that this was your left leg and that had to go down'.[138] In the end the team captains trained the little ones to keep in step and maintain the standard. At the mission's own sports day when the school divided into factions, the team from the 'Girls' House' beat the 'Boys' House' to win the Willaway Shield in three of the four years it was awarded.[139]

Music was also a feature of the public profile of St Joseph's and was highlighted in regular concerts. The large new hall also gave added impetus to activities Marie-Therese had sponsored from the start: folk dancing, drama and group recitations took their place in regular lessons and for special occasions. The concerts were reported first in the *Sunday Leaf*, a news-sheet for New Norcia only, and then picked up by the diocesan paper *Pax* with increasing enthusiasm as the years passed. In August 1953 the occasion was Abbot Catalan's jubilee. Glenys Benjamin, still 'a tiny little tot who had to be mounted and cushioned on the stool of the piano to enable her to reach the keyboard',[140] delighted the audience. 'How much Bishop Salvado would have enjoyed that number',[141] the *Sunday Leaf* applauded. Musical skill carried a heritage of respect at the mission.

The concert programs would not have been out of place in any Catholic school in the country. The 1957 event followed a trusted formula. From the opening 'God Bless Australia' through rhythmic drills, country dances both whirling and graceful with 'amazing lightness of step and agility of movement',[142] there was energy and talent but no specific attention to First Nations heritage at all.

The seniors recited 'The Old Bush School' and danced the 'Briar Rose Waltz' accompanied by Arthur Slater on accordion. Perhaps there was a faint hint of Aboriginal culture in the easy teamwork that meant Yvonne Anderson could substitute at short notice on the piano for Glenys Benjamin, who had broken her arm that year, and Shirley Egan could step up for Frances Yappo in a duet with Bella Cooper (harmonised so closely

---

138 Anne Moynihan, Interview, North Perth, 19 March 1999.
139 I am grateful to Dom Christopher Power, OSB, for this information on the trophies.
140 New Norcia *Sunday Leaf*, 23 August 1953.
141 *Sunday Leaf*, 23 August 1953.
142 *Pax*, 22 December 1957, 8. A photograph of girls dressed for folk dancing at a school concert has not been released for publication but see NNA W7-A3-4-489.

that *Pax* thought it had 'silken-spun quality'[143]). Otherwise, there was no sign of the mission context until the very end when Fr Prior spoke to encourage 'the parents of the children [to] be grateful to the Benedictine Sisters for all that they did'.[144]

The remark was surely jarring, if not for the local parents in the room who had no other educational options, then certainly for the children whose parents were not there and who had no choice at all. The teachers might have been grateful, but it was likely they also wondered who would be weeping after lights out. 'There now, there now. What is wrong with you?' Marie-Therese or Angelina would come to inquire quietly.[145] The end of the concert was not the end of the day and tears often followed family visits and big occasions.

Nevertheless, the investment of energy by the new teachers and new resources were making a difference in the school. Through the decade *Pax* reported on other success: the music examinations where Glenys Benjamin was consistently awarded marks in the 90s,[146] the one-off, now lost, edition of a school magazine,[147] and the state-wide essay competition of 1,000 entrants in which two St Joseph's students, Imelda Clinch and Elizabeth Papertalk, were highly commended.[148]

Alongside achievement, problems remained. Particular teachers took out their troubles on children, kicking chairs from under them, lashing out with physical and verbal abuse. Agnes is the focus for some of the worst memories. She had been sent to Teachers' College as the clever young niece of Hildegard, and it seems that her place in the Tapia family and her qualifications shielded her in circumstances where another sister would have been dismissed. The report awarding her teacher's certificate commented on a 'pleasant confident manner', but there was silence where other assessments commended trainees for 'natural aptitude' or 'good personal contact with children'. Agnes had simply 'shown good progress, control strengthening and preparation thorough'.[149] Back at New Norcia the emphasis in the classroom was on her authority, and students feared her temper.

---

143 *Pax*, 22 December 1957, 8.
144 *Pax*, 22 December 1957, 8.
145 Teresa González, Interview, Madrid, July 2002.
146 *Pax*, 9 September 1956, 2; 24 November 1957, 2.
147 *Pax*, 15 September 1957, 2.
148 *Pax*, 8 December 1957, 1.
149 Report on private student Sr Mary [Agnes] Ruiz, 13 December 1962, 'Training of Teachers for Non-departmental Schools', SROWA S24 cons1497 1958/1141.

Tension mounted in the community too. In 1963 and 1964, Agnes became infatuated with one favourite sister, Scholastica Carrillo, and routinely insulted the rest, disrupting recreation and meals. Rather than sending Agnes away, or helping her make good her own frequent threat to 'get a hat and leave',[150] there were 'various warnings and corrections' that 'proved fruitless'.[151] It was Scholastica who, with no inclination towards the relationship, as everyone knew, was given a canonical warning in the presence of the abbot and sent again to the north in 1964.[152] (It was, in fact, a 'banishment' she had been praying for since 1952 when she had been replaced after a brief stint at Drysdale River by the fervent but ill-suited Josefina. 'At every opportunity, every day, walking and working, I was praying: "St Joseph, send me back to Kalumburu".'[153])

The pattern repeated when in 1969 the children began to comment on the affection between Agnes and her teaching companion Sr Michael. Again it was the other sister who was moved. In 1970 Michael was switched out of the classroom to take up a role as cook for the Marist Brothers. Two years later the 'inordinate friendship' was part of the reason for her long stay with the Benedictine nuns at Pennant Hills near Sydney and ultimately an exit from the congregation. Agnes, far from 'regaining her senses' as Mary as superior had advised her, began to shadow a third sister who was also promptly sent away to Spain. Michael wrote in distress from Pennant Hills convinced that Agnes was risking her vocation, asking Mary to consider the need for love and trust and to remember what Agnes could bring to the community.[154] At this point, Mary wrote an account for the abbot concluding that Agnes should be dismissed. The decision came after 25 years at the mission, a decade after problems became obvious, and too late both for the sister whose unhappiness had wrought havoc and for those damaged in the wake. She found a temporary home with Michael's mother in Perth and ultimately moved to Darwin. The loss of the two trained teachers then stationed at New Norcia helped precipitate the sudden closure of St Joseph's between school terms in July 1973.[155]

---

150 Anne Moynihan, Interview, North Perth, 19 March 1999.
151 Mary Cidad, 'Razones para despedir a Sr. Agnes', c. 1972, ABTM.
152 Mary Cidad, 'Razones'; Scholastica Carrillo, Interview, Kalumburu, 1 May 1999.
153 Scholastica Carrillo, Interview, Kalumburu, 1 May 1999.
154 Michael to Mary, Michael to Bernard Rooney, both 22 November 1972, NNA S12-A5-4.
155 Michael to Mr Maine, Department of Community Welfare, 26 June 1973, 'Missions – Private – New Norcia – General Correspondence', SROWA S1099 cons2532 A403 v1.

Before this scandal unfolded, St Joseph's and an unnamed teaching sister who is most likely Michael featured positively in an account of the school published by the American educationalist Marianne Wolman about her visit in 1969.[156] Wolman worked with the Head Start program for disadvantaged children in the United States and sought out New Norcia because of its school. Writing in the well-established *Elementary School Journal*, she painted a bleak picture of New Norcia's dusty isolation but was inspired by the expectation of success at St Joseph's.

The visitor was surprised by the focus on formal learning and the levels of achievement. She remarked on the school uniform of blue cotton dresses, or blue shorts for the boys, with bare feet. The kindergarten room was lively and relaxed: 'There was no evidence of undue pressure on them; they were permitted to talk to one another which they did wholeheartedly; there was a good deal of laughter and shuffling of feet'.[157] With short lessons of 15 minutes broken up by play outside, the five- and six-year-olds impressed her with their level of reading and simple maths.

In the Grade 1 room, set up like 'any first grade room in the USA'[158] with work by the children on display around the room, Wolman was spellbound: all the children could read and '[t]here was not one child in that classroom who was not totally involved in learning'.[159] The young teaching sister explained her methods—a big stack of comics for the first few months, then flash cards, charts, simple stories, 'plenty of practice and a fair amount of drill'.[160] Wolman remarked that it was unusual for all the first grade to be able to read at the end of the year, but the teacher explained simply: 'I was very privileged to have received a fine education. I know how to teach. I expect all children to learn, and because I love them, they all do'.[161] It was a declaration that Wolman told readers she would always remember, though she wondered aloud if it really was that simple. There is no reason to doubt the gifts of the teacher, the sincerity of her comment, or the success among the early students; nevertheless, the wider history shows us that the story of the school is more complex.

---

156 Marianne Wolman, 'Visit to a Mission for Aboriginal Children', *Elementary School Journal* 70, no. 5 (February 1970): 261–66. I am grateful to Sharne Rolfe for this reference and for the photographs from the Wolman family. Copies of photographs of the visit showing 1970s classrooms and groups in the playground with triangular cartons of 'school milk' are with the Storylines project at the State Library of Western Australia.
157 Wolman, 'Visit to a Mission', 263.
158 Wolman, 'Visit to a Mission', 263.
159 Wolman, 'Visit to a Mission', 263.
160 Wolman, 'Visit to a Mission', 263.
161 Wolman, 'Visit to a Mission', 264.

In the same article, one of the monks underlined the early success, coupled with disappointment, that the children did not 'aspire' to more than farm work and homemaking. The American wondered instead 'whether it was … not rather a realistic evaluation of what Australian society would permit aboriginals [sic] to do in their country'.[162] Among the highly motivated first graders there were both girls and boys who would complete high school, undertake tertiary study, and pioneer work in nursing, in teaching and in many areas of the public service. From the standpoint of the convent, though, the most significant role models from the 1950s onwards were the former students who chose the Benedictine life.

Aboriginal Benedictines but 'the word was "native" and we were not that'

Cecilia Farrell was the first Aboriginal woman to enter a religious community in Australia and the only Aboriginal Benedictine woman or man since July 1849 when the two Yued boys, Francis Xavier Conaci and John Baptist Maria Dirimera, famously received the Benedictine habit from Pope Pius IX in Naples.[163] In the earliest days of New Norcia there had been hope among the missionaries that there would be many Aboriginal Benedictines. Against assumptions that Aboriginal people were 'incapable' of grasping religious training,[164] Salvado recognised the local sense of the sacred and was convinced of the possibility of an Indigenous priesthood. His hope came to nothing, but, occasionally, accounts of New Norcia recalled the four boys who travelled from New Norcia to European monasteries with Salvado and Serra.[165] More by accident or misunderstanding than any considered planning, Francis Xavier Conaci,

---

162 Wolman, 'Visit to a Mission', 264.
163 Rosendo Salvado, *Report of Rosendo Salvado to Propaganda Fide in 1883*, trans. Stefano Girola (Northcote, Vic.: Abbey Press, 2015), 36, 39–40; Anouk Ride, *The Grand Experiment: Two Boys, Two Cultures* (Sydney: Hachette, 2007) is a fictionalised account. Sr Beatrice Thardim of the Yetpela people joined the Daughters of Our Lady of the Sacred Heart (OLSH) in the 1960s; see Robyn Reynolds, OLSH, 'A Far Cry: Resounding Call to All Australians: "Missionary Turned Around: Bound to be Free"', Charles Strong Trust Lecture (Part 2), Adelaide, 2013, users.esc.net.au/~nhabel/lectures/2013Part2RobynReynoldsMissionaryTurnedAround.pdf; accessed 17 March 2016.
164 For example, *Freeman's Journal*, 19 August 1899, 21; *Mirror*, 21 March 1936, 15.
165 Most notably when Veronica Willaway was professed: 'Native Nun Takes Final Vows', *Record*, 24 March 1966, 12.

John Baptist Maria Dirimera, Benedict Upumera and Placid Cantagoro became members of Benedictine communities, but all died before they completed their studies. More than a century later, Vera took another step.

There is no story to tell about Vera Farrell or Sister Cecilia in her own words. With integrity and gentleness this elderly lady, now with some dementia, decided, 'I do not want to talk about that'.[166] We have memories of others, and the public record, but so close to the possibility of a richer account there is a choice for silence. Marie Willaway, who became Sister Veronica Therese, made a different choice, but like all the Benedictine Missionary Sisters whose conversation informs this work, the choice to speak involved revisiting realities that words do not capture well. The relationship between the mission culture and Aboriginal heritage is one of those realities.

When Veronica joined the community, she found what she knew Cecilia had found before her: that the choice for a Benedictine life was seen as a choice to silence all other claims of identity. In Veronica's experience, 'nobody talked about Aboriginality'.[167] The 'Aborigines' were tribal people in the north: 'it meant you were black, we didn't want to be black'.[168] Even the legal term for the peoples in the south who were assimilated or familiar with white ways was equivocal at St Joseph's: 'the word was *native* and we were not that'.[169] Being a St Joseph's girl was 'not that', at least not within the mission. Even more profoundly, being Benedictine was different again from being a St Joseph's girl, and both were somehow outside the negative categories on offer.

Nevertheless, when the Catholic press reported the milestones for Cecilia and later Veronica, it was to put 'native' in the headlines and to claim a bold success for assimilation. The distinctive, exceptional status of the sisters attracted comment. If St Joseph's quibbled about 'native', then *Pax* certainly did not, and even less the other newspapers in Western Australia. In a typical example, when Veronica made her final profession in the mid-1960s the *Record* claimed twin principles for New Norcia overall: the 'missionary vocation and assimilation programme for the

---

166 The polite refusal has been made many times through various channels, both Aboriginal and Benedictine, and definitively in a telephone conversation in August 2010.
167 Veronica Willaway, Interview, Nebraska, 8 July 2012.
168 Veronica Willaway, Interview, Nebraska, 8 July 2012.
169 Veronica Willaway, Interview, Nebraska, 8 July 2012, original emphasis.

natives'.¹⁷⁰ It claimed that Veronica's decision, like her brother Gabriel's election as team captain at St Ildephonsus, was 'a great demonstration of successful assimilation when a balanced atmosphere free from narrow prejudices can be found'.¹⁷¹ There was an affirmation, of sorts, of both the ancient culture the women represented and the ancient Rule they were committing to follow in the recognition that 'the ever-fresh Rule of St Benedict seems well-adapted to the needs and exigencies of one of the oldest races on earth'.¹⁷² The new phase was a success for the Benedictine women too, who were judged to be 'reaping the fruits of a field long and laboriously prepared by zeal for God and self-sacrifice'.¹⁷³ Their way of life now attracted 'unselfish generosity in young people to the extent of them asking for the Benedictine habit'.¹⁷⁴

In Veronica's assessment, the sisters' focus was simply on vocation, not race. The culture of the convent was assumed to be universal. 'Well, you know, they didn't stress "Aboriginal" back then. They just stressed that you went in as a postulant, that was "entering".' ¹⁷⁵ Her choice depended on everyone's conviction that human beings were equal before God. Paradoxically, it seemed to Veronica that it was a particularly Spanish trait not to discriminate between cultures:

> Now, you have to say one thing about the Spanish: they were never prejudiced. That was one of their best qualities. So, when I entered they didn't take me in because I was an Aboriginal person, Aboriginal girl, or because I was anything to do with Aboriginal, they just took me in as a young girl wanting to enter.¹⁷⁶

While she and Cecilia were celebrated publicly as past pupils and 'first of their people', privately there was the traditional corporate emphasis on not being distinctive. By the time Veronica entered, Cecilia's presence in habit and veil in the classroom and the playground was no longer novel; she had made a transition into the Benedictine world. For the girls at St Joseph's, Cecilia and Veronica were sisters who 'understood'.¹⁷⁷ They were

---

170   *Record*, 24 March 1966, 12.
171   *Record*, 24 March 1966, 12.
172   *Record*, 24 March 1966, 12.
173   *Record*, 24 March 1966, 12.
174   *Record*, 24 March 1966, 12.
175   Veronica Willaway, Interview, Nebraska, 7 July 2012.
176   Veronica Willaway, Interview, Nebraska, 7 July 2012.
177   Mary Nannup, Fatima Drayton, Gloria Drayton Interview, Moora, February 1999.

'like us',[178] members of families who had widespread connections through the Aboriginal community and they were embedded in St Joseph's already. According to the novice mistress at the time, there was a distinction to be created between the new members of the community and the girls they knew from school:

> [T]hey told me literally I had to change my attitude to the other girls. The girls wanted me to stay the same, but the sisters had a different idea: that I had to stay at a distance and in a certain way to think of myself above them as a Sister. This was one of the big things. ... [A]nd Cecilia yes, she had done the same.[179]

For these sisters, 'Aboriginal' and 'native' were both categories St Joseph's aimed to make irrelevant.

*****

The private dimension of Cecilia's vocation is no more available than the inner lives of the earlier sisters who left no writing, but it was particularly celebrated as a new stage in the history of New Norcia. If an aim to be 'not native' was part of the mission experience, it was nevertheless Cecilia's Aboriginal heritage that made her decision for the Benedictines memorable. Her choice would 'go into the records of the Mission',[180] because for the first time one of the mission women was received as a member of the Benedictine community.

When Vera Farrell made her choice to be a nun in 1953 she had been living at St Joseph's for five years and already the sisters appreciated her 'steadiness of mind'.[181] Vera's mother, Eileen Farrell, had written in 1944 from Walebing, 30 kilometres north of New Norcia, asking to place her daughter at the mission. There was a vacancy, and Abbot Catalan indicated he would hold the place for a fortnight, if the little girl was over eight and her mother would promise she would remain until she turned 19.[182] Eileen did not pursue the contact until two years later when Vera spent a month at New Norcia over the summer of 1946. Then in July 1948, aged 12, she was readmitted.[183] In mid-1952 Vera was one

---

178 Mary Nannup, Fatima Drayton, Interview, Moora, February 1999.
179 Veronica Willaway, Interview, Nebraska, 7 July 2012.
180 *Pax*, 15 October 1953.
181 *Sunday Leaf*, 5 April 1953.
182 Catalan to Mrs Eileen Farrell, 15 September 1944, NNA 01447/365.
183 Her birthday is listed as two different dates in the New Norcia records, but the date used most often is June 1936.

of three young women working at Bindoon when District Officer B. A. McLarty visited to inspect. His report raised a number of issues about the workload and indicated Vera wanted a new position near her family. Abbot Catalan assumed an inexperienced official had asked leading questions and dismissed follow-up enquiries from the department as an unjustified kerfuffle, but some changes followed at Bindoon. Explaining them to the department, Catalan advised that Vera had decided to stay at Bindoon until Christmas 1952 and then join her father in Geraldton.[184] Her life at Bindoon had struck the inspector as rather like the convent already, with an early start at 5.15 in the morning to join the sisters at Mass and routines until night prayers at 7.30 in the evening with further ironing sometimes until nine o'clock at night. McLarty was not persuaded by the assurance of Hildegard, as the sister-in-charge, that there was sufficient recreation because 'they are allowed to talk'.[185]

As Carmen recalled, the nuns also talked over the ironing. Chatting in the tiny laundry room a few months later, Vera stunned Carmen with a simple question, 'Did you know I am going to be a nun?'[186] Carmen liked this 'girl-helper' of 17 going on 18 but was frank about her surprise: 'I can't believe it. An Aborigine!'[187] She remembers Vera insisted, 'Truly yes! I am going from here. After a few days I am going to New Norcia. I want to be a nun'.[188] Carmen felt honoured to be the first of the ordinary sisters to know and acknowledged it was 'a good choice'.[189] Carmen's more immediate reaction of candid surprise underlined a reality. Vera's decision and the sisters' welcome challenged some stereotypes and carried wider and more public implications.

We do not know how the discussion of practical steps proceeded, but in April 1953 the *Sunday Leaf* announced Miss Vera Farrell had made the move to the convent and 'feels very much at home in the change and adapts herself well to the requirements of the new life'.[190] The standard six months of postulancy passed quickly. Visitación, not far from the experience herself, knew Vera was well-suited and was not surprised when

---

184 Catalan to Commissioner of Native Affairs, 30 June 1952, NNA 05050.
185 B. A. McLarty, 12 May 1952, summary report sent to Abbot Catalan for comment by Commissioner Middleton, 4 June 1952, NNA 05050.
186 Carmen Ruiz Besti, Interview, New Norcia, 28 July 1999.
187 Carmen Ruiz Besti, Interview in the Old Convent, New Norcia, October 2001.
188 Carmen Ruiz Besti, Interview in the Old Convent, New Norcia, October 2001.
189 Carmen Ruiz Besti, Interview, New Norcia, 1999.
190 *Sunday Leaf*, 5 April 1953.

'she was one of the ones I was closest to'.[191] When the time came for the community to affirm the decision and accept Vera as a novice, there was 'good hope that she will persevere to the end, and that her example might be followed by others'.[192]

At the ceremony where Vera was received formally and changed her name to Cecilia, many Aboriginal families crowded into the chapel to see 'the first [from] New Norcia to receive the gift of a religious vocation'.[193] They heard Abbot Catalan put her vocation on the world stage. The step she was taking was, he said, a local example of the dynamic of divine call that had drawn the Spanish sisters to New Norcia. They, too, had left the familiar behind as implicitly Vera was doing. The abbot stressed to the congregation that God's grace knew no boundaries:

> We have seen the example of many young ladies inspired by God and helped by his grace, [who] abandoned continent, native land, and homes and sailed for Australia to cooperate with Christ in the work of redemption and salvation of souls. In the ceremony this evening we find, however, that the grace of God is not tied to any colour, race or nationality.[194]

It was, the *Notebooks* recorded, 'very moving to see the chapel full of Indigenous women (*indigenas*) who had come to honour one of their own'[195] as she swapped her borrowed wedding dress for the Benedictine habit with the white veil of a novice. Vera's family hosted a generous spread afterwards with a big family gathering of her father's people from Carnarvon and her mother's family, the Narriers, who were well-connected over generations at New Norcia.

There were sombre reflections on the impact of her choice: 'From her the Lord will perhaps exact something above what he exacts from others', Abbot Catalan told the assembled crowd, '[and] her aid may count in the salvation of many native souls'.[196] Below the surface, by implication, Cecilia's decision to become a nun was a reordering of the relationship between the Indigenous and missionary communities at New Norcia.

---

191 Visitación Cidad in conversation, Madrid, 29 July 2010.
192 *Sunday Leaf*, 31 May 1953.
193 *Sunday Leaf*, 15 October 1953.
194 *Sunday Leaf*, 15 October 1953.
195 *Notebooks*, Madrid, 15 October 1953, 28.
196 *Sunday Leaf*, 15 October 1953.

Identity is about relationship.[197] Potentially, by committing her life to the Benedictine Missionary Sisters she was reframing the identity of Aboriginal people in the town.

Abbot Catalan knew Cecilia was 'the first of her class in these parts of W.A., a former pupil of St Joseph's Orphanage',[198] but he downplayed the claim for priority. He was probably familiar with the 'native sisterhood', the Daughters of Our Lady Queen of Apostles, founded in June 1939 by Bishop Raible of Broome and directed by the Pallottine Fathers and the Sisters of St John of God until its collapse in December 1951.[199] That relatively short-lived community, working at Beagle Bay and Balgo in the Kimberley, had been a 'Pious Union of Native Sisters'. Like New Norcia's sisters before 1935, they took private vows and were not a diocesan congregation as such. Membership was also restricted to Aboriginal women, similar to groups in the United States and Canada that were exclusively for Native American and African American women.[200] The abbot might not have known, as the Aboriginal families at New Norcia did, of at least one sister in another community in Western Australia whose family kept their Aboriginal descent private.[201]

As a public commitment to a diocesan congregation, Vera's move was different from the segregated congregations or undeclared Aboriginality. She was 'the first Native girl to apply' to the sisters, and the *Sunday Leaf* affirmed her confidently with a standard biblical allusion. Like Mary of Bethany who sat listening to Jesus: 'she has chosen the best part'.[202]

---

197 On identity as relational and its links to the understanding of space, see Doreen Massey, 'Geographies of Responsibility', *Geografiska Annaler: Series B, Human Geography* 86 (2004): 5–18.
198 *Sunday Leaf*, 15 October 1953.
199 'Aboriginal Nuns: First Congregation Establishment at Beagle Bay', *Geraldton Guardian and Express*, 29 April 1939, 1; Christine Choo, *Mission Girls: Aboriginal Women on Catholic Missions in the Kimberley, Western Australia 1900–1950* (Crawley, WA: University of Western Australia Press, 2001), 172–85; Hilary M. Carey, 'Subordination, Invisibility and Chosen Work: Missionary Nuns and Australian Aborigines, c.1900–1949', *Australian Feminist Studies* 13 (1998): 251–67.
200 'Aboriginal Nuns', *West Australian*, 11 October 1947; Brigida Nailon, *Nothing Is Wasted in the Household of God: Vincent Pallotti's Vision in Australia* (Richmond, Vic.: Spectrum Publications, 2001), 139.
201 Veronica Willaway, Interview, Nebraska, 9 July 2012.
202 *Sunday Leaf*, 11 October 1953.

Cecilia's new Benedictine identity and commitment emerged in the liturgy as a stern calling as well as a privilege. She was 'renouncing the blandishments and attractions of the world' for 'the total oblation of herself to God'[203] in a vowed commitment. There was talk not of joy but rather of the obedience that would sustain her in a unique vocation:

> God has given her the help of his grace; He expects her to co-operate with this grace by the faithful observance of the Rule, the Constitutions and Conventual Customs, not less than by the fulfilment of the vows.[204]

The focus was otherworldly. Cecilia was taught that her task was holiness above all, and the community were encouraged to pray for her:

> With her exemplary conduct, with the fulfilment of her vows and the practice of the virtues of humility and charity and the exercise of good sense, she may be instrumental in bringing many souls to the fold of the Church and ultimately to the mansions of heaven. Let us ask God through the intercession of Mary, the mother of Jesus, St Benedict the founder of monks, and his twin sister St. Scholastica to grant Miss Farrell the grace to persevere and to become some day a faithful spouse of Christ and a fervent Benedictine missionary.[205]

The community of sisters chanted the Latin hymns they had probably sung at their own clothing ceremonies, invoking the Holy Spirit in 'Veni Creator' and praising Jesus as inspiration and protector of virginity in 'Iesu, Corona Virginum'. The occasion was an emotional and historic first, but tradition and not innovation was to the fore.

Holding the occasion on 15 October, the feast day of Teresa of Avila, made a quiet connection with Sister Teresa Roca. Her death the previous February at the age of 85 had broken the community's direct link with their foundation history. It is significant that the *Notebooks* move directly from their tribute to the pioneer sister who had seen the arrivals and departures since 1904 to announce that Vera, '*alumna de San José*',[206] joined them in April to test her vocation.[207] Six months later, as she made her commitment as a novice, the community hoped Cecilia's decision

---

203 *Sunday Leaf*, 18 October 1953.
204 *Sunday Leaf*, 18 October 1953.
205 *Sunday Leaf*, 18 October 1953.
206 *Notebooks*, Madrid, 28.
207 *Sunday Leaf*, 31 May 1953.

might herald a new stage in their story, so that she would be 'a guide and beacon to many others who … will follow her footsteps'.[208] This vocation was more than a personal commitment: Cecilia represented a category for the monastery. When the new Sr Gertrude (Marina Diez from Villasilos, one of the 12) wrote from the north to say one of the young women at Kalumburu was interested in joining, Abbot Catalan responded clinically that this was entirely possible 'now we have professed the native Farrell'.[209]

There is a gap in the monastic *Chronicle* at New Norcia in the early 1950s, including the date of Cecilia's first profession, but the record had resumed by Saturday 22 November 1958, when she made a permanent commitment to the community. The diarist, Fr Boniface Gómez, was at the celebration, of course, and his entry recording it brought together the complex realities of New Norcia in a few brief sentences. Beginning with the ecclesiastical specifics, he noted: 'Sr Cecilia makes her perpetual profession. Fr Abbot celebrates Mass at St Joseph's Orphanage. Fr Basil gave the sermon'.[210]

The next detail located the new sister in her family of origin and offered an almost inadvertent glimpse of the impact of her choice and the interactions of the mission town: 'Her mother who is a daughter of Alec Narrier was present and Alec himself was seen coming out of the chapel with very red eyes. He told me he could not hold back his tears of emotion'.[211] The diarist's hint at Cecilia's grandfather's feeling is evocative. It could have been mirrored any number of times in Catholic Australia as parents and grandparents left convent chapels moved with pride, thanksgiving and grief at a daughter's choice.

The *Chronicle* did not pursue the train of thought but shifted attention to the federal election on the same day: 'We all went to cast our votes in the Commonwealth elections'.[212] 'All' in this case referred to the naturalised Australians in the Benedictine communities. The need to get to the polling booth did not distract 22-year-old Cecilia or her family or many of the other Aboriginal people at the service who had no voting

---

208 *Sunday Leaf*, 8 November 1953.
209 Anselm Catalan to Gertrude Diez, 5 December 1955, NNA 01457.
210 'Chronicle of the Benedictine Community of New Norcia' (hereafter *Chronicle*), 22 November 1958.
211 *Chronicle*, 22 November 1958.
212 *Chronicle*, 22 November 1958.

rights in federal elections until 1962.[213] Some Aboriginal families at New Norcia had 'certificates of exemption' under the state *Native Welfare Act 1954* to guarantee they were not associating with 'tribal Aborigines' and therefore had some voting rights, but many regarded the certificates as degrading and did not apply. On the one hand, they offended against family networks; on the other, they were an affront to people who did not categorise themselves as 'native' in the sense of the Act in the first place.

New Norcia's *Chronicle* did not comment on the question of justice or the politics of the day but returned the focus to the sisters with further news from another Aboriginal family, also framed as a formal announcement: 'On this day also the eldest daughter of Harrold [sic] Willaway, Marie, was admitted as a postulant'.[214] For Marie, this was not a 'native' story but a Catholic one. Named Marie Terese by her parents after the French Carmelite nun who had likewise insisted on joining the convent at a young age, Marie valued the precedent of child saints who had made heroic choices: 'All along, I claimed all the young saints, St Agnes, all those young ones, like the Little Flower. It was like they were on the same path as I was, centuries before'.[215] She cast her choices in the narrative of the Catholic quest for holiness.

*****

Marie Willaway became Sister Veronica Therese in a series of decisions that she traces to a defining story of her birth and a 'path God led me on with the angels'.[216] More self-revealing than the accounts offered by the Spanish sisters, Veronica's story traverses mysticism and the psychology of her earliest experiences to explain a conviction that her vocation emerged because 'God had paved this and the angels had helped'.[217] The first round of discussion is light; her vocation was 'out of the blue'.[218] But then the conversation deepens and goes back to the beginning.

---

213 The *Commonwealth Electoral Act 1962* extended voting rights to Aboriginal Australians in all federal elections; see also Australian Federal Election Speeches, Herbert Evatt, 1958, Museum of Australian Democracy, electionspeeches.moadoph.gov.au/speeches/1958-herbert-evatt; accessed 19 March 2016. (After a citizenship ceremony on 30 May 1956 in which two members of the Calingari Road Board astonished each of the 14 who had arrived after the Second World War with an English New Testament and bouquet of flowers, all the Spanish sisters were now required to vote.)
214 *Chronicle*, 22 November 1958.
215 Veronica Willaway, Interview, Nebraska, 7 July 2012.
216 Veronica Willaway, Interview, Nebraska, 16 June 2013.
217 Veronica Willaway, Interview, Nebraska, 16 June 2013.
218 Veronica Willaway, Interview, Nebraska, 16 June 2013.

Veronica was her father Harold's first child with his second wife, Philomena Nettles. The labour at the notorious Moore River hospital was slow and long. The baby was in breech position. After 72 hours, Dr Miles, who attended from Moora, asked Harold to make a choice:

> And so, the doctor … said to my father, 'You're going to lose one of them. We can't save them both.' So my father had just lost his first wife, Peter's mother, so he wasn't about to lose his second wife, so he said, 'Well, maybe the baby. At least the baby will go to heaven.' So they left it at that.[219]

Veronica pauses and takes a sip of water. Her own memory of what happened next is sure. It has crystallised over years of her own reflection, though she acknowledges, laughing, that 'somebody said it would be a good case for a psychologist'.[220] The doctor left them. Though not yet born, Veronica remembers a defining experience of being abandoned by her mother. 'I can still see it in my own mind. … I was just waiting for her to say goodbye to me. And nothing. She never said a word to me. … [M]aybe she was praying, I don't know.'[221] The sequel takes the experience out of the earthly realm. Her mother's account of the dramatic resolution became the more public part of the family story. The baby was delivered with supernatural intervention:

> She told me that three women she had never seen came inside the room, gently touched her on the belly, and she said I plopped out bottom first and made a mess of her. She said they came in, they touched me, I plopped down and they walked out and she's never seen them since. We presume they were angels. … So, that was the birth.[222]

The miraculous survival of both mother and baby did not heal the rift between them.

The clearest consequence for Veronica was an anger she couldn't resolve, especially towards her mother: 'I couldn't get it out of my system. And so, you know she tried her best, but the damage was done, way back then'.[223]

---

219 Veronica Willaway, Interview, Nebraska, 20 June 2013.
220 Veronica Willaway, Interview, Nebraska, 20 June 2013.
221 Veronica Willaway, Interview, Nebraska, 20 June 2013.
222 Veronica Willaway, Interview, Nebraska, 20 June 2013.
223 Veronica Willaway, Interview, Nebraska, 20 June 2013.

In her own mind, she was convinced 'I was nobody's child'.[224] She had nearly been consigned to heaven already, and God offered a welcome she felt she had been denied:

> As I grew older, then I said to my little self, 'Well, if my mother doesn't care, nobody cares, at least God cares.' So that from that time I got detached, and I was kind of like only God's child, because you don't trust anybody else because they're not going to help you. So you trust God.[225]

It was that clarity that prompted Veronica to 'leave home' for St Joseph's as a five-year-old, and it sustained her decision to join the sisters.

Most of the sisters had joined the Benedictine community aged about 18, and several had been 15 or 16, so they recognised youthful idealism as an advantage. Veronica, however, was pushing the limits. Most records adjust her entry to 8 December 1958, the day before her fourteenth birthday, but she had been intent on the convent since she finished primary school at 12. Her mother saw the possibility that her bright first-born might go to high school, but Veronica resisted the idea of college:

> So, I was ready, I had finished school when I was twelve and then my mother came and she said 'Do you want to go to St Gertrude's College?' But I was so anxious, and maybe because she said that I decided, 'No, I want to go to the convent.'[226]

The sisters hesitated but Veronica was 'stubborn enough' by her own account[227] and, as others remember, 'would not leave'.[228] There was always work for older girls to do at St Joseph's. Some correspondence lessons in English, human biology and business eventually overtook the anxiety-inducing prospect of St Gertrude's. Rose's memory of Veronica leaving in 'one-lap for the convent' fades beside the longer story of her persistence.

---

224 Veronica Willaway, Interview, Nebraska, 20 June 2013.
225 Veronica Willaway, Interview, Nebraska, 20 June 2013.
226 Veronica Willaway, Interview, Nebraska, 7 July 2012.
227 Veronica Willaway, Interview, Nebraska, 16 June 2013.
228 Anne Moynihan, Interview, North Perth, 19 March 1999.

Figure 9.8: The novices and postulants playing hockey at the back of St Joseph's—Imelda and Josephine in white veils, Veronica centre and Pius right, c. 1959. Fowl yard in the background.
Source: ABTM.

The community recognised her as an 'aspirant' on the understanding that she would be received as a postulant when she was older. Veronica's companions were two young women who had arrived from Spain in June 1958. Isolina Ruiz and Natividad Montero had met Sister Felicitas and Abbot Gregory in 1957 when they were in Spain promoting the work of New Norcia to potential recruits. The journey was prompted (at least in the opinion of the *Notebooks*) because 'there were no Australian entrants'.[229] The two who came 'after a lot of waiting'[230] were received as novices Sister Imelda and Sister Josephine on 14 February 1959. Veronica was judged still too young to take that step.

---

229 *Notebooks*, Madrid, 39.
230 *Notebooks*, Madrid, 39.

Figure 9.9: Sr Veronica Therese with her family on the day of her final profession, 12 March 1966; left to right: Rose, Philomena, Veronica, Peter, Harold, Gabriel and Isobel.
Source: Courtesy of Anne Moynihan and the Willaway family. Author's Collection.

Around the same time, Anne Moynihan from Perth began to visit the convent. Spurred on by a conversation with her brother Tom, a novice with the monks at the time, she came in her early twenties to see this group who seemed to fit her hopes so well: 'I always wanted to be a nun, I wanted to stay in Western Australia and I wanted to work with Aborigines. I did not want to be sent anywhere else'.[231] She got to know some of the Benedictine women who had better English, especially the lively teacher Marie-Therese, who often entertained the visitor in the parlour. Rather like Marie-Therese herself 10 years earlier, Anne decided to 'go for it'.[232] She took 12 months leave of absence from her job at the Department of

---

231 Anne Moynihan, Interview, North Perth, 19 March 1999.
232 Anne Moynihan, Interview, North Perth, 19 March 1999.

Social Services in June 1959 and was admitted as a postulant on 10 July.[233] This time the community judged Veronica Willaway could also move to more formal status. The two were companions through the process of formation and Josephine Montero, herself only a new novice, took them under her wing in the 'little Spain'[234] that was the convent. With Imelda they were the new quartet, and then, from August 1960 when Imelda decided the life was not for her and moved to Perth, a firm trio. There was plenty to adjust to for each of them. At one level, Anne confronted more that was unfamiliar than Veronica: notices and timetables in Spanish, a diet rich in olive oil and routines of thrift that seemed absurd. Veronica had known all this from childhood. She had also already internalised the need to conform, even if she recognised hers was the deeper challenge, already familiar from mission life, of 'turning white in order to blend in'.[235] As they learnt to chant the psalms and set the altar, mend the sheets and starch the linen, to follow the routines in the hope of finding a role for the future, the three in the novitiate—Aboriginal, Australian and Spanish—seemed to Anne a microcosm of the mission itself.

Turning towards Spain

Among the professed sisters at the same time, momentum was growing away from New Norcia and towards Spain. There was anxiety that numbers were not increasing in Australia, and Felicitas began to act on the idea of setting up a permanent house in Spain to encourage vocations in their traditional stronghold. Able and experienced sisters were already spread thinly between the three Australian houses, so the first step was to withdraw from Bindoon. In November 1958 Felicitas wrote to Brother Quilligan hoping he could contact a community of European nuns she had heard about who were coming from China, 'ready to accept any work offered to them',[236] as replacements for the Benedictine women. She assured him of her good intention and gratitude and that she needed to close the branch house to 'solve a problem which no other way could be resolved'.[237] There is no record of a reply. In a further letter on 15 June

---

233 *Notebooks*, Madrid, 39. See also 'Profession of Sister Pius', *Pax*, March 1965, 1.
234 Anne Moynihan, Interview, North Perth, 19 March 1999.
235 Veronica Willaway, Interview, Nebraska, 16 June 2013.
236 Felicitas to Brother Quilligan, Bindoon, 10 November 1958, ABTM.
237 Felicitas to Brother Quilligan, Bindoon, 10 November 1958, ABTM.

1959 she apologised for 'so much trouble' and assured him of prayers that he would find 'other Sisters who will be as good or better than ours'.[238] By this time the community's decision was imminent.

At an all-day meeting of the New Norcia and Bindoon communities on 26 July 1959 a majority supported a proposal to establish a 'junior house' in Spain for girls who wanted to explore a vocation to the Australian missions.[239] Abbot Gregory was strongly encouraging of the proposal. He presented two possible locations supported by other Benedictine abbots: one near the Spanish capital and the other in Galicia.

The first option would have linked the sisters with the Benedictine monks of Cuelgamuros at the Nationalist war memorial to Franco's fighters at the Valley of the Fallen, 70 kilometres from Madrid. Discussion about entrusting the busy international guesthouse to New Norcia's sisters stalled.[240] Felicitas wrote to Abbot Justo Pérez in October 1959 asking six practical questions. Her concerns ranged from what the duties would be and whether there would be time for prayer to how many sisters would be needed and whether compensation of £100 each would be reasonable.[241] Felicitas raised doubts about how much contact the sisters and the juniors should have with 'secular persons', through accompanying visitors or serving in the refectory, for example. On reflection, the intensity of that work also seemed to the monks in charge an unlikely fit for New Norcia's house of formation. According to Teresa, Abbot Pérez intended to offer the community other work, but 'before he came to a decision they went to Samos'.[242]

Samos was a village in the mountainous east of Galicia remote from everything except a community of Benedictine monks who needed help with their laundry. Surely in a failure of imagination, by June 1960 Felicitas was writing to the bishop of Lugo asking his permission to accept an offer of 'work and economic means of subsistence' in his diocese. She said the foundation was intended for 'the great glory of God and to the benefit of young women endowed with a religious vocation who wish to join our Congregation'.[243] Benita and Gema left Australia on 28 June

---

238 Felicitas to Brother Quilligan, Bindoon, 15 June 1959, ABTM.
239 *Notebooks*, Madrid.
240 Teresa González, Interview, Madrid, 25 May 1999.
241 Felicitas to Abbot Justo Pérez, Madrid, 22 October 1959, ABTM.
242 Teresa González, Interview, Madrid, 25 May 1999.
243 Felicitas to Dr D. Rafael Baloza, Lugo, Spain, 23 June 1960, ABTM.

1960, five days after the letter to the bishop to establish the community in Galicia. 'I am not sure what I would have done if I had been making the decision,' Teresa González observes, 'but I do not think I would have gone to Samos to live in a farmhouse in the country away from everybody'.[244] The choice suggested not so much the hope of meeting aspiring members as a readiness to continue domestic work. It was also a reorientation towards ministry in the Spanish context and financial independence. Significantly, this work and later arrangements with the St John of God Brothers in Zaragoza and Madrid would attract an independent stipend for the Benedictine women.

---

244 Teresa González, Interview, Madrid, 25 May 1999.

10

Spinning Apart

The 1959 decision to establish a house of formation in Spain was a turning point, although the Benedictine sisters did not realise it at the time. The immediate aim was to resource the Australian mission more reliably than visits to the villages around Burgos ever had. This hope went unfulfilled, but there were other consequences of the move. Being Spanish, missionary as well as monastic, and women rather than monks at New Norcia had always presented challenges. Gradually these realities reoriented the group away from Western Australia. Paradoxically, as the Second Vatican Council encouraged religious communities to remember their foundational goals, the touchstones of identity that had defined the sisters' presence in the mission town evolved through the 1960s and 1970s to become the reasons for their leaving. Being Spanish gradually superseded the claims of new missionary work and the community's significance in the monastic town. Through these decades there was still energy invested at St Joseph's and at Kalumburu, particularly in the innovative childcare centre at Girrawheen in Perth, but, subtly, the foundations at Samos, then Zaragoza, then Barcelona and Madrid began to define the future.

This chapter traces the commitment to the new initiatives in Spain and Australia and changes at New Norcia as new funding models opened choices for Aboriginal people. No less than other stages in their history, this last chapter of the Benedictine sisters' story in Australia was marked by contrast. An ambitious effort to step away from New Norcia coincided with a corrosive loss of confidence among the Spanish women about the viability of their community in Australia. Just as the new venture seemed to be flourishing, they made the decision to leave.

New foundations in Spain

In Spain at first, the work of formation for new members was itself relegated to the background as the sisters struggled to find a base for their ministry of household work, first in Samos and then in Zaragoza through the 1960s. Benita and Gema were dismayed that the promised convent in Samos was delayed and delayed again. They spent three months with Benedictine nuns in Madrid before they took up residence in a country farmhouse in the Galician village of Villadetres. Nevertheless, they were joined by Hildegard and Francisca in January 1961, and when the convent was finally finished in August the community included two potential new members. Benita returned to Australia in the same year, replaced by Francisca as superior so that by March 1962, when Teresa and Matilda arrived to work with the aspirants, there were five experienced sisters in the new Spanish base. Less than two years into the arrangement, however, there was an opportunity to do similar domestic work in Zaragoza for a more generous stipend in more suitable accommodation with the St John of God Brothers, so the community divided. The work with newcomers was moved to the larger town, a centre of pilgrimage in the northeast.

In Zaragoza, the house of formation became a community of nine at the end of 1963, when Angelina arrived as superior to join Teresa, Matilda, Hildegard and, after a regular turnover of hopefuls, five aspirants. Financial negotiations with the brothers continued until 6 July, when an agreement was reached that would enable the congregation to save enough to build a convent in the future.[1] We can imagine those conversations with the meticulous Angelina, holding the line on remuneration, urged on by Teresa, and both encouraged by the new mother general at New Norcia, Magdalena Ruiz de la Barga, and her councillors, Mary Cidad and Felicitas Pampliega. A year later Francisca and Gema, who had remained behind in Samos, closed the house there, the *Notebooks* record, as conditions were still not what had been guaranteed. They joined the others in Zaragoza, where the community considered itself happy, both well-provided for and appreciated by their employers.[2]

---

1 'Origen de la Congregacion de las Hermanas Benedictinas Misioneras de New Norcia, Western Australia', unpublished typescript from the notebooks of Sister Felicitas Pampliega c.1921–c. 1967, transcribed and edited by Sister Teresa González, Madrid c. 1980 (*Notebooks,* Madrid), 36.
2 *Notebooks*, Madrid, 36.

10. SPINNING APART

The good working arrangement with the St John of God Brothers expanded further in 1964 when the Benedictine sisters moved to Carabanchel on the outskirts of Madrid to take up roles within St Joseph's Refuge. This institute to care for epileptic boys had been built in extensive gardens by the Marqués of Vallejo at the turn of the twentieth century as the first of its kind in Spain and had been run by the community of nursing brothers from the outset.[3] In March 1961 they expanded to register a school for children and adolescents who needed help with 'social integration'.[4] Their invitation in July 1964 to the Benedictine sisters to assist them could have included some work in the school, but the vanguard community in Madrid of Francisca, Gema and four of the aspirants was probably focused on domestic work and initially provided a solution to overcrowding in Zaragoza as the number of hopeful candidates increased there. According to the *Notebooks*, it was only a few days before a similar increase in Madrid, with 16 aspirants by September 1964, when Teresa was transferred to Carabanchel to assist with the program.[5] Lucia also arrived in Zaragoza from New Norcia to help Hildegard run the kitchen there.

It seemed the sisters had been right to expect that there would be vocations for the community in Spain. Just a few months after Josephine Montero made her final profession at New Norcia on 12 March 1964, Ana Maria Lopez was received as a novice in Zaragoza on the feast of St Benedict in July. The *Notebooks* note the moving ceremony as she became the first to take the habit for the community in Spain. Three other aspirants were also received as postulants that day. As the community grew, the mood was buoyant. Even when Hildegard died in 1966, unexpectedly young at 57 years old, a photograph of half a dozen new members clustered around the headstone of the Drysdale River pioneer comforted her niece Visitación in the Kimberley, suggesting the future of the work was secure.

When the promising new candidates asked Teresa how they would manage in Australia if they did not speak English, however, she could not give them an answer that made sense to them or to her. Language study was expensive and rare in Franco's Spain, and even today only 12 per cent

---

3   Francisco Javier Faucha Perez and Jesus Fernandez Sanz, 'La Fundacion Instituto San José de Carabanchel Alto', *Madrid Historico* (2011): 73–80.
4   'Asilo de San José', Karabanchel.com: Una Pagina de Nuestro Barrio, karabanchel.com/asilo-de-san-jose-2/; accessed 2 January 2017.
5   *Notebooks*, Madrid, 37.

of Spaniards have a working knowledge of English.[6] Given the choice between Spain and a context where they could not speak, Teresa knew as well as they did that learning English haphazardly was a shaky foundation for ministry. In the end, out of more than 20 hopefuls, only Ana Maria remained to make a permanent commitment to the community.

In Teresa's mind domestic work for another community had always been a trap and a distraction from more significant work with people. She advocated for new initiatives in childcare that would link the foundations in Spain and Australia. In January 1970, looking to balance the history of the congregation with opportunities for the new members, they scaled back Zaragoza to open a kindergarten and weekly boarding house for children of working parents on the outskirts of Barcelona. Josephine Montero had completed her nursing training in Perth and come to Spain in 1969 to begin this work; financial support flowed from Kalumburu where Florentina was being paid by the Commonwealth Government as the nursing sister at the clinic. It was hard work, as usual. Some children were very young indeed, and the old house in Rasabada Road outside Barcelona's centre needed repairs, but they attracted a full complement of 34 by January 1971. Mary wrote enthusiastically to General Franco as head of state as well as to Propaganda Fide in Rome to seek financial support.[7] Discussions about a daycare centre were also well-advanced in Perth by the end of 1970, with funding already in place from state and church authorities,[8] and in April 1973 support from local benefactors made the land available at Parla on the outskirts of Madrid to establish a similar kindergarten, open only during the working day. Barcelona remained a boarding facility and was 'a difficult job for older people, as are the Sisters there', and 'even worse for young people with no training'.[9] Nevertheless, a promising cohort of eight or more newcomers remained, mostly connected to the community in Madrid.

---

6   European Union Directorate General for Education and Culture, *Europeans and Their Languages*, Special Eurobarometer 386 (Brussels: European Commission, June 2012), 29, ec.europa.eu/public_opinion/archives/ebs/ebs_386_en.pdf; accessed 3 January 2017.
7   Mary Cidad to His Excellency, General Franco, 12 January 1971, Archives of the Benedictine Missionary Sisters of Tutzing (ABTM).
8   Mary Cidad to Angelina Cerezo, 14 November 1970, ABTM.
9   Fr José Luis Cortega, OSB, to Mary Cidad, 1 June 1972, trans. Kerry Mullan, ABTM.

Figure 10.1: Young members from the Spanish house of formation in the late 1960s at Hildegard's tombstone in Zaragoza.
Source: ABTM.

Figure 10.2: Natividad Montero makes her profession as Sister Josephine, March 1964 at New Norcia. Students from St Gertrude's College and one of their teachers to her left, Felicitas, Veronica and Antonia to her right.
Source: ABTM.

When Mary Cidad was elected superior in October 1970, the new mother general wrote to the houses in Spain with a clear sense of urgency to clarify organisation and focus. Mary had plans to consolidate the novitiate in either Madrid or Barcelona (or even a proposed new location at the historic town of Castrojerez in Burgos),[10] whichever place that 'most guarantees the best offering of good formation and education for the young ones … as within a few years they will have to keep our Congregation afloat'.[11] She presented Girrawheen to the Spanish houses as an agreed new focus for ministry in Australia and similarly sought a single focus in Spain, instructing that 'everyone, even the Novices, must give me their opinion, which kind of apostolate interests you',[12] and urging Angelina and Matilda as local superiors to keep all the newcomers informed 'to give them courage and confidence'. Time might be short and her term was limited: 'pray often to our Lord to give me health; it is my wish to do all this in these three years'.[13] Above all, a common purpose was fundamental to her hopes: 'try to be united, otherwise you will ruin everything and I won't be able to do anything'.[14] She was writing not only to the sisters who had been her novices in the 1940s and 1950s at New Norcia but also to the new members born in the years since they had left for Australia.

Life at New Norcia had not prepared the sisters for a cross-generational community in urban Spain. The average age of the community had risen to 52, with most members in their forties. One of the monks from Cuelgamuros outside Madrid wrote to Mary in May 1972 with frank advice: she needed to announce plans for the six young sisters in temporary vows in Carabanchel, or they would leave. He assumed these young women recruited in Spain were the future of the community and urged Mary to give them full responsibility especially in the work among other newcomers. It was clear to him 'that the young people have no confidence in the older Sisters'.[15] Along with the simple fact of an age difference, he named the chief barrier to understanding as the pattern of life learnt at the mission:

---

10   Mary Cidad to Angelina Cerezo, 14 November 1970, trans. Kerry Mullan, ABTM.
11   Mary Cidad to Angelina Cerezo, 14 November 1970.
12   Mary Cidad to Matilda Arroyo, 14 November 1970, ABTM.
13   Mary Cidad to Matilda Arroyo, 14 November 1970.
14   Mary Cidad to Matilda Arroyo, 14 November 1970.
15   Fr José Luis Cortega to Mary Cidad, 1 June 1972, ABTM.

10. SPINNING APART

> [M]ost of [the New Norcia sisters] are already quite old, they were trained in a different environment from the one in which they live today. They lived almost like cloistered nuns and the impact from the outside has turned out to be very hard for them. We must give way to youth, give them a sense of responsibility.[16]

The 'good, very hardworking Sisters' had no aptitude for work with young people, 'especially in these times'. The exception was Teresa González, who could still 'kill the most robust person and tire out the most dynamic'. He warned that she had too much to do 'everyday and at all hours' so that she was becoming bitter even while she remained 'a great merit in the house and in the young ones' training'.[17] He proposed that she should share the role in formation with one of the Spanish recruits whom he felt the group also trusted. He argued strongly against closing the house at Carabanchel in Madrid.

Mary took at least some of this advice and did not close Carabanchel. She asked the community in Barcelona for their thoughts about moving the novitiate (which had been formally transferred from New Norcia to Barcelona the year before) to Madrid.[18] The community there had already welcomed the proposal. She referred them to St Benedict's understanding of authority: 'As you will understand, I have to listen to everyone, but listening is one thing and deciding is another',[19] and updated them on administrative arrangements. Two final matters—questions about their dress and their pattern of prayer—gave an indication of the context of change this community shared with other communities of vowed women after the Second Vatican Council.

The details of daily life were in flux. Mary sent instructions about the habit: postulants were to wear their own clothes; for novices, she was sending a new pattern with Florentina, who was transferring from Kalumburu to Barcelona, asking that Josephine might bring a spare white veil in the new design with her when she, in turn, travelled back to take up the duties in the clinic in the Kimberley 'in case someone enters here'.[20] It was still a possibility. Then, concerned about the format of prayers the community should follow, she reported that the Benedictine abbots would meet in 1973 to make a decision on the best of three new breviaries:

---

16   Fr José Luis Cortega to Mary Cidad, 1 June 1972.
17   Fr José Luis Cortega to Mary Cidad, 1 June 1972.
18   Mary Cidad to Matilda Arroyo and Community, 24 June 1972, trans. Kerry Mullan, ABTM.
19   Mary Cidad to Matilda Arroyo and Community, 24 June 1972.
20   Mary Cidad to Matilda Arroyo and Community, 24 June 1972.

> I asked if this will affect us and I have been told it will ... For the moment it is more practical to wait, there is no point wasting money now, only to have to change it [the prayer book] again in 2 years time; it won't take that long to translate it.[21]

It would be the same format for the whole community, in Spanish and in English, she observed, 'and that's ideal', but in the meantime they should make do. While bold about change in local matters, Mary consistently advocated caution in relation to the Council:

> I understand that many Nuns went further than the Council wanted and one also hears the nuns making many critical remarks; they say that [ordinary] people instead of admiring them [are] doing the opposite, and they do not get the respect they used to. Therefore let us learn this for ourselves, and let us be among the more careful ones.[22]

An unruly ferment of renewal held no attraction for Mary.

There had been few precursors to Vatican II at New Norcia.[23] The rigid collar introduced to the habit in the early 1950s was a symbol of their interaction with the modern world. Ungainly and hot but made of up-to-the-minute plastic, the great advantage of the innovation was supposed to be that it was easy to clean. Most sisters actually found it unhygienic and impractical.[24] At Kalumburu they wore it for photos and special occasions.

It was replaced with a rolled collar of normal fabric in 1962 in a secret ballot on modifying the habit, to the great rejoicing of the *Notebooks*.[25] That the community persisted with 'the bib' for close to a decade says something, perhaps about a lack of capacity to evaluate change.

The need to adapt sensibly was part of the advice given to the fourth Congress of Religious Sisters that gathered 200 representatives from Australia and New Zealand at the Loreto Convent in Claremont in January 1965.[26] The Benedictine Missionary Sisters were among the 50 groups

---

21 Mary Cidad to Matilda Arroyo and Community, 24 June 1972.
22 Mary Cidad to Matilda Arroyo, 25 June 1971, trans. Kerry Mullan, ABTM.
23 David Barry, 'New Norcia', in *Historical Encyclopedia of Western Australia*, ed. Jenny Gregory and Jan Gothard (Crawley, WA: University of Western Australia Press, 2009), 629–30; John H. Smith, ed., *The Story of New Norcia. The Western Australian Benedictine Mission* (New Norcia, WA: Benedictine Community of New Norcia, 2015), 32.
24 *Notebooks*, Madrid, 13 February 1962.
25 *Notebooks*, Madrid, 13 February 1962.
26 *Record*, 28 January 1965, 10.

represented, and it would have been Magdalena with Felicitas and Mary who heard the Apostolic Delegate, Fr Domenico Enrici, remind the women of the power of unity. Sharing 'the same love for Christ and His Church, and the same resolve to work for the salvation of the world', they were to be 'an army, compact and invincible fighting the good battle' and 'a family, united together by the sweet bonds of charity'.[27] Both metaphors suited the sensibilities of the Spanish Benedictines.

While the conference was underway, the Benedictine delegates returned to New Norcia to celebrate the final profession of Pius Moynihan with liturgical reforms made possible by the Council. On 21 January 1965 Sr Pius vowed a permanent commitment to the Benedictine life, and then, with Abbot Gregory presiding, she became the first woman in Catholic Australia to receive not only bread but also wine at the Eucharist. The Council's decree on the liturgy had been promulgated on 4 December 1963, but according to the *Record*, this was the first occasion 'that we know of in Australia'[28] to draw on its provisions to make the cup available to others, not only the priest.[29] The following March, when Veronica Therese had turned 21 and was also able to make a life commitment, she also received both bread and wine, and the *Record* remarked on it again: 'The returning to the spirit and practice of the Last Supper by the use of this rite is highly recommended by the Council Fathers'.[30] Innovation in the interests of tradition was a thoroughly Benedictine trait.

In keeping with the Roman directive to all religious communities following the Council, the Benedictine sisters had held a general chapter to consider their constitutions in July 1969. These were provisionally approved in 1970, but in July 1971 Mary took advantage of the formal visit to New Norcia of the abbot president and former abbot of Montserrat, Gabriel Brasó, to ask him to bring them further into line with the Council. Abbot Brasó's visit coincided with the resignation of Gregory Gomez as abbot of New Norcia and his replacement by the first Australian to hold the post: Fr Bernard Rooney. The change in leadership increased Mary Cidad's reliance on the Spanish-speaking Abbot Brasó for administrative advice. Although he occasionally referred her back to the more than

---

27   *Record*, 21 January 1965, 1.
28   *Record*, 11 February 1965, 5.
29   Constitution on the Sacred Liturgy, *Sacrosanctum Concilium*, 4 December 1963, para. 55, www.vatican.va/archive/hist_councils/ii_vatican_council/documents/vat-ii_const_19631204_sacro sanctum-concilium_en.html; accessed 9 January 2017.
30   *Record*, 24 March 1966, 12.

competent canon lawyers at New Norcia, Brasó became an important link to the Spanish church. Mary confided that 'as I don't know who else to turn to, naturally I am turning to Your reverence as our protector'.[31] It was a significant shift in the relationships between the Benedictine communities in the mission town.

Considering the constitution, the abbot president made a number of suggestions in person and in the correspondence that followed through 1972 to make the document 'more rounded and richer in doctrine'.[32] Then in some confusion about the drafts, apparently triggered by a letter from Mary, the Congregation for Religious suspended work on the new statements from New Norcia until January 1973,[33] and a process of revision continued until after July 1977.[34] If they stopped to think about it, New Norcia's sisters had been waiting carefully for similar determinations about their constitutions for most of their history.

Defining the New Norcia charism—again?

When Felicitas had adapted the constitutions from Maredsous to her own community in the 1930s, she had added local references while keeping the European model intact. Like the skilled seamstress she was, she made thoughtful adjustments to a trusted pattern rather than design from scratch. Both the Belgian and Australian groups aimed for 'the sanctification of their members', and their main work was with children in need. Felicitas broadened the scope (and reflected the reality at New Norcia), noting that commitment did not exclude 'other benevolent work such as working in the Missions, serving in hospitals or providing domestic service to another religious Community'.[35] She added Joseph to the patrons they shared with Belgium—Benedict and Scholastica— and retained the claim to 'protection' under 'the Sacred Hearts of Jesus and Mary', although that more typically French and Irish devotion did

---

31   Mary Cidad to Gabriel Brasó, 6 January 1973, ABTM.
32   For example, Gabriel Brasó to Mary Cidad, 15 December 1973, ABTM.
33   Gabriel Brasó to Mary Cidad, 23 January 1973, ABTM.
34   Teresa González, 'Summary of the Meeting and Notice to the Communities in Madrid and Barcelona', 7 July 1977, ABTM.
35   *Constitutiones de la Congregación de Religiosas Oblatas Regulares Benedictinas de Nueva Nursia*, handwritten copy, n.d.. Madrid, I (2), ABTM; *Constitutions de las Congrégation des Soeurs de la Misericorde des Sacrés Coeurs de Jésus et de Marie d'Héverlé Oblates Reguliéres de Saint Benôit*, printed copy, n.d., Madrid, 1 (2), ABTM.

not feature strongly in the Spanish heritage of New Norcia.[36] Similarly, the maternal image of the convent itself remained: the 'mother-house' at New Norcia was a spiritual 'cradle' and a gathering place that nurtured a 'faithful image' of the 'religious family' in its other houses.[37] Both groups were 'not strictly cloistered because of their mission',[38] and it was also specified that there was no distinction into classes of sisters as 'Choir' or 'Lay'; instead, all members had 'equal rights'.[39]

There was one remarkable difference from the European model as finally approved by Abbot Gomez in 1954: these Benedictines made five vows. This provision was in neither the Belgian original nor Felicitas's handwritten translation, but appeared in the later typescript. At their first profession the New Norcia sisters committed themselves to poverty, chastity and obedience. These were the vows made at first temporarily and then for life by the Belgian sisters and by other 'active' religious congregations. In the handwritten version of the New Norcia constitutions, these three vows were sufficient to frame the life commitment of the Benedictine community.[40] The later, typed copy specified 'additionally' that when the Benedictine Missionary Sisters at New Norcia made their perpetual profession they added the two Benedictine promises of 'Stability in the Congregation' and 'Conversion of Customs and Habits'.[41] Felicitas had written originally for the 1936 community who were already oblates and had probably taken these Benedictine attributes for granted in the first draft. The tangle points to the community's hybrid identity, but if the addition came later maybe Abbot Catalan had been waiting for some particular Benedictine statement of identity, never dreaming it could be added to the 'simple vows' of the active sisters. In summary, this was a group in the Benedictine tradition dedicated to the missionary work supported by New Norcia and other wider apostolates that seemed appropriate. Significantly, the constitutions did not specify their connection with Aboriginal children and families.

---

36 *Constituciones ... Nueva Nursia*, I (4); *Constitutions ... Héverlé*, 1 (4).
37 *Constituciones ... Nueva Nursia*, I (6); *Constitutions ... Héverlé*, 1 (6).
38 *Constituciones ... Nueva Nursia*, I (4); *Constitutions ... Héverlé*, 1 (4).
39 *Constituciones ... Nueva Nursia*, I (7); *Constitutions ... Héverlé*, 1 (7).
40 *Constitutiones de la Congregación de Religiosas Oblatas Regulares Benedictinas de Nueva Nursia*, handwritten copy, n.d., ABTM.
41 *Constitutiones de la Congregación de Religiosas Benedictinas Misioneras de Nueva Nursia*, typewritten copy, 1962, of the version approved in 1954, ABTM.

The status of the community had haunted Felicitas through her long tenure in authority: first, as the novice mistress training the community for public vows from 1936; then, as the prioress appointed by Abbot Catalan in 1942 and 1945; and, finally, as the elected superior for 12 years from 1949. She had been succeeded in 1961 by her trusted adviser, Magdalena Ruiz. Wise and astute, 'with the milk of human kindness',[42] Magdalena had always shied away from formal roles because she felt her lack of English, but she was trusted and respected by both monks and sisters at New Norcia and at Kalumburu,[43] and now she successfully managed the new foundations in Spain. Then, in a push to see the next generation of leaders, Angelina Cerezo was elected in 1967. The transition to the younger sisters proved too sudden, however, and to resolve tensions Felicitas became local superior at New Norcia again in 1968. Following the general chapter for the renewal of the constitutions in 1969 (resulting in the draft that would be referred to Gabriel Brasó), Mary Cidad was elected superior in October 1970 for three years. Mary's ambition for clarity and order was linked to the long history of awkwardness about the status of the community. As events played out, independence from the monks and payment for the work of the sisters came to be crucial in her eyes. In Australia that quest for financial autonomy emerged alongside increased access to funds for Aboriginal people.

Money and authority to choose

Through the middle years of the twentieth century, Aboriginal Australians were gradually able to access social welfare payments available to other Australians, beginning with child endowment allowances in 1944 through to the old-age pension and other substantial benefits in 1959, including for people on reserves or at missions, and finally also including those classified as 'primitive and nomadic' in 1966.[44] Frequently, however, and especially in remote areas, payments were made to a third party—such as a mission or an employer—that was legally entitled to control the funds on behalf of individuals and to pass on only what was deemed appropriate and necessary. This was very much the arrangement in place at Kalumburu

---

42 Veronica Willaway, Interview, Nebraska, 13 June 2013.
43 Fr Seraphim Sanz, personal communication, October 2002.
44 J. C. Altman and W. Sanders, 'From Exclusion to Dependence: Aborigines and the Welfare State in Australia', in *Social Welfare with Indigenous Peoples*, ed. John Dixon and Robert P. Sheurell (London and New York: Routledge, 1995), 209.

and, to a lesser extent, at New Norcia. Total Commonwealth expenditure on Aboriginal welfare almost tripled between 1969 and 1971, more than doubled again in 1972 and 1973, and continued to rise under both Labor and Liberal federal ministers. In 1974 and 1975 the Commonwealth allocated $186.1 million, more than 10 times the amount in real terms that had been allocated in 1969.[45]

In 1962 the Benedictine Missionary Sisters became an incorporated body under that more streamlined name and in their own right, rather than as a dimension of the monastery. They opened their first bank account and, through Br Anthony McAlinden, a young Australian monk in charge at St Mary's, they were able to charge purchases independently at Ahern's, the Catholic department store in Perth.[46] Previously, all provisions had come via the monks, with the exception of what could be purchased with proceeds of the annual embroidery sale and the income from eggs and poultry sold to the New Norcia hotel. ('This is because you cannot ask monks to buy the underwear', Scholastica Carrillo observed.[47]) Salaries began to flow to the mission at Kalumburu for the work of Araceli, Florentina and Josephine, all trained nurses who were responsible in turn for the health clinic in the 1960s and 1970s, and also for the work of Visitación teaching sewing.

After strenuous negotiation in exclamatory Spanish, the superintendent at Kalumburu, Fr Seraphim Sanz, agreed to a portion of this income being transferred to the Benedictine sisters, with other funds held against the in-kind support of the community. By 1974 this annual payment was $1,000 for each of the sisters at Kalumburu.[48] (At the time, the average annual wage for a woman working full time in Western Australia was around $3,700, and the minimum award was $3,010.80,[49] but as Seraphim put it to Mary: 'How many lay men or women save $1000 [net per annum]? There are many lay missionaries who work for much less

---

45 'Table 1, Identifiable Commonwealth Expenditure on Indigenous Affairs, 1968–1969 to 2009–2010', in John Gardiner-Gaden and Joanne Simon-Davies, *Commonwealth Indigenous-Specific Expenditure 1968–2012* (Canberra: Parliament of Australia, 2012), www.aph.gov.au/About_Parliament/Parliamentary_Departments/Parliamentary_Library/pubs/BN/2012-2013/Indigenous Expend#Table1; accessed 9 January 2017.
46 Anthony McAlinden, Interview, New Norcia, 2002.
47 Scholastica Carrillo, Interview, Kalumburu, April 1999.
48 Seraphim Sanz to Mary Cidad, 10 January 1974, trans. Kerry Mullan, ABTM.
49 *Western Australian Year Book 1975* (Canberra: Australian Bureau of Statistics), 501, 503, www.abs.gov.au/AUSSTATS/abs@.nsf/DetailsPage/1300.51975?OpenDocument; accessed 10 January 2017.

that this!!!'[50] He drew no comparison with the Aboriginal workers who, like the Benedictine women, were still paid mostly in kind.) Additionally, when the Marist Brothers withdrew from the boys' college at New Norcia at the end of 1964 and the Benedictine monks took on responsibility for that school, renaming it St Benedict's, they turned to the Benedictine sisters to take over the kitchen. If Abbot Catalan had occasionally expected the Marists to manage with school fees paid in bags of wheat, there was now a more generous cash economy. The school fees supported payment for the cooks within the community. Later, there was also state sponsorship of adult education classes at New Norcia. Together, these funds made it possible for the Benedictine Missionary Sisters to buy a modest house at 55 View Street, North Perth, for £4,750 in 1965 (or roughly $9,500 in the decimal currency introduced the following year).[51] It was an important step to have a base that was separate from the monastery's own house in Perth and, financially, View Street was a foundation for other ventures.

Figure 10.3: Scholastica, Florentina and Visitación, and Kalumburu's cat, with chorizo made from the local wild boar that fed on the monastery's figs.
Source: ABTM.

---

50   Seraphim Sanz to Mary Cidad, 10 January 1974, ABTM.
51   *Notebooks*, Madrid, 27 April 1965.

As predictable cash flow increased, both the mission and Aboriginal families could make different decisions. Families were able to support and educate their children in Perth and elsewhere, and numbers fell at St Joseph's from 120 in 1959 to 24 in 1973.[52] The relative proportion of children placed by state authorities rather than by families also increased at St Joseph's as a result, reaching 58 per cent in the final year.[53] As funding became available for direct payment of fees and uniforms, other schools also increasingly enrolled Aboriginal students. For example, in an arrangement Pius Moynihan forged with St Gertrude's, it became the norm for older girls at St Joseph's to go on to high school as full-time boarders there. The connection with the college closed the gap that had opened up after the departure of the Teresians, but it did not escape the attention of the Benedictine sisters that the St Joseph's girls fared much better when there were teachers in charge who had enough history in the town to relate to them well:

> Sister Gregory [Leonie Maine] and Sister Georgina [West] were both very good to our girls when they eventually went to St Gertrude's. They made them feel welcome … keeping an eye on them and telling them off when they needed to be pulled into line with certain things. It was interesting when those two sisters left the next year, [two others] had no idea how to handle the girls so they were all expelled. I was wild about it.[54]

Later years were calmer, and when the Girrawheen community opened, at least one of the girls boarding at St Gertrude's caught the bus to Perth to stay with Pius and the community 'as the colleges are having a long-weekend'.[55] Such a visit fitted with the shift the Australian sisters hoped to see: away from the large institution of St Joseph's and towards group homes, to be run by Aboriginal families but with the sisters and monks involved. The question of how such a change in structure could be made to fit with the Benedictine pattern of religious life remained unresolved and troubled the older Spanish sisters.

---

52   See Appendix 1.
53   Report of Trevor Ewers, District Officer Moora, to the Director, 31 May 1973, 'Native Education – Reports from Officers of Native Welfare Department', State Records Office of Western Australia (SROWA) S24 cons1497 1951/0953.
54   Anne Moynihan, Interview, North Perth, 19 March 1999.
55   'Chronicle of the Benedictine Missionary Sisters, Girrawheen' (*Girrawheen Chronicle*), 4 July 1974, NNA 05505. Photographs of the Girrawheen community and a visiting child, and others from this period at New Norcia showing small groups of Benedictine sisters with the girls at a birthday party are with the Storylines project at the State Library of Western Australia.

There was no divide about initiatives in 'Adult Native Education'. The Benedictine sisters across the board strongly supported classes, from direct involvement as teachers to encouraging men and women from the town to participate, providing refreshments and offering other behind-the-scenes support. These classes were sponsored by the state government, first to provide information about voting rights and the repeal of discriminatory restrictions under the *Native Welfare Act 1963*,[56] and then expanded to include courses in personal development.[57] New Norcia's involvement began when Sister Michael saw an invitation in the paper; it grew in conversation with Brother Anthony McAlinden and the two took their interest to the Education Department. By 1970 there were nine classes running at New Norcia, including Community Obligations, Personal Grooming, Mothercraft, Home Renovation and Maintenance, and Dressmaking.

The program became a landmark success based on collaboration between the sisters, the monastery, the Aboriginal people and the government. Initially, the idea had been to base the work at the convent, but 'then it became quite evident that really the nuns couldn't carry it because they didn't have the connections … [T]hey never went out'.[58] Instead St Joseph's became the nucleus for sewing and dressmaking classes, and Brother Anthony coordinated a wider overall program resourced by schoolteachers and other skilled locals.

One of those involved as a teacher was Philomena Drayton, one of the St Joseph's girls. Early in 1965 she had joined the sisters as a postulant but returned to her family after two months and was still living in town. Well trained by Felicitas, she was an excellent seamstress and ideal to have involved: 'we set her up because she could do some teaching up there too'.[59] Communication with the department ensured funding flowed smoothly for the coordinator and the teachers and the equipment, and New Norcia's people were keen participants:

---

56   *My Voice for My Country: Changing Images of Aboriginal and Torres Strait Islander Voter Participation* [online exhibition], AIATSIS, 'A Growing Demographic', aiatsis.gov.au/exhibitions/my-voice-my-country; accessed 11 January 2017.
57   *My Voice for My Country*.
58   Anthony McAlinden, Interview, New Norcia, 2002.
59   Anthony McAlinden, Interview, New Norcia, 2002.

> I used to get the government department man [Peter Cuffley] to come up here; he was thrilled to come. [H]e told us at one stage that we were the biggest operation in the State. And we had all these classes going. The same people going to different classes, and then we'd bring people in from round about … [I]t was great.[60]

A dinner dance in August 1970, initially suggested by the Community Obligations group to mark Abbot Gregory's fiftieth jubilee, became a celebration of the program itself.

The Minister for Native Welfare in the Brand Liberal Government, Edgar Lewis, was also the local member for Moore and a regular at sports days and other events. He sent 'warm thanks for the interest taken over so many years by the Benedictine Community and the Sisters of New Norcia' and particularly the 'encouragement towards social assimilation'.[61] He forwarded the glowing reports of the event sent by Peter Cuffley and Mrs Michael Beaton of Native Welfare at Moora. Funded by sales of refurbished washing machines and toffee apples, between 50 and 60 Aboriginal guests gathered at New Norcia's hotel.[62] For Aboriginal people to join the abbot for sherry in the hotel that had excluded them was in keeping with the repeal of legal restrictions on drinking[63] and a significant shift. The formal dinner with matching wines, coffee and speeches was followed by a dance that included all age groups in the St Joseph's hall.[64] The Megatones, a local group led by Meg and Tony Phelan, provided the music: from 'old-time ballroom to modern popular dances'.[65] Overall, it was 'the conduct and appearance of the people present, the children's behaviour, and the evidence of organisation displayed'[66] that Cuffley underlined. The positive atmosphere of 'fellowship plus good organisation' among the 'well-dressed and socially mature community' also impressed Beaton.[67]

---

60 Anthony McAlinden, Interview, New Norcia, 2002.
61 Minister Lewis to Gomez, 8 October 1970, NNA 05100.
62 Adult Native Education, Visit to New Norcia by P. J. Cuffley on 22 August 1970, forwarded to Abbot Gregory by Edgar Lewis, Minister for Native Welfare, 8 October 1970, NNA 05100.
63 Lyn Furnell, *Report of the Royal Commission upon All Matters Affecting the Wellbeing of Persons of Aboriginal Descent in Western Australia*, 26, cited in Kayla Calladine, 'Liquor Restrictions in Western Australia', *Indigenous Law Bulletin* 15 (2009), www.austlii.edu.au/au/journals/IndigLawB/2009/15.html; accessed 13 January 2017.
64 Adult Native Education, Visit to New Norcia by P. J. Cuffley on 22 August 1970, forwarded to Abbot Gregory by Edgar Lewis, Minister for Native Welfare, 8 October 1970, NNA 05100.
65 Cuffley, 22 August 1970; Anthony McAlinden, Interview, New Norcia, 2002.
66 Cuffley, 22 August 1970. Photographs of young women and girls at a 1970s dance and of action on the dance floor are with the Storylines project at the State Library of Western Australia.
67 Mrs Michael Beaton, District Officer Moora to Superintendent of Native Welfare, 27 August 1970, forwarded to Abbot Gregory by Edgar Lewis, Minister for Native Welfare, 8 October 1970, NNA 05100.

Figure 10.4: Speeches during an annual dinner at the New Norcia hotel to celebrate the adult education classes, 1970s. Mr Peter Cuffley standing, Abbot Gregory Gomez and Br Anthony McAlinden to his right.
Source: Courtesy of Tony McAlinden. Author's collection.

The sisters were not especially surprised at any of this. The relationships across the groups were strong; they knew the women could sew and dress well and that, as Br Anthony recalls, 'they always come up to the mark, never miss'.[68] The ball became an annual event. The sisters were always there, in the thick of the preparation for supper, served with panache by the St Joseph's girls: 'it was a great night for the nuns'.[69] Pius continued to promote social confidence at St Joseph's, arranging for senior girls to have dinner together in the hotel dining room once or twice a year.[70] Similarly, before a school trip to the southwest over Easter in 1973, she saw the significance of contemporary casual clothes and secured a small government grant so that each girl, as well as the boys, had a pair of jeans.[71]

The question of how St Joseph's primary school itself would move forward was becoming sharper for the community. In June 1970 the Department of Native Welfare had gone out of its way to affirm the work. As minister, Edgar Lewis wrote to 'reassure' the sisters that all were 'totally satisfied' with arrangements for the children, following a full inspection by Mr Wallace, Director of Primary Education.[72] In the timeline of their history that the sisters created in Carabanchel in the 1980s they preserved the letter in full. Immediately after noting the government's warm support for the

---

68   Anthony McAlinden, Interview, New Norcia, 2002.
69   Anthony McAlinden, Interview, New Norcia, 2002.
70   Anne Moynihan, Interview, North Perth, 19 March 1999.
71   J. M. Bailey, Liaison Officer Midland, 'Issue of Clothing to New Norcia', n.d. but c. February 1973, SROWA S24 cons1497, 1951/0953.
72   Katharine Massam, 'Notes on the Timeline', 1999, ABTM.

school, however, they also record that 'owing to this matter the Sisters attended a course of 8 Meetings arranged by the Department on Child Care'.[73] In Barcelona, Casa del Niño had been open two months. Talk of a new kindergarten in Perth seemed timely.

At New Norcia, St Joseph's was short-staffed. Teresa had been transferred to Kalumburu in 1959 and implemented changes in the school there, including connecting the mission to the radio transmissions of the School of the Air from the state Education Department, before being transferred again to Spain. Dolores, who replaced her at New Norcia, was her equal in strength of character ('the only one who could make me change me mind',[74] Teresa would recall), but she had only natural talent, no training as a teacher, and was often overwhelmed in the classroom. With Angelina moving between Spain and leadership responsibility in Australia, Michael in the kitchen, Agnes in unpredictable crisis, Damien, the promising young Australian, still studying at the Holy Spirit Institute for Religious Formation in Perth, and talented young women in Spain baulking at the journey to Australia,[75] the schools at St Joseph's and Kalumburu were depending on sisters without formal qualifications. In the Kimberley the mission moved towards lay teaching staff, while at New Norcia, as numbers fell, there was a reconsideration of the need for a primary school at all.

In late October 1970 Mary received a letter from Minister Lewis responding to her interest in the government's budget announcement about financial support for new 'child-minding centres' in partnership with local authorities. She had asked specifically about plans for the Balga area north of Perth, and Lewis forwarded the premier's three-page summary offering to arrange for Mary to meet with the right people in Treasury and the Department of Child Welfare to take the discussion further.[76] Two weeks later, Mary was writing to Angelina in Madrid and Matilda in Barcelona about the plans for the future that had been agreed in Western Australia.[77]

---

73 'Notes on the Timeline', 1999, ABTM.
74 Teresa González, Interview, Madrid, 26 October 2013.
75 On 6 December 1971 Mary announced new assignments for 1972 (to be implemented by Christmas if possible), including posting one of the Spanish recruits, Sr Pilar Iñiguez, to Australia. Pilar made the journey but returned to Spain to leave the congregation. Teresa González in conversation, Madrid, 7 July 2017.
76 Edgar Lewis to Mary Cidad, 28 October 1970, NNA 01646.
77 Mary Cidad to Angelina Cerezo, 14 November 1970; Mary Cidad to Matilda Arroyo, 14 November 1970, ABTM.

The decision to open a childcare centre in Perth was not initially a decision to close New Norcia's convent or even necessarily St Joseph's school. On the contrary, as planning for Girrawheen continued over the next two years there were also discussions about what would be viable at New Norcia.

Brother Anthony McAlinden represented New Norcia in a series of meetings with government officials through 1972. The Benedictine Missionary Sisters were not involved directly in the negotiations about what would emerge in the mission town; neither did the conversations include the Aboriginal families, although commitment to continuing to work with Aboriginal people was fundamental to the hopes that Br Anthony brought to the table. His main partner in the plan to find a new role was the Department of Child Welfare (or Community Welfare from 1972). A meeting in June 1972 set out some principles on 'New Norcia's continuing contribution to Aboriginal Welfare'[78] that had been agreed to at that point. Noting first the reversal of government assumptions from earlier decades that 'contemporary child care practice on a long term basis requires that children be placed in as normal a home life setting as possible and then only after every attempt has been made to support the natural family itself',[79] the judgement was that New Norcia was now 'basically unsuited to long-term child-care work'.[80] Both the communal life of the Benedictines and the physical layout of the existing buildings were barriers to their hope for small family-group homes 'where children can relate to permanent parent figures'.[81]

The department was willing to explore an ongoing role in education, probably for children who were 'retarded scholastically but not intellectually',[82] but it also pointed out that other programs of the same kind had not worked well. The notes of the meetings suggest Brother Anthony was struggling to establish New Norcia's credibility in relating to Aboriginal people and that the long history of local involvement was seen to amount to paternalism and no more. He persisted. Eventually the department conceded that 'positive thinking on your part certainly

---

78   J. Goerke, Acting Chief Supervisor Metropolitan, 'A New Role for New Norcia Mission', 27 June – 5 July 1972, Department of Child Welfare, 'Missions – Private – New Norcia – General Correspondence', SROWA S1099 cons2532 A0403 v1.
79   Goerke, 'A New Role for New Norcia Mission'.
80   Goerke, 'A New Role for New Norcia Mission'.
81   Goerke, 'A New Role for New Norcia Mission'.
82   Goerke, 'A New Role for New Norcia Mission'.

inspires confidence that, no matter how unpredictable the future is, you will attempt to provide a service based on the real but changing needs in the area of aboriginal welfare'.[83]

As the discussion continued, a plan emerged to establish two group homes, despite misgivings. They would be run by two local Aboriginal women, one married, one single. A meeting between the monastery and the Department of Community Welfare in July 1973 heard that land for the homes had been gazetted by the state Housing Department, but the plans had not yet been discussed formally with the five Aboriginal families resident at New Norcia.[84] Although Pius and others were firm advocates for the proposal and imagined a role for the elderly Spanish sisters as 'grandmothers and aunties' that would not cut across their community life,[85] they were not around the table. This may have been because Pius was close to collapse.

Sister Pius Moynihan was, in the opinion of the Department of Community Welfare but as her own community would never dream of telling her, 'an outstanding person in child care'.[86] In May 1973 Mr T. C. Ewers, the District Officer at Moora, judged she alone at New Norcia had 'the resources to provide for the needs of these developing children', and she was consequently seriously overworked and ill, 'from her exacting role as mother to all'.[87] In June that year he heard that Pius was off-duty and triggered a meeting at New Norcia with Mary and Mrs Rosemary Cant—crucially, a woman as well as a psychologist with the department.[88] The sisters were 'coping', but Mary apparently reported there was no one else 'capable of providing a permanent back up for Sister Pius'.[89] They hoped Pius would be able to take up normal duties again in a fortnight. The crisis put the future of St Joseph's in doubt, and Mary advised they 'would probably not be re-opening after the Christmas holidays'.[90] Mrs Cant,

---

83 Goerke to Prior Bernard Rooney, following a meeting with him and Br Anthony, 18 October 1972, SROWA S1099 cons2532 A0403 v1/188.
84 Minutes of a Meeting Held on 20 July 1973, NNA S12-A5-4.
85 Anne Moynihan, Interview, North Perth, 19 March 1999.
86 Report of Trevor Ewers, District Officer Moora, to the Director, 31 May 1973, 'Liaison – New Norcia Mission', SROWA S1099 cons2532 A0403 v2.
87 Ewers to the Director, 31 May 1973.
88 Mr T. C. Ewers to Social Work Supervisor, Mr K. Monsen, 7 June 1973, SROWA S1099 cons2532 A0403 v2.
89 Mrs R. L. Cant to Mr F. Bell, Chief of Institutional Services, Riverbank, 7 June 1973, SROWA S1099 cons2532 A0403 v2.
90 Cant to Bell, 7 June 1973.

involved in negotiations for the group homes, saw the closure as no bad thing. The department began to make plans to relocate the state wards at the end of the year.

Before the month was out, however, a handwritten letter from Sister Michael, still secretary to the superior, hit the director's desk. Four crisp, polite sentences brought the last day of the school forward to the following week, 29 June 1973. The children would be bussed to the state primary school at Gillangarra, 25 kilometres east. St Joseph's would close completely after the school holidays in August.[91] She announced a change of direction:

> As far as we are concerned, the chapter in the History of our Order which deals with Aborigines is finished and all our energies are now directed towards our new Apostolate.[92]

The stark assumption that Girrawheen had nothing to do with the previous work would have shaken most of the Benedictines involved.

The department received the letter on the very day the school closed and stamped it urgent. District officers prepared a letter of thanks from the director to the Benedictine sisters for their long-standing and full-time involvement with Aboriginal people from 'long before official bodies such as ours were expected to take an interest'.[93] The letter was addressed to Sister Michael but by the time it was sent she had left the convent. Internally then, the sisters knew the decision to close was linked directly to an acute staffing crisis: Pius overworked, Michael gone, and also, by early July, Damien granted a dispensation from her vows.[94] The monks, on the other hand, were shocked to have had no more warning than the government.[95] Their diarist allowed himself a comment on 10 July when he marked the departure of the last Aboriginal girls to leave St Joseph's: 'In many ways it is a sad day'.[96] The implications were biggest for the Aboriginal families affected. The official record is silent on that impact. Like much that had gone before, the abrupt closure left evaluation until later.

---

91   Michael to Maine, Director of Community Welfare, 26 June 1973, SROWA S1099 cons2532 A0403 v2.
92   Michael to Maine, 26 June 1973.
93   Director, Community Welfare Department, to Michael, 3 August 1973, SROWA S1099 cons2532 A0403 v2.
94   Sr Damien Gould, granted exclaustration on 18 May 1973 and dispensation from vows on 6 July 1973; request for dispensation from Sr Michael Allen to Abbot Bernard Rooney, 28 July 1973, NNA S12-A5-4.
95   Anthony McAlinden, Interview, New Norcia, 2002.
96   'Chronicle of the Benedictine Community of New Norcia' (hereafter *Chronicle*), 10 July 1973.

The Girrawheen story

The Benedictine Missionary Sisters' Child Care Centre in Girrawheen was an initiative made possible by a network of support the Benedictine women enlisted beyond New Norcia itself. It put them 'beyond' rather than 'between' competing spheres of influence because the enterprise was recognised as their own. The opening on 15 September 1973 was a grand diocesan occasion organised by the Catholic network of businessmen, the Knights of the Southern Cross, and covered extensively by the *Record*.[97] About 180 people gathered on a fine spring Saturday to see Perth's auxiliary Bishop Peter Quinn bless the rooms, and Joe Berinson, the Labor member for Perth representing Kim Beazley Snr, the federal Minister for Education, declare the complex open.[98] The site of three acres adjoined land reserved for a future parish church and Catholic school and a steady flow of Catholic visitors keen to help kept the foundation community busy.[99]

The Benedictine sisters' enquiries about establishing a childcare centre had coincided with land being opened up 15 kilometres north of Perth's business district to offer affordable housing. The new area of Girrawheen, meaning 'place of flowers' in one of the Aboriginal languages of Queensland, adjoined Balga, the suburb Mary had originally nominated, named with the Noongar word for 'grass tree', where there was a high proportion of social housing and a number of Aboriginal families, including some from New Norcia.[100] The *Record* reported that the sisters had taken advice from both the state Housing Commission and the Department of Community Welfare on the location for the new ministry and were committed to helping single-parent families, migrants, and 'those in special need'. At the end of 1970, Mary had detailed the promised funding of $15,000 from the state government, a matching amount from the local Wanneroo Shire Council along with a gardener to help out as needed and cash flow to cover repairs on the property, together with a grant from the state Lotteries Commission to equip the classrooms.[101] The sisters sold their house in North Perth to contribute close to another $15,000 to the new project.

---

97 *Record*, 20 September 1973, 6.
98 *Girrawheen Chronicle*, 15 September 1973.
99 Anne Moynihan, Interview, North Perth, 19 March 1999; Philomena Roche, Interview, Nebraska, 2010.
100 *Girrawheen Chronicle*, 14 December 1974.
101 Mary Cidad to Angelina Cerezo and Sisters, 14 November 1970, ABTM.

A recurrent grant from the Commonwealth Department of Education added a further $20,000 annually, enabling the community to take on the project with a total cost of over $150,000. When Archbishop Goody proposed to Mary that in time the Benedictine women might take on the primary school and 'look after' the church too, she agreed, 'very probably, yes'.[102] Her vision and ambition were expansive.

The facilities were planned carefully with an eye on the future too. The 3-acre site included a large adventure playground for 50 children from two to five years old, with separate areas for each age cohort in the airy building, and a convent to accommodate 10 sisters with provision for visitors, all on a domestic rather than institutional scale to integrate with the surrounding suburb as it expanded. The purpose-built centre and convent had been designed by prominent Catholic architect Iris Rossen.[103] It featured white rendered brickwork and red terracotta tiles echoing Spain, with exposed jarrah timber inside and out. The chapel in particular was a showpiece of sensitive liturgical decisions informed by the Second Vatican Council: 'contemporary in character but containing a warmth of history'.[104] Rossen gathered friends to the project. A wall cross and the door of the tabernacle were designed and donated by the artist Robert Juniper, altar vessels and candleholders were ceramics by Janet Kovesi, and windows were by the Perth stained-glass firm of Gowers, Brown and Wildy.

Iris Rossen herself spent many hours designing and painting a large banner of Benedict and Scholastica that the community particularly liked, with the motto 'Ora et Labora' above them and 'Pax' below. Photographs of the chapel reflect her appreciation of monastic simplicity and a strong arts and crafts influence with everything fit for purpose. 'Description is not enough,' commented Sr Philomena Roche, the enthusiastic if frequently unspecific diarist, 'one needs to see it'.[105]

---

102   Mary Cidad to Angelina Cerezo and Sisters, 14 November 1970.
103   Western Australian Museum, 'Welcome Walls: ROSSEN, Ernest & Iris', museum.wa.gov.au/welcomewalls/names/rossen-ernest-iris; Rossen designed a number of Catholic churches in the area and would also design the neighbouring parish church and school: 'Our Lady of Mercy Church', inHerit Our Heritage Places, 1 January 2017, inherit.stateheritage.wa.gov.au/Public/Inventory/Print SingleRecord/7f1e9d39-bdf7-4a4d-80b3-7cbaca3bfc76. See also www.artefacts.co.za/main/Buildings/archframes.php?archid=3284&countadd=0; all accessed 7 March 2017.
104   *Record*, 20 September 1973.
105   *Girrawheen Chronicle*, 19 August 1973.

Figure 10.5: Chapel at the Girrawheen convent, showing tabernacle and wall cross by Robert Juniper.
Source: Photo courtesy of Paul Rossen. Author's collection.

Figure 10.6: *Ora et Labora* banner by Iris Rossen, now in the chapel of the Benedictine Missionary Sisters of Tutzing in Madrid.
Source: Author's collection.

Philomena Roche was the newest member of the Benedictine Missionary Sisters. She had transferred to the New Norcia community from the enclosed Benedictine convent at Pennant Hills in August 1971 after a nine-month trial and just before her fortieth birthday. A New Zealander, she joined Pius Moynihan, Cecilia Farrell, Dolores Vallejo and Carmen Ruiz as the foundation community in Girrawheen: another community where, as Pius had felt so strongly during her novitiate, Spanish, Aboriginal and Anglo-Celts worked together. Preparing for the new community and with the same hospitality from the Sisters of Mercy in Perth as when the primary teachers were studying in the 1950s, Cecilia and Philomena had completed qualifications in 'mothercraft nursing' at Ngala, the training centre in South Perth, under the guidance of long-time director Beryl Grant. It had been significant for Ngala to have an Aboriginal graduate. Cecilia had excelled. As Matron Grant saw it, she was well-suited to the work she was to do with the children and likely to continue in it.[106]

With Cecilia, Philomena, Dolores and two lay teachers, Mrs Kinsella and Mrs Park (and later Miss Anne Doig),[107] Pius as the (still overworked) administrator, and Carmen running the kitchen, the centre celebrated the end of its first week with a picnic. In the New Norcia tradition they took the 27 children across the road to the uncleared bushland for a picnic lunch of sandwiches, cold chicken and salad. Enrolments were close to 50 for 1974, and the community expanded to six with the arrival of Veronica from New Norcia; a management committee of four unnamed 'gentlemen' from the shire council met monthly with Pius and Dolores, and there was a flow of visits from both state and federal governments, including Mrs Walter whose advice on the Commonwealth grants scheme had been crucial. It had been a flourishing start.

The Girrawheen convent was a hub for both sisters and monks travelling from New Norcia and Kalumburu to Perth, as well as former students at St Joseph's who visited or occasionally came to stay.[108] Fr Joseph Carr, OSB, was in residence as chaplain, and they also maintained links with the parishes of Mirrabooka, Joondanna and the Redemptorist Monastery in North Perth. Pius and Philomena both held driver's licences, the community had a car as well as a small van, and with two connecting buses the centre of the city was about half an hour away. In-service days, evening lectures, medical appointments, grocery and other shopping, parish functions and visits with friends were becoming routine. Excursions with

---

106 Beryl Grant, Interview, Floreat, WA, 2000. For Cecilia's ongoing work, see her publications under her married name Vera Budby: *A Resource Catalogue for Aboriginal and Islander Early Childhood Education Centres*, ed. Vera Budby ([Brisbane]: Creche and Kindergarten Association of Queensland, 1983); *Establishment, Membership, Role and Function of the National Aboriginal Education Committee and the State Aboriginal Education Consultative Groups*, ed. Vera Budby (Canberra: Department of Aboriginal Affairs, 1982); *Draft National Workshop Report: Aboriginal Independent Schools*, ed. John Budby with sketches by Vera Budby (Woden, ACT: National Aboriginal Education Committee, 1982).
107 *Girrawheen Chronicle*, 5 October 1973, 5 May 1974. A photograph of children and staff at Girrawheen in 1974 is with the Storylines project at the State Library of Western Australia.
108 *Girrawheen Chronicle*, Glenys Benjamin Miles and her family, 30 June 1974, the Willaway family, Margaret Jacobs and her baby.

the children to the beach and the zoo could be managed easily in small groups, and, at Fr Joseph's instigation, the sisters themselves saw the hit musical *Godspell* on stage and ventured to the cinema to see both *Brother Sun, Sister Moon* and *Jesus Christ Superstar*.[109] New Norcia had always had a network of visitors, but Girrawheen made interaction easier. Ironically, even tragically, just as publicity increased and the sisters' circle widened, communication within the community broke apart.

'Let us approve the three points put forward by the Mother General'

In January 1974 New Norcia remained the motherhouse for the diocesan congregation of Benedictine Missionary Sisters, administering five communities: Girrawheen and Kalumburu in Western Australia, and Carabanchel, Parla and Barcelona in Spain. There were 27 members in total. In Girrawheen there were six, and in Kalumburu, four (Scholastica, Visitación, Francisca and Josephine). The communities in Spain included a number of novices and six temporarily professed sisters, together with the seven who had returned to Spain from Australia. At New Norcia the death of Ludivina in April 1973, after 42 years at the mission, and Agnes's final departure following the closure of the school[110] made the motherhouse a small community of six. It was also the most elderly house, with an average age just over 65 years. Despite the flourishing centre in Perth, Mary Cidad feared for the future of the congregation.

When planning for Girrawheen had begun, Mary had put great faith in the Australian sisters, especially Michael. If Felicitas had a blind spot and could insist on 'whatever the girls wanted', the Spanish sisters thought Mary lacked judgement about the younger Australians.[111] She deferred to their capacity in English, their good education and work experience, their networks of family and friends, and their understanding of life in the Perth community, and she relied on them. Girrawheen was an initiative the five of them had been meant to carry, with Michael as administrator. All through the tumult of letters from Pennant Hills, Mary had expected to find a way for Michael to continue in the congregation. The crisis had

---

109 *Girrawheen Chronicle*, 1 December 1973, 19 January 1974, 6 July 1974.
110 Remarkably, the *Girrawheen Chronicle* initially expects Agnes will be joining the community in 1973.
111 Teresa González, Interview, Madrid, 27 May 1999.

'broken her heart',[112] and when Damien, younger and so much more outwardly compliant, also sought to leave, Mary was shocked to the core. Her own lack of discernment had betrayed her.

Mary flipped from admiration for the Australians to distrust. With Girrawheen barely open, she began actively seeking a separation between the Spanish and Australian members. In November 1973 Sister Mary De Lourdes, the Superior General of the Good Samaritan Sisters, was visiting Rome. She was surprised to receive a letter from Mary Cidad, forwarded on from Sydney. In it Mary advised that the Spanish sisters were hoping to return to Spain and raised the prospect that three of the New Norcia sisters might transfer to an Australian group, specifically the Good Samaritans who shared the Benedictine tradition.[113] There was more than a little subterfuge in this: the three Australian sisters had no idea such enquiries were being made on their behalf, and among the Spanish at New Norcia the prospect of a permanent move to Spain was hardly even gossip.

De Lourdes, insightful and steady, sought advice first from a canon lawyer at Sant'Anselmo in Rome, Fr Damien Kraus. Ironically, his suggestion was to establish a diocesan congregation responsible to the local bishop— the structure that was already in place although neither he nor De Lourdes seemed to realise that. Back in Sydney, and following Kraus's recommendation, she tried without success to contact Abbot Bernard Rooney, as the local bishop, by telephone. When a second letter from Mary arrived on 3 January 1974 asking if the Good Samaritans would also be responsible for the centre at Girrawheen and renewing an invitation to visit New Norcia to discuss the issues, De Lourdes wrote to Bernard to ask if they could meet when he visited Sydney for the bishops' conference in January.[114] They did have a conversation but, as Rooney's files note, 'with little hope of the amalgamation'.[115] As De Lourdes wrote to Mary in the end, the Good Samaritans needed to consolidate, not expand into Western Australia. Accepting the Benedictine Missionary Sisters into the congregation would mean 'for them to move east out of their own environment'.[116] All the practicalities were against it.

---

112 Michael to Mary, 22 November 1972, referring to Mary's previous letter (not extant), NNA S12-A5-4.
113 De Lourdes Ronayne to Bernard Rooney, 4 January 1974, NNA S12-A5-4.
114 De Lourdes Ronayne to Bernard Rooney, 4 January 1974.
115 Marginal comment in the index to this correspondence, 21 January 1974, NNA S12-A5-4.
116 De Lourdes Ronayne to Bernard Rooney, 4 January 1974.

10. SPINNING APART

Also as 1974 began, Mary Cidad resumed her correspondence with Abbot President Gabriel Brasó. He was expected to visit New Norcia in February, and she hoped to speak confidentially with him then. She confided her view that the Australian phase of the community was over: 'of the few Australians that there were, two have left, and there is no hope that any more will enter'.[117] She sought his help to transfer the motherhouse to Spain. She told him, presumably truthfully, that the sisters there had petitioned her to do so although there is no formal record of any such request. Nevertheless: 'I see [their request] as quite natural, and given the circumstances, not only natural but also advisable, and we all believe that it will be better'.[118] It is not clear who in the community knew what Mary intended at this stage. Word spread gradually, informally as well as in ordered channels, and eluded some sisters altogether until the very end.

Moving the motherhouse would not have meant necessarily also closing New Norcia, but that was the proposal it seems Mary put to the sisters in Spain by letter, although only their consolidated response survives.[119] Their reply was not immediate acceptance; rather, Mary told the abbot president, 'things have been a bit delayed because of our Sisters in Spain who could not understand our situation'.[120] The Kalumburu sisters also resisted. Scholastica wrote a blistering letter that argued for the ongoing need of a community there and the validity of her own vocation. Strategically, and she believed decisively, she also urged that if they allowed her to remain in Australia she would become eligible for an Australian pension, an ongoing asset.[121] Scholastica was counting on the leadership changing at the next round of elections due in 1976 and had already determined 'to leave her bones in Kalumburu'.[122] Mary visited Kalumburu for two weeks in May and came round to this view. 'I thought I was in paradise,' she wrote to Abbot Brasó and, distancing herself from the proposals that were by this stage under consideration in Spain and in the north, she added, 'what a shame if they have to close this Mission, but I have a feeling it [the proposal] won't go far'.[123]

---

117 Mary Cidad to Gabriel Brasó, 6 January 1974, ABTM.
118 Mary Cidad to Gabriel Brasó, 6 January 1974.
119 Teresa González, 'Summary of the Meeting and Notice to the Communities in Madrid and Barcelona', 7 July 1977, ABTM.
120 Mary Cidad to Gabriel Brasó, 15 May [in fact June] 1974, ABTM.
121 Scholastica Carrillo, Interview, Kalumburu, 25 April 1999.
122 Scholastica Carrillo, Interview, Kalumburu, 25 April 1999.
123 Mary Cidad to Gabriel Brasó, 15 May [June] 1974.

On her return she stayed at Girrawheen for the week leading up to 24 May but said nothing to the community there of what was in train.[124] She did, however, meet with the bishop (presumably Bishop Quinn, responsible for religious) who passed on the welcome news of the solution he had found: that the Sisters of Mercy 'will gladly take Girrawheen Centre'.[125] To meet the conditions of the Commonwealth grant in particular, the childcare service needed to continue and Mary could not leave the country until responsibility for it had been formally transferred to someone else.[126]

Mary called an extraordinary meeting of the General Chapter for Sunday 16 June 1974 at New Norcia. The *Girrawheen Chronicle* notes blandly:

> We all went to N.Norcia today for a Community Meeting, as there were some matters concerning which Mother Mary wished us all to vote. We left mid-morning and arrived back about 6 pm.[127]

What Philomena could not bring herself to say was that the searing meeting had stretched the community to the limit. Putting three proposals, Mary spoke vehemently against the Australian sisters as a group, accusing them of 'lack of obedience' more and more stridently until at last Felicitas intervened, rising from her seat in the tiny chapter room and raising her voice in turn to tell Mary to stop, she had said enough, she was being unfair.[128] There would be a secret ballot to determine the decision on questions that had been put two months before to the two houses in Spain (Carabanchel–Parla in Madrid and Barcelona) and to the sisters in Kalumburu. Votes had been sent to New Norcia to arrive by 14 June.

Carmen could not stand it. She knew what was coming and fled out of the convent and up to the fowl yard. There was more sympathy there. She maintains she did not vote, but the totals counted her in, mistakenly assuming she agreed with the majority. The questions were:

1. If it was judged to be suitable to close the New Norcia House and to transfer the Mother House to Spain;
2. If the Congregation should retain Kalumburu Mission;
3. If they agreed that the Girrawheen Centre should pass to another Congregation.[129]

---

124 *Girrawheen Chronicle*, 24 May 1974.
125 Mary Cidad to Gabriel Brasó, 15 May [June] 1974, NNA 05505.
126 'Child Care Act—Sisters of Mercy, Girrawheen Child Care Centre (formerly Benedictine Child Care Centre)', National Archives of Australia, NAA K317, 53/78/945.
127 *Girrawheen Chronicle*, 16 June 1974.
128 Anne Moynihan in conversation, New Norcia, 12 October 2001.
129 'Questions for Decision', ABTM.

All the proposals passed comfortably. Two sisters out of 27 held out against closing New Norcia and three against closing Girrawheen. One voted against keeping Kalumburu open, but perhaps that was Pius, too shattered to think straight, or one of the four recruited in Spain cautious against any Australian link.

It was over by four o'clock in the afternoon, in plenty of time for the monks to hear before Sunday Vespers. Abbot Rooney who might have otherwise presided at the meeting was sick in bed, but the diarist knew the sisters had decided 'to withdraw from the Child Care Centre at Girrawheen, and at the end of the year to close their house at New Norcia, but to keep open Kalumburu Mission as long as possible'.[130] The next day, Mary wrote to Abbot Brasó bringing him up to date 'with how our affairs are going, certainly better than I had hoped'.[131] There was no disguising the fracture in the community though: of the four non-Spaniards, 'two … one of them indigenous, have decided to go with us; the other two don't yet know what they are going to do'.[132] The rift in the Benedictine town was clear too: Abbot Rooney had asked for a few months notice to find replacements for the sisters still cooking and washing for New Norcia. Mary responded, 'they don't deserve it, but we will do it'.[133] Then she reported the question that had stung and unrepentantly asked Brasó for help to ensure her bitter reply bore fruit:

> He asked me who was going to pay for our travel. I replied [those] who we have worked for for 60 years without charging a cent. See if you can do something for us about this.[134]

Mary hoped to leave in July, the community would stay through until March 1975.

---

130 *Chronicle*, 16 June 1974.
131 Mary Cidad to Gabriel Brasó, 17 May [actually June] 1974, ABTM.
132 Mary Cidad to Gabriel Brasó, 17 May [June] 1974.
133 Mary Cidad to Gabriel Brasó, 17 May [June] 1974.
134 Mary Cidad to Gabriel Brasó, 17 May [June] 1974.

Leaving

Veronica would reflect later on the six-week journey by ship to Europe:

> The choice was 'Come with us or leave'. Well, I'd joined them, I was a Benedictine, so I went with them. I didn't think too much about it. Of course I knew others were upset. For me, it was only when we were sailing into Barcelona, into that harbour and all that ocean behind us, then I realised. 'What have I done?'[135]

Four decades later, the question is fresh and unresolved. In the large convent in Nebraska where she has worked as liturgical director, in the laundry, and with First Nations people at Winnebago Mission, there is a period of extended home leave in view: Veronica's eyes fill with tears.

The ritual of Benedictine life had sustained the community through the tension of the decision and the departure. Mary came to Perth three times in July 1974 on business and frequently after that to meet the superior of the West Perth Sisters of Mercy and the officers of the Commonwealth Education Department as they worked through the requirements of the recurrent grant.[136] Other sisters and monks from New Norcia came with her for appointments, or to see the centre if they had not had a chance before, or to visit after other errands. Prayer in common, the psalms that ran the gamut of human emotion, the daily celebration of the Eucharist in all the houses, and the assumption that they were called to live the Gospel even if the community was splitting apart provided a container for the anger and distress of the Australians and the more simple sense of loss that confronted many of the Spanish.

Cecilia and Pius saw they were out of step with the community. They were both clear that moving to Spain made no sense for them, but what an alternative would look like was anybody's guess. They would have no community in Perth. They knew nothing of Mary's attempt to talk about transfer with the Good Samaritans, and the distinctive Benedictine tradition worked against any simple merger with another group in Perth. They felt it was a problem they were being asked to solve alone. Pius spent mid-August to mid-September away from Girrawheen with her brother's family in Albany, on 'holiday' the *Chronicle* suggested, no doubt aiming

---

135 Veronica Willaway, Interview, Nebraska, 9 July 2012.
136 *Girrawheen Chronicle*, 9, 16, 30 July 1974.

to come to terms with events.¹³⁷ On the weekend after she returned, the community assembled at New Norcia again to hear more of the future of Girrawheen: 'The West Perth Mercy Sisters will be taking it, but the exact date has not been settled yet'.¹³⁸ Mary travelled back to Perth with them to continue the process of transfer.

In hindsight, it is a puzzle that the choice facing the Australians was so stark. Any number of alternatives seem promising now. Could the sisters who wanted to remain have been attached to the Kalumburu house but working in Perth? Could they have followed the path Maria Harispe had found of pursuing religious life but with informal status as oblates? Could another Perth congregation have offered a lifeline of hospitality, as Mary had clearly been hoping when she approached the Good Samaritans? Could Girrawheen have continued to be a base, even a house of the congregations, supported by more lay staff? Could the monks have refocused their work at St Mary's to share and support the centre in Girrawheen? Religious communities were not yet as open to adaptation or even to news of each other as they would be just a few more years after the Council. It was by chance that Sister Gregory from St Gertrude's ran into Cecilia one Sunday at Midland and learnt of the ultimatum: come with us or leave. It seemed non-negotiable. Later, there might have been more lateral thinking.¹³⁹

As it was, the farewells were beginning. Mary wrote to Bernard to give him the notice she had promised, advising that they would wash and cook until the end of February 1975, and she planned for the final group to leave on 20 March 1975.¹⁴⁰ Josephine came down from Kalumburu for a refresher course at one of the hospitals and also wrote to Bernard after two weekend visits to New Norcia to spend time with those who were leaving. She had been sorry not to see him: 'Please pray for us as we are very upset at the return of the New Norcia Sisters to Spain', she concluded.¹⁴¹ For the Aboriginal families, the sisters leaving went much deeper than the closure of St Joseph's:

> 'They were Spanish, they had to go back.'
>
> 'But after so long? what changed? They came for the people. What changed?'

---

137 *Girrawheen Chronicle*, 14 August 1974, 19 September 1974.
138 *Girrawheen Chronicle*, 22 September 1974.
139 Leonie Mayne, telephone conversation, Perth, May 1999.
140 Mary Cidad to Bernard Rooney, 5 November 1974, NNA S12-A5-4.
141 Josephine Montero to Bernard Rooney, 11 November 1974, NNA S12-A5-4.

The decision was contested through and beyond the reunion of 2001.

In November 1974 Pius and Cecilia both wrote to Abbot Bernard asking for leave of absence from the congregation to consider their future. Cecilia put it simply: 'Being an Australian Aboriginal I believe my future is here where I wish to serve my own people with help of the Holy Spirit'.[142] Pius put it more bluntly in the negative, 'I do not believe my future is there [Spain]'.[143] At this point Pius had a clearer plan and knew she was casting in her lot with an experimental foundation, the Institute for Human Development, being established by Sr Patrice Cook from the Sisters of the Good Shepherd. Her letter focused simply on her wish to remain 'in this country, serving my own people' and her hope 'to find out how best this could be achieved—with the help of the Holy Spirit!'[144]

At the end of the month, Mrs Philomena Willaway arranged a farewell from the St Joseph's old girls. The *Chronicle* captured her key role in initiating the event, even as it repeated the mission terminology that was by that time outdated:

> We all went to New Norcia today as Philomena Willaway had organised a day of reunion for natives with the Sisters before we go to Spain. Many were former children from the Orphanage.[145]

It was a forerunner of many 're-unions' the former students would host in coming decades and perhaps even held seeds for the extraordinary occasion of 2001. The details are scant, but it was a poignant day of shared food and stories where the bonds between the women and the long-time missionaries were part of the social fabric. For Veronica's family it was a lead-up to the hard parting on 20 March: 'with Aunty Veronica leaving, we were sure we would never see her again'.[146] And as it would prove in 2001, the occasion also reflected the bonds forged beyond family by the common experience of life at St Joseph's and in the mission town. When the time came, it was Felicitas and Margaret, who had arrived together in 1921, the first two to join from the villages near Burgos, who sailed from Fremantle with Veronica and Dolores.

---

142 Cecilia Farrell to Bernard Rooney, 17 November 1974, NNA S12-A5-4.
143 Pius Moynihan to Bernard Rooney, 1 November 1974, NNA S12-A5-4.
144 Pius Moynihan to Bernard Rooney, 1 November 1974.
145 *Girrawheen Chronicle*, 23 November 1974.
146 Paul Willaway and Veronica Willaway, in conversation, Perth, November 2014.

Figure 10.7: The last of the community from New Norcia embarks for Barcelona, 20 March 1975; left to right: Margaret, Veronica, Dolores and Felicitas.
Source: NNA W7-a5-5-134.

By Easter 1975 the convent at New Norcia was empty. The Sisters of Mercy had been at Girrawheen since Christmas. Pius was with the new institute. Cecilia had gone to her brother's house in Midland. Carmen had gone to Barcelona inwardly pledged to return and certain 'my vocation was for Australia'.[147] The Kimberley community would reduce to three, Scholastica, Visitación and Josephine, when Francisca joined the sisters in Spain in 1976. She was superior at Kalumburu through 1975, deferring awkward correspondence about remuneration until the abbot

---

147 Carmen Ruiz Besti, Interview, New Norcia, 14 October 2001. In 1981, after five years in Barcelona, she initiated a process of transfer to the Benedictine nuns at Jamberoo Abbey in New South Wales.

could visit, gracefully refusing to be drawn into the argument about stipends that was raging around her but asserting her obedience to side with Mary: 'nevertheless I say my Lord I am subject to the Congregation. I have notified Rev Mother Mary … [S]he will be the one to agreed [sic], or to decide, of what we have to do'.[148] The tension between missionary labour 'for ultimate rewards, sufficient in themselves'[149] and community awareness that 'in this days [sic] of rising costs a certain amount for each Sister is an absolute necessity'[150] was one small instance of the many dimensions in which the Benedictine women still faced competing demands and expectations.

In making the decisions to close New Norcia they had faced hard choices between competing hopes: between the practical reality that the work they were doing at New Norcia was beyond the capacity of the community and the emotional (even cultural) reality that their lives were embedded in the town; between the reality that there were enduring relationships formed by the mission and the need to renegotiate those relationships towards better autonomy both for the sisters in relation to the monastery and for the Aboriginal people in relation to the Benedictine communities and the church itself; between the hope that Spain would furnish new members and the reality that contemporary missionary work in Australia was impractical for non-English speakers. For Francisca the tension resolved in obedience to the decision once made; she trusted the community's choice even though departure came at a cost.

Before she left Australia, Francisca spent some weeks with her brother who had come to Australia as a postulant for New Norcia, too, but who now had a family in Perth. They all visited New Norcia one last time so she could say goodbye. In the parlour at the monastery, everyone encouraged her to take some time to walk across to the convent, perhaps to get a sense of the museum and art gallery already being discussed for the newest sections.[151] The kitchen and laundry would be quiet as the new lay cook worked from the college kitchen to cater for the monastery as well ('a lowering of quantity as well as quality'[152]) and the washing came up by bus from the Good Shepherd Sisters in Perth ('They do a good job,

---

148 Francisca Pardo to Bernard Rooney, 23 March 1975, NNA S12-A5-4.
149 Bernard Rooney to Francisca Pardo, 17 February 1975, NNA S12-A5-4.
150 Mary Cidad to Bernard Rooney, 9 March 1975, NNA S12-A5-4.
151 'Governments Grant $20,000 for Cultural Centre at New Norcia', *Beverley Times*, 6 December 1973, 3.
152 Bernard Rooney to Felicitas Pampliega, 29 September 1975, ABTM.

but at rather high expense'[153]). She could take the impression of these changes with her and tell the others. Francisca left the parlour with her own thoughts:

> I did not say anything to anyone but I could not go. I went to the cemetery to see the sisters. But I could not go to our place. Too much. Too much.[154]

She could never farewell New Norcia, not really, though there were no words to say so.

Imagining reconciliation

An ongoing connection to New Norcia remained for the Benedictine women, despite the distance, as they adjusted to Spain again. In Carabanchel the community wore their title as 'the Australian Sisters' with pride. The tag recognised the formative role of Australia in their religious imagination, their long sojourn in that remote country, their ability to manage more than most in English as well as their ongoing work in the Kimberley. Correspondence between Madrid and New Norcia continued on financial matters as the community at Kalumburu continued, and beyond the practical matters some sisters also understood their bond with New Norcia theologically.

In September 1975 Felicitas wrote a reflective letter to Abbot Bernard. She had been back in Madrid six months or so. Writing in English with the whole community gathered at evening recreation, her simple phrases built on the Catholic understanding of being drawn into the heart of God through prayer and especially the Eucharist. She knew others also felt that the distance had not disrupted their involvement with the people:

> After all when leaving Australia especially New Norcia, I still remainded [sic] with everyone I ever met, lived with and loved in Christ. (I should perhaps speak in the plural taking advantage of my Sisters' feelings.) Yes, our hearts were deposited in that of Jesus together with all of you.

---

153 Bernard Rooney to Felicitas Pampliega, 29 September 1975.
154 Francisca Pardo, Interview, Madrid, 31 May 1999.

They remained united, Felicitas believed, because Jesus paradoxically transcended time and place:

> Therefore since He, remaining there, yet came with us, He also brought you with Him. Thus we are still with you. Realising this fact there is no need of many letters to believe in our close spiritual union and physical remembrance. While looking at Him we see everybody.[155]

Felicitas offered a vision of the church as the Mystical Body of Christ connected sacramentally. The image came from the heart of Catholic tradition. It opens out another horizon of reflection and, like the reunion of the Benedictine women with their former students at St Joseph's in 2001 where this account began, it embraces the reality of the material world of travel and events, as it also goes beyond it.

Felicitas's emphasis on the absence of boundaries for the community 'deposited in that [heart] of Jesus' shares a theological conviction that the Eucharist and the story it tells are keys for understanding the church in the world.[156] The celebration of the Eucharist collapses boundaries.[157] As the ritual of the prayer itself constitutes the church, it forms a mutual community of 'solidarity and resistance', beyond barriers of time and space, drawing members together as the Body of Christ. Taking the mystical reality for granted, Felicitas's letter opens up discussion of the ways in which Christian faith offers resources for reconciliation itself.

When the Benedictine women left for Spain, 'reconciliation' was not yet part of the political vocabulary in Australia. In the years following, it came to stand for addressing the schism between Aboriginal and non-Aboriginal Australia, especially with the foundation in 1991 of the Council for Aboriginal Reconciliation under the leadership of Patrick Dodson. In 1975 Dodson had been a member of the Missionaries of the Sacred Heart, a Catholic religious order, and the first Aboriginal man ordained as a Catholic priest, remaining active in that role until 1981.[158] In at least one interview he traced a link between the political 'reconciliation …

---

155 Felicitas Pampliega to Bernard Rooney, 17 September 1975, NNA S12-A5-4.
156 For example William Cavanaugh, *Theopolitical Imagination: Discovery the Liturgy as a Political Act in an Age of Global Consumerism* (London and New York: T & T Clark, 2008); James Alison, *The Joy of Being Wrong: Original Sin through Easter Eyes* (New York: Crossroad, 1998); James Alison, *Raising Abel: The Recovery of the Eschatological Imagination*, 2nd ed. (London: SPCK, 2010).
157 Cavanaugh, *Theopolitical Imagination*, 4, 5.
158 Kevin Keefe, *Paddy's Road: Life Stories of Patrick Dodson* (Canberra: Aboriginal Studies Press, 2003), 218–66.

a mitigation of the kinds of injuries that were done to Aborigines' and the Catholic spirituality that taught 'no matter how bad ... or how rejected ... you were still an important being in the eyes of Christ'.[159] Beyond politics or ethics, for Christians reconciliation has a spiritual core.

At the heart of Christian conviction, the death and resurrection of Jesus Christ solves the riddle of reconciliation for people of faith. Often in the unashamedly bloody iconography of Spain the cross stands for 'God's punishment' of human sinfulness, borne by Jesus in our place. The language of the liturgy, of 'sacrifice' especially, can seem to confirm this. Through much of the sisters' time in Australia and in many Catholic classrooms, the self-giving love of the cross was lost in popular understanding. As Catholic theologians in the ancient world made clear, the emphasis throughout should have been on radical grace, on the forgiveness that breaks out of reciprocity, returning good for evil, and on hope that blooms out of fear.[160] This is the theological imperative that offers transformation in the Christian world view.

In the prayer of every Eucharist, every time the Benedictine sisters and the St Joseph's girls went to Mass, believers are 'tilted towards' a 'memory of the future' where love already defines reality.[161] If Jesus is the Christ, truly as much God as God is, and equally as human as we are, then the cross and resurrection are not God's punishment. Rather, the eyes of faith see that, in Jesus, God as God's self steps freely and willingly into the deepest experience of humiliation. On the cross, God-with-us occupies that place of desolation and powerlessness and chooses to suffer its full brunt without divine magic. This is not so as to model the value of suffering as an end in itself but to break out of the cycle of revenge. Freely suffering the worst that humanity can offer, Jesus broke the cycle of retribution and defined a new reality. As the Aboriginal Catholic writer Elizabeth Pike envisages it, this new reality makes possible the renewal of relationships and the sharing of the deepest stories that are fundamental to genuine community.[162]

---

159 Rex Scambary, 'Dodson Talks', *Catholic Leader*, 1985, cited in Keefe, *Paddy's Road*, 265.
160 Alison, *The Joy of Being Wrong*, 104; Miroslav Volf, 'A Religion of Love', *Nova prisutnost* 12 (2014): 458–71, hrcak.srce.hr/file/192078.
161 On 'tilting', Alison, *Raising Abel*, 109–16; and on 'memory', Cavanaugh, *Theopolitical Imagination*, 5, quoting John Zizioulas.
162 Elizabeth Pike, 'Reconciliation, or Conciliation through Restoration?', in Developing an Australian Theology, ed. Peter Malone (Strathfield, NSW: St Paul's Publications, 1999), 38–42.

In this reality, reconciliation is a new way of being to be entered into. It follows from the 'vivacity, power and deathlessness of God in a way that seems almost unimaginable to us'.[163] The 'dangerous memory' of the death and resurrection of Jesus, celebrated at the Eucharist, enables, or perhaps even compels, people to embody mercy and justice.[164] This perspective informed Archbishop Desmond Tutu's campaign against apartheid in South Africa as well as his work there as chair of the Truth and Reconciliation Commission (1995–98). He claims a central place for the church's worship in the authentic transformation of culture.

For Tutu, the liturgy speaks of the possibility of God's new creation even in contexts that apparently deny it. By celebrating the Eucharist together, believers form an 'alternative society', throwing into relief the corruption and injustice that surround it and enabling those who participate to see reality clearly and move towards relationships of justice and peace:[165]

> If our worship is authentic and relevant, it prepares us for combat with the forces of evil, the principalities and powers. It prepares us to be involved where God's children are hurt, where they spend most of their lives: at work, in the market place, in schools, on the factory floor, in Parliament, in the courts of law, everywhere they live and work and play. Jesus refused to remain on the mountain top of the transfiguration. He came down into the valley of human need and misunderstanding.[166]

A sacramental imagination trusts there is a new dispensation where love already defines reality. Outside physical time, participation in the cosmic narrative binds believers to an alternative way of being. In that reality, injustice cannot be ignored, precisely because the hope for transformation is secure and guaranteed in the forgiveness of the crucified and risen Christ. Faith spurs remembering, the lament for and confession of, and casting away of all that should not be, as it promises a new reality.[167] Faith does not circumvent the call for justice in the here and now. In the face of political complexity and repeated failure, faith keeps alive the hope that justice is possible.

---

163 Alison, *Raising Abel*, 40.
164 Michael Battle, *Reconciliation: The Ubuntu Theology of Desmond Tutu* (Cleveland, OH: Pilgrim Press, 2009), 118.
165 Battle, *Reconciliation*, 118.
166 Desmond Tutu, 'Spirituality. Christian and African', in *Resistance and Hope*, ed. Charles Villa-Vicencio and John de Gruchy (Cape Town and Grand Rapids, MI: Eerdmans, 1985), 162.
167 Peter Sherlock, 'Reflections from the Vice-Chancellor on the Health and Integrity Conference', Melbourne, 27–29 August 2018, VOX, University of Divinity, www.healthandintegrity.org.au/post-conference-communiques; accessed 28 May 2019.

Perhaps it did not seem such a mystical occasion on the Saturday of the reunion in October 2001 when the Benedictine women and their former students gathered with the Aboriginal families and the monks. The community assembled that day in the open air. The liturgy began as the church bells rang and the sixth abbot of New Norcia, Placid Spearritt, greeted the Benedictine women at the monastery gate. Recalling the sisters' arrival at New Norcia when the monks and Aboriginal people would escort the newcomers into the church, he called the crowd of well-wishers to do the same, processing and singing the same Latin hymn of praise that had met so many of the groups from Spain. As the women moved towards honoured seats in the sanctuary with Sheila Humphries's painting in pride of place, the congregation followed—some to the front pews, others just to the porch to come and go, and still others on the grass to wait. The organ flared out in welcome beyond the doors, and tears flowed. When since the closure of the schools had there been so many Aboriginal people gathered with the missionaries? When since the time of Salvado had there ever been so many Aboriginal people in town across three and four generations of their families?

The readings from scripture revolved around reconciliation: Teresa read in Spanish of Isaiah's vision of weapons turned to gardening tools; we sang a psalm of justice revealed to 'all the ends of the earth'; Veronica read from Paul's letter to the Ephesians of grace flowing in Christ to bring together everything in the heavens and everything on earth; and the community stood to hear how Jesus prayed for his followers to be consecrated in the truth, asking God for disciples as united 'as you are in me and I am in you … that the world will realise it was you who sent me and that I have loved them as much as you loved me'.[168] For believers, that realisation of unity comes from being drawn into the process of being forgiven, of being welcomed into the place of the Other.

The local story followed the scripture. In a narrative of the Benedictine sisters' history, former students brought symbols of the life of the community forward. The telling had its own rhythm, weaving together themes of race and ethnicity, religious community, manual work and the school with traditions of feminine gentility summed up in needlework. A refrain was too simple but still rang true: 'This is a story of hard work,

---

168 Isaiah 2:1–5; Psalm 97; Ephesians 1:3–10; John 17:11, 17–23. Booklet for the Mass of Thanksgiving, Reunion of the Benedictine Sisters and Past Pupils of St Joseph's and St Mary's, 20 October 2001, NNA 07078.

and suffering, of much courage and of love'. Chant interspersed the action as the central display was assembled. The image of Mary, Our Lady of Good Counsel, lent against Sheila's painting as embroidered cloths, metal wash troughs and a washboard, baskets that held oranges from the orchard, school books and sporting trophies were all laid in place with dignity and quiet tears. The yellow parasol from the 1950s school concert came towards the end, perched jauntily near the vase that mixed European blossoms with local wildflowers and a candle painted with the Aboriginal colours, a gift from the Benedictine nuns at Jamberoo. As well as the parasol, the storeroom had yielded an embroidered chasuble, part of a full set of eucharistic vestments that the novices of 1948 had worked on together, following the custom of many religious communities. Teresa González had designed the riot of pink and rose flowers stitched onto white silk for the priests of the monastery to wear at Mass, and at the end of the narration she presented the garment again, this time to Abbot Placid. The simple gesture brought the years together. He donned it and moved to the lectern to preach.

Abbot Placid's homily traced the Gospel through the local story, thanking God for the life shared at New Norcia and acknowledging the suffering inflicted and received. Using the politically charged phrase 'I am sorry', he apologised not once but twice, 'to everybody who has ever felt hurt at New Norcia'. The recent days had brought memories to the surface, some happy and some 'so sad that we are never going to hear them at all'.[169] It was an important moment of acknowledgment of how deep the hurt had been. Like Felicitas's letter it wore its theology lightly but insistently:

> Of course I am sorry, and since we are a Christian community, I am confident that I can say we are sorry, all of us, that anybody should ever have been hurt here ... because we know that all human beings have been chosen in Christ before the world was made, because we know that Jesus loves us as much as his Father loves him, because we know he wants us to be one in him.[170]

---

169 'Nuns Reunion with Aborigines 20 October 2001', NNA 07078. Photographs of the reunion that show the procession of the St Joseph's banner into the church and the building of the liturgical display are NNA W7-A5-3-005, W7-A5-3-054, W7-A5-3-118.
170 'Nuns Reunion with Aborigines 20 October 2001'.

Figure 10.8: Benedictines and community assembled for the reunion liturgy, October 2001.
Source: NNA W7-a5-3-028.

Figure 10.9: The abbot greets the sisters at the monastery gate as the liturgy begins, Abbot Placid Spearritt and Sister Carmen Ruiz Besti.
Source: NNA W7-A5-3-006.

The homily was a plea to make real the hope of scripture for a community of truth and grace. Prayers followed, led by members of the Aboriginal Corporation (Rose Narkle, Norma Stack, Bernie Starr, Margaret Drayton and Georgina Taylor); Sister Carmen and Sister Hilda (representing Carmen's Benedictine community at Jamberoo) prepared the altar, setting linen and vessels in place; Mae Taylor and Sister Anne Moynihan brought the bread and wine forward; and Abbot Placid took up the prayer, recounting the action of God in Jesus, doing as Jesus did, breaking bread and sharing the cup, in memory of the self-giving of the cross and, according to the ancient ritual, in the presence of Jesus, risen and forgiving.

Felicitas would not have doubted that the reunion Eucharist was a cosmic event, bringing together the past, present and future. When the members of the reunion moved towards the sanctuary to join the sisters for Abbot Placid's final blessing, divisions blurred. In the eyes of faith they were surrounded by a 'great cloud of witnesses' (Heb 12:1). They were all there: Maria Harispe, Teresa Roca, Consuelo Batiz, Escolastica Martinez, all the girls who refused to answer their part in the rosary; Katie Yappo who decided it was time to leave, Grace Williams who never could; the parents from nearby cottages and those too far away; the mothers who wrote and those who could not; the children who flourished and those robbed of their childhoods; and, yes, those who committed those crimes as well as those who could not imagine them. Alongside the congregation gathered physically in the church, flowing over the sanctuary steps where Felicitas and Margaret had pledged their commitment in 1921, faith knew them gathered; all tilted in the eucharistic reality towards a future where reconciliation has already been enacted.

In the present, as people came forward in a confusion of recognition and greeting there were layers in the interaction. In the aisle one man paused at the end of a pew inviting a schoolmate with a gesture, waiting quietly until they went forward together. Grandkids went forward. Cameras flashed. The blessing was choked in sobs. Between the verses of the singing, Sr Carmen's delighted voice was resonant through the hubbub, calling out names in recognition. The sanctuary contained them all, and when the time seemed right the organ struck up the recessional hymn, an old favourite of the St Joseph's girls, often used at funerals. The unsophisticated, lilting lyrics called on 'Mary, Mother of Christ, Star of the Sea', to 'pray for the wanderer … the sinner … your children … for me'. In the same way as the extraordinary gathering had celebrated with an ancient and familiar ritual, here was a thread of familiarity in the unique occasion.

Figure 10.10: Benedictine sisters (Veronica, Visitación and Carmen) with the congregation in the church for the reunion liturgy.
Source: NNA W7-A5-3-055.

That reconciliation has a theological core does not give people of faith magical solutions to dissolve injustice or cancel heartbreak. The promise of a future that *already is* calls forth a new imagination, sometimes embraced swiftly and easily but usually learnt and relearnt slowly in community. Nevertheless, reconciliation as a spiritual value opens up a realm of much deeper political engagement because believers are shaped by an imagination that is not captive to the power of the state or the fear of the other. In this dispensation, discipleship does not replace citizenship in the political reality but galvanises it. In this dispensation, faith does not protect the institution but holds it to a standard of self-giving. The congregation at the reunion liturgy dispersed, but the prayerful occasion generated more than private resolutions. It was a key act of public acknowledgment of the complex history of St Joseph's and the Spanish missionary women in Australia.

Figure 10.11: Mae Taylor (left) and Anne Moynihan (Sr Pius) bring bread and wine for the Eucharist to Abbot Placid Spearritt and Dom Chris Power. The abbot is wearing the chasuble made by the novices in 1948.
Source: NNA W7-A5-3-128.

Figure 10.12: Praying the Lord's Prayer during the Eucharist.
Source: NNA W7-A5-3-056.

New Norcia's story of reconciliation did not start or end at the reunion. The event was part of a much larger narrative being enacted through stories heard accurately and received deeply. Within that larger narrative the story of the Benedictine women at New Norcia is about crossing boundaries and about falling between them, about the good intentions of the mission and its blindness to the racism it condoned. The story of the missionary women bridges the domestic and the institutional, public and private. The gap, the space, was a place of paradox, of tragedy and hope, and also of prayer. New Norcia remains a town built on a fault line between cultures. Any shift in culture is by definition communal and built on relationships.

The story of the Benedictine Missionary Sisters of New Norcia is one strand in the complex past of the town. It gives a close, but far from narrow, focus to a longer story of missionary encounter in Australia. It also opens out a wider story of the significance of relationships for reconciliation and the place of a community of memory and hope to support and sustain a process of reconciliation. The Benedictine women of New Norcia gave their lives to a vision that moved towards wholeness, but they knew well they had not attained it. Their story is woven through the lives of many others. They did not want a triumphal history. They hope for an account that empowers others to risk their own stories of remembering in sincerity and truth.

Bibliography

Archival holdings[1]

New Norcia Archives (NNA)

Aboriginal Families Index

'Chronicle of the Benedictine Community of New Norcia'. [*Chronicle*]

'Chronicle of the Benedictine Community of Kalumburu'. [*Chronicle*, Kalumburu]

Photograph Collection – Series P.

The Golden Career of St Gertrude's College, New Norcia. New Norcia: The Abbey Press, [1958].

NNA D7:89, Sketch Plan: St Gertrude's and St Joseph's.

NNA S12 – A5 – 4, Correspondence of Abbot Bernard Rooney, 1972–1975.

NNA S13.A3.4, Ros, Eladio. 'Music at New Norcia: A Historical Survey, First Period'. Unpublished manuscript.

NNA 00033, 'Viaje de Génova a Nueva-Norsia (Australia)'. [*Viaje*]

NNA 00918, Correspondence between Abbot Catalan and Religious of Various Orders.

NNA 01061, Drysdale River Mission Correspondence.

NNA 01123, Honour List – St Mary's Dominican Convent, Cabra.

NNA 01144, Correspondence: Lands and Surveys: Leases.

---

1   Abbreviations: OSB – Order of St Benedict; RSJ – Religious Sister of St Joseph.

NNA 01159, Land – Melbourne Loc. 1 – New Norcia, Historical Notes.

NNA 01341, Correspondence from Religious Sisters.

NNA 01360, Correspondence from Secular People and Family.

NNA 01365, Correspondence and Forms.

NNA 01418–01440, Correspondence of Abbot Anselm Catalan, 1916–1939.

NNA 01418–01421, Correspondence with Index [Abbot Catalan].

NNA 01434, Correspondence with Index [Abbot Catalan].

NNA 01441, Correspondence of Abbot Anselm Catalan, 1952–1956.

NNA 01442–01456, Correspondence with Index [Abbot Catalan], 1940–1951.

NNA 01457, Correspondence with Religious, 1953–1955.

NNA 01458, Correspondence with Religious & others, 1956–1958.

NNA 01646, Education Department Perth, Western Australia.

NNA 01717, 'Canonical Visitation to the Community of Teresians of St Gertrude's New Norcia, October 1907'. Translated by David Barry OSB. [*Visitation*]

NNA 01849, Correspondence – Apostolic Delegation to New Norcia Copies from Propaganda Fide.

NNA 2234A-41—023/024, Diary of Abbot Torres.

NNA 05505, 'Chronicle of the Benedictine Missionary Sisters, Girrawheen'. [*Girrawheen Chronicle*]

NNA 05513, 'Benedictine Missionary Sisters', handwritten summary from the notebooks of Sister Felicitas Pampliega c. 1921–c. 1967, previously held at the convent of the Benedictine Missionary Sisters Kalumburu. [*Notebooks, Kalumburu*]

NNA 05050, Annual Report of the Commissioner of Native Affairs for the Year Ended 30-Jun-1953.

NNA 05100, Correspondence [1970–1973].

NNA 05120, Correspondence Relating to Aboriginals between Native Affairs and the Benedictine Community 1885–1952.

NNA 05132, Correspondence Copy Book [1893–1906].

NNA 05496, Letters of the Sisters. Translations by David Barry OSB.

NNA 05517, Past Monks of New Norcia.

NNA 07078, 'Reunion of the Benedictine Sisters and Past Pupils of St Joseph's and St Mary's, 20 October 2001', Personal papers of Abbot Placid Spearritt. NN General Series: NNHT – OBL (Box 130) General / N.

NNA 2-2234A, Salvado Correspondence: Summaries by Teresa De Castro and David Barry OSB.

NNA 2969A/48, Wages and Goods 1914–1915.

Benedictine Missionary Sisters of Tutzing, Carabanchel, Madrid (ABTM)

New Norcia Folders: correspondence of Felicitas Pampliega OSB, correspondence of Maria [Mary] Cidad OSB, correspondence of Teresa González OSB.

'Las Necrologias', [Obituaries] Benedictinas Misioneras de Tutzing.

'Notes on the Timeline [of the Benedictine Missionary Sisters of New Norcia]', 1999.

'Origen de la Congregacion de las Hermanas Benedictinas Misioneras de New Norcia, Western Australia', unpublished typescript from the notebooks of Sister Felicitas Pampliega c.1921–c. 1967. Transcribed and edited by Sister Teresa González, Madrid c. 1980. [*Notebooks,* Madrid]

Photograph Albums

'Benedictine Missionary Sisters: Foundation and Progress', unpublished typescript summary in English from the notebooks of Sister Felicitas Pampliega c.1921– c.1967. [*Notebooks in English*, Madrid]

National Archives of Australia (NAA)

'Biographical Cuttings on Mary Pandilow, First Child to Be Born at the Old Pago Pago Mission', nla.gov.au/nla.cat-vn1991118.

M. C. [Consuelo] Batiz to Secretary of Home and Territories Department, 24 June 1918, National Archives of Australia, NAA A1, 1919/1216 37354 f.20.

Incoming passenger list, Osterley, National Archives of Australia, NAA K269 (Barcode 30151233).

'Child Care Act—Sisters of Mercy, Girrawheen Child Care Centre (formerly Benedictine Child Care Centre)', National Archives of Australia, NAA K317, 53/78/945.

Other Archival Collections

Documentation and Research Centre on Religion and Culture (KADOC), Catholic University of Louvain, Belgium.

Sisters of St Joseph of the Sacred Heart, South Perth.

Collection of the Royal Western Australian Historical Society, State Library of Western Australia, 02131PD.

State Record Office of Western Australia (SROWA)

SROWA S24 cons1497 1951/0953, 'Native Education – Reports from Officers of Native Welfare Department'.

SROWA S24 cons1497 1958/1141, 'Training of Teachers for Non-departmental Schools'.

SROWA S116 cons652 1916/1592, 'Returns of Children at New Norcia Mission'.

SROWA S1099 cons2532 A403 v1, 'Missions – Private – New Norcia – General Correspondence'.

SROWA S1099 cons2532 A0403 v2, 'Liaison – New Norcia Mission'.

SROWA S1644 cons652 1909/0171, Torres, 'New Norcia Mission – Annual Report for 1908'.

SROWA S1644 cons652 1911/0473, 'Treatment of Natives. New Norcia. Complaints re George Shaw and Felix Jackimarra'.

SROWA S1644 cons652 1911/1475, Rt. Rev. F. Torres. O.S.B., 'New Norcia Mission: Annual Report 12 months ended 30 June 1911'.

SROWA S1644 cons652 1913/0213, George S. Olivey, Travelling Inspector, 'Report on New Norcia Mission'.

SROWA S1644 cons652 1913/1273, 'New Norcia Mission. Annual Report for Year ending 30 June 1913'.

SROWA S1644 cons652 1917/0331, 'Sr Consuelo. New Norcia. Reporting That Native Woman Recently Living with Indian John Michael Is in a Destitute Condition'.

SROWA S2030 cons993 1926/0350, 'New Norcia Mission – Subsidy and General'.

SROWA S2030 cons993 1940/0904, 'New Norcia Mission – Education of Natives'.

SROWA S3005 cons255 1907/0108, 'Police, New Norcia Re: Arrests'.

SROWA S3054 cons968 1907/0505, 'New Norcia: Case against George Shaw and Others'.

Interviews

All inteviews, conversations and personal communications are with the author unless otherwise indicated.

Carrillo, Scholastica, OSB. Kalumburu: 25 April 1999, 1 May 1999; Madrid: 7 June 1999, 8 June 1999.

Catalan, Pilar, OSB. Madrid: 9 June 1999; New Norcia: 18 October 2001; Madrid: 29 July 2010.

Cidad, Visitación, OSB. Kalumburu: 24 April 1999, 27 April 1999, 3 May 1999; Madrid: 29 July 2010, 3 August 2010, 26 October 2013, 28 September 2014.

Cidad, Visitación, OSB, and Scholastica Carrillo, OSB. Kalumburu: 29 April 1999, 30 April 1999.

Cidad, Visitación, OSB, and Teresa González, OSB. Madrid: 6 October 2010.

Diez, Josefina, OSB. Benedictinas de San José, Burgos: 2 October 2010.

Drayton, Mrs Margaret. Perth: 19 April 1999.

González, Teresa, OSB. Madrid: 17 May 1999, 21 May 1999, 22 May 1999, 25 May 1999, 27 May 1999, 31 May 1999, 3 June 1999; New Norcia, WA: 30 August 2000, 17 October 2001; Madrid: July 2002, 10 July 2004, 26 October 2013, 7 July 2017, 8 July 2017, 10 July 2017, 19 March 2018.

González, Teresa, OSB, with her sister and nephews. Villaquirán, Burgos, 30 May 1999.

González, Teresa, OSB, with Mae Taylor. New Norcia and Moora: 30 August 1999.

González, Teresa, OSB, Pilar Catalan, OSB, Francisca Pardo, OSB, and Maria Gratia Balagot. Madrid: 9 July 2004.

González, Teresa, OSB and Visitación Cidad, OSB Interview, Madrid, 30 September 2010.

González, Teresa, OSB, Visitación Cidad, OSB, and Pilar Catalan, OSB. Madrid: 4 October 2010.

Grant, Ms Beryl. Perth: 15 February 2000.

Herbert, John, OSB, in conversation with Katharine Massam and Sharne Rolfe: 27 April 2010.

Humphries, Ms Sheila. New Norcia: May 1999, July 1999.

Humphries, Ms Sheila. Interview with Sr Anne Carter. New Norcia: 10 June 2002. *New Norcia Studies* 10 (2002): 36–37.

Humphries, Ms Sheila. Interview with Katharine Massam and students of the United Faculty of Theology, New Norcia: 15 July 2003.

Mayne, Leonie, RSJ. Perth (by telephone): May 1999.

McAlinden, Mr Anthony. New Norcia: October 2002.

Miles, Mrs Glenys Benjamin, and Mrs Phyllis Brennan. Perth: June 1999.

Moynihan, Sr Anne. North Perth: 19 March 1999; New Norcia: 12 October 2001.

Nannup, Mrs Mary. Moora: March 1999.

Nannup, Mrs Mary, with Ms Fatima Drayton and Ms Gloria Drayton. Moora: February 1999.

Narkle, Mrs Rose. Langford: 2001.

Narkle, Mrs Rose, and Veronica Willaway, OSB. Langford: 2001.

Pardo, Francisca, OSB. Madrid: 31 May 1999, 4 June 1999.

Pardo, Francisca, OSB, Teresa González, OSB, and Pilar Catalan, OSB. Madrid: 10 July 2004, 11 July 2004, 12 July 2004.

Perez, Illuminada [Sr Florentina]. Burgos: September 2010.

Reunion Group, Interview in the Old Convent, New Norcia, October 2001.

Roche, Philomena, OSB. Nebraska: 9 July 2010.

Rossen, Mr Paul. West Perth: 2017.

Ruiz Besti, Carmen, OSB. Interview with Sr Hilda Scott and Katharine Massam, New Norcia: 28 July 1999.

Ruiz Besti, Carmen, OSB. Old Convent, New Norcia: 14 October 2001.

Ruiz, Isolina, in conversation at New Norcia: October 2001.

Sanz, Seraphim, OSB. New Norcia: October 2002.

Taylor, Ms Mae. New Norcia: October 2001, 2003.

Taylor, Ms Georgina. Old Convent, New Norcia: 17 October 2001.

Taylor, Ms Georgina, and Ms Mae Taylor. New Norcia: May 2017.

Sr Theophane, RSM. Perth: April 1999.

Villaño, Lucia, OSB. Benedictinas de San José, Burgos: 2 October 2010.

Willaway, Veronica, OSB. New Norcia: October 2001; Nebraska: 7 July 2012, 8 July 2012, 9 July 2012; 13 June 2013, 16 June 2013, 20 June 2013, June 2014; New Norcia: September 2015.

Willaway, Mr Paul, and Veronica Willaway, OSB. Perth: November 2014.

Newspapers and periodicals

Beverley Times (Beverley, WA)
Daily News (Perth, WA)
Diario de Burgos (Burgos, Spain)
Freeman's Journal (Sydney, NSW)
Geraldton Guardian and Express (Geraldton, WA)
Mirror (Sydney, NSW)
New Norcia Studies (New Norcia, WA)
Northern Times (Carnarvon, WA)
Pax (New Norcia, WA)
Recorder (Port Pirie, SA)
St Ildephonsus College Magazine (New Norcia, WA)
Sunday Leaf (New Norcia, WA)
Sunday Times (Perth, WA)
Tablet (London)
West Australian (Perth, WA)
West Australian Catholic Record [*Record*] (Perth, WA)
Western Mail (Perth, WA)
Yorgum Newsletter (Perth, WA)

Published primary sources

Aboriginal Corporation of New Norcia. *Newsletter of the Aboriginal Corporation of New Norcia*, 2008.

[Benedict of Nursia]. *RB 1980: The Rule of St. Benedict in Latin and English with Notes*. Edited by Timothy Fry. Collegeville, MN: Liturgical Press, 1980.

Beréngier, Théophile. *New Norcia: The History of a Benedictine Colony in Western Australia 1846–1878*. Translated by Peter Gilet. Northcote, Vic.: Abbey Press, 2014.

Budby, John, ed. With sketches by Vera Budby. *Draft National Workshop Report: Aboriginal Independent Schools*. Woden, ACT: National Aboriginal Education Committee, 1982.

Budby, Vera, ed. *Establishment, Membership, Role and Function of the National Aboriginal Education Committee and the State Aboriginal Education Consultative Groups*. Canberra: Department of Aboriginal Affairs, 1982.

———, ed. *A Resource Catalogue for Aboriginal and Islander Early Childhood Education Centres*. [Brisbane]: Creche and Kindergarten Association of Queensland, 1983.

Catalan, Anselm. 'Drysdale River Mission'. In *The National Eucharistic Congress, Melbourne, Australia, December 2nd–9th, 1934*. Edited by J. M. Murphy and F. Moynihan, 179–89. The Advocate Press: Melbourne, 1938.

Catholic Commission for Justice and Peace for the Catholic Bishops of Australia. *Aborigines: A Statement of Concern*. Sydney: E. J. Dwyer, 1978.

Commonwealth Bureau of Census and Statistics. *Official Year Book of the Commonwealth of Australia Containing Authoritative Statistics for the Period 1901–1913*. No. 7. Canberra: Government Printer, 1914.

Constituciones de la Compañia de Santa Teresa de Jesús. Barcelona: Tipografia Tersiana, Calle de los Angeles 22 y 24, 1903.

Constitution on the Sacred Liturgy. *Sacrosantum Concilium*. 4 December 1963. www.vatican.va/archive/hist_councils/ii_vatican_council/documents/vat-ii_const_19631204_sacrosanctum-concilium_en.html.

Dasey, M. Edward. *The Story of the Regional Missionary and Eucharistic Congress, Newcastle, NSW*. Newcastle: Speciality Publications, 1938.

European Union Directorate General for Education and Culture. *Europeans and Their Languages*. Special Eurobarometer 386. Brussels: European Commission, June 2012. ec.europa.eu/commfrontoffice/publicopinion/archives/ebs/ebs_386_en.pdf.

Golden Wattle Cookery Book. Compiled by Margaret A. Wylie. Perth: E. S. Wigg and Son, 1924.

Harrison, Mary. *The Skillful Cook: A Practical Manual of Modern Experience*. London: J. M. Dent and Sons, 1906.

John Paul II. 'Canonización de Enrique de Oss y Cervelló'. Homily preached 16 June 1993. w2.vatican.va/content/john-paul-ii/es/homilies/1993/documents/hf_jp-ii_hom_19930616_canonizzazione-madrid.html.

Metcalf, Theodore. 'Carmel in India'. *Tablet*, 2 October 1900, 20.

Montessori, Maria. *The Child in the Church: Essays on the Religious Education of Children and the Training of Character*. Edited by Mortimer Standing. London: Sands and Co., 1930.

Murphy, J. M., and F. Moynihan, eds. *The National Eucharistic Congress, Melbourne, Australia, December 2nd–9th 1934*. Melbourne: The Advocate Press, 1936.

Pius XII. *Evangelii Praecones*. 2 June 1951. w2.vatican.va/content/pius-xii/en/encyclicals/documents/hf_p-xii_enc_02061951_evangelii-praecones.html.

Provisional Curriculum for Coloured Pupils in Caste Schools. Perth: Education Department of Western Australia, 1953.

Ros, Eladio. *La Musica en la Nueva Nursia*. Translated by Mercedes Utray. Madrid: Ministerio de Asuntos Exteriores, 1992.

Royal Commission into Institutional Responses to Child Sexual Abuse. *Analysis of Claims of Child Sexual Abuse Made with Respect to Catholic Church Institutions in Australia*. Sydney: Commonwealth of Australia, December 2017. www.childabuseroyalcommission.gov.au/sites/default/files/REPT.0012.001.0001.pdf.

———. *Final Report*. Sydney: Commonwealth of Australia. December 2017. www.childabuseroyalcommission.gov.au/final-report.

———. *Proportion of Priests and Non-Ordained Religious Subject to a Claim of Child Sexual Abuse 1950–2010*. Report 0011.001.0001. Sydney: Commonwealth of Australia, February 2017. www.childabuseroyalcommission.gov.au/sites/default/files/REPT.0011.001.0001.pdf.

———. *Report of Case Study Number 11, Congregation of the Christian Brothers in Western Australia Response to Child Sexual Abuse at Castledare Junior Orphanage, St Vincent's Orphanage Clontarf, St Mary's Agricultural School and Bindoon Farm School*. Sydney: Commonwealth of Australia, December 2014. www.childabuse royalcommission.gov.au/case-studies/case-study-11-christian-brothers.

Salvado, Rosendo. *Report of Rosendo Salvado to Propaganda Fide in 1883*. Translated by Stefano Girola. Northcote, Vic.: Abbey Press, 2015.

———. *Report of Rosendo Salvado to Propaganda Fide in 1900*. Translated by Stefano Girola. Northcote, Vic.: Abbey Press, 2016.

———. *The Salvado Memoirs: Historical Memoirs of Australia and Particularly of the Benedictine Mission of New Norcia and of the Habits and Customs of the Australian Natives*. Translated by E. J. Storman. Nedlands, WA: University of Western Australia Press, 1977.

Sanz de Galdeano, Seraphim. *Memoirs of a Spanish Missionary Monk*. Carlisle, WA: Hesperian Press, 2006.

Souvenir of the Centenary of Holy Angels. Kerala, India: Congregation of the Carmelite Religious, n.d.

[Thérèse Martin]. *Soeur Thérèse of Lisieux*. London: Burns, Oates and Washbourne, 1912.

[Torres, Fulgentius]. *The Torres Diaries, 1901–1914: Diaries of Dom Fulgentius (Anthony) Torres y Mayans, O.S.B., Abbot Nullius of New Norcia, Bishop Titular of Dorylaeum, Administrator Apostolic of the Kimberley Vicariate in North Western Australia*. Translated by Eugene Perez. Edited by Rosemary Pratt and John Millington. Perth: Artlook Books, 1987.

Western Australian Year Book 1975. Canberra: Australian Bureau of Statistics, 1976. www.abs.gov.au/AUSSTATS/abs@.nsf/DetailsPage/1300.51975?Open Document.

Secondary sources

Website resources

All Saints College, Trivandrum, India. www.allsaintscollege.in/allSaints/ccr.php (expired domain).

'Asilo de San José [Carabanchel, Madrid]', Karabanchel.com: Una Pagina de Nuestro Barrio, karabanchel.com/asilo-de-san-jose-2.

Australian Federal Election Speeches, Museum of Australian Democracy at Old Parliament House, electionspeeches.moadoph.gov.au.

British Food in America, www.britishfoodinamerica.com/The-Hardship-War-Austerity-Number-Part-2/the-lyrical/An-Appreciation-of-the-sheep-s-head-both-at-the-table-and-on-the-page/#.X3QPeVllNTY.

Colegio de las Teresianas, Gaudi Barcelona Club, www.gaudiclub.com/esp/e_vida/teresian2.html.

Company of St Teresa of Jesus, www.teresians.org.

Compañia de Santa Teresa de Jesús, www.stjteresianas.org.

Conference on the History of Women Religious, www.chwr.org.

Congregation of the Apostolic Carmel, www.apostolic-carmel.org/index.htm.

Congregation of the Carmelite Religious, www.ccr.ind.in.

Creative Spirits, 'Some History of Redfern', www.creativespirits.info/australia/new-south-wales/sydney/redfern.

De priorij Onze-Lieve-Vrouw van Bethanië [Priory of Our Lady of Bethany], www.priorijbethanie.be.

FamilySearch, The Church of Jesus Christ of Latter-Day Saints, familysearch.org.

Goan Churches: Carmelites of Trivandrum C.C.R., goanchurches.info/orders/carmelites-of-trivandrum-c-c-r/.

Health and Integrity in Church and Ministry: An Ecumenical Conversation on the Task of Rebuilding and Renewal after the Royal Commission into Institutional Responses to Child Sexual Abuse, Melbourne, 27–29 August 2018, VOX, University of Divinity, www.healthandintegrity.org.au.

Heritage Council, State Heritage Office [WA], inherit.stateheritage.wa.gov.au.

History of Women Religious of Britain and Ireland, historyofwomenreligious.org.

Holy Angels Convent, Our History, www.holyangelstvm.org/history.aspx.

'Introduction to Lord Curzon's Education Policy', Krishna Kanta Handiqui State Open University, kkhsou.in/main/education/education_policy.html.

Japanese bombing of Darwin, Broome, and northern Australia, www.australia.gov.au/about-australia/australian-story/japanese-bombing-of-darwin (site discontinued).

Kaartidijin Noongar–Noongar Knowledge, South West Aboriginal Land & Sea Council, www.noongarculture.org.au.

Kalumburu Mission, www.kalumburumission.org.au/main/history.html.

Kalumburu Mission – The Bombing of Kalumburu, www.kalumburumission.org.au/main/bombing.html.

Monasterio San Pedro de Cardeña, www.monasteriosanpedrodecardena.com.

Monasterio de San Salvador, www.benedictinaspalacios.com.

My Voice for My Country: Changing Images of Aboriginal and Torres Strait Islander Voter Participation [online exhibition], AIATSIS, aiatsis.gov.au/exhibitions/my-voice-my-country.

Patrimonio Industrial Arquitectonico, patrindustrialquitectonico.blogspot.com.

Redress, WA (2008–2011), Find & Connect, www.findandconnect.gov.au/guide/wa/WE00505#tab1.

St Andriesabdij Zevenkerken, www.abdijzevenkerken.be/abdij/geschiedenis.

Theodore Neve, OSB, Webpage created for a workshop held at Saint Andrew's Abbey, Valyermo, California in 1990, ldysinger.stjohnsem.edu/@texts2/1910_neve/00a_start.htm.

'Towards Healing'. Truth, Justice and Healing Council, www.tjhcouncil.org.au/support/towards-healing.aspx.

Vivian Iris Rossen, Artefacts, www.artefacts.co.za/main/Buildings/archframes.php?archid=3284&countadd=0.

Western Australia. Parliament. Hansard Archive, 1870–, www.parliament.wa.gov.au/hansard/hansard.nsf/NewAdvancedSearch.

Western Australian Legislation, Government of Western Australia, www.legislation.wa.gov.au.

Western Australian Museum, Welcome Walls, museum.wa.gov.au/welcomewalls/names/.

Westaustralianae, Rosendo Salvado Correspondence, summarised by Teresa De Castro, www.geocities.ws/CollegePark/Field/4664/Historyserver/westraliana/index.htm.

Books, articles, theses and film

Alison, James. *The Joy of Being Wrong: Original Sin through Easter Eyes*. New York: Crossroad, 1998.

——. *Raising Abel: The Recovery of the Eschatological Imagination*. 2nd ed. London: SPCK, 2010.

Almond, Philip. 'Oblati'. In *The Catholic Encyclopedia: An International Work of Reference*, edited by Charles Herbermann. New York: Appleton, 1911. www.newadvent.org/cathen/11188a.htm.

Altman, J. C., and W. Sanders. 'From Exclusion to Dependence: Aborigines and the Welfare State in Australia'. In *Social Welfare with Indigenous Peoples*, edited by John Dixon and Robert P. Sheurell, 206–29. London and New York: Routledge, 1995.

Arnold, D. 'The Place of "the Tropics" in Western Medical Ideas since 1750'. *Tropical Medicine and International Health* 2 (1997): 303–13.

Atkinson, Judy. *Trauma Trail, Recreating Song Lines: The Transgenerational Effects of Trauma in Indigenous Australia*. North Geelong, Vic.: Spinifex Press, 2002.

Ballhatchet, Kenneth. *Class, Caste and Catholicism in India, 1789–1914*. London: Curzon Press, 1998.

Barry, David. 'New Norcia'. In *Historical Encyclopedia of Western Australia*, edited by Jenny Gregory and Jan Gothard, 629–30. Crawley, WA: University of Western Australia Press, 2009.

Bashford, Alison. *Imperial Hygiene: A Critical History of Colonialism, Nationalism and Public Health*. London: Palgrave McMillan, 2014.

Battle, Michael. *Reconciliation: The Ubuntu Theology of Desmond Tutu*. Cleveland, OH: Pilgrim Press, 2009.

Besse, Martial. 'The Spanish Benedictines'. *Downside Review* 16 (1897): 268–97.

Birt, H. N. *Benedictine Pioneers in Australia*. London: Polding Press, 1911.

Biskup, Peter. *Not Slaves, Not Citizens: The Aboriginal Problem in Western Australia 1898–1954*. St Lucia: University of Queensland Press, 1973.

Borrás Llop, José María. *Historia de la infancia en la España contemporánea, 1834–1936*. Madrid: Ministerio de Trabajo y Asuntos Sociales, Fundación Germán Sánchez Ruipérez, 1996.

Bowie, Fiona, Deborah Kirkwood, and Shirley Ardener, eds. *Women and Missions: Past and Present; Anthropological and Historical Perceptions.* Providence, RI: Berg: 1993.

Bridge, Catherine. 'Midwifery Care for Australian Aboriginal Women'. *Australian College of Midwives Incorporated Journal* 12 (1999): 7–11.

Brock, Peggy. *Outback Ghettos: A History of Aboriginal Institutionalisation and Survival.* Cambridge: Cambridge University Press, 1993.

Bruno-Jofré, Rosa. *The Missionary Oblate Sisters: Vision and Mission.* Montreal: McGill-Queen's University Press, 2005.

Burley, Stephanie. 'An Overview of the Historiography of Women Religious in Australia'. *Journal of the Australian Catholic Historical Society* 26 (2005): 43–60.

Calladine, Kayla. 'Liquor Restrictions in Western Australia'. *Indigenous Law Bulletin* 15 (2009). www.austlii.edu.au/au/journals/IndigLawB/2009/15.html.

Callahan, William J. 'The Spanish Parish Clergy, 1874–1930'. *Catholic Historical Review* 75 (1989): 405–22.

Carey, Hilary. 'Subordination, Invisibility and Chosen Work: Missionary Nuns and Australian Aborigines, c.1900–1949'. *Australian Feminist Studies* 13 (1998): 251–67. doi.org/10.1080/08164649.1998.9994913.

Carter, Anne, and Elizabeth Murphy. *A Rich Harvest—St Gertrude's College.* South Perth: Sisters of St Joseph of the Sacred Heart, 2006.

Cavanaugh, William. *Theopolitical Imagination: Discovering the Liturgy as a Political Act in an Age of Global Consumerism.* London and New York: T & T Clark, 2008.

Chin, Catherine. 'Marvellous Things Heard: On Finding Historical Radiance'. *The Massachusetts Review* 58 (2017): 478–91.

Choo, Christine. *Mission Girls: Aboriginal Women on Catholic Missions in the Kimberley, Western Australia, 1900–1950.* Crawley, WA: University of Western Australia Press, 2001.

———. 'The Role of the Catholic Missionaries at Beagle Bay in the Removal of Aboriginal Children from Their Families in the Kimberley Region from the 1890s'. *Aboriginal History* 21 (1997): 14–29.

Clark, Mary Ryllis. *Loreto in Australia.* Sydney: University of New South Wales Press, 2009.

Clendinnen, Inga. *True Stories*. Sydney: ABC Books for the Australian Broadcasting Commission, 1999.

Cole, Anna with Victoria Haskins and Fiona Paisley, eds. *Uncommon Ground: White Women in Aboriginal History*. Canberra, ACT: Aboriginal Studies Press, 2005.

Copeland, M. Shawn. 'A Cadre of Women Religious Committed to Black Liberation: The National Black Sisters' Conference'. *U.S. Catholic Historian* 14, no. 1 (1996): 123–44. www.jstor.org/stable/25154544.

———. 'Building up a Household of Faith: Dom Cyprian Davis OSB and the Work of History'. *US Catholic Historian* 28, no. 1 (2010): 53–63. doi.org/10.1353/cht.0.0028.

Cowlishaw, Gillian. 'On "Getting It Wrong": Collateral Damage in the History Wars'. *Australian Historical Studies* 37 (2006): 181–202. doi.org/10.1080/10314610608601210.

Crăciun, Maria, and Elaine Fulton. *Communities of Devotion: Religious Orders and Society in East Central Europe, 1450–1800*. Farnham, Surrey: Ashgate, 2011.

Crawford, Ian. *We Won the Victory: Aborigines and Outsiders on the North-West Coast of the Kimberley*. Fremantle, WA, Fremantle Arts Centre Press, 2001.

De Castro, Teresa. 'New Norcia's Golden Decade: Rosendo Salvado's Correspondence in the Last Years of the 19th Century (1891–1900)'. *New Norcia Studies* 14 (2006): 64–107.

De la Cruz, Valentin. *El Monasterio de Las Huelgas de Burgos*. Léon: Editorial Everest, 2005.

De Serio, Barbara. 'The Profile of the Montessori Assistant: Historical Paths and New Education Projects'. *Studi sulla Formazione* 19 (2006): 171–85.

Delgado, Jessica. *Laywomen and the Making of Colonial Catholicism in New Spain*. Cambridge: Cambridge University Press, 2018. doi.org/10.1017/9781108185639.

Dickens, A. G. *Late Monasticism and the Reformation*. London: Hambledon Press, 1994.

Djuric, Bonny, Lily Hibberd, and Linda Steele. 'Transforming the Parramatta Female Factory Institutional Precinct into a Site of Conscience'. *The Conversation*, 4 January 2018. theconversation.com/transforming-the-parramatta-female-factory-institutional-precinct-into-a-site-of-conscience-88875.

Faucha Perez, Francisco Javier, and Jesus Fernandez Sanz. 'La Fundacion Instituto San José de Carabanchel Alto'. *Madrid Historico* (2011): 73–80.

Fernandez Pombo, Alejandro. *Saturnina Jassá de la Compañia de Santa Teresa de Jesús*. Barcelona: Ediciones STJ, 1991.

Flecha Garcia, Consuelo. 'Education in Spain: Close-Up of Its History in the 20th Century'. *Analytical Reports in International Education* 4 (2011): 17–42.

Flemming, Leslie A., ed. *Women's Work for Women: Missionaries and Social Change in Asia*. Boulder, CO: Westview Press, 1989.

Foale, Marie Therese. *The Josephites Go West: The Sisters of St Joseph in Western Australia 1887–1920*. Fremantle, WA: University of Notre Dame Press, 1995.

Foucault, Michel. *Histoire de la sexualité*. Vol. 3: *Le souci de soi*. Paris: Gallimand, 1984.

——. *The History of Sexuality*. Vol. 3: *The Care of the Self*. Translated by Robert Hurley. New York: Vintage Books, 1978–86.

Fox, Charlie. 'The Fourteen Powers Referendum of 1944 and the Federalisation of Aboriginal Affairs'. *Aboriginal History* 32 (2008): 27–48. doi.org/10.22459/AH.32.2011.02.

Frisch, Michael. *A Shared Authority: Essays on the Craft and Meaning of Oral and Public History*. Albany: State University of New York Press, 1990.

Gadamer, Hans-Georg. *Hans-Georg Gadamer on Education, Poetry, and History: Applied Hermeneutics*. Edited by Dieter Misgeld, Graeme Nicholson, Lawrence Schmidt, and Monica Reuss. Albany: State University of New York Press, 1992.

——. *Truth and Method*. Translated by J. Weinsheimer and D. G. Marshall. 2nd rev. ed. New York: Crossroad, 1989.

Ganter, Regina, and Patricia Grimshaw. 'Introduction: Reading the Lives of White Mission Women'. *Journal of Australian Studies* 39 (2015): 1–6. doi.org/10.1080/14443058.2014.1001308.

Garaty, Janice, Lesley Hughes, and Megan Brock. 'Seeking the Voices of Catholic Teaching Sisters: Challenges in the Research Process'. *History of Education Review* 44 (2015): 71–84. doi.org/10.1108/HER-03-2014-0022.

Gardiner-Gaden, John, and Joanne Simon-Davies. *Commonwealth Indigenous-Specific Expenditure 1968–2012*. Canberra: Parliament of Australia, 2012.

Ghosh, Suresh Chandra. 'The Genesis of Curzon's University Reforms, 1899–1905'. *Minerva* 26 (1988): 463–92. doi.org/10.1007/BF01096494.

Girola, Stefano. 'Rhetoric and Action: The Policies and Attitudes of the Catholic Church with Regard to Australia's Indigenous Peoples, 1885–1967'. PhD thesis, School of History, Philosophy, Religion and Classics, University of Queensland, 2006.

Green, Neville, and Lois Tilbrook, eds. *Aborigines of New Norcia 1845–1914*. Crawley, WA: University of Western Australia Press, 1989.

Grimshaw, Patricia. 'Rethinking Approaches to Women in Missions: The Case of Colonial Australia'. *History Australia* 8 (2011): 7–24. doi.org/10.1080/14490854.2011.11668386.

The Habits of New Norcia. Directed by Frank Rijavec, with Harry Taylor and Carmelo Musca. Eight Mile Plains, Qld: CM Film Productions, 2000.

Hadot, Pierre. 'Reflections on the Idea of the "Cultivation of Self"'. In *Philosophy as a Way of Life: Spiritual Exercises from Socrates to Foucault*, translated by M. Chase, 206-14. Oxford and New York: Blackwell, 1995.

Haebich, Anna. *Broken Circles: Fragmenting Indigenous Families 1800–2000*. Fremantle: Fremantle Arts Centre Press, 2000.

———. *Dancing in Shadows: Histories of Nyungar Performance*. Crawley, WA: UWA Publishing, 2018.

———. *For Their Own Good: Aborigines and Government in the South West of Western Australia, 1900–1940*. Nedlands, WA: University of Western Australia Press for the Charles and Joy Staples South West Region Publications Fund, 1988.

———. 'No Man Is an Island: Bishop Salvado's Vision for Mission Work with the Aboriginal People of Western Australia'. *New Norcia Studies* 9 (2001): 20–28.

Hancock, W. K. *Professing History*. Sydney: Sydney University Press, 1976.

Harris, John. *One Blood: 200 Years of Aboriginal Encounter with Christianity; A Story of Hope*. Sutherland, NSW: Albatross Books, 1990.

Hetherington, Penelope. *Paupers, Poor Relief and Poor Houses in Western Australia 1829–1910*. Crawley, WA: University of Western Australia Publishing, 2009.

Hilliard, David. 'Church, Family and Sexuality in Australia in the 1950s'. *Australian Historical Studies* 27 (1997): 133–46. doi.org/10.1080/10314619708596048.

———. 'God in the Suburbs: The Religious Culture of Australian Cities in the 1950s'. *Australian Historical Studies* 24 (1991): 399–419. doi.org/10.1080/10314619108595856.

Hodson, Sally. 'Making a Rural Labour Force: The Intervention of the State in the Working Lives of Nyungars in the Great Southern, 1936/1948'. In 'Historical Refractions', edited by Charlie Fox, special issue, *Studies in Western Australian History* 14 (1993): 26–41.

Holland, Alison. 'Mary Bennett and the Feminists: A Response'. *Australian Historical Studies* 33 (2002): 398–400. doi.org/10.1080/10314610208596228.

——. '"Wives and Mothers Like Ourselves"? Exploring White Women's Intervention in the Politics of Race, 1920s–1940s'. *Australian Historical Studies* 32 (2001): 292–310. doi.org/10.1080/10314610108596166.

Humble, Nicola. 'Little Swans with Luxette and Loved Boy Pudding: Changing Fashions in Cookery Books'. *Women: A Cultural Review* 13 (2000): 322–38.

Hutchinson, David, ed. *A Town Like No Other: The Living Tradition of New Norcia*. Fremantle, WA: Fremantle Arts Centre Press, 1995.

Irrera, Orazio. 'Pleasure and Transcendence of the Self: Notes on "a Dialogue Too Soon Interrupted" between Michel Foucault and Pierre Hadot'. *Philosophy and Social Criticism* 36 (2010): 995–1017. doi.org/10.1177/0191453710379026.

Kardong, Terrence. *Benedict's Rule: A Translation and Commentary*. Collegeville, MN: Liturgical Press, 1996.

Keefe, Kevin. *Paddy's Road: Life Stories of Patrick Dodson*. Canberra: Aboriginal Studies Press, 2003.

Kinder, John. 'I'm Writing Simply to Say I Have Nothing to Write About: The Martelli Letters 1854–1864'. *New Norcia Studies* 19 (2011): 19–33.

Kinder, John, and Joshua Brown. *Canon Raffaele Martelli in Western Australia, 1853–1864: Life and Letters*. Northcote, Vic.: Abbey Press, 2014.

Koselleck, Reinhart. *Futures Past: On the Semantics of Historical Time*. Translated by Keith Tribe. Cambridge, MA: MIT Press, 2004.

Kulp, Philip M., ed. *Women Missionaries and Cultural Change*. Studies in Third World Societies 40. Williamsburg, VA: Department of Anthropology, College of William and Mary, June 1987.

Kulzer, Linda, and Roberta C. Bondi. *Benedict in the World: Portraits of Monastic Oblates*. Collegeville, MN: Liturgical Press, 2002.

Lake, Marilyn. 'Feminism and the Gendered Politics of Antiracism, Australia 1927–1957'. *Australian Historical Studies* 29 (1998): 91–108. doi.org/10.1080/10314619808596062.

Lake, Marilyn, and Henry Reynolds. *Drawing the Global Colour Line: White Men's Countries and the Question of Racial Equality*. Melbourne: Melbourne University Press, 2008. doi.org/10.1017/CBO9780511805363.

Lannon, Frances. *Privilege, Persecution, and Prophecy: The Catholic Church in Spain, 1875–1975*. Oxford: Clarendon Press, 1987.

——. 'Women and Images of Women in the Spanish Civil War'. *Transactions of the Royal Historical Society*, 6th series 1 (1991): 213–28.

——. 'Identity and Reform in the Second Republic'. In *A Companion to Spanish Women's Studies*, edited by X. de Ros and G. Hazburn, 273–86. Woodbridge, Suffolk: Tamesis, 2011.

Laudan, Rachel. 'Convent Sweets'. In *Oxford Companion to Sugar and Sweets*, edited by Darra Goldstein. Oxford: Oxford University Press, 2015.

Leggott, Sarah. *The Workings of Memory: Life Writing by Women in Twentieth-Century Spain*. Lewisburg, PA: Bucknell University Press, 2008.

Lerner, Gerda. *The Majority Finds Its Past*. Oxford: Oxford University Press, 1981.

Link, Gertrud. *My Way with God: Experiences of a Missionary Sister on Five Continents*. Translated by Matilda Handl. St Ottilien: EOS-Verl, 1998.

Lyng, J. *Non-Britishers in Australia: Influence on Population and Progress*. Melbourne: Macmillan and Melbourne University Press, 1927.

MacGinley, M. Rosa. *A Dynamic of Hope: Institutes of Women Religious in Australia*. Darlinghurst, NSW: Crossing Press, 2002.

Macintyre, Stuart, and Anna Clark, eds. *The History Wars*. Melbourne: Melbourne University Press, 2004.

Mangion, Carmen. '"To Console, to Nurse, to Prepare for Eternity": The Catholic Sickroom in Late Nineteenth-Century England'. *Women's History Review* 21 (2012): 657–78. doi.org/10.1080/09612025.2012.658175.

——. 'Developing Alliances: Faith, Philanthropy and Fundraising in Nineteenth-Century England'. In *The Economics of Providence: Management, Finances and Patrimony of Religious Orders and Congregations in Europe 1773–1931*, edited by Maarten van Dijck, Jan de Maeyer, Jimmy Koppen, and Jeffrey Tyssens, 205–26. Leuven: Leuven University Press, 2013.

Maschietto, Francesco Ludovico. *Elena Lucrezia Cornaro Piscopia (1646–1684): The First Woman in the World to Earn a University Degree*. Philadelphia: St Joseph's University Press, 2007.

Massam, Katharine. 'Benedictine Missionary Women at New Norcia'. In *Monasticism Between Culture and Cultures*, edited by P. Nouzille and M. Pfeiffer, 287–95. Rome: Pontifical Athenaeum S.Anselmo, 2013.

———. 'The Blue Army and the Cold War: Anti-Communist Devotion to the Blessed Virgin Mary in Australia'. *Australian Historical Studies* 24 (1991): 420–28. doi.org/10.1080/10314619108595857.

———. 'Cloistering the Mission: Abbot Torres and Changes at New Norcia 1901–1910'. *Australasian Catholic Record* 89 (2012): 13–25.

———. 'Missionary Women and Holy Work: Benedictine Women in Western Australia'. *Journal of Australian Studies* 39 (2015): 44–53.

———. *Sacred Threads: Catholic Spirituality in Australia, 1922–1962*. Sydney: University of New South Wales Press, 1996.

———. 'The Spiritual and the Material: Women and Work at the New Norcia Mission 1860–1910'. *New Norcia Studies* 22 (2015): 53–61.

———. '"That There Was Love in This Home": The Benedictine Missionary Sisters at New Norcia'. In *Evangelists of Empire? Missionaries in Colonial History*, edited by Amanda Barry, Joanna Cruickshank, Andrew Brown-May, and Patricia Grimshaw, 201–14. Melbourne: eScholarship Research Centre in collaboration with the School of Historical Studies, 2008.

———. '"To Know How to Be All for All": The Company of St Teresa of Jesus at New Norcia 1904–1910'. *New Norcia Studies* 15 (2007): 44–52.

———. 'Work in the Benedictine Monastery of New Norcia 1860–1910'. *Tjurunga: An Australasian Benedictine Review* 87 (2015): 33–47.

Massam, Katharine, and John H. Smith. 'New Norcia and Federation: A Story of Nation, Church and Race'. *New Norcia Studies* 9 (2001): 7–19.

Massey, Doreen. 'Geographies of Responsibility'. *Geografiska Annaler: Series B, Human Geography* 86 (2004): 5–18. doi.org/10.1111/j.0435-3684.2004.00150.x.

Mellor, Doreen, and Anna Haebich, eds. *Many Voices: Reflections on Experience of Indigenous Child Separation*. Canberra: National Library of Australia, 2002.

Misonne, Daniel. *En parcourant l'historie de Maredsous*. Maredsous: Editions de Maredsous, 2005.

Montaño, Mary Caroline. *Tradiciones Nuevomexicanas: Hispano arts and culture of New Mexico*. Albuquerque: University of New Mexico Press, 2001.

Moore, Robin J. 'Curzon and Indian Reform'. *Modern Asian Studies* 27 (1993): 719–40. doi.org/10.1017/S0026749X0000127X.

Morrow, Diane Batts. *Persons of color and religious at the same time the Oblate Sisters of Providence, 1828–1860*. Chapel Hill: University of North Carolina Press, 2002.

Mosso, Lauren. '"Your Very Affectionate Father in the Lord": The Letters of Abbot Anselmo Catalan during His Visit to Spain, July–August 1933'. *New Norcia Studies* 19 (2011): 53–62.

Nailon, Brigida. *Nothing Is Wasted in the Household of God: Vincent Pallotti's Vision in Australia*. Richmond, Vic.: Spectrum Publications, 2001.

Oblate Formation Booklet for Oblates Associated with St Vincent Archabbey. Latrobe, PA: The Abbey, 2002.

O'Brien, Anne. *God's Willing Workers: Women and Religion in Australia*. Sydney: University of New South Wales Press, 2005.

O'Brien, Susan. *Leaving God for God: The Daughters of Charity of St Vincent de Paul in Britain, 1847–2017*. London: Darton, Longman & Todd, 2017.

Orsi, Robert. *Between Heaven and Earth: The Religious Worlds People Make and the Scholars That Study Them*. Princeton, NJ: Princeton University Press, 2005.

Paisley, Fiona. *Loving Protection? Australian Feminism and Aboriginal Women's Rights 1919–1939*. Carlton, Vic.: Melbourne University Press, 2000.

Pallath, Paul. *The Catholic Church in India*. Kerala: Oriental Institute of Religious Studies, 2010.

Peramos, Francisco. *Un Grad Pegagogo: El padre Manjón. Temas Españoles*, no. 117. Madrid: Publicaciones Españolas, 1954.

Pike, Elizabeth (Aunty Betty). 'Reconciliation, or Conciliation through Restoration?' In *Developing an Australian Theology*, edited by Peter Malone, 27–42. Strathfield, NSW: St Paul's Publications, 1999.

Plamper, Jan. 'The History of Emotions: An Interview with William Reddy, Barbara Rosenwein, and Peter Stearns'. *History and Theory* 49 (2010): 237–65. doi.org/10.1111/j.1468-2303.2010.00541.x.

——. *The History of Emotions: An Introduction*. Translated by Keith Tribe. Oxford: Oxford University Press, 2015.

Proeve, Michael, Catia Malvaso, and Paul DelFabbro. *Evidence and Frameworks for Understanding Perpetrators of Institutional Child Sexual Abuse: A Report Commissioned and Funded by the Royal Commission into Institutional Responses to Child Sexual Abuse.* University of Adelaide, September 2016.

Rademaker, Laura. '"We Want a Good Mission Not Rubbish Please": Aboriginal Petitions and Mission Nostalgia'. *Aboriginal History* 40 (2016): 119–43. doi.org/10.22459/AH.40.2016.05.

Raftery, Deirdre. '"Je suis d'aucune Nation": The Recruitment and Identity of Irish Women Religious in the International Mission Field, c. 1840–1940'. *Paedagogica Historica: International Journal of the History of Education* 49, no. 4 (2013): 513–30. doi.org/10.1080/00309230.2013.800123.

——. 'The "Third Wave" Is Digital: Researching Histories of Women Religious in the Twenty-First Century'. *American Catholic Studies* 128 (2017): 29–50. doi.org/10.1353/acs.2017.0030.

Reece, Bob. '"Killing with Kindness": Daisy Bates and New Norcia'. *Aboriginal History* 32 (2008): 128–45.

Reynolds, Robyn. 'A Far Cry: Resounding Call to All Australians: Missionary Turned Around: Bound to be Free'. Charles Strong Trust Lecture (Part 2), Adelaide, 2013. users.esc.net.au/~nhabel/lectures/2013Part2RobynReynolds MissionaryTurnedAround.pdf.

Ride, Anouk. *The Grand Experiment: Two Boys, Two Cultures.* Sydney: Hachette, 2007.

Rooney, Bernard. *The Way of the Boorna-Waangki: A Tale of Cultural Endurance.* Melbourne: Abbey Press, 2014.

Rowse, Tim. *Indigenous and Other Australians since 1901.* Sydney: NewSouth Publishing, 2017.

Russo, George. *Lord Abbot of the Wilderness: The Life and Times of Bishop Salvado.* Melbourne: Polding Press, 1980.

Santos y Ganges, Luis and José Luis Lalana Sotot. 'La antigua estación de Burgos y el precario papel del patrimonio en los proyectos urbanos y arquitectónicos. Arquitecturavia.com. Accessed 20 October 2019.

Schneiders, Sandra M. *The Revelatory Text: Interpreting the New Testament as Sacred Scripture.* San Francisco: HarperSanFrancisco, 1991.

Schreiter, Robert J. *Reconciliation: Mission and Ministry in a Changing Social Order.* Maryknoll, NY: Orbis Books, 1992.

Schyrgens, Andre. 'Notes et Documents, Maredsous—Les soeurs bénédictine de la maison d'Emmaüs'. *Revue Liturgique et Monastique* 17 (1931–32): 243–45.

Serrano, Luciano. *Una fundación medieval de la Casa de Lara el Monasterio de Palacios de Benaber*. Burgos, 1941. Digital Copy, Valladolid: Junta de Castilla y León. Consejería de Cultura y Turismo, 2009–10.

Shellam, Tiffany. '"On My Ground": Indigenous Farmers at New Norcia 1860s–1900s'. In *Indigenous Communities and Settler Colonialism: Land Holding, Loss and Survival in an Interconnected World*, edited by Zoë Laidlaw and Alan Lester, 62–85. Houndsmills: Palgrave Macmillan, 2015.

Smart, Judith. 'The Evangelist as Star: The Billy Graham Crusade in Australia, 1959'. *Journal of Popular Culture* 33 (1999): 165–75. doi.org/10.1111/j.0022-3840.1999.3301_165.x.

Smith, John H. 'Grace and Grumbling: With Reference to the Rule of St Benedict'. In *Immense, Unfathomed, Unconfined: Essays in Honour of Norman Young*, edited by Sean Winter, 309–21. Melbourne: Uniting Academic Press, 2013.

——, ed. *Rosendo Salvado: Commemorating Two Hundred Years*. New Norcia: Benedictine Community of New Norcia, 2014. www.salvado.wa.edu.au/pdf/patron_bicentenarybrochure.pdf.

——. ed. *The Story of New Norcia. The Western Australian Benedictine Mission*. New Norcia, WA: Benedictine Community of New Norcia, 2015.

South West Land & Sea Council, John Host, with Chris Owens. *'It Is Still in My Heart, This Is My Country': The Single Noongar Claim History*. Crawley, WA: University of Western Australia Press, 2009.

Spearritt, Abbot Placid. *Friends of New Norcia Newsletter*, 23 December 2001.

Stannage, Tom. 'New Norcia in History'. *Studies in Western Australian History* 29 (2015): 125–30.

Stibi, Frances. 'Cathedral Construction: Building the Cathedral of the Immaculate Conception'. *New Norcia Studies* 14 (2006): 1–13.

Stockwell, R. F. 'Henderson, Gilbert Dowling (1890–1977)'. *Australian Dictionary of Biography*, National Centre of Biography, The Australian National University. adb.anu.edu.au/biography/henderson-gilbert-dowling-12975/text23449; published first in hardcopy 2005.

Stols, Eddy. 'The Expansion of the Sugar Market in Western Europe'. In *Tropical Babylons: Sugar and the Making of the Atlantic World, 1450–1680*, edited by Stuart B. Schwartz, 237–88. Chapel Hill, NC: University of North Carolina, 2011.

Sutera, Judith. 'The Origins and History of the Oblate Movement'. In *The Oblate Life*, edited by Gervase Holdaway, 33–34. Collegeville, MN: Liturgical Press, 2008.

Tilbrook, Lois. *Nyungar Tradition: Glimpses of Aborigines of South-Western Australia 1829–1914*. Nedlands, WA: University of Western Australia Press, 1983.

Tomlinson, Derrick. 'Too White to Be Regarded as Aborigines: An Historical Analysis of the Policies for the Protection of Aborigines and the Assimilation of Aborigines of Mixed Descent and the Role of Chief Protectors of Aborigines in the Formulation of these Policies in Western Australia from 1898 to 1940'. PhD thesis, University of Notre Dame Australia, 2008.

Tully, Kaye. 'State Secondary Education in Western Australia, 1912–1972'. *Education Research and Perspectives* 29 (2002): 1–141.

Tutu, Desmond. 'Spirituality: Christian and African'. In *Resistance and Hope*, edited by Charles Villa-Vicencio and John de Gruchy, 159-64. Cape Town and Grand Rapids, MI: Eerdmans, 1985.

Ungunmerr-Baumann, Miriam-Rose. '*Dadirri*'. *Compass Theology Review* 22 (1988): 9–11.

———. '*Dadirri*: Listening to One Another'. In *A Spirituality of Catholic Aborigines and the Struggle for Justice*, edited by Joan Hendricks and Gerry Heffernan, 34–37. Brisbane: Aborigines and Torres Strait Islander Apostolate, Catholic Archdiocese of Brisbane, 1993.

Venarde, Bruce L. 'Recent Western Christian Historiography'. In *Encyclopedia of Monasticism*. Vol. 1: *A–L*, edited by William Johnston, 596–99. Chicago and London: Fitzroy Dearborn, 2000.

Veracini, Lorenzo. 'Of "Contested Ground" and an "Indelible Stain": A Difficult Reconciliation between Australian and Its Aboriginal History during the 1990s and 2000s'. *Aboriginal History* 27 (2003): 225–39.

Verdina, Frederica. 'The Depiction of Indigenous Australians in Catholic Missionary Epistolarity'. Paper presented at the Eighth Biennial Conference of the Australasian Centre for Italian Studies (ACIS), Sydney, 1–4 July 2015.

Villa-Vicencio, Charles. 'Telling One Another Stories: Towards a Theology of Reconciliation'. In *The Reconciliation of Peoples: Challenge to the Churches*, edited by Gregory Baum and Harold Wells, 30–42. Maryknoll, NY: Orbis Books, 1997.

Volf, Miroslav. *The End of Memory: Remembering Rightly in a Violent World*. Grand Rapids, MI: William B. Eerdmans, 2006.

———. 'A Religion of Love'. *Nova prisutnost* 12 (2014): 458–71.

Walsh, Margaret. *The Good Sams: Sisters of the Good Samaritan 1857–1969*. Mulgrave, Vic.: John Garrett Pub., 2001.

Williams, Rowan. *Why Study the Past? The Quest for the Historical Church*. London: Darton, Longman and Todd, 2005.

Wimberly, Cory. 'The Joy of Difference: Foucault and Hadot on the Aesthetic and the Universal in Philosophy'. *Philosophy Today* 53 (2009): 191–202. doi.org/10.5840/philtoday200953261.

Wolman, Marianne. 'Visit to a Mission for Aboriginal Children'. *Elementary School Journal* 70, no. 5 (February 1970): 261–66. doi.org/10.1086/460577.

Appendix 1: Numbers at a Glance

St Joseph's Native School and Orphanage, St Mary's Native School and Orphanage, Benedictine Missionary Sisters of New Norcia.

Data for Aboriginal children compiled by Peter Hocking, Archivist, New Norcia, and Mark Chambers, Department of Aboriginal Affairs, Western Australia. Data for Benedictine Missionary Sisters compiled by Katharine Massam.

Year	St Joseph's	St Mary's	Total children	Benedictine Sisters
1900	14	3	17	0 [Br Miró and matrons from 1870s until 1904]
1901	13	3	16	0
1902	13	4	17	0
1903	13	6	19	0
1904	26	9	35	Teresians 7
1905	7	33	40	Teresians 7
1906	11	45	56	Teresians 7
1907	17	34	51	Teresians 6
1908	17	26	43	Teresians 6
1909	18	20	38	Teresians 3
1910	23	16	39	1
1911	32	22	54	1
1912	34	26	60	3
1913	29	29	58	3
1914	28	24	52	3
1915	28	22	50	4
1916	35	24	59	4

Year	St Joseph's	St Mary's	Total children	Benedictine Sisters
1917	36	20	56	4
1918	35	17	52	4
1919	36	18	54	4
1920	40	24	64	5
1921	45	23	68	7
1922	46	23	69	7
1923	49	25	74	7
1924	45	31	76	7
1925	46	30	76	9
1926	44	32	76	8
1927	47	35	82	8
1928	42	35	77	8
1929	43	37	80	11
1930	52	38	90	11
1931	51	43	94	13
1932	50	33	83	13
1933	33	40	73	15
1934	37	39	76	14
1935	41	28	69	14
1936	21	39	60	14
1937	29	31	60	14
1938	29	41	70	14
1939	32	29	61	14
1940	31	33	64	14
1941	45	34	79	14
1942	47	41	88	13
1943	46	45	91	13
1944	46	44	90	13
1945	48	46	94	13
1946	50	45	95	13
1947	25	20	45	13
1948	37	19	56	24
1949	32	13	45	25
1950	33	4	37	30
1951	35	4	39	29

APPENDIX 1

Year	St Joseph's	St Mary's	Total children	Benedictine Sisters
1952	49	21	70	28
1953	53	10	63	27
1954	61	20	81	27
1955	75	35	110	28
1956	95	54	149	28
1957	117	81	198	28
1958	104	83	187	28
1959	120	97	217	31
1960	119	81	200	31
1961	117	74	191	30
1962	106	84	190	32
1963	91	97	188	32
1964	87	116	203	32
1965	95	110	205	32
1966	89	94	183	32
1967	108	79	187	31
1968	109	54	163	31
1969	91	27	118	31
1970	75	22	97	30
1971	59	43–51	112–120	31
1972	46	19–26	65–72	30
1973	24	14–19	38–43	30
1974				28

Appendix 2: Benedictine Missionary Sisters of New Norcia

Compiled from the New Norcia Archives and the Archives of the Benedictine Missionary Sisters of Tutzing, Madrid, by Katharine Massam.

Company of St Teresa of Jesus, New Norcia, August 1904 – February 1910

	Arrival	Departure	Return
Montserrat Fito	25 August 1904	11 July 1907	
Consuelo de la Cruz Batiz	25 August 1904	11 July 1907	5 September 1912 – 28 November 1917
Felipa Sanjuan	25 August 1904	10 October 1908	
Maria Teresa Vilar	25 August 1904	10 October 1908	
Leonor Bargallo	25 August 1904	5 February 1910	
Teresa Roca	25 August 1904	5 February 1910	19 September 1915 – d. February 1953
Carmen Mayordom	25 August 1904	10 October 1908	
Crisanta Lopez	19 August 1907	23 November 1907	
Luz Castañada	19 August 1907	23 November 1907	
Dolores Sol de Vila	19 August 1907	10 October 1908	
Maria Harispe	19 August 1907		

Benedictine Missionary Sisters of New Norcia, arriving before November 1933

	Arrival New Norcia	Origin
Maria Harispe Quilliri (14 July 1880 – 16 November 1925)	19 August 1907 as a Teresian	Montevidio, Uruguay (French citizen)

	Arrival New Norcia	Origin
Elias (Teresa) Devine (15 April 1839 – 20 October 1933) Retained her Carmelite identity	16 April 1912	Tipperary, Ireland
Mary Consuelo Batiz Abelleyra (15 December 1877 – ?) left Australia c. 1921	25 August 1904 – 11 July 1907, returned 5 September 1912	Chalchicomula, Mexico
Teresa Roca Lluch (21 December 1867 – February 1953)	25 August 1904 – 6 February 1910 as a Teresian, returned 19 September 1915	Beniccarlo, Castellon de la Plana, Spain
Gertrude (Ellen) Banks (21 November 1878 – 26 July 1961) left New Norcia 14 July 1937	c. 15 October 1920 – 14 July 1937	Sydney, New South Wales, Australia
Felicitas (Maria Isobel) Pampliega (11 November 1902 – 1995)	17 February 1921	Cañizar de los Ajos, Burgos, Spain
Margarita (Perpetua) Perez Santamaria Usually known as Margaret (8 March 1899 – 4 May 1985)	17 February 1921	Palacios de Benaver, Burgos, Spain
Benita (Ernestina) Gozalo Puente (11 November 1907 – 1 May 1990)	23 December 1925	Cavia, Burgos, Spain
Escolastica (Conceptión) Martinez (December 1908 – 4 December 1941)	23 December 1925	Cavia, Burgos, Spain
Hildegard (Benilde) Ruiz Berbere (14 June 1909 – 14 October 1966)	15 August 1928	Tapia de Villadiego, Burgos, Spain
Maria (Martina) Cidad Simón Also known as Mary (10 November 1911 – 2001)	15 August 1928	Sasamón, Burgos, Spain
Matilde (Carmen) de la Fuente Amo (?1913 – 3 April 1948)	15 August 1928	Tapia de Villadiego, Burgos, Spain
Ludivina (Aurora) Marcos Perez (16 July 1899 – 1973)	28 April 1931	Palacios de Benaver, Burgos, Spain
Edita (Trinidad) López (1915 – ?) left New Norcia 24 September 1934	28 April 1931	Tapia de Villadiego, Burgos, Spain
Magdalena (Felisa) Ruiz de la Barga (20 January 1907 – 20 April 1989)	2 October 1933	Cavia, Burgos, Spain
Francisca (Andrea) Pardo Lopez (3 February 1917 – 2004)	2 October 1933	Villorejo, Burgos, Spain
Placida (Pilar) Catalan Catalan (1 January 1918 – March 2016)	2 October 1933	Corella, Navarra, Spain

APPENDIX 2

Benedictine Missionary Sisters arriving from November 1948

	Arrival	Origin
Scholastica (Josefina) Carrillo Barea Also Schollie (17 March 1917 – 2008)	23 November 1948	San Sebastian de Guipucoa, Spain
Teresa (Amalia) González Lozano Also known as Marie-Therese (7 March 1924 –)	23 November 1948	Villaquirán, Burgos, Spain
Gema (Josefina/Josefa) Liroz Giminez Often spelt Gemma in Australia (23 July 1923 – 1991)	23 November 1948	Corella, Navarra, Spain
Cecilia (Milagros) Ruiz Nozal (November 1923 – 1951)	23 November 1948	Villaneuva de Odra, Villadiego, Burgos
Josefina (Otilia) Diez Cidad (13 December 1927 – ?) left New Norcia 28 April 1957	23 November 1948	Sandoval de la Reina, Villadiego, Burgos, Spain
Gertrude (Marina) Diez Ramos Sometimes Gertrudis (24 February 1929 – 31 January 1969)	23 November 1948	Villasilos, Burgos, Spain
Angelina (Angelina) Cerezo Cabañes (31 May 1928 – ?) after 1980 in a French congregation	23 November 1948	Lerma, Burgos, Spain
Isabel (Francisca) Alfaro Valles (19 September 1929 – ?) left New Norcia 19 April 1954	23 November 1948	Corella, Navarra, Spain
Matilda (Florencia) Arroyo Ruiz (27 October 1930 – ?) after 1980 Benedictinas de San José, Burgos	23 November 1948	Tapia de Villadiego, Burgos, Spain
Edita (Josefa) Rubio Lazaro (17 March 1932 – ?) returned to Spain	23 November 1948	Sotopalacios Burgos, Spain
Agnes (Carmen) Ruiz Ruiz (14 January 1933 – ?) left New Norcia 1972	23 November 1948	Tapia de Villadiego, Burgos, Spain
Florentina (Illuminada) Perez Perez (14 January 1933 –)	23 November 1948	Villorejo, Burgos, Spain
Bernada/Araceli (Ines) Herce Menendez (29 January 1934 – 2 January 1994)	6 January 1950	Calahorra, Rioja, Spain
Dolores (Clementina) Vallejo Rodriguez (23 January 1935 – 14 July 1996)	6 January 1950	Tapia de Villadiego, Burgos, Spain
Visitación (Visitación) Cidad Ruiz Also Visi (1 July 1931 – February 2016)	6 January 1950	Tapia de Villadiego, Burgos, Spain

	Arrival	Origin
Carmen (Maria Carmen) Ruiz Besti (20 December 1923 – 2014, Jamberoo Abbey)	6 January 1950	Calahorra, Rioja, Spain
Lucia (Maria) Villaño Cereceda In Australia: Lucy (27 August 1928 – 2011, Benedictinas de San José, Burgos)	6 January 1950	b. San Pantaleon de Losa, Burgos, entered from San Sebastien, Spain
Casilda (Julia) Rubio Lazaro (21 August 1935 – ?)	6 January 1950 – 5 November 1951	Spain
Cecilia (Vera) Farrell (9 June 1935 –)	5 April 1953	Moore River, Western Australia
Mary of the Rosary	24 May 1953 – January 1955	Australia
Rosario (Crescentia) Vazquez	19 September 1955 – 30 May 1956	Philippines
Josephine (Natividad) Montero	2 January 1958	Spain
Imelda (Isolina) Ruiz	2 January 1958	Spain
Veronica Therese (Marie) Willaway (9 December 1944 –)	10 July 1959	Moore River, Western Australia
Pius (Anne) Moynihan (1935 –)	10 July 1959	Perth, Western Australia
Bernadetta (Alicia) Ruiz	11 March 1960 – 13 March 1961	Spain
Antonia (Norma) Stack	30 August 1960 – c. 1962	Western Australia
Philomena Drayton	16 March 1965 – c. May 1965	Western Australia
Michael (Barbara) Allen	1964–1973	Western Australia
Damien (Carolyn) Gould	1964–1973	Western Australia
Philomena (Verna) Roche Hart (17 November 1931 – ? 2017)	1971–2017	New Zealand
As well as aspirants, postulants and novices in Australia not listed here and some who joined through the House of Formation in Spain but did not travel to Australia		

www.ingramcontent.com/pod-product-compliance
Lightning Source LLC
Chambersburg PA
CBHW040337300426
44112CB00027B/2858